Religious Differences in France

Habent sua fata libelli

Religious Differences in France

PAST AND PRESENT

*To Grace and Ed,
With my love
and admiration.
— Kath*

Edited by
Kathleen Perry Long

Sixteenth Century Essays & Studies 74
Truman State University Press

Copyright 2006 by Truman State University Press, Kirksville, Missouri
All rights reserved. Published 2006.
Sixteenth Century Essays & Studies Series
tsup.truman.edu

Cover illustration: François Dubois, *Massacre of Saint Bartholomew's Day,* ca. 1572–84. Oil
on wood. ©Musée cantonal des Beaux-Arts de Lausanne. Photo courtesy of Musée cantonal
des Beaux-Arts de Lausanne.

Cover and title page design: Teresa Wheeler
Type: Minion Pro © Adobe Systems Inc.
Printed by Thomson-Shore, Dexter, Michigan USA

Library of Congress Cataloging-in-Publication Data

Religious differences in France : past and present / edited by Kathleen Perry Long.
    p. cm. — (Sixteenth century essays & studies ; v. 74)
    Includes bibliographical references and index.
    ISBN-13: 978-1-931112-57-4 (alk. paper)
    ISBN-10: 1-931112-57-6 (alk. paper)
    1. Religious pluralism—France—History—Congresses. 2. Religion and state—
France—History—Congresses. 3. France—Religion—congresses. I. Long, Kathleen P.,
1957– II. Series.
BL980.F8R38 2006
201'.50944—dc22

                                                                    2006001494

Contents

Illustrations

Abbreviations

ACP	Archives du Carmel de Pontoise
AN	Archives Nationales
BN	Bibliothèque Nationale
BPF	Bibliothèque du Protestantisme Français
BMP	Bibliothèque Municipale de Poitiers
BPR	Bibliothèque de Port Royal
BSHPF	Bibliothèque de la société de l'histoire du Protestantisme français
DBF	Dictionnaire de biographie française
HUA	Het Utrechts Archief
Mss. Fr.	Manuscrits français
Nouv. Acq.	Nouvelles Acquisitions

Acknowledgments

The colloquium that led to this collection would never have taken place without the support of my colleague Steve Kaplan, who inspired the event and assured that it would happen, and of Nelly Furman, whose hard work helped me obtain funding for the colloquium and whose advice both guided me through the colloquium and helped me improve the presentation of the manuscript. I must also thank the Office of the Provost at Cornell University for its generous support of this event, as well as the Florence Gould Foundation and the Lucius N. Littauer Foundation. Other support came from the Jewish Studies Program at Cornell, the Dean's Office, the French Studies Program, the Peace Studies program, Cornell United Religious Work, the Society for the Humanities at Cornell, the Department of Modern Languages, the Religious Studies Program, Near Eastern Studies, the Department of History, the Department of Romance Studies, the Renaissance Colloquium, the Institute for European Studies, the Department of Government, and the Women's Studies Program. I would like to thank my patient contributors to this volume; their advice and understanding helped me see this project through. My thanks go as well to Duane Rudolph, who translated the essays by Denis Crouzet, Christian Jouhaud, and Carmen Bernand. I am grateful to Susette Newberry, and the rest of the staff of the Rare Book and Manuscript Collection at Cornell, for their help in finding illustrations for this volume. I thank Douglas Long, my in-house computer support, my mapmaker, and my most trusted advisor. But most of all, I thank Ray Mentzer, whose advice was crucial to the completion of this project, and the staff at Truman State University Press, who guided me through the process of preparation of this manuscript.

A version of Dale K. Van Kley's essay, "Catholic Conciliar Reform in an Age of Anti-Catholic Revolution," appeared in *Religion and Politics in Enlightenment Europe*, ed. James E. Bradley and Dale K. Van Kley (Notre Dame, IN: Notre Dame University Press, 2001), 46–118.

Aron Rodrigue's article, "Totems, Taboos, and Jews: Salomon Reinach and the Politics of Scholarship in Fin-de-Siècle France," appeared in *Jewish Social Studies: History, Culture, and Society* n.s. 10 (Winter 2004): 1–19.

A version of Philip Nord's article, "Catholic Culture in Interwar France," appeared in *French Politics, Culture and Society* 21 (Fall 2003):1–20.

INTRODUCTION

Kathleen Perry Long

In a speech given at Orléans at the 1560 opening of the Estates General of France, Michel de L'Hospital spoke words that ring ominously for the history of France and of the world:

> [W]e cannot deny that religion, good or bad, creates such a passion in man that a greater one cannot exist.
>
> … It is folly to hope for peace, repose, and friendship between people who are of different religions. And there is no opinion so deeply held in the heart of men as the opinion of religion, nor one that separates them so much from each other.…
>
> We have experienced it today and see that a Frenchman and an Englishman who are of the same religion have more affection and friendship for each other than two citizens of the same city, subject to the same lord, who are of diverse religions. This is the extent to which the unity caused by religion surpasses that caused by country. On the other hand, the division caused by religion is greater and wider than any other. It is what separates the father from the son, the brother from the brother, the husband from his wife. *Non veni pacem mittere, sed gladium* [I have not come to make peace, but war]. It is what keeps a subject from obeying his king, and what causes rebellions.[1]

This volume explores the history of religion in France from two fundamental perspectives: the assessment and renegotiation of the relationship between

Unless otherwise noted, all translations are the author's.

[1]Michel de L'Hospital, "Harangue prononcée à l'ouverture de la session des Etats généraux à Orléans le 13 décembre 1560" ("Discours d'Orléans"), in *Discours pour la majorité de Charles IX,* ed. Robert Descimon (Paris: Imprimerie nationale, 1993), 83–84: "Mais aussi ne pouvons nier que la religion, bonne ou mauvaise, ne donne une telle passion aux hommes que plus grande ne peut estre. C'est follie d'esperer paix, repos et amitié entre les personnes qui sont de diverses religions. Et n'y a opinion qui tant perfonde dedans le cœur des hommes que l'oppinion de religion, ny qui tant les separe les uns des autres.… Nous l'experimentons aujourd'huy et voyons que deux François et Anglois qui sont d'une mesme religion ont plus d'affection et d'amitié entre'eux que deux citoyens d'une mesme ville, sujets a un mesme seigneur, qui seroient de diverses religions. Tellement que la conjonction de religion passe celle qui est a cause du pais. Par contraire, la division de religion est plus grande et loingtaine que nulle autre. C'est ce qui separe le pere du fils, le frere du frere, le mari de la femme. *Non veni pacem mittere, sed gladium.* C'est ce qui eslongne le sujet de porter obeissance a son roy et qui engendre les rebellions."

church(es) and state over the course of the last four hundred years, offering a variety of models for resolving the tensions caused by religious differences; and the elaboration of individual religious identities relative to the state and to religious institutions. These two perspectives allow us to sketch out the personal and institutional accommodations of religious diversity, as well as some of the personal and institutional causes of religious violence.

Religious debates in France are not at all new. Over the course of the last decade or so, the fifteen hundredth anniversary of the baptism of Clovis and the four hundredth anniversary of the Edict of Nantes (the edict permitting French Protestants to practice their religion to some limited degree) have passed, as has the hundredth anniversary of the Dreyfus affair, the two hundredth anniversary of the Concordat between the regime of Napoleon Bonaparte and the papacy, and the sixtieth anniversary of the Vélodrome d'Hiver, the first massive roundup of Jews in France. The fall of 2001 saw the first official recognition of the massacre of Algerians in Paris that took place on the night of 17 October 1961 under the watch of Maurice Papon, then prefect of police in Paris, and secretary general of the Gironde during the Nazi Occupation when he was responsible for the deportation of thousands of Jews. The centennial of the Law of 1905 separating church and state has passed, as has the fiftieth anniversary of the Battle of Algiers. In this context, historians of France have been reexamining its religious history, which reveals rich diversity and intractable differences. Many solutions to the problems raised by religious difference have been tried: persecution and massacre, but also tolerance, assimilation and integration, laïcité and republican universalism, and pluralism or multiculturalism. While some of these approaches are linked to a very precise period, their roots can be found in earlier periods and their significance extends much further than their own time. This collection of essays is very much focused on the interactions between diverse religions, as well as between religion and secularism, but it is also focused on interactions between historical periods, differences as well as resemblances. In particular, the essays examine not only how the major minority religions in France—Protestantism, Judaism, Islam, and even Jansenism, a major dissenting branch of Catholicism—were treated by the state and by the Catholic Church, but also how they perceived themselves in the context of religious tensions and Catholic hegemony. The essays also deal with the importance of secularism, or its particular avatar in France, laïcité, for religious diversity in France. Today, by far the largest religious minority is Muslim. It is impossible to accurately count the number of Muslims in France; various estimates hover around 4 million, although this may be well short of the actual number.[2] This significant presence is testing the flexibility of the secular model of

---

[2]Alain Boyer, L'Islam en France (Paris: Presses Universitaires de France, 1998), 18.

society established by the Law of 1905. The recent law (2004) banning Muslim headscarves and other conspicuous religious symbols in French schools is a sign of this confrontation between the secular state and its religiously diverse population. The resulting tensions recall previous conflicts over public displays of religious adherence, such as the riots that erupted periodically over the course of the sixteenth century when Protestants refused to doff their hats as processions carrying images of the Virgin Mary or of Christ passed in front of them, or when they gathered to sing the Psalms. In order to allow the reader to place these essays in their historical context, this introduction will give a brief overview of religious issues and events in France from the late sixteenth century up to the present day.

The concept of tolerance, debated in France from the sixteenth century on, is still hotly discussed in terms of *intégrisme,* assimilation (both terms evoking the desire for Muslims and others to adapt to the French culture), and *le droit à la différence* (the right to be different). These terms highlight the question of religious identity and its expression and repression enfolded in the notion of tolerance itself. The religious "other"—whether Jewish, Protestant, Jansenist, or Muslim, depending on the period of French history under discussion—is tagged and marginalized as such, and set aside; but under the regime of tolerance, it is untouched. Nonetheless, this marking of the other, which in France often took the form of geographic or social isolation (this latter in the form of exclusion from certain professions and from political activity), poses a menace. The Protestants were granted fortified towns known as *places de sûreté,* where they could gather in the event of renewed hostilities after the Edict of Nantes, as well as precise places to worship; the Jews gathered in particular neighborhoods and were eventually forced into transit camps; the Muslims, concentrated first in the *bidonvilles,* or shantytowns, surrounding most large cities in France, and later in the *banlieux,* have been easily identified and targeted. Before the 1685 Revocation of the Edict of Nantes, in particular regions of France known to harbor large numbers of Protestants, suspected families were targeted for *dragonnades,* a practice in which soldiers were billeted with these families to harass and perhaps convert them.[3] In the Second World War, particular *quartiers,* or neighborhoods, of cities and towns in France were more frequently subjected to the *rafle* because they were known to have significant Jewish populations. Beyond these more obvious examples of religious violence, marginalizing of the religious other can both enable the eradication of the other, or itself be enabled by cultural effacement, as Jean Baubérot points out:

> Four hundred years after the Edict of Nantes, Protestantism enjoys total
> freedom ... and nonetheless is regularly reduced to silence implicitly by the

[3]See Barbara de Negroni, "Les missionaires bottés sur les murailles de Babylone," in *Intolérances: Catholiques et Protestants en France, 1560–1787* (Paris: Hachette, 1996), 105–25.

media, which speak of "the Church" for "the Catholic Church" and which attribute the title "leader of Christianity" to the pope.[4]

Such effacement, whether by means of violence or of cultural constructions of religious practices, has profound and complex implications for religious identity, which is the primary focus of this anthology. Faced with violent menace, such as massacres or *dragonnades,* many Protestants feigned conversion, outwardly practicing a faith that inwardly they rejected. This duplicity saved them and may have enabled them centuries later to save some Jews, as was the case in the village of Le Chambon during the Vichy regime as well as of a number of Protestant communities in the Cévennes.[5] But this double identity also increased the distance between social practice and personal belief, undermining the sense of community that the king and his officers attempted to enforce. This separation of public and private becomes a crucial basis for the elaboration of *laïcité,* as Steven Hause demonstrates in his essay on the contribution of French Protestants to the elaboration of secular models of government and education over the course of the nineteenth century. It is also a crucial element of the current debate over pluralism versus integration (*intégrisme*).

The added complexity that forced conversion brings to the question of identity is the inevitable suspicion that the Jewish *conversos,* a number of whom moved to France, as well as converted Protestants, were not truly Catholic. This lingering suspicion echoes the later difficulty Jews encountered in their attempts to assimilate into French culture,[6] as well as the invasive and extended nature of the seventeenth-century *dragonnades* to control suspected Protestants. Under these circumstances, the newly converted become "the enemy within," sometimes seen as more menacing than their more recalcitrant coreligionists.[7] This attitude, extending from the Middle Ages, informs the willingness on the part of many

---

[4]Jean Baubérot, "La tolérance dans la France actuelle," in *Tolérance et intolérance de l'édit de Nantes à nos jours,* ed. Guy Saupin (Rennes: Presses Universitaires de Rennes, 1998), 123: "Quatre cents ans après l'Edit de Nantes, le protestantisme jouit d'une liberté totale…et pourtant est régulièrement réduit implicitement au silence par des médias qui parlent de 'l'Eglise' pour 'Eglise catholique' et qui attribuent le titre de 'chef des chrétiens' au pape."

[5]Philippe Joutard, Jacques Poujol, and Patrick Cabanel, *Cévennes terre de refuge, 1940–1944* (Montpellier: Les Presses du Languedoc, 1994).

[6]Philip Nord, "Jewish Republicanism," in *The Republican Moment: Struggles for Democracy in Nineteenth-Century France* (Cambridge, MA: Harvard University Press, 1995), esp. 67. See also Michael Graetz, "Breaking Stereotypes," in *The Jews in Nineteenth-Century France: From the French Revolution to the Alliance Israélite Universelle,* trans. Jane Marie Todd (Stanford: Stanford University Press, 1996), 110–42; and Pierre Birnbaum, "Les Juifs et l'Affaire," in *Les Juifs de France: De la Révolution française à nos jours,* ed. Jean-Jacques Becker and Annette Wieviorka (Paris: Liana Levi, 1998), 75–101.

[7]This issue has been brought up by James Carroll in *Constantine's Sword: The Church and the Jews* (New York: Houghton Mifflin, 2001), 346.

officials to deport anyone of Jewish origin in the course of the Nazi Occupation. Whereas French Jews often identified themselves as French before they did as Jewish, in the eyes of the Catholic Church, this Jewish lineage could never be effaced.

One of the legacies of the French monarchy is a complex relationship between religion and national identity. Denis Crouzet points out in his article, "A Law of Difference in the History of Difference: The First Edict of 'Tolerance,'" that although the framers of the so-called January Edict of 1562 envisioned a France eventually reunited under the aegis of one true religion, the edict calls for a suspension of the debate (and of the wars) over which religion is "true" in the interest of civil peace. The edict envisions a primarily political solution to the religious differences wreaking havoc on France; civil order is by necessity and in a limited way valued over religious "truth." While bringing Protestantism to some degree under the protection of the Crown, the January Edict also makes the authorities of the new religion answerable to the royal officers and thus places the churches themselves under government scrutiny. This subordination of church to state, even if only applicable to Protestant synods, marks a new conception of the relationship between spiritual and governmental institutions, and is significant for later renegotiations of the relationship between church and state (such as the Civil Constitution of the Clergy in 1790). This, more than any protection or tolerance of Protestantism, is the contribution of the January Edict to the tangled history of church and state in France.

The elaboration of a complex relationship between church and state is retraced by Christian Jouhaud in his article on "Religion and Politics in France during the Period of the Edict of Nantes (1598–1685)." The victory at La Rochelle in 1628 gave new life to the Catholic cause, and the *parti dévot* was able to call for the rejection of any policy that would privilege national interests over religious ones. But more Gallican-minded Catholics proposed that no spiritual or temporal power could release the king's subjects from their loyalty and obedience to him. Jouhaud presents Richelieu and Mazarin, the cardinal-ministers who largely governed France for forty years, as negotiating the shoals of these two views. Richelieu succeeded in defining a vision of the state's present, temporal salvation that freed its subjects to seek their own spiritual salvation. But he also inscribed the sacred as a matter of state that justified secrecy in the elaboration of policies and blind obedience in the enforcement of those policies; the sacred rests hidden at the center of temporal policies. This elaboration of the *raison d'etat* reinforced the mechanisms of absolutism and possibly prevented the evolution of a constitutional monarchy.

The cardinal-minister held personal responsibility for sins committed by officials working in the interests of the state; this system of spiritual patronage bound officials to the minister. But Jansenism, with its emphasis on solitary contemplation, renunciation of worldly ties, and personal responsibility, threatened to dissolve the ties between individuals and the state. The Compagnie du Saint-Sacrement was founded by lay aristocrats as a potential solution to the conflict between individual spirituality and the interests of the state. This solution, interestingly, also involved a sort of doubling of identities between a secretive spiritual life and the more worldly engagement in public life. This doubling seems to echo Richelieu's solution to the potential conflict of interest royal officers might face between the interests of the state and their own spiritual needs. It also echoes the doubling of many Protestant identities, between public conformity to Catholic orthodoxy and personal beliefs that contradicted that orthodoxy. This separation between public and private spirituality, later echoed by that between church and state, was the necessary basis for the elaboration of a secular state.

Expression of individual religious identity in the context of these political accommodations remains fraught with peril and difficulty. Barbara Diefendorf's essay, "Waging Peace," explores the relationship between the various political accommodations of religious difference and the formation of religious identity among Protestants and Catholics in the sixteenth and seventeenth centuries. The various edicts of toleration promulgated in the sixteenth century were met with increasingly hardened Catholic resistance, beginning with the first War of Religion in 1562, to be followed by seven more civil wars that tore France apart until the Edict of Nantes in 1598. This increased resistance eventually led to the 1584 revival of the Catholic League. Each of the wars also hardened Protestant resolve and enabled them to form a more militant identity as the beleaguered people of God who would survive in the face of adversity. The various edicts, not the least the Edict of Nantes itself, seem based on a utopian vision of France reunited in peace under the banner of one religion; yet the hardened stances of Catholics and Protestants alike underscore the fantastical nature of this goal. For such an idealistic vision to function, a great deal of forgetting would have to take place; this "oblivion" was officially demanded at the end of each of the Wars of Religion. But the very nature of the violence of these wars suggests that forgetting was ill advised; the cause of these wars continued to be present and thus the violence itself was constantly renewed. The wars themselves contributed to the consolidation of those very differences that had caused them. The revisionist history of the Wars of Religion that Théodore-Agrippa d'Aubigné offered in his epic, *Les Tragiques*—in particular his reworking of the story of Richard de Gastines, which makes the boy a Huguenot hero—is a spectacular example of this formation of a militant identity. Even in the course of the seventeenth century, it became clear that tolerance and coexistence were not sufficient models to heal religious divisions and stabilize the country. The persecution and clandestine worship of the post-Revocation period known as the Désert became the focal point of French Protestant identity, as it reinforced the notion of Protestantism as separate from official political and social structures, as a sort of people's movement. Thus, French Protestantism became closely identified with French Republicanism and heavily invested in it, as many influential Protestants participated in the nineteenth-century movement toward secularization of the state.

In turn, Roman Catholic identity seemed to be reconfirmed, often in the form of penitential devotion, by priests and confraternities in the wake of concessions made in various treaties and edicts over the course of the sixteenth century. These groups lay the groundwork for the Catholic League and for the seventeenth-century *dévot* party. Their taste for confrontational piety, mirroring the Huguenots' public declamation of Psalms, often threatened public order and the stability of the state.

Keith Luria's essay on "Sharing Sacred Space" considers the framework that the Edict of Nantes created for religious coexistence in France. As with the January Edict, this solution was political and was functional only inasmuch as it maintained or restored public order. Where the perceived need for order and harmony in the community was greatest—often where there was a significant and/or powerful Huguenot presence and where the two religious communities had strong ties, as in Parthenay—compromises were formed and accommodations made on both sides to make the exercise of religious belief accessible to all. Clearly, the early years after the promulgation of the edict and the creation of commissions to assure its enforcement saw more successful attempts at coexistence. When it was politically expedient for the state to tolerate Protestant worship, as during the Fronde, it confirmed privileges and protections extended by the edict. But the personal reign of Louis XIV saw increased restrictions on Protestants, even harassment in the form of *dragonnades,* beginning in 1681. Temples were closed and destroyed and congregations were increasingly banned from worship over the course of the second half of the seventeenth century. The Revocation of the Edict of Nantes in 1685, prohibiting Reformed worship in France, did not eliminate all cooperation between Catholics and Protestants, but such tolerance could no longer be expressed on a public, communal level. This brief experiment in coexistence came to a close.

Significantly, Richelieu's construction of separate but intertwined church and state, in the interests of Catholicism and the monarchy, was reconfigured in Enlightenment thought as a clearer distinction between civic/political interests and those of the Catholic Church. Eventually, in the course of the Revolution, the nation took over the central role of moral arbiter and guardian of conscience. This shift from church to state or nation as the primary site toward which individual loyalty was directed, while prepared gradually, had a tremendous impact on the history of religious differences in France.

In 1764, King Louis XVI signed an edict prohibiting the Jesuits, an order whose rules seemed to undermine notions of absolute monarchy and obedience to the king, from reorganizing in France. Their colleges had been closed in 1762. At this time, the king declared that reform of secular colleges would be placed under the aegis of offices consisting of local officials rather than controlled by bishops. The gradual detachment of the monarchy and other institutions from the Catholic Church was supported by the more secular civil practices of the *nouveaux convertis,* Protestants whose conversion to Catholicism had often been forced by *dragonnades* or other means. These newly converted followed Catholic ritual only to the degree necessary to assure their freedom from prison as well as their control over their own property; otherwise, in many marriages, wills, and other circumstances that formerly carried a religious charge, they used notaries and other professionals to create secular versions of these documents. Finally, the state recognized Protestant difference, and the validation of civil marriages and regularization of questions of civil status were established by the Edict of Tolerance of 1787. Steven Hause's essay shows that as Protestants participated more and more in the governance of France over the course of the nineteenth century, they helped to elaborate a model of the secular state that led quite logically to the 1905 law separating the state from the Roman Catholic Church (or any churches).

But this eventual separation of church and state only followed upon a destructive period fueled by a dangerously manipulative symbiosis between church and state, one that arguably contributed to the forces leading to the French Revolution. To suppress the Jansenist movement, which Louis XIV saw as politically dangerous, the monarchy solicited a series of papal bulls that established Jansenism as heretical. The most damaging of these bulls was the *Unigenitus* (1713), which mandated an unprecedented level of papal control over the lives of the faithful and the practices of the French clergy. The attempt to impose *Unigenitus* on all representatives of the Catholic Church in France and thus, in essence, on all of the French, resulted in increased persecution of Jansenists in particular. This attempt extended even to the point of refusal of last rites to those who did not have a letter of confession attesting to their orthodoxy, written by a priest approved by the archbishop of Paris (for several years from 1746 on).[8] The unrest caused by such draconian actions caused the king and the Parlement to distance themselves from the religious authorities, as they saw that their interests were not furthered by excessive repression. The reaction of the Jansenists to this heightened persecution was to republish the polemical, frequently antimonarchical literature of the Wars of Religion, both Huguenot (Protestant) and Catholic League

---

[8]Dominique Julia, "L'affaiblissement de l'Église gallicane," *Histoire de la France religieuse,* ed. Jacques le Goff (Paris: Seuil, 1991), 3:35–36.

material. The Protestant *Vindiciae contra tyrannos* and similar works from the League, such as Jean Boucher's *Justa abdicatione Henricus tertius,* delineated a more republican form of government based on the will of the people.

Not even a year after the *Déclaration des Droits de l'Homme* of 26 August 1789, the Civil Constitution of the Clergy was promulgated (24 August 1790). The tenth article in the *Déclaration* states that "nul ne doit être inquiété pour ses opinions, même religieuses...." This tolerance is then translated into freedom of religion in the 1791 constitution, in which each man was granted "liberté... d'exercer le culte religieux auquel il est attaché."[9] The Civil Constitution of the Clergy forms a part of this process, redefining the Catholic Church's relationship to the state by suppressing institutions purely linked to the church in favor of those dependent upon the state: parishes would be linked in number to the *départements* and the clergy would be paid by the state. The sovereign would have the power to dictate reform as he deemed necessary.

As Dale Van Kley's work demonstrates, the French Catholic Church's internal debate over ultramontane (papist) governance as opposed to Gallican self-governance, fueled by the Jansenist and Jesuit controversies, created models not only for revolutionary notions of government, but also for the relationship between the church and the state. His essay on "Catholic Conciliar Reform in an Age of Anti-Catholic Revolution" traces the trajectory from the Jansenist struggles to church councils around Europe that served as models of Republican governance and through revolutionary redefinition of the relationship between church and state to the dawn of secularization. The Catholic Church had to redefine itself relative to the state in order to survive the destruction of the Revolution. Struggles between the Catholic Church and the Republic became particularly acute again in the period between following 1876 and leading up to the 1905 law separating church and state.

Hause's essay on "French Protestants, Laicization, and the Separation of the Churches and the State," traces the role of Protestants in the nineteenth-century debate over the separation of church and state, and in the formulation of the separation itself. State support for Protestantism grew steadily over the course of the nineteenth century. It was in these more comfortable circumstances that Protestants began to support the separation of church and state; this was in part a legacy of French Republicanism, long linked to Protestantism. But Protestant arguments for separation can be more clearly linked to the movement known as le Réveil toward a return to earlier forms of faith. Hause also traces the importance of individuals such as Alexandre Vinet, who elaborated a theory of the separation of

---

[9]Michel Vovelle, "La politique religieuse de la Révolution française," in *Histoire de la France religieuse,* ed. Le Goff, 3:81.

church and state in 1826, basing his argument on the notion of moral individualism, related to the Reformed notion of the direct relationship between the individual and God. The focal point of this movement became the Eglise Taitbout (1830), the first major church not subject to the Concordat of 1801, and thus not the property of the state. The founding families were mostly comprised of descendants of French Huguenot refugees. The Eglise Taitbout was the origin of a number of *églises libres,* but also served as a clearinghouse for thought concerning the secularization of the state since its leaders, Henri Lutteroth and Edmond de Pressensé, maintained contact with Vinet and others. The Monod family of pastors also preached separation, and, under the aegis of François Guizot, Adolphe Monod became a professor at the Protestant Faculty of Theology at Montauban, thus forming a generation of Protestant pastors. Although small in numbers, the *églises libres* (free of Concordat restrictions) exercised profound influence. The establishment of the Third Republic (1873) reopened debate on the separation of church and state. In relation to laicization, Protestants are best known for their considerable involvement in the establishment of a secular public school system. Also, as budgets for state support of churches were cut, these churches were weaned from their dependence on the state; but this process was slow and uneven. Eventually, other sources of funding were found to replace these cuts. The Dreyfus affair led to general support of the separation of church and state. Francis de Pressensé, grandson of the founder of the Eglise Taitbout, authored the bill separating churches and the state that was finally adopted in modified form in 1905.

This law declared freedom of religion, but established the fact that the state would neither recognize any religion as officially sanctioned nor give a salary to its adherents. As both its independence and its status as the state religion crumbled away, the Catholic Church began a long process of self-evaluation and reconstruction that would last well into the twentieth century, as Philip Nord's essay suggests.

Separated by law from the political sphere in 1905, the Catholic Church sought to tighten its hold on the social sphere by means of youth groups, social activities, and other outreach programs Nord discusses in his essay on "Catholic Culture in Interwar France." They succeeded, particularly between the two wars, by fostering associations. These associations reveal a church capable of allying itself either with more democratic or more authoritarian regimes, but a number of these groups that formed after the First World War had as their aim the fostering of solidarity between Catholics and workers.

The Fédération nationale catholique was founded in 1924 as a response to elections that swept the Cartel des Gauches (the Leftist Cartel) into office; by the late twenties, the membership of this federation was nearly two million, a figure attesting to the continued importance and strength of Catholicism in France. The Vatican also made the crucial move of placing the Action française under interdict, thus separating itself not only from monarchism in particular, but from political engagement in general. This nearly unprecedented decision led to the formation of a large number of nonpartisan associations, youth groups for the most part. This movement in turn fostered an explosion of Catholic culture: theater groups, music festivals, radio shows, and magazines. In music and literature, Paul Claudel, François Mauriac, Georges Bernanos, Francis Poulenc, and others fostered a religious (Catholic) renaissance. *Ateliers d'art sacré* were founded by Maurice Denis and others.

This use of modern culture as a means of reconnecting with the faithful did not mean that the Catholic Church accepted the current ways of the world. Catholics looked to an idealized past (golden age Spain, medieval France) to inform its goals and morals. The scout movement was seen as a revival of medieval chivalry and the cult of saints similarly looked to the past for inspiring figures. Choral singing, open-air theater, and spectacular mass events drew the faithful by the thousands. While theatrical events drew Catholics together, innovators were also incorporating theatrical elements into various aspects of Catholic ceremony.

As Nord points out, Catholic culture became central to public life under Vichy. Many of the Vichy government's aims were similar to those of the church: strengthening the family and containing the spread of liberalism, Jewish influence, and communism. Catholic activists largely supported Pétain, as did the Catholic Church hierarchy, and Catholic culture intersected with increasing frequency with Nazi culture. But the role of Catholic groups was more complex. Members of a number of these groups, for example of Jeune France, joined the Resistance. Témoignage chrétien was the most significant group of Catholic *résistants*. This rupture with Vichy brought Catholic activists into dialogue with secular movements they had previously labored against.

After the war, the Catholic Resistance formed an influential political party that shaped many policies, those concerning the family in particular. Catholic activism grew closer to certain basic republican principles. Postwar Catholicism was a religion of renewal; the promise of that renewal may have been lost, but it also cast the relationship between church and state in yet another light, easing republican interdictions to some degree.

Of course, the centrality of Catholic culture stands in strong contrast to the marginalization of religious minorities throughout French history. We have seen how Protestants in the ancien régime even pretended to be Catholics, often attending Mass and observing other Catholic rituals as long as royal soldiers were in town,

only to return to their usual observances once the army had left. The marginalization of Jews throughout French history is even more striking. Clearly, Jews had
been present in France from Roman times. They were proscribed in France in
1306 by Philip the Fair, and settled in Lorraine, Alsace, Burgundy, Dauphiné,
Provence, Spain, and even as far away as Hungary and Poland.[10] Recalled and re-
expelled at regular intervals, Jews were definitively expelled by Charles VI in
1394, not to return for about a century. Conversos fleeing Spain began to settle in
portions of France after 1492 and, although Marie de Médicis renewed the interdiction in 1615, even unconverted Jews continued to live in France from the end
of the fifteenth century on. The marranos from Spain, as they were called, converted to Christianity, but often practiced Judaism in secret. They were authorized to settle in France in the sixteenth and seventeenth centuries. Jews were
expelled from Lorraine in the fifteenth century, but returned throughout the sixteenth century and settled particularly in Metz, Toul, and Verdun, which had by
the end of the century come under the control of the French Crown. In Alsace,
the urban Jewish communities were eradicated in the mid-fourteenth century, but
a minimal presence continued in the countryside. Just before the Revolution, the
Jewish population numbered about forty thousand in France: there were twenty
thousand in Alsace, seven thousand in Lorraine, and about five thousand in
southwestern France, with several thousand in the papal territories. Jews were
forbidden to live in Paris by royal interdiction, but as many as five hundred settled
there anyway.[11] For the most part, Jews had to pay special taxes, sometimes one
that designated them as "cattle," and were forbidden to own land or practice certain trades. Frequently, their language, clothing, diet, and customs marked them
as different from the general population. The Jews of southwestern France, the
marranos, had assimilated more completely into French culture by means of conversion, yet were still often designated as conversos rather than simply as Catholics. The Catholic Church maintained its doctrine of anti-Semitism, viewing the
Jewish people as those who killed Christ. But the Enlightenment's rise of tolerance
gave rise as well to other voices, among them the abbé Grégoire and Cerf-Berr,
who convinced Malesherbes to work to improve the condition of Jews in France.

   The emancipation of the Jews did not occur until 27 September 1791, when
they were granted French citizenship and all the rights that accompanied it. They
could then, in theory at least, live wherever they wished and exercise whatever
profession they chose, but with the new requirement that they serve in the military whenever called upon to do so. This new freedom did not occur without
causing some resentment. Even the most enlightened spirits of the Assemblée

---

[10]Becker, "A la veille de l'émancipation," in *Juifs de France,* ed. Becker and Wieviorka, 12.
   [11]Freddy Raphaël, "Les juifs de l'Ancien Régime," in *Histoire de la France religieuse,* ed. Le Goff,
3:65.

nationale saw the emancipation of the Jews as a step toward assimilation into French culture; others saw them purely as a threat to life or livelihood. The anti-Semitic backlash prevented the Jews of Alsace and Lorraine in particular from partaking of their full rights as French citizens.

Napoleon undertook the unprecedented task of reforming Judaic religious practices and regularizing the relationship between Judaism and the state, first convoking an *assemblée de notables,* that is, an assembly of Jewish leaders, from July to September 1806, and then reviving the Grand Sanhedrin, the highest order of Judaic representation, for meetings taking place between December 1806 and April 1807. The assembly was to answer a series of questions directed at resolving the issue of whether Judaism and common law could coexist. The Grand Sanhedrin gave weight to these answers. Napoleon then, in 1808, signed decrees centralizing the Jewish religion by the creation of the Central Consistory as well as departmental consistories. These consistories were responsible for assuring obedience not only to Jewish law, but also to the Empire, and also for assuring order and morality. Alsatian Jews had particular difficulty assimilating into the new French nation and avoided conscription by any means possible,[12] as did many other French men. But in their case, every accusation was taken as proof positive of the Jews' vile and degraded state. And, more menacing still, Napoleon saw them as a nation within a nation.

Napoleon's decree of 17 March 1808 established a synagogue and a consistory in each department with a population of two thousand or more Jews. A great rabbi assisted by another rabbi and three laymen chosen by local dignitaries and approved by the government presided over each consistory. The Central Consistory in Paris, established by a decree of 11 December 1808, was run by three chief rabbis and two laymen, and was responsible for managing the other consistories. All Jewish immigration into Alsace was forbidden and military service was obligatory, without the possibility of replacement. This decree applied only to the Jews of Alsace, occasionally of Lorraine, but the Jews of Paris and the Midi were exempted. Another decree, of 20 July 1808, called for Jews to register their family names and given names with the authorities. All of these decrees were made with the goal of assimilating Jews into French law and society. The perpetuation of many aspects of these decrees allowed the government to keep track of Jews, a practice renewed during the Nazi Occupation.

Restoration France seemed more favorably disposed toward the Jews, and the government did not renew the 1808 decrees, although the consistory structure remained. Over the course of the nineteenth century, through various changes of government, the measurable Jewish population doubled. The nineteenth century

---

[12]Becker, "De la Révolution aux années 1880," in *Juifs de France,* ed. Becker and Wieviorka, 33.

can be seen as a period of assimilation for the Jews of France, as they progressively moved into the cities and into the bourgeoisie. As this movement took place, Jews, particularly in the south, lost their ties to their religion. By the end of the century, Parisian Jews had moved from artisanal work into various professions, including medicine, law, and teaching. The Alliance Israélite Universelle was founded in 1860 to advance Jewish solidarity in conjunction with the ideals of republicanism, and was particularly active in fostering educational opportunities, defending human rights, protecting minorities, and encouraging communication between religious groups.

Parallel with this double movement toward assimilation and community-building, however, was continued virulent anti-Semitism. Not sanctioned by the government for the most part in the nineteenth century, this hatred was still prevalent in the doctrine of the Catholic Church. The prevalent view of the church was that Jews could neither be citizens nor be saved unless they converted to Christianity. Some saw the secularized Jews as the most dangerous since they were so difficult to distinguish from Christians. At the same time, some prominent financiers were from Jewish families, and some, like the Rothschilds, remained closely connected to their Jewish identity. This and other factors (still the usury issue, for example) linked Judaism closely to modern capitalism. For a number of reasons, including a rise in immigration from the East, anti-Semitism became quite virulent in the period immediately preceding the Dreyfus affair.

Alfred Dreyfus was accused of spying for Germany on 15 October 1894. He was from a family that had fled the German occupation of Alsace and had been a gifted officer in the French army. This event and the subsequent reactions put the possibility of assimilation into question. French Jews had attained certain rights and a certain place in society, in return for abandoning particularism—the outward social practices that set them apart from the ambiguously secular/Catholic society that surrounded them—in favor of private religious observances. Franco-Judaism took on the mantle of the Republic.[13] French Jews were very much engaged in the civil service and in politics.

Jewish leaders did not respond to the Dreyfus affair only as Jews, but also as French citizens working in the interest of basic human rights. But the Dreyfus affair did lead to new explorations of Jewish particularism and how it intersected with republican universalism, and to new articulations of Franco-Jewish identity. The course of Salomon Reinach's career, delineated and analyzed by Aron Rodrigue in his essay on "Totems, Taboos, and Jews: Salomon Reinach and the Politics of Scholarship in Fin-de-Siècle France," reflects the problematic choices many

---

[13]Nord, "Jewish Republicanism," in *Republican Moment*, 64–89. See also Michael Marrus, *The Politics of Assimilation: A Study of the French Jewish Community at the Time of the Dreyfus Affair* (Oxford: Oxford University Press, 1971).

French Jews faced concerning their identity, and also shows the fault lines of republican universalism.

Reinach, from a well-to-do Jewish family, was a consummate classicist and philologist. At the same time, he was deeply involved in a number of Jewish organizations, including as vice president of the Alliance Israélite Universelle. He was one of the first Dreyfusards, committed to the exoneration of Captain Dreyfus. Reinach, like many Jewish intellectuals of his time, saw Jews as the creators of "the foundations of universal morality and justice."[14] In this, it could be said that Reinach was creating an "archaeology" of republican universalism.

French republicanism had served Jews well, allowing them to enjoy greater professional advancement than elsewhere in Europe. Jewish intellectuals were influential in virtually every field of study. At the same time, Judaism was legitimated by the state in the form of consistories and organizations. To Reinach, the French language and culture were a further step toward the advancement of Jews, and modernism had benefited them greatly. But the anti-Semitism preceding and following the Dreyfus affair demonstrated some severe flaws in republican universalism, haunted by a new form of nationalism. With few alternatives, most French Jewish intellectuals maintained their support of universalist ideals.

The anti-Semitism surrounding the Dreyfus affair changed Reinach's scholarship in important ways. In the domains of linguistics, archaeology, and anthropology, a racial version of the origins of Western culture was being developed, with the Aryan race as the primary point of origin. This marginalized Semitic races, although some concession was made to the importance of Judaism for religious aspects of this culture. Reinach rejected these racial designations and moved more toward British anthropological approaches, applying them to religious studies. Religion, according to Reinach, did not originate in one specific location, but rather was a natural instinct in men and thus arose everywhere. But religion also evolved into purer forms of morality. Reinach's work became a critique of all religion as a primitive version of morality, with secularism as the evolved version of moral codes. His reaction to contemporary anti-Semitism was to push universalism to the extreme and reject any aspects of Judaism that hinted at the particular. Reinach in essence erased all distinctiveness from Judaism. His Jewish colleagues were not prepared to go this far, and Reinach's attacks on Zionism as an especially dangerous form of particularism caused him to be further marginalized by the Jewish intellectual community. As Jewish organizations defended more and more the particular practices of Judaism, Reinach found it impossible to continue his engagement in public service and was forced into the domain of pure scholarship. Similarly, Jewish militancy and republican universalism became somewhat more disengaged from each other even though they had served each other well at the end of the century.

[14]Rodrigue, "Totems, Taboos, and Jews," 162.

It is not within the scope of this volume to give a detailed history of the Nazi
Occupation; interested readers should consult the work of Annette Wieviorka,
among others, for an excellent introduction to this period.[15] But certain moments
of the Occupation are particularly significant for this volume, such as the German
law of 27 September 1940, which defined Jews as those belonging to the Jewish
faith or having more than two grandparents of the Jewish faith. Jews who fled the
Occupied Zone were forbidden to return; all remaining Jews had to register with
the subprefect of their *arrondissement*. It is worth noting that this latter practice
echoes one of the Napoleonic decrees of 1808, promulgated purportedly to stabilize family names in the Jewish community so that individuals could be easily
identified (and conscripted into the army). The registration did two things: it
identified Jews and tracked them. These points of information were crucial to the
1941 and 1942 roundups (*rafles*), but they also signal a recurrent fear expressed by
anti-Semites from as early as the eighteenth century: that the Jews were among
the French, a nation within a nation, and they were not distinguishable from the
French (ironically, an assimilation that Napoleon strove to achieve). The organization of this program to identify Jews is chilling in its efficiency; the chaotic violence of the massacres of Saint Bartholomew's Day in 1572, supposedly directed at
Protestants but catching many others in its wake, had been replaced in the case of
the Occupation with a systematic elimination of members of one religious group.
The insufficiency of the political models brought to bear on the problems of religious diversity inevitably leads in French history to large-scale violence: the massacres of the Wars of Religion, the anticlerical violence of the Revolution, and
French participation in the Holocaust. It should be added that France is not alone
in this dilemma; current events make clear that religious issues, when ignored or
inadequately addressed, often lead to horrifying violence. The problem remains of
whether these issues can be addressed effectively.

Three out of four French Jews survived the Occupation, according to
Wieviorka, who attributes this rate to the tradition of republican individualism.
Largely assimilated, many French Jews were able to seek means of escape from the
peril.[16] They were sometimes aided by non-Jews who had absorbed the principles
of French republicanism, particularly the basic concept of human rights. The era
of World War II saw a significant shift in the character of the Jewish population in
France from an Ashkenazi majority (of eastern European origin), dominant since
the Enlightenment, to a Sephardic majority of southern European origin. To some
extent, this was because the Sephardic Jews had more completely assimilated to
French culture.

---

[15]See, for example, Annette Wieviorka, "Les années noires," in *Juifs de France,* ed. Becker and
Wieviorka, 197–247.

[16]Wieviorka, "Années noires," in *Juifs de France,* ed. Becker and Wieviorka, 236.

The issue of assimilation also continues to haunt France today, as the French attempt to come to terms with a growing and significant Islamic minority. The term more frequently used is *intégrisme*, but this notion is more or less synonymous with assimilation. The Crusades defined Catholic France's stance towards Islam as conflictual from the Middle Ages on; France was heavily invested in the (re)conquest of Jerusalem. Yet, as the 1526 alliance between Francis I and Süleyman the Magnificent demonstrates, France was capable of maintaining diplomatic relations with Islamic powers. Alliances between the French and the Turks continued to thrive well into the eighteenth century. But the relationship between France and Islam shifted dramatically when the French embarked on a colonial enterprise in North Africa in the nineteenth century, and Algiers was captured in 1830.[17]

Whereas France was somewhat less invasive concerning religious practices in Morocco and Egypt, it treated Algeria as an extension of France in every respect, trying to impose French culture and the model of *laïcité* on many aspects of Algerian society, particularly the political structures. Also, Algerian Jews gained French nationality by means of the Crémieux Decree of 1871, while Algerian Muslims never became French citizens and remained largely excluded from the colonial government. The situation in Algeria after World War II left little hope for a more egalitarian society. At the same time, increased industrialization during the war and for the *trente glorieuses* (thirty glorious years) after called for a larger workforce, one taken for the most part from North Africa. The workers, generally men, either unmarried or leaving their families behind, came on limited contracts with the assumption that they would return to their country of origin when they were no longer needed. Because of the temporary nature of this assignment, the presence of Islam in France did not seem to be much of an issue.

But French colonization had a powerful impact, both on Algeria and on France. Recent religious violence in Algeria echoes the past colonial government's use of massacres and torture to gain and maintain political control. The tendency of some French citizens to see Islam as a subversive element can be seen as the expression of a lingering resentment over the Algerian war for independence as well as a reaction to recent terrorist acts. Just as Protestants were treated from the sixteenth through the eighteenth centuries and Jews were treated under Napoleon and during the Occupation (and in many other instances between these two periods), Muslims are currently marginalized by a number of public policies. This marginalization widens the gap between expectations of assimilation into French culture and the development of a Muslim particularism potentially susceptible to fundamentalist influences. Jocelyne Césari points out that, as Islam has become

---

[17]For historical background on France and Islam, see Boyer, *L'Islam en France*, 38–72.

increasingly—and visibly—politicized in certain parts of the Arab world, the suspicion of a nascent Islamic fundamentalism in France has increased. The events of 11 September 2001 led to a discussion of the status of Islam in France throughout the media. More recent events call for a rethinking of French *intégrisme* and for the possibility of more pluralistic approaches, as well as for a thorough reevaluation of the social status of Muslims in France.

Laws passed in 1976 concerning Islam reflected the still predominant assumption that Muslims were merely temporary workers in France. But the 1980s saw a strong shift in attitudes, in part as a result of the political ascendancy of Islamic fundamentalism in Iran. In 1989, in the wake of the first *affaire des foulards* in which Muslim girls wearing headscarves were expelled from school, Pierre Joxe named a commission of six Muslim experts, expanded in 1990 to form the Conseil de réflexion sur l'Islam de France (CORIF): "Its goal was to unify Muslim populations in order for the government to be able to interact with one well-informed interlocutor."[18] This goal resembles closely Napoleon's in resurrecting the Grand Sanhedrin after centuries of disuse. As Césari points out, this desire to place Islam under the aegis or control of the state does seem to go against the spirit of the Law of 1905. In 1993, the CORIF was abandoned in favor of using the Mosque of Paris, controlled by Algerian Muslims, as the site of exchange with the government. In 1995, the High Muslim Council of France was founded as a result of dissent against the Mosque of Paris. As of December 1999, Jean-Pierre Chevènement began again the attempt to organize Islam in France. Muslim leaders have been required to sign a document enumerating the rights and responsibilities of Muslims under the constitution and the Law of 1905; this document has caused some tension, as it is seen as evoking suspicion of Muslims and of their loyalty to the state. The most recent law regulating the wearing of headscarves has only stirred up this debate even more.

One of the difficulties that prevent an easy solution from presenting itself is the status of imams, figures of spiritual authority (and particularly leaders of prayer), who, nonetheless, do not have a precise place in a religious hierarchy in the manner of priests or even rabbis. The emphasis on individual responsibilities and on the individual's importance for the religion itself creates a situation not easily comprehended by a society accustomed to religious hierarchies and to well-defined religious institutions, even if this model of individualism would seem to suit the republican spirit well. Furthermore, the imams in France are for the most part foreign-born and trained, thus heightening the perception of Islam as a foreign religion being imposed on French citizens. Both of these factors test the limits of French pluralism. The imams do not have official status; they do not receive a salary and are sometimes relatively uneducated. Their marginalization in French

---

[18]Césari, "Islam in a Secular Context," in this volume, 225.

society—and relative to each other—also pushes Islamic pluralism to its own limits, making effective organization difficult.

Misunderstandings have also arisen from misinterpretations of French *laïcité*, a concept that is comprised both of the separation of church and state, and the guarantee of freedom of religious expression. Socially, however, many interpret *laïcité* as forbidding public expression of religious belief, particularly for minority religions (and thus headscarves, not crucifixes, are grounds for suspension). Césari points out that *laïcité* and the separation of church and state in France are the result of long efforts to repudiate religious tradition. Reason and science were meant to replace religion as the forces that held society together. The school system was envisioned as a means of erasing religious doctrine from the collective conscience. In essence, the Law of 1905 privatized religion and delegitimized any government involvement in religious matters. But religion has lost social legitimacy in this process. Republicans founded a universal morality opposed to religious particularism with science as a foundation for that morality. The school became the institution most involved in promulgating this morality; hence, the conflicts that have boiled over in the late 1980s and throughout the 1990s concern the wearing of headscarves in school, religious holidays, and religious instruction.

The relegation of religion purely to the private sphere is impossible in the context of Islam—and of a number of other religions. The visibility of Islam in France, its reflection of a troubling colonial history, and the European association of the veil with lingering questions concerning the status of women in Islam have all led to an intensification of the most extreme principles of *laïcité*—and their most extreme expression, calling for an exclusion of public display of religious adherence, which would seem to contradict the principle of freedom of religious expression. The reaction to Islam in France has revealed once again the fault lines of republican *laïcité* as it is legally formulated and as it is socially manifested. One can only hope that the principles of *laïcité* have the flexibility to adapt to a new set of religious differences. The problems raised by religious particularism in the context of republican universalism are still being worked through in France, as the current law and accompanying debates concerning headscarves demonstrate. Religion is inextricably linked to French culture, as is the republicanism that often opposes it and that sometimes seems itself to be a religion.

Carmen Bernand's essay on "The Right to Be Different" situates religious diversity in the context of cultural diversity and of fundamental human rights as defined by the revolutionary Déclaration des Droits de l'Homme (Declaration of the Rights of Man). Bernand particularly addresses the issue of whether universalism obscures the right to be different, and whether French secularism is in confrontation with multiculturalism. The French universalism that has evolved over the intervening centuries does not condemn diverse traditions, but rather their impinging on the public sphere. What is at stake in many current debates over religion in France is this distinction between public and private, a distinction that many intellectuals see as defining modern life. It should be noted, as Bernand does, that some of the most heated points of tension and debate arise over this distinction, which is not universal to all cultures. In particular, Islamic beliefs reflect a closer relationship between the individual and the religious community at large, one in which the Koran serves as a judicial as well as religious code and in which public expression of religious belief is frequent.

One precise use of the notion of "people" as a "collectivity of humans equal before the law"[19] is crucial to universalism. As Bernand notes, "It is in the name of a group of citizens that religious minorities disappear as distinctive groups."[20] Clearly, there was an antireligious element to the French Revolution, heightened by the Catholic Church's involvement in the counterrevolution. Bernand notes a period of iconoclasm when any public representation of any religion was forbidden. Some of this emphasis on the rights of the individual over those of any collectivity is now echoed by the Catholic Church's condemnation of sects that violate individual rights.

If French universalism is dependent on the separation of public (collectivity) and private (individuality), few people's lives are lived in such neat compartments. The Muslim community (as the Protestants and Jews did before) seems to be testing the flexibility of this universalist model in a situation complicated by racism and the renewal of Catholic ascendancy, as well as more strident interpretations of French republicanism. Still, universalism lives on (and no doubt will continue to thrive) in discussions of human rights in a number of international forums. While its limitations must be recognized, universalism still has a significant contribution to make. But there is no end in sight to the debate between universalism and communitarianism, and French culture remains—particularly in relation to religious differences—a work in progress.

And so, many different solutions to the problems raised by religious differences have been tried: the massacre of religious minorities from the Cathars to the Jews; geographical separation and privatization of the minority religion to quell the civil wars of the sixteenth century; the separation of official action from religious morality in the establishment of absolutism; imprisonment, torture, and other forms of coercion. The particularly French elaboration of secularism, both political and social, that is, as a model for institutions such as schools as well as for the state that administers them, must be seen in the context of past violence. France has a rich history of events and debates concerning religion's place in state

[19]Bernand, "The Right to Be Different," in this volume, 203.
[20]Bernand, "The Right to Be Different," 204.

and society, and relative to the individual. Some obvious truths appear from this history: no law, no threat, no act of violence—no matter how massive or horrible—can separate all fervent believers from their religion; nor can such means persuade all nonbelievers to convert to a particular religion. Therefore, religious difference will always exist, in the form of atheism, religious skepticism, or diverse religions. Such difference may be hidden in times of extreme menace, but throughout French history, religious differences stubbornly remain. Tolerance of religious minorities—a concept that falls short of acceptance, even if some of the more forward-thinking Enlightenment philosophers saw in it the potential for such acceptance—is not sufficient. Assimilation and integration, which assume that an individual will abandon much if not all of the culture surrounding his or her religion, function well only in relation to extremely secularized forms of religion. Pluralism or multiculturalism often strain the limits of the universal Declaration of the Rights of Man. But, glancing at the past as these essays do, the present situation, if religious and political leaders could only reject violence, offers at least some small hope for the future. As Luria's essay suggests, coexistence is possible. And France's past torments and present impasse can offer valuable insights to much of the world, still trapped in the solutions of the past: war, persecution, and religious violence.

A Law of Difference in the History of Difference

THE FIRST EDICT OF "TOLERANCE"

Denis Crouzet

THE JANUARY EDICT OF 1562, also sometimes called the Edict of Saint-Germain, represented a significant change in royal policy given the events immediately preceding its elaboration. The edict offered a political solution for the unrest caused by religious tensions and it offered, for the first time, limited recognition of the Protestants' right to worship. But instead of assuming the revolutionary nature of this edict, as many historians have, scholars must consider it in its precise historical context, as a document closely related to the time in which it was created. After Henri II died in 1559 in a jousting accident, his successor, fifteen-year-old François II (who was married to Mary Stuart, niece of François, duc de Guise) fell under the control of the Guise family. A Protestant attempt in March 1560 to wrest François II from the hands of the Guise (called the Conspiracy of Amboise) was suppressed in bloody fashion by the duc de Guise. The Guises and their followers used this opportunity to portray all Protestants as traitors to the Crown. But in December 1560, François II died and his eleven-year-old brother, Charles IX, succeeded to the throne; his mother, Catherine de Médicis, declared herself regent and expelled the Guise family from the court. Catherine's primary objective was the restoration of order in the kingdom; she tried repeatedly to mediate between Catholic and Protestant leaders, whose positions were already hardened, particularly in the ultimately unsuccessful Colloque de Poissy of September 1561. These attempts at mediation culminated in the January Edict of 1562. Unfortunately, the massacre at Vassy on 1 March 1562, in which troops led by François, duc de Guise, massacred unarmed Protestants, can be seen as a response to this edict, as well as the incitement to the first War of Religion (8 April 1562).[1]

This essay was translated from the French by Duane Rudolph.

[1]For an excellent basic review of this period, see Mack P. Holt, *The French Wars of Religion, 1562–1629* (Cambridge: Cambridge University Press, 1995).

1

"The Edict of King Charles IX…on the most proper means of pacifying the troubles and revolts concerning Religion"[2] of 17 January 1562 brought to a close the long first period of the Reformation by elaborating political solutions to the tensions caused by religious divisions and by leading to the civil war that it was designed to avoid. The edict also represented a break with the age-old belief that the state must be founded on religious unity. The edict noted that previous attempts to forbid public expression of Calvinist belief had led only to more violent and frequent seditious acts, and that the effort to maintain the king's subjects in "union and concord" only resulted in more division.[3] The king and his council hoped to "maintain our subjects in a state of peace and concord, as we wait for God to grant us the grace to bring them together and to restore them to the same sheepfold, which is all our desire and our principal intent."[4] The edict divided the spiritual from the worldly, the religious from the political. The problem and its solutions were presented as political, and not spiritual matters, from the perspective of the king and his council, rather than that of the prelates. This document seemed to contradict the idea that a state in which several religions would be tolerated would incur the curse of God and would only be destined for ruin and destruction. In fact, the January Edict allowed the Calvinists liberty of conscience and worship under precisely limited circumstances.

Many prominent Catholics immediately flew into a rage because of the edict, while the Parlement of Paris reprimanded the king with prophecies of the inevitable desolation of the kingdom. Just as many of its contemporaries saw the January Edict as a work of innovation and a rupture with past enforcement of religious orthodoxy, many historians have also been swayed by the opinions of adherents to religious unity, resulting in a vision of a chancellor ahead of his times and destined for failure because of his "tolerance," and seen as modern in a way that would have been impossible to imagine at the time.

But it is only an enticing anachronism to identify as modern an element of sixteenth-century politics and see it as a genuine rupture related to the secularization of authority, when in fact the edict should be viewed more accurately in light of its author's desire to use the political realm as a tool for religious strategy. It would probably be too tempting to perceive the so-called edict of tolerance as a revolutionary act, which could have been a part of a process of synchronous and parallel "autonomization of political reason in the middle of the sixteenth

[2]Quoted from André Stegmann, ed., *Edits des Guerres de Religion* (Paris: J. Vrin, 1979), 8: "Edit du Roi Charles neuvième de ce nom…sur les moyens les plus propres d'apaiser les troubles et séditions survenus pour le fait de la Religion.…"

[3]Stegmann, *Edits*, 9.

[4]Stegmann, *Edits*, 10: "[P]our entretenir nos sujets en paix et concorde, en attendant que Dieu nous fasse la grâce de les pouvoir réunir et remettre en une même Bergerie, qui est tout notre désir et principale intention."

century."[5] Apart from the negative or pejorative connotations that the word "tolerance" has today, and which make it in no way an ideal expression in the law, historians should be wary of the ambiguity of the Renaissance imagination, which,
above all, always takes into consideration the reverse of what it might want to do or
say. Thus, that which would seem to have given way to a modern "tolerance" could
in fact have been rather distant from the modern notion of "tolerance," or could
even have been its absolute antithesis.[6] The fact that the edict was drawn up by one
of the most prominent jurists of the French Renaissance has directed historical
analysis toward this early attempt to reconcile civil order and an emphasis on the
individual. In this view, the judiciary, already motivated by social demand for a
reduction in religious conflict, would therefore have shaped absolutism and Michel
de L'Hospital would be one of the architects of this articulation.

To be brief, there would be certain danger in reading the Edict of January
teleologically when one considers its meaning for readers of its time and its failure, or in reading it from the perspective of a modern cultural system based on
difference. This document does not represent an acceptance of difference; it must
be read in the context of the piety of its authors, L'Hospital, Catherine de Médicis,
Jean de Monluc, and others, who certainly dreamed more of an imminent restoration of Christian unity made possible by an act of kindness that would grant all
men peace and that would thus bring God's blessings upon them, than they did of
"tolerance" in the modern sense of the word. They expected this reunification to
occur after an intermediary period of limited duration, during which religious
coexistence would be accepted. The January Edict was the tangible expression of
nothing more than the advancing of a pious desire for reformation in the mores of
mankind, a desire that rejected any violence toward "those of the new religion,"[7]
and wished to "summon, search for, and seek" them so as to allow God's power to
recapture them. In this tradition, faith is primarily composed of love and hope.
Such love and hope could only cause tension directed at those who doubted the
Catholic Church, a tension that would not find its expression in violence but in a
reform that would please God.

Thus, the edict comprised a deceptive discourse that concealed a confession of
faith, and executed a strategy of reducing in the kingdom the very difference that it
authorizes.[8] It was the product of a paradoxical imagination that infused French

[5]The designation is Olivier Christin's in his "Sortir des guerres de Religion: L'autonomisation de
la raison politique au milieu du XVIe siècle," *Actes de la Recherche en Sciences Sociales: Histoire de
l'Etat* (March 1997): 24–38.

[6]For a sustained analysis of the history of tolerance—the term and the practice—in France, see
Negroni, *Intolérances*.

[7]Stegmann, Edits, 9: "ceux de la nouvelle Religion."

[8]Robert Descimon, ed., "Présentation," in Michel de L'Hospital, *Discours pour la majorité de
Charles IX* (Paris: Imprimerie Nationale, 1993), 24–25.

evangelical writings with life, persuaded that everything originating with sinful man was bad and that God alone was capable of mastering human history. The object of the edict was to authorize the return of God among men by abstracting them from their passions and their dreams of violence and anguish, and separating them from the diabolical illusion that made them believe they could accomplish God's will through their own strength. Civil peace could be, for L'Hospital, the only future of the kingdom, as only civil peace could permit the development of a period during which the French, in religious coexistence, would improve and be in a position to accept God's forgiveness. The French would also be in a position to witness a return to religious unity through the application and restoration of their lost virtues, among which friendship and charity to the Calvinists, who had certainly lost their way, was essential. The events of 17 January 1562 should not be understood anachronistically, viewing religious coexistence as an end, but seeing it instead as a means to another end. Religious coexistence should only be understood within the limits of a mentality that believed completely in the justice and the mercy of a God who one day would render judgment and grant mercy as he revived the unity of the Christians that had flourished before for many centuries.

L'Hospital was arguably a man endowed with a great capacity to fight for the maintenance of the royal estate. Such a capacity sprang not only from a belief in the primacy of reason, but above all from a personal mysticism and from a sense of mission ordained by God. Likewise, the eruption of violence and aggression that sustained the Wars of Religion cannot be analyzed without reference to religious structures and to the religious motivations and imaginations of the participants.[9] In the same way, the attempt to impose peace in order to reduce the number of conflicts must be analyzed in the light of the piety of the edict's authors. There is an excessive tendency to treat the confrontations among religious denominations in the second half of the sixteenth century as nothing other than confrontations between the opposing forces of Calvinist reform and those promoting the notion of the exclusivity of the Roman Catholic Church. Facing these two denominations, however, was a third force, that of a very precise form of evangelism, which undeniably had its origins in a powerful fideist movement.

The *évangéliques* of the 1530s and the post-*évangéliques* of the beginning of the 1560s believed that, as Rabelais says, "for God nothing is impossible."[10] Indeed, to have faith is to know that all is possible for God and is therefore to attempt to put the world back on the road to peace, for God's sake. The politician must do every-

---

[9]Denis Crouzet, *Les Guerriers de Dieu: La violence au temps des troubles de religion* (Seyssel: Champ Vallon, 1990).

[10]François Rabelais, *Gargantua*, ch. 6. Although Rabelais is quite sarcastic in this passage, he is parodying a certain evangelical discourse of his time.

thing to ensure that God, in his unbounded omnipotence, can be recognized and glorified. The January Edict therefore does not articulate a secularized political state of affairs. Rather, it shows politics to be an instrument of God's glory as it calls for a mystifying of the will of a fathomless and omnipotent God.

It would be useful for the purposes of this argument to review the clauses of the January Edict. In them, L'Hospital never evoked the word "tolerance." More-over, "tolerance" is a word that he never uttered in any of his speeches. He pre-ferred the terms "union and concord," in the sense of a joining of the hearts and of fraternity.

THE ARTICLES OF THE JANUARY EDICT

The January Edict, which was made up of sixteen articles, was addressed to the members of the Reformed Church, and commanded them to return to the Roman Catholic Church the religious edifices, houses, assets, and income that they had seized at the expense of the clerics. They were also obliged to return the reliquar-ies and the liturgical objects that they took. They were prohibited from seizing or building churches, from hindering the collection of tithes and other forms of ecclesiastical revenue as well as from imposing their own, and, above all, from attacking the crucifix and other images and doing "other scandalous deeds." The prohibitory measures above all dealt with the problems of freedom of worship of the new cult and forbade its members from meeting in private and in public inside the walls of any city for the purpose of preaching.[11] The law of the king therefore remained a law that rejected religious difference.

In its main clauses, the law did not appear to contradict the law promulgated in July 1561, which outlawed both the private meetings and public and private assemblies for the purpose of preaching and distributing sacraments in the Cal-vinist fashion "as we await the decision of a general Council, to arrest the progress of the diversity of opinions; and to gather by this means our subjects in union and concord, in order to bring to a halt all of the troubles and seditions."[12] L'Hospital insisted that the convening of this council could not be delayed if religious reform was to be effected. As Nicola Sutherland has argued, the edict was limited in scope and had a strong Catholic tone, with the exception of a vital concession of the free-dom to preach, which Catherine de Médicis admitted was intended to satisfy "at least in some way those regrettable souls."[13]

[11]Stegmann, *Edits*, 9–10, 15–17.

[12]Stegmann, *Edits*, 9: "[E]n attendant la détermination d'un Concile général, pour rompre le cours à la diversité desdites Opinions; et en contenant par ce moyen nos sujets en union et concorde, faire cesser tous troubles et séditions."

[13]Nicola M. Sutherland, *The Huguenot Struggle for Recognition* (New Haven: Yale University Press, 1980), 134.

The law of the king did take into consideration what it had already considered in 1561, which was "the malice of the times and the diversity of opinions,"[14] as well as the political failures of the policies of François I, Henri II, and François II, whether those policies were harsh or mild. One reality could not be eclipsed, however: "The thing [heresy] has so penetrated into our said kingdom and into the spirits of a number of our subjects of all sexes, estates, qualities, and conditions...."[15] Because of the inadequacy of previous legislation, Charles IX affirmed that his political choice was only "provisional"—therefore temporary and necessitated by the times—and suspended the prohibitory measures evoked in the Edict of July and in all of its predecessors.[16] Although Reformed religious assemblies were still prohibited inside the city walls, they were permitted outside the city walls. The king's decision was also made in anticipation of a meeting of a General Council. The Edict of January allowed household prayers without any hindrance whatsoever; this concession was presented as a response to the situation at hand, but did not deny that religious unity was at the foundation of the royal estate. This explains why the Calvinist request to build churches, rejected by Catherine de Médicis herself, was not taken into consideration.[17] The Huguenots received only the right to preach.

Based on this instance of a suspension of the law by a law, and in the light of the condition initially offered to the members of the Reformed Church—that they return to legality and abstain from all acts of subversion and appropriation that they had hitherto perpetrated—the king addressed himself to all those who had the authority of his hand and, more universally, to "other persons, be they of whatever estate, quality, or condition,"[18] asking them to arrest those of the new religion should they not assemble according to previously outlined conditions. On the other hand, the restoration of public order by means of even this limited assurance of freedom of assembly had two prerequisites: first, that Protestantism itself no longer be prohibited by the king's law, and second, that the officers and magistrates apply a policy that would permit public worship by assuring protection against those who, by means of "troubles and sedition," would wish to prevent Protestants from gathering. The edict underscored the restoration of justice and thus the punishment to be handed down to the seditious "be they of whatever religion."[19] This principle was repeated several times in the articles. The aim of the January Edict

[14]Stegmann, *Edits*, 8: "La malice du temps, et de la diversité des opinions."
[15]Stegmann, *Edits*, 8: "La chose a pénétré si avant en notredit Royaume, et dedans les esprits d'une partie de nos sujets, de tous sexes, états, qualities et conditions."
[16]Stegmann, *Edits*, 8.
[17]Sutherland, *Huguenot Struggle*, 133.
[18]Stegmann, *Edits*, 13.
[19]Stegmann, *Edits*, 11: "de quelque Religion qu'ils soient."

was to disarm the protagonists of religious antagonisms and to this end, the articles focused explicitly on Catholics.

Next followed a new injunction that affirmed the sovereign's wish to reestablish civil peace and to defuse the wave of violence. The king wanted to see his kingdom disarm, both militarily and in discourse, so that his subjects could "live and interact with each other gently and graciously."[20] Only the nobility was exempt from the demilitarization of the social body. Priests were instructed not to use their sermons for attacks and to avoid other invectives against the ministers of the new religion and their followers; by using the pulpit in such a manner in the past, the edict added, clerics had induced the populace to sedition. Added to clauses controlling governance and speech was an order concerning printed materials that endeavored to warn printers and all those who might distribute and sell "broadsheets and defamatory pamphlets" (Placards et Libelles diffamatoires) of the whipping that awaited them for the first offense, and the death penalty for the second time they contravened the law. The objective of the edict was to bring the kingdom to a state of "general and universal repose" (repos général et universel), and the king declared that, since his officers had a duty to accomplish that objective, all those who did not execute their duties would be relieved of their positions. All holders of public offices were required to inform the appropriate authorities and to institute legal proceedings against the offender(s); verdicts should be delivered without the possibility of appeal and carried out immediately. In cases where the holders of such offices were told of some evil deed, nothing was to hinder the exemplary punishment that the lower judiciary had the duty to mete out.[21]

Even while enumerating the conditions for the restoration of civil order, the January Edict focused on sorting out the relationship between the state and the churches of the new religion. It created, at least on paper, a concordat-like structure, while imposing a certain number of responsibilities and obligations on the structures that framed the churches. First it demanded an inspection by the ministers and the "leaders of the new religion" (principaux de ladite Religion nouvelle).[22] The latter were to obtain information regarding the life and character of those who attended their gatherings, "so that if they are pursued by the law, or found guilty in absentia or by default of a crime meriting punishment, they take them and give them over to our officers, so that they may be punished."[23] The preachers of the new religion were also required to welcome, with due reverence,

---

[20]Stegmann, *Edits*, 11: "Vivent et se comportent les uns avec les autres doucement et gracieusement."

[21]Stegmann, *Edits*, 13.

[22]Stegmann, *Edits*, 11.

[23]Stegmann, *Edits*, 11: "A fin que si elles sont poursuivies en Justice, ou condamnées par défaut ou contumace de crime méritant punition, ils les mettent et rendent à nos Officiers, pour en faire la punition."

officers of the king who might wish to attend the gatherings and "see what doctrine shall be preached there" (voir quelle Doctrine y sera annoncée).[24] They were even obliged to help the officers apprehend a criminal at the officers' request. Churches were to submit to royal decree and they were not to provide, as they had been able to during the crisis of previous months, social spaces of resistance to the law. Religious matters are alluded to in a demand for submission to civil law.

Apart from the requirement that the king's representatives be allowed to attend gatherings, the articles made a more important demand: that the meetings of synods and, above all, of consistories only take place with the approval of a royal officer or in the presence of one who is to be informed of both the time and place of these meetings.[25] Therefore, the functioning of Protestant churches was subject to royal control and a kind of concordat was imposed on them, which limited their range of autonomy. The state considered itself the regulator and controller of the "new" religion. One of its more fundamental specifications was that, should the ministers and religious leaders wish to elaborate regulations concerning religious practices, they were first required to reveal these rules to royal officers who could either agree to them or ask for royal permission.[26] The Edict of January therefore established state control over the activities of Protestant churches in a very strict manner. This particular aspect of the edict was probably part of a royal project, the aim of which was to curtail, in the short or intermediate term, religious dissidence by providing the state with the possibility of intervention in the activities of churches.

This subjection of church to state was underscored by the obligation imposed upon ministers to make a feudal gesture of obeisance to royal officers. This gesture signaled a promise to observe the articles of the edict. Above all, ministers were "to promise not to preach a doctrine that contravened the pure word of God, according to the manner in which it is contained in the symbol of the Nicene Creed and in the canonic books of the Old and New Testaments."[27] The ministers were also prohibited from attacking the Mass and the liturgical ceremonies of the Roman Catholic Church in their sermons, as well as from forcefully proselytizing the men and women of the kingdom.[28] The document subsequently made it clear that each new church was to be accepted and acknowledged by a magistrate when its minister arrived. The aim of the edict was primarily to eliminate the use of

---

[24]Stegmann, *Edits*, 11.

[25]Stegmann, *Edits*, 11, 17.

[26]Stegmann, *Edits*, 11–12, 17.

[27]Stegmann, *Edits*, 12: "Et promettre de ne prêcher Doctrine qui contrevienne à la pure parole de Dieu, selon qu'elle est contenue au Symbole du Concile 'Nicene,' et ès Livres Canoniques du vieil et nouveau Testament."

[28]Stegmann, *Edits*, 12, 18–19.

force through the last clarification: "and they [the ministers] are not to go from one place to the other, from village to village, to preach by force, contrary to the liking and consent of the lords, priests, vicars, and the churchwardens of the parishes."[29] One aspect of the January Edict that has been understated all too often is its implicit attempt to stabilize the status quo by limiting the freedom given ministers in their preaching.

In the framework of these requirements, religion was neither allowed to encroach upon the political power under whose aegis it was placed nor to replace that power in the appropriation of royal rights. Those of the Reformed religion also did not have the power to choose magistrates, to enact laws, statutes, or ordinances, to enlist people for the purpose of war, to "strengthen and help each other" (pour se fortifier et aider les uns les autres), or to exact taxes. In this framework, the followers of the new religion were required to submit to the laws of a political state. They were also to submit to the laws "that are received in our Catholic Church, regarding celebrations and days of inactivity; as well as those of marriage, for the degrees of consanguinity and affinity."[30] This attempt to stabilize the social and political situation could not be clearer.

The last article of the edict concerned its diffusion. The king stated that the task of all of his officers, from those in the Parlement down to minor judges, was to have the edict published, read, registered, and adhered to without variation or restriction.[31] The edict established a system of coexistence among denominations that seemed to modify completely the relationship between the political and the religious spheres. Indeed, it completed the process of the legalization of heresy under civil law that was first undertaken in March 1560 and continued in progressive fashion by L'Hospital. The system of coexistence, temporary in principle, that was enunciated in the January Edict implied the institutionalization of Reformed churches, as their ministers had to swear to a loyal officer of the king (while making the gesture of obeisance) that they were going to observe every article of the edict, including the one commanding ministers to admonish their followers to obey the edict itself. This was certainly both a pragmatic and an ideological act, the result of the failure of religious persecution, which brought in its wake the evident risk of civil war.

However, one point should be underscored. The Parlement of Paris, which only registered the edict on 6 March, was able to obtain a royal declaration and

---

[29]Stegmann, *Edits*, 12–13: "Et de n'aller de lieu en autre, et de village en village, pour y prêcher par force, contre le gré et consentement des seigneurs, curés, vicaires et marguilliers des Paroisses."

[30]Stegmann, *Edits*, 12: "Même celles qui sont reçues en notre Eglise Catholique, en fait des fêtes et jours chômables; et de marriage, pour les degrés de consanguinité et affinité." See also Théodore de Bèze, *Histoire ecclésiastique des Eglises reformées au Royaume de France* (Anvers: Jean Remy, 1580), 1:674–80.

[31]Stegmann, *Edits*, 14.

interpretation, made public on 14 February, that dealt with the role of royal officers in controlling the activities of churches. If the monarchy reiterated that its law
only had provisional meaning, it also added to this statement a crucial point: that
it had made neither the choice nor the decision to approve two religions in the
kingdom. Though necessity had dictated acceptance of freedom of worship and of
conscience, the edict was not so much an acknowledgment of religious difference
as it was an affirmation of the absolute power of the monarchy as guardian of civil
order and as structuring history to guarantee a return to unity of faith.[32]

THE FORM AND CONTEXT OF THE JANUARY EDICT

Christ spoke through the law of the king; that is, in the conventions adhered to
and in force before the writing of the January Edict, everything was done to stage
the theater of royal power in a manner consonant with religious ceremony. Thus,
during the Renaissance, the discourse of power was liturgical in nature. The monarchy was one way of making a public ceremony of this discourse. The edict was
initially elaborated within a very precise framework of a large consultation
attended by the Queen Mother, lieutenant general, princes of royal blood, members of the privy council, and representatives of Parlement. Undoubtedly, at this
meeting opinions were initially solicited from the likes of Paul de Foix, Chris-
tophe de Harlay, or Arnaud du Ferrier.[33] This was the monarchy's immediate ceremony of dissemination, since the symbolic principle of the meeting of January
1562 could be seen as directly inspired by an ideal of Christlike power of council
as it had been defined in the 1519 edition of *La Grant Monarchie de France*. A
more recent edition of the text had just been printed by Galiot du Pré in 1557/58.
Although Claude de Seyssel had remarked that the good prince, on whom everything depends and who has absolute power at his disposition, is a prince who has
the full obedience of his subjects, he also argued that the prince's duty, beyond
assuring that the laws were adhered to even as he himself observed the limits of
his power, was to "correct and annul useless or imperfect laws, and to make newer
laws if it was expedient to do so."[34]

The monarch was therefore compared to a doctor, who has some experience
and who listens to his patient in order to cure the illness. Seyssel's ideal prince was
therefore a prince who acted in accordance with his council, thus avoiding acting

---

[32]Sutherland, *Huguenot Struggle*, 135.

[33]Noted moderate jurists already consulted by Henri II concerning the persecution of Protestants in the 1550s. See Théodore Agrippa d'Aubigné, *Histoire universelle*, ed. André Thierry (Geneva:
Droz, 1981), 1.2:246.

[34]Claude de Seyssel, *La Monarchie de France et deux autres fragments politiques*, ed. Jacques
Pujol (Paris: Librairie d'Argences, 1961), 130: "Car ayant l'obéissance entière des sujets, il peut sans dif-
ficulté faire observer et garder les bonnes lois, ordonnances et coutumes, corriger et annuler celles qui
ne sont utiles ou assez accomplies, et en faire de nouvelles s'il est expedient."

"either as a result of a disorderly will or suddenly."[35] The council, another check to royal authority, was therefore an instance of the mediation of the royal will, a custom by which the sovereign attained wisdom and through which he realized his potential qualities and virtues in their entirety, bringing his absolute power into being. The council drew absolute power to the concept of Christlike identity that the sovereign claimed, particularly since François I. For Seyssel, the importance of the council was derived from both pragmatic and biblical evidence. There was, first, the striking example that God himself made when he commanded that Moses have counselors, chosen from among the wisest and most renowned men of his people.[36] There were also limits to one man's—even the king's—power of comprehension. One man, when faced by many, did not suffice by himself. The council was a practical necessity in the management of a state conceived of as a complex space that was intrinsically dangerous. It allowed the sovereign to actualize that divine election immanent in him. The danger lay in the monarch's ruling his kingdom in too cursory a manner without the reflection that the complexity of matters required and, above all, without taking into consideration the future ramifications of a present decision. It was therefore necessary that he proceed after deliberation and counsel, and Seyssel was interested in those who would constitute the assembly of men called upon to bring their clear-sightedness and experience to the prince. Seyssel also indicated that they should not be too many. The selected model of governance was presented as being based on the New Testament, as it fundamentally identified the king of France with Christ and made a soteriological figure of his person. Therefore, to identify the January Edict in the context of a reduced assembly that discussed and reflected upon the edict, it had to be understood that the king, in whose name the assembly was convened, received his kingdom from God and was therefore God's representative in his kingdom. Seyssel added that Christ had three councils and that government by council created the spectacle of an evolution of the prince toward Christ, making the prince the earthly equivalent of Christ and giving evidence of a sacred monarchy. Seyssel indicated that Christ first had a great council of seventy-two disciples, which was completed by the twelve apostles who were often sent out to preach. He stated that there was also a council comprising the twelve apostles, who dealt with nothing but secret things, as well as the inner council comprising Peter, John, and James "to whom he told the most secret things as well as the highest mysteries, such as the transfiguration, and whom he called to witness his greatest deeds and works, such as the hour that he prayed to God to let him avoid the Passion that he saw

[35]Seyssel, *Monarchie,* 133: "C'est que le Monarque ne fasse aucune chose par volonté désordonnée ni soudaine."
[36]Seyssel, *Monarchie,* 134.

Portrait of Michel de L'Hospital, from Jean Simon Lévesque de Pouilly, *Vie de Michel de L'Hôpital, chancelier de France* (London: D. Wilson, 1764). Reprinted with the kind permission of the Cornell University Library, Rare Book and Manuscript Division.

ahead."[37] Added to these three councils was a final one that witnessed the revelation of secrets to John that were never divulged to the others.[38]

The staging of the Assembly of Notables at Saint-Germain was meant to convey the edict as an expression of God's will, a confession of faith, and a product of the divine power delegated to Charles IX. Yet, for L'Hospital, power had restraints different from those underscored by Seyssel and the primary of these was ethical. L'Hospital believed the virtue of humility demanded that the sovereign protect his people from violence and wars, fight against his passions, and solicit counsel. This virtue referred to the position of the sovereign in the face of God's omnipotence.[39]

By publishing the January Edict, the king enunciated a Christlike word. The edict was the word and thus a sacred text; it was both a confession of faith and a revelation, as the procedure from which it issued referred to the monarch's Christlike identity, evidenced by its absolutist moderation. His power was absolute, yet he moderated his behavior through the self-consciousness that he exercised in the manner of his governance, by listening to his best subjects, by respecting the laws of the state, and by creating new laws that responded to the needs of the civic community. L'Hospital's king was a king who ruled by council.[40]

The ideal of power, absolute power, was one of *mediocritas,* moderation that identifies the king with a mediating Christ, and authority emanating to him from his subjects. The opening speech at the assembly at Saint-Germain, delivered by L'Hospital, was clearly in this vein as it entreated those summoned, cognizant of the impossibility of effecting extreme solutions, to give proof of *modus,* of this moderation. L'Hospital situated his speech, which followed the king's, in the context of a scriptural invocation (in this case Psalms 32:10), which invited the just to make a joyful sound unto a God who loved justice and truth, a God, the creator, who from the heavens above observed all the people of the Earth and watched over their every action.[41]

L'Hospital began by tracing the history of religious dissent, which for him dated back to Luther's critique of indulgences in 1517. Although God had wanted, through the sins of men, to make known the necessity of amendment, nothing was done to this end and religious difference could only increase. L'Hospital reiterated his belief that nothing had checked this increase in religious division because insufficient means—that is, fire and the sword—had been used where instead it was most necessary to assuage God's wrath by a correction of lifestyles and more

---

[37]Seyssel, *Monarchie,* 135: "Auxquels il communiquait les choses les plus intrinsèques et les plus hauts mystères—comme celui de sa Transfiguration,—qu'il appelait à ses plus grands travaux et affaires—comme à l'heure qu'Il pria Dieu Son père pour éviter la Passion qu'Il veait prochaine."

[38]Seyssel, *Monarchie,* 134–35.

[39]See, for example, L'Hospital, "Discours d'Orléans," esp. 71–76.

[40]L'Hospital, "Discours d'Orléans," 75.

[41]Jacques-Auguste de Thou, *Histoire universelle…* (The Hague: Henri Scheurleer, 1740), 3:118–21.

attentive and present pastoral care. The crisis at hand was by no means surprising for L'Hospital. He inveighed against the episcopate. It is clear that L'Hospital considered religion to be at the basis of the crisis in the kingdom, as religion had held the kingdom captive in ignorance of God's will. The crisis would therefore be eradicated through the work of the men of the Roman Catholic Church, work that they would initially have to do themselves. Clearly, if the cause of dissent was religious, then the remedy, in spite of all appearances, could only be religious.[42]

Moreover, if the followers of the new religion had become, for L'Hospital, more daring during the first few months of Charles IX's reign, this was due to divine permission, the goal of which had always been and still was to extract the French from their state of blindness. It follows that those who would want to recommend a violent solution to the problems of the kingdom by supporting one of the two opposing parties were struck with blindness.[43] For L'Hospital, to follow their advice would be to take up arms, to promote the ruin of the (civic) body—which would amount to a disavowal of moderation and therefore of the will of Christ.

The correct choice would be a compromise, a positioning of the political between the two parties beyond any passion and, therefore, according to Christ's will. For L'Hospital, the counsel solicited from those summoned to Saint-Germain should have been the result of prudent and measured reflection—counsel informed by the wisdom of God. That counsel should have been nourished less by human reason than by the fear of God and by his truth; failing that, those who offered counsel would incur God's wrath. It was God who gave the *judicium* (the power of judging and therefore of ruling) to the king, over and above their own wisdom.

The theme of God's wisdom is essential for our understanding of L'Hospital's almost mystical expectations, the mystical impulse that structured the law he decreed for the kingdom of France after the meeting at Fontainebleau. The wisdom of God was analogous to the wisdom of the man who gave himself up to God because he was cognizant of man's original sin, and because he knew that man was a vessel of iniquity. This view of wisdom is drawn from 1 Corinthians 1:18–31. The wisdom of God was the knowledge of one's weakness, which induced man not to be overconfident in his own wisdom. God's wisdom atoned for man's sins through the sacrifice of Christ; this was the love of God, who freely gave his grace to the man who placed his hope in him after having declared his own worthlessness. It was also the wisdom of God that those summoned to Saint-Germain had as their final goal as they approached the king to promulgate the January Edict.

---

[42]See also L'Hospital, "Discours d'Orléans," 83–86, which underscores this same point.

[43]L'Hospital, "Discours d'Orléans," 82–83: "Ne vaut l'argument dont ils s'aident qu'ils prenent les armes pour la cause de Dieu. Car la cause de Dieu ne veut estre defendue avec armes…" (The argument that they are taking up arms for God's cause is worthless, because God's cause does not wish to be defended by arms).

The ceremonial staging would therefore formalize this one part of the meaning of that law, the sacred context in which it was elaborated.

THE MEANING OF THE JANUARY EDICT

This wisdom, according to L'Hospital, was to be found in the word of God, and the opinions that those summoned to Saint-Germain would give after some reflection would therefore have to be in harmony with their respect for Christ. L'Hospital wished to impose the belief in a way that depended on Christ for all its thought and acts by beginning with the apparently paradoxical intention of disassociating the political and the religious. Yet, in the belief system of L'Hospital, the wisdom of God probably also referred to "the justice of God" of Paul's Epistle to the Romans. To be part of God's justice therefore meant to be part of a consciousness that lived in faith and humility. For L'Hospital, Christ never advocated violence, because he always wanted concord and union.

Without considering the letters posthumously published at the beginning of the 1580s—many infused with a clear religious sentiment, undoubtedly L'Hospital's own—it would be possible to misunderstand the Edict of January and the reasoning that brought the chancellor to produce it.[44] Man was sin and, in his history, there was the burden of sin that rendered empty all knowledge that came from man. L'Hospital affirmed that to know oneself was to know the inanity and vanity of one's own being. Connected to these flaws were presumptuousness and pride, the Erasmian notion of self-love whose influence was evident, and the Erasmian theme of *curiositas impia* (impious curiosity). Human wisdom was merely the appearance of wisdom and, therefore, it was impudence. L'Hospital compared the man who believed that knowledge could bring him closer to God to Narcissus falling in love with his own reflection. Such vanity concerning human knowledge independent of God met its match in the jealousy of God, which did not tolerate man's love for his own sin. God did not suffer being compared to anyone else in the love that he inspired. He demanded to be adored wholeheartedly. As in the work of Rabelais, God demanded that man assume a *mediocritas* and realize he was nothing. Nevertheless, if God was a jealous God, he was also overflowing with love. He showed his love more negatively than positively, sending disease and calamity to mankind, even war, to remind mankind that they were to adore him wholeheartedly by showing their weakness. To be loved by God was to be tried and to suffer.

The God of love was, above all, the God of Calvary, who sent Christ down to earth to redeem mankind. Christ redeemed ungrateful man through a gift that

---

[44]See Denis Crouzet, *La Sagesse et le malheur: Michel de L'Hospital chancelier de France* (Seyssel: Champ Vallon, 1998), 101–88.

extinguished the power of sin, a gift that affected everyone. L'Hospital was a believer in the freeness of salvation, which was given universally and without restriction to all humanity on the condition that they be receptive to God's love and not try to accomplish by their own deeds what is possible only through God's grace. This formulation recalled neither Calvin, nor Luther, nor Trent, but was closer to the ideas of Erasmus. Faith was the acceptance of God's love, with absolute trust, by a free being who cooperated with God's grace. Christ wished the man of faith to believe in nothing but his goodness and to free himself from his own self-interest to live in Christ alone. L'Hospital designated faith as *alma fides,* through which man no longer lived through anything other than Christ. The motion that brought man closer to God was one born of free will. L'Hospital, having placed all of his faith in God's justice and mercy, was a believer in man's freedom to move toward God of his own will.

The man who possesses God's wisdom is obligated to his utmost to make others learn the path that took him from tempestuous waters to a port made sunny by nourishing faith. To govern was to work in synergy with the love of God to fight evil and sin, to struggle to put humanity on the path toward God's love. Charity was, for L'Hospital, the foremost virtue and had to inform everything the prince and his counselors did. The world had to be at peace before anything else, because only in peace could it encounter divine love. L'Hospital's Christ, who ordered mankind not to resort to war and to suffer threats and torture without complaint, who forbade use of the sword and of terror, and who set an example through his death, was the Pauline Christ who subjugated the turbulence of history to the discipline of rhetoric, thus controlling men's passions. To men saved by grace in exchange for their faith "he ordered, on the other hand, that they calm the insubordinate souls and hearts through their words."[45] Law was a gift from the self to the community, bereft of any private sentiment, to bring the civic community to a state of order that would allow it to grasp God's mercy and justice.

This was an image of a fraternal and charitable world that arose from evangelical times, when Christ taught his followers to ask no one but God for forgiveness and peace of life. This does not mean, however, that L'Hospital approved of the Calvinists' rupture from Rome; quite the contrary, for in one letter, he referred to them as "wolves." His portrayal of religious sentiment was also very derisive of piety of the papacy and other corrupt prelates.

L'Hospital added that Christ wanted the rich to help the poor and the blind to be helped to find their way, and that it was by such show of brotherhood that religion, in the time of the early Christians, had become widespread. An important

---

[45]L'Hospital, quoted in Henri Amphoux, *Michel de L'Hospital et la liberté de conscience au XVIe siècle* (Paris: Librairie Fischbacher, 1900), 269–70: "Il ordonna, en revanche, de calmer par la parole les esprits et les coeurs insoumis."

source that echoed this system of thought was Cicero, who made it possible to apply Christian ideals to the governance of the civic entity. From Cicero came the notion of the impartial sage who should not adhere to any political parties, was beyond political affiliation, and did not favor anyone.[46] To favor one of the parties would be to deny one's friendship to everyone, and to yield to the fear that the opposing party might get the upper hand. L'Hospital elaborated a mode of power that relied on a strategy of overcoming divisions and opinions, of the sharing of friendship, and of a moderation nurtured by that friendship. Politics, for the chancellor, was a universal friendship that reflected Christ's universal love as shown in his gift to mankind. L'Hospital added that politics should remove men from their state of presumptuousness that makes them believe they can do what only God can, relying on their enfeebled understanding to decide which are the truths of faith.

The edict was a direct application, the hidden writing-into-law of this particular evangelism of the *amicitia-caritas.* Therefore, the edict intended to sever men from the temptation to appropriate any realm of action that did not depend on God and to stop them from playing God by imposing their faith on others. God was omnipotent; only he knew the meaning of history. Through peace, men were able to distance themselves from their passions, which were the root of all their quarrels, and to implore God for his forgiveness. Therefore, if men placed all their faith in God's mercy, God would bring them all together as a single flock at a time only he knew. L'Hospital's work aimed at creating an intermediary period during which men, specifically through acts of charity, would help God to exercise his justice mixed with mercy. That would neither mean an autonomous nor secularized period, but a period of preparation for society's return to a complete state of holiness. L'Hospital did not believe in tolerance in the modern sense of the term; he was not a precursor of the Enlightenment *philosophes,* at least not in that direct a manner. Rather, he believed in the concord that existed in peace. Such concord was the first stage that would prepare mankind for a return to unity, bring reform to the Roman Catholic Church, and cause a reformation of mores. Consequently, such change would place mankind in a position to receive God's forgiveness. The meaning of the edict, as its content and formal framework suggest, had the sense of a confession of faith, conveying an immense amount of faith in a just and merciful God. As this study has suggested, this was much more an edict of moderation than one of toleration in the modern sense.

---

[46]Cicero *De officiis* 1.25.85–89.

Jacques Chomarat has underscored a point that could prove important in understanding the intellectual mechanisms behind Michel de L'Hospital's desire for
peace. Chomarat indicates that Erasmus lingered over Christ's prudence and dis-
sembling to the pilgrims on their way to Emmaus. Christ could have gone as far as
beguiling or cheating, even as far as trapping the tempter, as there could have
been some Christian cheating in the face of Satan's lies. However, such cheating
would have been only temporary and would have been infused with charity. It
would amount to a desire to do good to one's neighbor in spite of himself, without
his being clearly aware of it. For Erasmus, *tolerantia* was not to be understood as a
"sharing of errors." Rather, *tolerantia* was an active decision to "bear patiently" the
faults of another, as only God was in any position to put an end to such faults:
"[t]his 'tolerance' does not signify that one shares their error or that one views it
with indifference, but that one counts on time and kindness to make it disappear,
and not upon violence."[47] This was certainly L'Hospital's main line of thought
when he conceived of a law of difference, a law that was understood by his contemporaries as a discourse of difference, not of acceptance. The historian's task,
however, is to analyze with precision from the viewpoint of difference in relation
to his own universe of representation, while taking into account the particular
faith that motivated Charles IX's chancellor.

---

[47]Jacques Chomarat, *Grammaire et rhétorique chez Erasme* (Paris: Belles lettres, 1981), 2:661:
"cette 'tolérance' ne signifie pas qu'on partage leur erreur ou qu'on la voie avec indifférence, mais que
l'on compte sur le temps et la douceur pour la faire disparaître et non sur la violence." On Erasmus's
rebuttal of intolerance, cf. Thierry Wanegffelen, *L'Edit de Nantes: Une Histoire européenne de la Tolérance du XVIe au XXe siècle* (Paris: Livre de poche, 1998), 77–87.

Waging Peace

MEMORY, IDENTITY, AND THE EDICT OF NANTES

Barbara B. Diefendorf

Injury has a long memory. From Ireland to the Balkan states to India, parties to ethnic and religious quarrels justify their behavior by citing grievances that date back hundreds of years. Stories of forced conversion and dispossession vie with incidents of rape and murder as catalogs of old injustices warn against even the possibility of trust. The power of collective memory complicates any attempt to negotiate peace after the turmoil of ethnic or religious clashes or the violent rupture of civil war. But should we remember or should we forget? When is it healthy to learn the truth about past enmities and when does rehashing old injuries merely perpetuate the chain of mutual recriminations and act as a barrier to peace? South Africa's Truth and Reconciliation Commission was founded on the premise that "without memory, there is no healing," and that healing may be more important than justice before a court of law. The commission offers amnesty to those who confess to racial crimes. "There is no point exacting vengeance now, knowing that it will be the cause for future vengeance by the offspring of those we punish," explains Bishop Desmond Tutu. And yet, for the sake of the victims—for their injured self-worth and dignity—the past cannot simply be forgotten. "Denial doesn't work," adds Bishop Tutu. "It can never lead to forgiveness and reconciliation. Amnesia is no solution. If a nation is going to be healed, it has to come to grips with the past. This has been true of the concentration camp experience for Jews all over the world."[1]

As Bishop Tutu recognizes, the idea that only in acknowledging memory can one do justice to suffering is in many respects a legacy of the Holocaust, a corollary to the lesson that only by remembering crimes against humanity can we prevent

---

Unless otherwise indicated, all translations from foreign language sources are the author's.

[1]Bishop Desmond Tutu, interview by Colin Greer, *Parade Magazine* (11 January 1998): 4–6. The article is significant because it presents to a popular audience debates over how to deal with a troubled past often reserved for more specialized venues. Also general, but more substantial, is Timothy Garton Ash, "The Truth about Dictatorship," *The New York Review of Books* 45 (19 February 1998): 35–40.

their recurrence. As a sign above the exit to the Monument to the Deportation in
Paris reminds us, "Pardonne, mais n'oublie pas." The idea that remembering past
injuries can be divorced from the desire for vengeance is nevertheless a recent
one, a product of our "psychological" age. Four hundred years ago, when Henri
IV sought a peaceful end to forty years of religious war, no one dreamed that
recalling the wounds each side inflicted on the other could do anything except
perpetuate the quarrels by rekindling still smouldering hatreds. As a means of
healing his wounded kingdom, Henri prescribed not memory but rather oblivion—*oubliance*. Indeed, the very first clause of the Edict of Nantes provides "that
the memory of all things passed on the one part and the other [during the wars of
the League] and also during the other precedent troubles...shall remain extinguished and suppressed, as things that had never been."[2] Henri not only forbade
both the public and private pursuit of grievances arising from the religious conflicts, he went so far as to prohibit any reference to past quarrels that might tend
to stir up old animosities.[3]

But outlawing memory does not in fact suppress it. Earlier attempts at settling the religious conflicts had proved that one could not simply legislate forget-
fulness; positive guarantees and protective measures against retribution were also
necessary. Time and experience also proved that some injuries should not simply
be forgotten. If the state was to return to any semblance of order, a line had to be
drawn between acts of war, for which amnesty should apply, and criminal acts, for
which it should not, although admittedly the distinction is not always clear. The
requirement to extinguish all memory of the troubles thus existed in tension with
the need to remember them as part of Henri's strategy for the waging of peace,
and this tension between memory and forgetting may be explored through the
earlier, unsuccessful attempts to end the religious conflicts.

If memory existed in tension with forgetting, it also existed in defiance of it.
The sufferings endured in the wars were not forgotten but were rather memorialized in history and legend. Religious boundaries and religious identity were still
fluid in the mid-sixteenth century. A distinctive Huguenot identity was forged only
under the pressure of civil war, the need for self-definition being part and parcel of
self-defense. Collective memory operated in various ways to forge among French
Protestants an identity premised on separation, or difference, that remained in tension with the unified national identity ardently desired by the centralizing state.

[2]Quotes from the Edict of Nantes are taken from the now antiquated but still most accessible
English translation, E. Everard, *The Great Pressures and Grievances of the Protestants in France* (London, 1681), republished as appendix 4 of Roland Mousnier's *The Assassination of Henri IV: The Tyrannicide Problem & the Consolidation of the French Absolute Monarchy in the Early 17th Century*, trans.
Joan Spencer (New York: Scribner, 1973), 318. Spelling and punctuation have been modernized for
clarity.
[3]Mousnier, *Assassination of Henri IV*, 319.

In reaction to the challenge of the Protestant Reformation, Catholic identity also acquired greater definition. But the dilemmas of memory and identity did not just affect Protestant-Catholic divisions in France. The wars of the League created a deep rupture within the Catholic faith. Henri IV's command to forget past divisions applied to internecine quarrels between ultra-Catholics and Catholic moderates, or *politiques,* as well as to Protestant-Catholic quarrels, and here too the persistence of memory threatened the legal requirement to forget. This study will also explore some of the tensions that arose within French Catholicism as a result of the quarrels of the League and suggest some consequences of these quarrels for Catholic identity in France.

THE TENSION BETWEEN MEMORY AND OBLIVION
The policy of relegating past quarrels to oblivion did not originate with the Edict of Nantes. It has precedents in medieval peace treaties, which similarly forbade any rehashing of old wrongs. Moreover, like almost all of the provisions of the treaty concluded at Nantes, the clauses on *oubliance,* or oblivion, can be found in the edicts of pacification issued in the wake of previous religious wars. Indeed, the passages quoted above occur almost word for word in the Edict of Amboise, which settled the first War of Religion in March 1563, and in every subsequent edict of pacification down to the Edict of Nantes. The only difference is that the passages forbidding memory of the quarrels occurred toward the end of the first two peace treaties. They were moved to the front with the Edict of Saint-Germain (1570) and remained there in the Edicts of Boulogne (1573) and Beaulieu (1576), and the Peace of Bergerac (1577).[4] In other respects, however, the edicts changed significantly over time. Most important, they became more complex. Each new war added to the accumulated grievances that divided the parties; at the same time, those negotiating peace were forced to recognize that a return to prewar circumstances was impossible, and increasingly elaborate provisions had to be made to allow the two faiths to attempt a peaceful coexistence.

In surveying the provisions made for religious peace, it is useful to begin not with the edict of pacification issued after the first War of Religion ended in March 1563, but rather with the edicts issued by Catherine de Médicis when she assumed the regency for her second son, ten-year-old Charles IX, in December 1560. The policies that culminated in the Edict of Nantes in fact began here, before the outbreak of war. The persecutions initiated by François I and his son Henri II, even the latter's institution of a *chambre ardente* in Parlement for the prosecution of

---

[4]Stegmann, *Edits,* 35–36 (Edit d'Amboise), 56 (Paix de Longjumeau, 1568), 69 (Edit de Saint-Germain, 1570), 87 (Edit de Boulogne, 1573), 97 (Edit de Beaulieu, 1576), and 132 (Paix de Bergerac, 1577).

religious crimes, are less relevant here than is the intensification of religious persecutions under Henri II's son, François II, whose brief reign (1559–60) was dominated by his wife's ultra-Catholic uncles, François, duc de Guise, and Charles,
cardinal of Lorraine. The new policies increased religious tensions without at the
same time halting the new religion's spread. When François II died in December
1560, Catherine, in seizing the regency, hoped to alleviate both the factional rivalries aggravated by Guise domination and the religious tensions aggravated by their
persecutions by adopting a more flexible policy of limited toleration of religious
dissent. She seems, however, to have misjudged just how much advantage the
Huguenots might derive from the slightest easing of the pressure of persecution.

Having long chafed under the restrictive laws that forbade them to assemble
openly, members of the Reformed churches responded eagerly to Catherine's easing of restrictive policies. As ever larger audiences turned out for religious services, the Huguenots grew more confident, took more risks, and assembled more
openly. As Huguenots grew bolder, Catholics grew more restive. Taught to view
Reformed theology as heresy and Reformed Church meetings as seditious, Catholics responded with harassment and incidents of popular violence. In April 1561,
Catherine tried to calm the situation by declaring that no one should be injured or
provoked on account of religion. She hoped that a church council would resolve
the theological differences between proponents of the new faith and the old, fostering a return to religious uniformity. In the meantime, each side should exercise
restraint. In fact, just the opposite occurred. Protestants took advantage of the situation to meet still more openly; Catholics reacted with increasing anger. Clashes
between the two groups increased in number and severity.

A royal edict issued in July 1561 attempted to clarify the April law by
expressly forbidding public meetings at which the new doctrines were preached,
but as the edict also forbade provoking or injuring anyone on account of their
religious opinions, it did not put a stop to Calvinist preaching and even, in the
opinion of many Catholics, encouraged a further expansion of the Reformed
Church movement. In January 1562, Catherine took a further risk and issued in
her son's name an edict that retracted the prohibition on assemblies of the new
faith. It is hard to overstate the momentous importance of this edict, which for the
first time authorized the practice of two religions side by side within the state. The
edict did set geographical limits on where Huguenots might worship, expressly
permitting such assemblies only as long as they were held outside town walls. And
it set at least an implicit temporal limit to the arrangement. Like the Edict of July,
the January law was qualified as provisional, serving only until a church council
could meet to reconcile differences between the two confessions. It was nevethe-
less represented as a concession of such major proportions to the Huguenots that,
right up until the Edict of Nantes, their very first demand in the negotiation of any

peace (that they came to from a position of strength) was for the restoration of the January Edict. By the same logic, this edict was totally unacceptable to many French Catholics, convinced by the message from the pulpit that heresy was a cancer that would destroy the social body if not promptly rooted out. The edict's concessions to the Huguenots, moreover, prompted Catholics to direct their rage against the Crown, which was accused of passively accepting—or even encouraging—the infection of heresy, as well as against the Huguenots, who were considered the source of the pernicious infection.

The religious divisions in turn exacerbated political factionalism and undermined monarchical authority, already weakened by the absence of a mature, adult king. Militant Protestants demanding freedom of worship, on the one hand, and an alliance of hard-line Catholics intent on the elimination of heresy at any price, on the other, posed a threat to the Crown. Both factions, moreover, were headed by ambitious aristocrats whose personal rivalries were inseparable from their political and religious allegiances. The Catholic alliance, or Triumvirate, also enjoyed broad popular support, and the threat of popular insurrection posed an additional danger to royal policy making. Paris, fiercely Catholic and ever volatile, was a particularly sensitive trouble spot.[5] When the religious tensions erupted into war in 1562, the royal family was caught between the opposing factions. Catherine solicited the protection of Louis, prince of Condé, the Huguenot leader, but he failed to respond and with his troops seized Orléans and other key towns. Catherine reluctantly accepted the protection the Triumvirate offered her, but continued to attempt to negotiate peace.

Thus began the first of the eight civil wars that fractured the French state and reduced it to near anarchy before a relatively stable peace was achieved with the Edict of Nantes in 1598. The Protestant population of France was small, comprising at most 10 to 15 percent of the kingdom's roughly twenty million souls. The Huguenots' strategy of seizing broadly scattered and defensible towns, coupled with the hiring of foreign mercenaries to supplement locally raised troops, gave them a military strength disproportionate to their numbers. In each of the wars, the Huguenot position in the field remained strong enough to force a compromise peace upon the Catholics. At the end of each war, the Huguenots managed to retain a right to worship too limited for their own satisfaction and yet unacceptable in principle to their ultra-Catholic opponents.

The Peace of Amboise, which settled the first war in March 1563, embodied the essential compromises that marked every subsequent peace down to and including the Edict of Nantes. It promised freedom of conscience to all, but limited

[5]The nature and seriousness of this threat is the subject of my *Beneath the Cross: Catholics and Huguenots in Sixteenth-Century Paris* (New York: Oxford University Press, 1991).

RELIGIOUS DIFFERENCES IN FRANCE

the right to worship according to specific social and geographical criteria. Only noble households above a certain rank might establish religious services for their dependents and not just their immediate families. In addition, the Calvinists were permitted to hold services in the suburbs of one town in each judicial district, or *bailliage*, and in those towns they had held at the time the fighting ceased. These services had to be held in members' homes or other private properties; Protestants were forbidden to build temples and were required to return all buildings and furnishings seized from the Catholic Church. In recognition of the Parisians' vociferous opposition to the compromise peace, Paris was exempted from the provisions for urban worship. Protestant services were strictly forbidden in both the city and its suburbs. Each of the subsequent peace treaties contained a similar provision.

Later treaties differed on just where and how broadly Calvinist worship might be established. When the Huguenots finished a war in a strong position, forcing a settlement upon the Crown, they naturally took advantage of the situation to push for further concessions, such as additional sites for religious services. But the converse was also true: when the ultra-Catholics were in the ascendancy, they pushed back the Huguenots' privileges. Most of the wars resulted from a kind of pendulum effect whereby the party that felt most aggrieved by the deficiencies of one settlement rallied its forces, initiated a new round of warfare, and hoped to gain sufficient advantage that the next peace treaty would operate in its favor. All of the treaties were compromises, but none were equally acceptable to both sides. This was the essential mechanism that perpetuated the wars.

In addition to regulating the conditions for Huguenot worship, the treaties subsequent to the 1563 Edict of Amboise adopted increasingly complex provisions intended to guarantee the peace by attempting to short-circuit the bad feelings that inevitably arose from the wars and by providing venues in which complaints about the nonexecution of the peace could be aired. Beginning with the Edict of Amboise, all the treaties explicitly pardoned participants in the war, forbade recriminatory acts, and insisted that members of both faiths "live peacefully together, as brothers, friends, and fellow citizens."[6] The edict ordered the release of all religious prisoners and prisoners of war, but it made no explicit provision for the return of properties, offices, or titles taken from Huguenots as a result of the war. Like medieval peace treaties, it seemed to assume that ordering a return to the *status quo ante bellum,* along with the prohibitions against renewing or even recollecting mutual injuries, would suffice to guarantee the peace. This oversight was remedied in the Peace of Longjumeau, which settled the second war in March 1568. Subsequent treaties similarly promised that possessions, offices,

[6]Stegmann, *Edits,* 35–36.

and titles taken from the Huguenots during the war should be returned to them. The king also, beginning with Longjumeau, usually agreed to pay the cost of the foreign mercenaries hired to fight the war. The latter provision was a pragmatic one—the sooner the mercenaries were paid, the sooner they would leave France and stop preying upon the countryside—but, as can be imagined, it caused no end of anger among the citizens who found themselves taxed to pay off the armies that had so recently made war against them.

Catholic resistance to the Peace of Longjumeau meant that neither side disarmed. The third War of Religion broke out just five months later and continued for more than two years. When peace was finally signed at Saint-Germain in August 1570, the Huguenots, who at one point had appeared the sure losers in the war, had rallied sufficiently to negotiate once again from a position of strength. They retained the rights promised in the previous peace treaties, but gained an additional place of worship in every province. The treaty represented an important advance over the Edict of Amboise and the Peace of Longjumeau in the concrete steps it took to secure civil order by eliminating obvious causes of popular violence. It laid down rules governing Protestant burials, putting an end to Catholics' disinterments of what they considered to be heretics buried on hallowed ground. It also ordered the destruction of any monuments to the quarrels, a clause intended among other things to force the removal of a pyramid erected in central Paris to commemorate the execution for heresy of several bourgeois notables in 1569. In exchange, the Huguenots promised to respect Catholic customs by closing their shops on designated feast days and refraining from selling meat during Lent. For the first time, an edict of pacification recognized the persistent tensions deriving not just from doctrinal or factional differences between Catholics and Huguenots, but from the elaboration of distinctive customs and religious identities, and it tried to find ways to relieve these tensions.

The Edict of Saint-Germain also recognized for the first time that the courts of justice might not deal equitably with lawsuits brought by Protestants—or at least that the Protestants might fear this to be the case—and included special provisions intended to allow Huguenots to level the scales of justice either by recusing a certain proportion of their judges or by having their cases evoked to other courts. In exchange, Catholics were allowed to recuse any Protestant judges and prevent them from taking part in their trials. These provisions mark a first recognition of a problem that was to result in later edicts of pacification in the creation of special courts—*chambres de l'édit* or *chambres mi-parties*.[7]

---

[7]See Diane Margolf, "Adjudicating Memory: Law and Religious Difference in Early Seventeenth-Century France," *Sixteenth Century Journal* 27 (1996): 399–418.

Equally important, the Edict of Saint-Germain (or the Paix de Saint-Germain) explicitly recognized that memory of the quarrels could not simply be suppressed "because some people have received and still suffer such injuries and harm to their properties and persons that only with great difficulty will they be able to forget."[8] Many Huguenots feared to return to their homes and concrete measures had to be taken to guarantee their security. Charles IX accordingly promised the Huguenots four *places de sûreté,* fortified cities they might hold and use as places of refuge for a period of two years before surrendering them back to the king. An innovation in 1570, the principle of holding fortified cities as *places de sûreté* was something that the Huguenots tried to insist upon in each subsequent peace. It should be noted, however, that from the beginning the *places de sûreté* were intended to be temporary measures. When the designated period was over, the Huguenots could continue to live freely and practice their faith in the appointed cities, but they had to turn political control over to whomever the king chose to name and permit the free exercise of the Catholic faith.

The Saint Bartholomew's Massacre, which began on 24 August 1572, initiated the fourth religious war. The order that gave rise to the massacre appears to have had its origins in Charles IX's fear of a Huguenot coup, but the precise role Charles IX and other members of his family played in the events of Saint Bartholomew's Day will never be known for certain. The Huguenot leaders who escaped the killing in Paris took refuge in La Rochelle, one of their designated *places de sûreté,* and directed a war for their very survival. Besieged for seven months, they yielded in July of 1573 and signed a peace that, although superficially resembling the Peace of Saint-Germain, severely restricted practice of the Reformed faith. Reformed worship was allowed only in La Rochelle, Montauban, and Nîmes, and even in these places it was permitted only in private.

The Huguenots were not satisfied with these conditions and began to plot a new offensive. Huguenot propagandists publicized the horrors of Saint Bartholomew's Day and wrote treatises arguing that resistance to monarchical authority was justified when the king behaved like a tyrant. Huguenots in the south, where the Protestant population was strongest, took the more radical step of drawing up a republican constitution effectively separating them from the monarchy. In 1574 they forged an alliance with the Catholic governor of Languedoc, Henri de Montmorency, sieur de Damville. Damville typifies the emergence among Catholics of a new advocacy of religious coexistence as a means of resolving the kingdom's quarrels. Derisively nicknamed *politiques* by ultra-Catholics (who believed they sacrificed religious truth to political ends), men like Damville never formed a unified party. They nevertheless shared a belief that serious political and economic

[8]Stegmann, *Edicts,* 78.

reforms were needed to repair the damage done by the wars and ensure lasting peace. At the same time, they saw peace as a precondition for reform and were willing to ally themselves with the Huguenots in pursuit of these goals.

Charles IX died in May 1574 and was succeeded by his brother Henri, recently elected king of Poland. Everyone tensely awaited his return. Known as an ardent Catholic, Henri disappointed the militants who hoped he would lead them to triumph over the Huguenots. The Crown's debts were so enormous that he could not have raised an effective army had he wanted to. A fitful war broke out in which Henri's brother, François, duc d'Alençon, became the figurehead of the Huguenot-*politique* alliance. Alençon was heir to the throne, and his rebellion threatened irreparable harm to the state. Henri III was forced to negotiate peace in May 1576.

As might be predicted from the king's humiliation, the Peace of Beaulieu made more concessions to the Huguenots than in any other war. Signed in May 1576, the edict permitted the Huguenots to worship and even to build churches in any places that belonged to them or whose owners consented, except Paris and its immediate surroundings. It gave them eight *places de sûreté,* twice the number accorded by the Peace of Saint-Germain, and it created special chambers in Parlement to hear cases where religious differences might otherwise impede the rendering of justice. The king also submitted to Huguenot demands in publicly expressing his "very great regret and displeasure" over the events of Saint Bartholomew's Day and reversing legal judgments against Admiral Coligny and others convicted as rebels in the wake of these events. He restored Damville and other *politique* leaders to their offices and honors and awarded the governorships of Picardy and Guyenne to Huguenot leaders—Henri, prince of Condé, and Henri, king of Navarre, respectively—thereby leaving an important power base in the Huguenots' hands. Alençon was rewarded with the title of duc d'Anjou and given a large swath of lands across central France to hold in *apanage.* Finally, Henri III agreed to convoke the Estates General at Blois within six months to hear his subjects' remonstrances and reestablish the good order necessary for lasting peace.

The generous terms of the Peace of Beaulieu angered ultra-Catholics, who formed a league in defense of the faith under the leadership of Henri, duc de Guise (son François, duc de Guise, assassinated in 1563). Henri III attempted to co-opt the League, hoping thereby to raise money and troops to reverse the humiliating Peace of Beaulieu. The Huguenots fought again and lost some of their gains. The Peace of Bergerac, concluded in September 1577, rolled back their freedom of worship and reduced the proportion of Protestant judges in the special courts designated to try cases involving religious differences. Moreover, for the first time since the January Edict of 1562, the settlement was explicitly described as provisional and intended to last only until "a good, free, and legitimate general council could reunite all of [the king's] subjects in the Catholic Church."[9] Despite these limitations, the concessions made to the Huguenots were too generous to satisfy the ultra-Catholics. Another brief war in 1580 failed to change the status quo. Henri III grew increasingly unpopular. Debts mounted; popular rebellions and disorders troubled the countryside.

The death of François, duc d'Anjou, in 1584 caused a succession crisis. It seemed increasingly unlikely that Henri III would produce a son. The Protestant Henri de Bourbon, king of Navarre, was by Salic law heir to the throne. Ultra-Catholics revived the League to oppose this prospect and signed an alliance with Spain (December 1584) to finance a new war against heresy. While the Guises recruited aristocrats, urban Leagues formed in the cities. Bowing to League power in July 1585, Henri III signed the Treaty of Nemours. Promising to eradicate heresy, he revoked the edicts of pacification, forbade practice of the Reformed faith, and ordered Protestant ministers to leave France. Their hard-won rights revoked, the Huguenots again prepared for war; the League prepared to fight them. Caught between, Henri temporized, hoping that the League forces would exhaust themselves in battle and the Huguenots likewise, leaving only him to refill the vacuum. It did not happen this way. The royal army that Henri sent against the Huguenots lost a key battle; the League won one he expected them to lose. Henri de Guise's star continued to rise, Henri III's to decline. Desperate to reverse this situation, Henri III ordered the assassination of the duc de Guise. This fatal move, carried out 23 December 1588, only hastened his path toward disaster. Instead of a tenuous alliance with the all-too-powerful League, Henri was faced with outright revolt. Beginning with Paris, cities across the country renounced their loyalty to the "murderous tyrant." They celebrated the fallen duc de Guise as a martyr and looked to his kin for leadership where the king had failed them. Henri III had no choice but to turn to Henri de Navarre and create an alliance with him to put down the revolt of the League. He was engaged in just this process when, in August 1589, an assassin made him pay for Guise's life with his own. Among his last actions was formally to recognize Navarre as his heir.

Making good on the claim was something Navarre, now Henri IV, had to do for himself. This is not the place to recount the familiar story of his military victories and the key role that his conversion played both in securing him entry to his capital and in weakening popular enthusiasm for the League. It is important, however, to recognize that Henri's consolidation of power was a gradual process and depended as much on a policy of deliberate appeasement as on military victory. In fact, the essential conundrum that Henri IV faced in trying to impose

---

[9]Stegman, *Edits,* 132: "un bon, libre, et légitime concile général, de réunir tous nos sujets à notre église catholique."

peace on his troubled kingdom was the same one as his predecessors had tried unsuccessfully to resolve for nearly half a century. Despite the many successes of his policy of appeasement, powerful adversaries remained on both sides of the Crown. They included both the more militant of Henri's former Huguenot allies and the leaders of the Catholic League that had fought tooth and nail to prevent his accession to the throne. He had defeated (or, more often, bought off) the ultra-Catholic leaders one by one, but he knew that they remained powerful enough to thwart his efforts at a religious settlement if he made too many concessions to his former coreligionists. At the same time, he recognized that the Huguenots' loyalty had been sorely tested by his abjuration. Although some Huguenots had accepted his conversion as a political necessity required to secure the allegiance of moderate Catholics and to weaken the grounds for opposition on the part of the ultras, many could not overcome the conviction that he had betrayed not only his faith but also their common cause.

Six months after his abjuration and ceremonial promise in July 1593 to live and die in the Catholic faith, Henri IV was consecrated in Chartres Cathedral (Rheims was still in the hands of his enemies). His coronation oath, like that of his predecessors, explicitly required him to expel all heretics designated by the church. Would he live up to his oath? The ultra-Catholics insisted that he must; the Huguenots feared that he would. Both sides threatened to return to the battlefield if Henri did not deliver a satisfactory peace, and yet the demands that they considered essential to peace were mutually contradictory. The Huguenots required freedom of conscience and the right to practice their religion, but also civil rights and certain guarantees of military force they believed necessary to back up their other claims. The ultra-Catholics continued to insist on the extirpation of heresy and the formal return of religious dissidents to the unique practice of the Roman Catholic faith. They were, by extension, violently opposed to granting civil recognition to the Huguenots and to their creation of a defensible "state within the state."

In many respects, then, the religious situation in France had changed very little since 1562, when these same contradictory demands for religious liberty versus Catholic unanimity had first reduced the state to civil war. Indeed, if anything, it would seem that the years of violent conflict had only deepened the mutual distrust between the opposing parties, making it still more difficult to negotiate a workable religious settlement. It is true that all of the parties were tired of war. They were exhausted emotionally and economically by the devastations of marauding armies, the civil disorders occasioned by religious hatreds, and the financial exactions brought on by the wars. And yet both the ultra-Catholics and the Huguenots were serious in their threat to return to battle if Henri did not offer acceptable terms for peace.

RELIGIOUS DIFFERENCES IN FRANCE

In 1591, Henri IV had unilaterally reinstated the 1577 Peace of Bergerac abolished by Henri III on the demand of the League in 1585. In 1595, at the Huguenots' behest he coaxed Parlement to re-register "the deceased king's edict," that is to say, the Peace of Bergerac, and announced his firm intention to make it the law of the land. Parlement's hesitations and the quibbles over key provisions in the edict, such as the right of Huguenots to hold all honors and offices in the state, caused the latter to press for further concessions. Needing the Huguenots' assistance to drive the Spanish armies from the north of France, Henri reopened negotiations in 1596. His commissioners agreed to some liberalization in the terms of the peace. They added a large number of articles spelling out in detail how the special courts of Parlement were to operate and to otherwise guarantee that Huguenots should receive fair treatment under the law, but they held firm against the Huguenots' demand for the freedom of worship first accorded nearly forty years earlier with the January Edict of 1562.

If the Edict of Nantes closely resembles the Peace of Bergerac, this is because the latter document was on the table when further discussions were reopened. One big difference between Henri III's peacemaking and Henri IV's, however, was already apparent when Parlement consented to re-register the Peace of Bergerac in 1595. As one of the magistrates pointed out, "the edict of 1577 … was only a piece of paper with writing on it, which the king gave the Huguenots to content them on paper," whereas this time they could be quite certain that the king intended the edict to be observed.[10] But before the Edict of Nantes could be observed, Henri IV had to get it registered by Parlement, and this necessity dictated other differences between the peace made at Nantes and the Peace of Bergerac. The most inflammatory concessions to the Huguenots were contained not in the ninety-two general or fifty-six secret articles that made up the Edict of Nantes, but rather in two special warrants, or *brevets*, appended to the agreement that did not require Parlement's approval. The first of the *brevets* promised to pay the salaries of Reformed Church ministers and was intended to compensate for the fact that, by the general articles, Huguenots had to pay the ecclesiastical tithe, just as Catholics did. The second and even more controversial *brevet* concerned the *places de sûreté* left in Huguenot hands. Instead of just a handful of armed towns such as the earlier edicts provided, Henri allowed the Huguenots to maintain garrisons in "all the fortified places, towns, and châteaux that they held up to the end of last August [1597]."[11] This amounted to some two hundred towns, roughly half of which were to be garrisoned at the Crown's expense for a period of eight years. As Mack Holt points out, "By allowing the Huguenots to remain armed and in

[10]Pierre de L'Estoile, *Mémoires-journaux: Journal de Henri IV, 1595–1601* 7, ed. G. Brunet et al. (Paris: Librairie des Bibliophiles, 1879), 14.

[11]Mousnier, *Assassination of Henri IV,* 360.

possession of so many fortified towns, Henri was indirectly endorsing the Huguenot 'state within the state.' The king made it very clear, however, that this concession of fortified towns was purely temporary, as the *brevet* expired eight years
after its publication."[12]

Holt makes it clear, moreover, that "religious coexistence, like the 'state
within the state,' was never meant to be permanent," and this is indeed the conclusion of most recent scholars who have studied the Edict of Nantes.[13] Rendered
necessary by circumstances—by the overwhelming need for peace after nearly
forty years of civil war—the edict was intended pragmatically to provide rules for
living together peacefully until all the king's subjects might be reunited in one
church. As Henri expressed it in the edict's preamble:

> Now that it hath pleased God to give us a beginning of enjoying some rest, we
> think we cannot employ our self better than to apply to that which may tend
> to the glory and service of his holy name, and to provide that He may be
> adored and prayed unto by all our subjects: and if it hath not yet pleased him
> to permit it to be in one and the same form of Religion, that it may at the least
> be with one and the same intention, and with such rules that may prevent
> amongst them all troubles and tumults.[14]

The idea that the religious divisions were something that God permitted and
would someday bring to an end, the better to reveal his truth and glory, should
not be taken as a convenient platitude but rather as a sincere—and commonly
shared—statement of belief. Whatever their differences, Protestants and Catholics
believed that there was only one true faith, and if each side believed that it had
already identified that faith (that was, after all, what they were fighting about),
they had no doubt that God would in time offer abundant signs to make his truth
manifest. Some still held out the hope that the churches would be reunited
through a general council; others believed in a more gradual conversion process,
through which those floundering in error came to recognize the truth.[15] Either

---

[12]Holt, *French Wars of Religion,* 166.

[13]The fundamental article on the subject is Mario Turchetti, "'Concorde ou tolérance?' de 1562 à
1598," *Revue historique* 274 (1985): 341–55. Mack Holt and Philip Benedict, among others, also explicitly argue that the Edict of Nantes was never intended to be more than a temporary religious settlement and that Henri IV, as well as his Bourbon successors, ardently hoped that his subjects would
ultimately be reunited in one church. See Holt, *French Wars of Religion;* and Philip Benedict, "*Un roi,
une loi, deux fois:* Parameters for the History of Catholic-Reformed Coexistence in France, 1555–
1685," in *Tolerance and Intolerance in the European Reformation,* ed. Ole Peter Grell and Bob Scribner
(New York: Cambridge University Press, 1996), 65–93.

[14]Mousnier, *Assassination of Henri IV,* 317.

[15]The Reformed Church synod of Montpellier in May 1598, although recognizing "the duty of
all of the faithful heartily to desire the reunion of all of the subjects of this kingdom in the unity of
faith," nevertheless designated this reunion as "rather a matter of our prayers, than of our hopes" and
opposed any of the current attempts at reunion as utterly impossible and deserving of the most sincere

way, the fundamental assumption was that the circumstances requiring the edict
would eventually change. The designation of the edict as "perpetual and irrevocable," so often cited as evidence of Louis XIV's treachery in revoking the edict in
1685, is in fact misleading. It meant only that the edict could not be countermanded without the formal passage and registration of another edict. Just as the
Ordinances of Saint Maur, issued at the outbreak of the third War of Religion in
September 1568 that forbade all exercise of the Reformed faith by "a perpetual
and irrevocable edict" were countermanded by the equally "perpetual and irrevocable" Edict of Saint-Germain in 1570, so the Edict of Nantes was destined only to
last until a new law was passed.

The Huguenots knew this when they agreed to the edict. They bargained
hard to gain as much security as they could, but they knew that ultimately their
fate was in the hands of the king—and, they would have said, divine providence.
While the Revocation of the Edict of Nantes may have been a mistake, the idea
that it was the treacherous violation of a sacred promise is part of the myth and
not the history of the Edict of Nantes.[16] The Huguenots of course had an important part in the creation of this myth, but Catholic and secular opponents of absolutism played their part as well.

MEMORY AND HUGUENOT IDENTITY

"It is often said that history is written by the victors," notes Peter Burke. "It might
also be said that history is forgotten by the victors. They can afford to forget, while
the losers are unable to accept what happened and are condemned to brood over
it, relive it, and reflect how different it might have been." Burke cites the Irish and
the Poles as "particularly clear examples of the use of the past, the use of the social
memory, and the use of myth in order to define identity."[17] He might equally well
have cited the Huguenots. The story of their struggle for survival during the Wars
of Religion played a formative role in the shaping of a Huguenot identity and

---

censure. See John Quick, *Synodicon in Gallia Reformata, or, the Acts, Decisions, Decrees and Canons of
those Famous National Councils of the Reformed Churches in France* (London, 1692), 1:196. This official position was adopted precisely because there were members of the church still speaking and writing in favor of reunion.

[16]In writing about social memory and "the process by which the remembered past turns into
myth," Peter Burke distinguishes between myth in "the positivist sense of 'inaccurate history'" and
"the richer, more positive sense of a story with a symbolic meaning, made up of stereotyped incidents
and involving characters who are larger than life, whether they are heroes or villains." It is the latter,
richer meaning I am invoking here. Peter Burke, "History as Social Memory," in *Memory: History, Culture and the Mind,* Thomas Butler, ed. (Oxford: Oxford University Press, 1989), 97–112, quoted at
103–4. See also Maurice Halbwachs, *Les cadres sociaux de la mémoire* (Paris: Mouton, 1975), which
remains fundamental to historians' understanding of collective, or social, memory.

[17]Burke, "History as Social Memory," 106.

remains, more than four hundred years later, a key element in that identity. Retelling the story of the wars—reminding themselves of why they fought—taught the Huguenots who they were. It encouraged the formation of cultural practices and social boundaries that set them apart from French Catholics in ways that, at the start of the wars, were still only implicit in Calvinist theology.

One of the ironies, then, of the official demand for oblivion that ended each of the religious wars is that the demand was necessarily subverted by those who, even if they had no legal recourse for righting the wrongs that had been perpetrated against them, simply could not afford to forget. The demand for oblivion was premised on the notion that, with peace, the essential cause of the quarrels had been eliminated; in the Wars of Religion, this could not be the case. Fighting for the very right to exist as a separate church in a Catholic state, the Huguenots demanded not just to continue to worship separately but also to maintain the host of practices that, deriving from doctrinal differences, had come to separate them socially and culturally from their Catholic neighbors. At the same time, identifying themselves in all other ways as loyal subjects and citizens, they insisted on sharing fully the civil and legal rights, prerogatives, and honors accorded to those of the majority faith. The constant reminders of unacceptable differences, the demands for separateness and yet equality, were continual thorns in the Catholics' side. The elaboration of a distinctive Huguenot identity thus prompted a corresponding hardening of Catholic identity as Catholics acted out with new enthusiasm those rituals and gestures that set them apart from the Huguenots they despised.

It is important to remember that when the Wars of Religion broke out, religious identity in France was still fluid. The Reformed churches were not yet a decade old; the first national synod, which drafted the first Reformed Church Discipline for France, was held only in 1559. During the period before the religious wars, moreover, many of those who made up the audience for Reformed preaching were simple admirers or fellow travelers—people who were attracted to the Protestant message but had not achieved a level of conviction that impelled them to seek membership in the Reformed Church.[18] A large proportion of these fellow travelers never did convert, but rather ultimately retreated to the greater security of the traditional Catholic Church. Others converted but then found their faith shaken by the pressures of popular violence and the terrors of war. After the cataclysm of Saint Bartholomew's Day in particular, many Huguenots abandoned their faith. According to one Huguenot pastor, the French Reformed churches lost more than two-thirds of their members in the wake of the massacre and few of the apostates ever returned.[19]

[18]Diefendorf, *Beneath the Cross,* 115–18.
[19]Jean de L'Espine, *Traicté de l'apostasie* (n.p., 1583), Aii. See also Diefendorf, *Beneath the Cross,* 142–44.

There continued to be movement—conversion—both into and out of the Reformed Church, but what it meant to be a French Protestant necessarily changed once the church was under siege. Those who clung to the Reformed faith despite the adversities of war forged a distinctive and militant identity in the process. They found ready tools from which to create this identity in the Huguenot psalter. Identifying with David up against the Catholic Goliath, they learned to view persecution as a trial imposed by God and a special mark of his covenant. If the doctrine of predestination—or election to salvation—became more central to Calvinist than to Lutheran teaching, this is not just because of temperamental differences between Luther and Calvin or because of Calvin's more explicit discussion of this doctrine in his *Institutes*. French Protestants latched onto the idea of election because they needed to draw together in their adversity, and the greatest security they could find—the greatest assurance that the dangerous path they had chosen was the correct (indeed the only possible) one—lay in the notion of themselves as the chosen of God, the children of Israel, the elect.

The singing of psalms in Clement Marot's vernacular translation became a badge of French Protestant identity even before the religious wars, as bands of Protestants defied official prohibitions against the vernacular psalter by parading through city streets to the tune of the Psalms. During the wars, Huguenot congregations and Protestant regiments adopted particular psalms as their anthems, and songs celebrating Huguenot victories—or mourning defeats—were often written to their familiar tunes. After the shock of the Saint Bartholomew massacres, Huguenot pastors quite naturally turned to the rhythms and message of the Psalms as they attempted to reassure the faithful and reactivate the conscience of apostates to draw them back to the Reformed faith.[20] At the same time, the Huguenots built upon and expanded the image of themselves as a chosen people in their martyrologies, histories, and memoirs. Jean Crespin's *Histoire des martyrs,* first published in 1564, was expanded to include later tragedies and republished again and again. The *Histoire ecclésiastique* assembled under Théodore de Bèze's direction is in many respects also a martyrology, given the important place that the persecutions of the faithful have in the story it tells. Huguenot memoirs, such as Charlotte d'Arbaleste's life of her husband Philippe du Plessis de Mornay, worked the story of their trials into the reassuring message of God's providence to pass on to the next generation.[21] Popular songs and legends also memorialized the Huguenots'

[20]This discussion draws on my article "The Huguenot Psalter and the Faith of French Protestants," in *Culture and Identity in Early Modern Europe (1500–1800): Essays in Honor of Natalie Zemon Davis,* ed. Barbara Diefendorf and Carla Hesse (Ann Arbor: University of Michigan Press, 1993), 41–64.

[21]Charlotte d'Arbaleste, *Mémoires de Charlotte d'Arbaleste sur la vie de Duplessis-Mornay, son mari,* in Philippe Duplessis-Mornay, *Mémoires et correspondance* (Paris: Treuttel et Würtz, 1824), esp. 1:5–9, 39–46, 63–68, which d'Arbaleste addresses to her son and tells the story of her own and her husband's escape from the Saint Bartholomew's Day massacre.

sufferings during the religious wars, but most have been lost with the passage of time. Théodore-Agrippa d'Aubigné's stunning Huguenot epic, *Les Tragiques,* survives, and one episode in particular shows how the Huguenots transformed the memory of their sufferings into a mythic affirmation of identity and faith.

In the fourth book of the *Tragiques,* entitled "Les feux," d'Aubigné recounts how Richard de Gastines, arrested with several kinsmen for participating in clandestine Protestant rites in their house in Paris, preached the gospel within the very walls of the Conciergerie. D'Aubigné employs all of his poetic artistry to tell the story of this layman so moved by the spirit of God that he sought to bring the light of truth into the dark halls of his prison. He places in de Gastines's mouth a moving speech against the terrors of death, a speech by which the young man sought to breathe courage into the hearts of his fellow prisoners as they contemplated the painful death of execution by burning that would await them as convicted heretics, and he depicts him running joyously out to accept the martyrdom that was his fate.[22] This story does not appear in the standard Huguenot martyrologies. Jean Crespin's *Histoire des martyrs* and other Protestant histories tell of the arrest of Richard de Gastines, along with his father and their neighbor Nicolas Croquet, in January 1569 and their condemnation and execution six months later, but they make no mention of the sermon that d'Aubigné recounts.[23] It is possible that the whole episode sprang from the poet's fertile imagination, so well does it serve to insert into the heart of the poem (in the section devoted to the fires of martyrdom) a resounding statement of the Huguenots' conviction that in dying for their faith they would find eternal life. And yet there is archival evidence that Richard de Gastines did indeed preach an impromptu sermon within the walls of the Conciergerie.

The circumstances, however, were quite different from those that d'Aubigné recounts. Scholars will never know the full truth of what occurred, and it would be a mistake to naïvely suggest that archival evidence—in this case, testimony before Parlement—tells "the truth," while literary constructions like d'Aubigné's do not. Examination of the records shows two "truths" were manufactured, one that served the needs of de Gastines's Catholic jailors and one that served the needs of his coreligionists, while a third truth—or what Richard de Gastines himself alleged to have been true—was denied and ultimately forgotten. Two weeks after his arrest

[22]The incident is narrated in "Les Feux," the fourth book of "Les Tragiques," verses 719–996, as published in Agrippa d'Aubigné, *Oeuvres,* ed. Henri Weber, Jacques Bailbé, and Marguerite Soulié (Paris: Gallimard, 1969), 134–40.

[23]Jean Crespin, *Histoire des martyrs persecutez et mis à mort pour la verité de l'Evangile, depuis le temps des apostres jusques à présent (1619),* ed. Daniel Benoît and Matthieu Lelièvre (Toulouse: Société des livres religieux, 1889), 3:655–57. The story of the deaths of Nicolas Croquet and Philippe and Richard de Gastines is the last entry in the 1570 edition of the *Histoire des martyrs,* the last edition compiled by Crespin himself.

in January 1569 on the charge of having participated in clandestine services in his
family home in Paris's rue Saint-Denis, Richard de Gastines was summarily hauled
before the judges of the Tournelle, Parlement's criminal chamber, on the new accusation that, while in the Conciergerie chapel, he had preached heretical doctrine to
a fellow prisoner.[24] More specifically, he was accused of having accosted a condemned prisoner who had just made his final confession "so as to obtain grace,
remission, and pardon for his sins" and of having tried to "prevent and turn him
away from his salvation."[25]

Richard de Gastines was accused, then, not of preaching to his fellow Huguenots but rather of "dogmatizing," or teaching forbidden doctrines, to a man of the
Catholic faith, accusations that he energetically denied. Called upon to testify, he
tried to clear himself by insisting that, because "the poor penitent was fretting and
complaining that he had been wrongly judged, he had told him that he mustn't say
such things, and that he should think rather about his soul, and that it wasn't likely
that the gentlemen of the court would have condemned him to death if he didn't
deserve it, and he should thus patiently accept [his fate]." After giving this statement, he was led out of the courtroom, so that the witnesses against him might be
heard. Four men—two bailiffs, a clerk of the court, and a minor cleric attached to
the Conciergerie—then gave testimony against Richard de Gastines. Their stories
differed in minor details, but all agreed that they had seen the accused approach
the penitent and tell him that he must confess to God alone, or to Jesus Christ his
son. In other words, they accused him of denying the validity of the sacrament of
penitence. Returned to confront the witnesses against him, de Gastines repeated
that he did not remember having said anything to the man in question other than
these words: "My friend, you are tormenting yourself. Don't think about this any
longer but rather about your conscience." Asked if he had not said that one must
confess to Jesus Christ alone and not to anyone else, he replied emphatically that
he had not said such a thing and that he would not have said such a thing because,
as a prisoner, it would have put him in grave danger. The judges obviously did not
believe this denial and, after some delay, they accepted the prosecuting attorney's
recommendation that de Gastines be sentenced to a ritual apology, or *amende*

---

[24]The arrest record for the case has been published in Nathanaël Weiss, Charles Read, and Henri
Bordier, "Poursuites et condemnations à Paris pour hérésie de 1564 à 1572, d'après les registres d'écrou
de la Conciergerie du Palais," *Bulletin de la Société de l'histoire du protestantisme français* 50 (1901): 640.

[25]AN, X2a 933, 20 January 1569: *plumitif* of the *interrogatoire sur la sellette* of Michel [sic] de Gastines. This document is lengthier than most of the interrogations contained in the *plumitifs;* it is also
written in a somewhat clearer hand. The latter fact may indicate that, rather than being a shorthand
transcript of the proceedings written on the spot, it was copied into the record after the event. The fact
that testimony of witnesses and confrontations between the accused and the witnesses are included
here is another reason for thinking that this entry was copied later from stenographic notes made at the
time of the interrogation itself. It is not clear why this should be the case, but it is one of many indica-
tions that the arrest of the Gastines was not treated as a routine event by the judges of Parlement.

honorable, and a four hundred livre fine. The court also acted to prevent any repetition of the incident by threatening to send to the gallows any prisoner who entered the Conciergerie chapel and said scandalous things against the church to a condemned prisoner.[26] By this time, however, de Gastines's trial on the charges of attending illicit religious assemblies and receiving communion in the Protestant manner was drawing near, which no doubt distracted his attention from this earlier judgment while dashing any hopes that the judges might be lenient in deciding his case. On 1 July 1569, Richard de Gastines, his father, and brother-in-law were hanged on the Place de Grève.[27]

When Agrippa d'Aubigné memorialized Richard de Gastines by making of his martyrdom a triumphant assertion of faith, he elaborated upon a story that was doubtless circulating by word of mouth in Huguenot circles. Just how accurately the story was reported cannot be known, but neither the story related by de Gastines's Catholic jailors nor de Gastines's emphatic denial of the charges served d'Aubigné's purposes well. The act of consoling one lone prisoner had little drama to it and still less if, as de Gastines insisted, there was no doctrinal content to the words he spoke. But what actually might have occurred was not what mattered to d'Aubigné. Richard de Gastines, along with his fellow prisoners in the Conciergerie, died a martyr's death. By magnifying the courage that he showed in life to match the courage that he showed in his death, d'Aubigné fashioned a larger-than-life figure that fit the Huguenots' need for heroes on whom to pattern their own behavior in giving witness for their faith.

It is worth noting that the Huguenots were not alone in memorializing the Gastines. Parisian Catholics not only razed their house, where Reformed Church services were alleged to have taken place, they also erected a pyramid commemorating their destruction of the site. This tall pyramid topped by a crucifix became one of the major bones of contention in applying the clauses relating to memory in the 1570 Edict of Saint-Germain. Catholic resistance to the edict's mandate to remove all monuments related to the conflict came to a climax in riots in December 1571, when Charles IX, yielding to Huguenot pressure, prepared to have the cross quietly removed despite the vigorously expressed opposition of the Parisian populace.[28] Memory was embodied in images and in places, not just in words, and the episode of the Cross of Gastines testifies to the difficulty of legislating oblivion when symbolic remnants of the quarrels could command such vigorous defense.

---

[26]AN, X2b 56 (minutes of 16 May 1569). A secret final clause said that de Gastines would be held prisoner even after the fine was paid unless the court decided otherwise. See also Archives de la Préfecture de police, AB 3, fol. 45r (4 June 1569): order to hold Richard de Gastines prisoner until the fine of four hundred livres ordered by Parlement by *arrêt* of 23 May 1569 was paid.

[27]AN, X2b 56 (30 June 1569).

[28]Diefendorf, *Beneath the Cross,* 84–88.

Even though the Edict of Nantes succeeded in creating a relatively stable religious peace, memory of the violence perpetrated during the wars did not fade because religious violence continued to occur. As Philip Benedict has pointed out, "incidents were particularly frequent in the decade of renewed religious warfare in the 1620s and in the period immediately preceding the Revocation, but no decade was spared."[29] Although individual Catholics and Huguenots enjoyed friendly relations, mutual suspicion between the two faiths did not fade with coexistence but rather seems to have increased in the course of the seventeenth century.[30] The conceptual bases for religious toleration changed little. Each church continued to claim a monopoly on religious truth; religious coexistence was tolerated only out of necessity. Public debates and religious polemics addressed to an increasingly literate laity continued to polarize French society, with each confession responding by reinforcing the social boundaries that separated it from the other. Benedict's research on seventeenth-century Protestant communities suggests that both mixed marriage and interfaith godparentage declined and he concludes, perhaps overcautiously, that "the two confessions may have become increasingly sharply separated and self-enclosed communities as the century advanced."[31]

To take Benedict's conclusions further, it can be argued that history and memory of past persecutions helped to reinforce Huguenot separateness and, when persecutions began anew or flared up in the seventeenth century, provided the tools for interpreting them. Faith in God's providence to his chosen people provided the same reassurance when the *dragonnades* began and during the so-called Desert period of clandestine assemblies that followed the Revocation as it had during the Wars of Religion. Writing about the Museum of the Desert, which commemorates the eighteenth-century clandestine church, Philippe Joutard commented that "saturation in history...suffuses all of Protestant culture, as can be seen from an enumeration of oral legends."[32] Studying the use French Protestants make of their history through the articles published in the *Bulletin de la société de*

[29]Benedict, "*Un roi*," 86. The remainder of this paragraph also draws on Benedict's conclusions in this article.

[30]Bernard Dompnier, *Le venin de l'hérésie: Image du protestantisme et combat catholique au XVIIe siècle* (Paris: Le Centurion, 1985), esp. ch. 6, which summarizes the literature on coexistence and the strains to which it was subjected. To the literature Dompnier cites should be added Gregory Hanlon, *Confession and Community in Seventeenth-Century France: Catholic and Protestant Coexistence in Aquitaine* (Philadelphia: University of Pennsylvania Press, 1993).

[31]Benedict, "*Un roi*," 90. See also Keith Luria, "Rituals of Conversion: Catholics and Protestants in Seventeenth-Century Poitou," in *Culture and Identity in Early Modern Europe,* ed. Diefendorf and Hesse, 65–82.

[32]Philippe Joutard, "The Museum of the Desert, the Protestant Minority," in *Realms of Memory: Rethinking the French Past,* vol. 1, *Conflicts and Divisions,* ed. Pierre Nora, English edition, ed. Lawrence D. Kritzman, trans. Arthur Goldhammer (New York: Columbia University Press, 1996), 354–55.

l'histoire du Protestantisme français, Joutard has nevertheless made the interesting observation that, over time, the period of the Desert has overtaken the period of the religious wars as a focus for historical interest.

"Why," he asks, "should Protestants stubbornly persist in commemorating primarily their period of exclusion from national life?"[33] The answer he offers is revealing: "One reason why French Protestants spontaneously choose to remember the eighteenth-century Desert period rather than the sixteenth-century Wars of Religion, and the Revocation rather than Saint Bartholomew's Day, is that these choices help to form family as well as communal memories." Unlike the religious wars, which were fought by great nobles, the sufferings of the Desert belonged to all. "The long repression of an entire population had given rise to a large number of oral traditions piously transmitted from generation to generation, so that every Protestant felt that his or her ancestors had been historical actors."[34]

Joutard's article is also useful for his observation that "the memory of the French Protestant minority has not been at odds with French national memory since the nineteenth century." Protestant resistance to the repressive excesses of absolutism came to be seen as a precursor to the Revolution and integrated itself well into the republican tradition. More recently, Huguenot resistance—especially the Camisards—came more broadly to symbolize resistance against intolerance and even to prefigure "people's liberation" movements. For Joutard, this suggests that, for the Huguenots, collective memory has favored the period of the Desert because it was in this period that

> the persecuted, rejected minority became a precursor of liberty...the battles of the sixteenth century...left the Huguenots trapped in defeat and misfortune with no prospects for the future. Victims in 1572, French Protestants could not even cling to the Edict of Nantes, because 1685 wiped out 1598: all they had was the Cross without the Resurrection. Then, too, the Revocation made victims of the Huguenots, but their resistance turned them into a "triumphant people."[35]

Insightful as these conclusions are, Huguenot memory does make an important place for the sixteenth-century Wars of Religion. This was demonstrated vividly in 1997 in the loud cry of shock and anger the French Protestant community emitted upon learning that Pope John Paul II's visit to France would climax with a rally and Mass at Notre-Dame Cathedral on 24 August. That this day, which will forever in the Protestant mind be synonymous with the Massacre of Saint Bartholomew, could have been chosen by accident and with no intention of insulting

[33]Joutard, "Museum of the Desert," 364–67.
[34]Joutard, "Museum of the Desert," 370.
[35]Joutard, "Museum of the Desert," 376.

France's Protestant minority was no consolation to those for whom 24 August is a date that cannot and should not be forgotten. The fact that Huguenots were victims of the massacre is of course inseparable from the memory of that day, but this is a cause for remembering and not for trying vainly to forget. Collective memory long ago transformed the negative associations of victimization into positive ones by incorporating them into the longer struggle for liberty and freedom of conscience.

MEMORY AND CATHOLIC IDENTITY

The Wars of Religion did not just divide Protestants from Catholics, they also deeply divided Catholics among themselves, especially during the final decades of the sixteenth century, during the wars of the League. The term Counter-Reformation is in disfavor today among many historians who prefer, by using the term Catholic Reformation, to stress the impulses for reform and renewal that came from within the late fifteenth- and early sixteenth-century Catholic Church as opposed to the church's reaction to the challenge from Martin Luther and his Protestant followers. Without denying the revival that began and remained within orthodox Catholic tradition, it is nevertheless important to recognize that the Catholic Church also changed in response to the Protestant challenge. If there was a Catholic Reformation, there was also a Counter-Reformation, and if sometimes one term or definition is clearly more accurate, there are also other moments when revival, reform, and reaction are so closely entwined that it is pointless to try to separate them. Equally important, however it is termed, the Catholic renewal in France was a long-term process that continued through and had important roots in the Wars of Religion.

The continuities have tended to be obscured by historians writing in a confessional tradition, who have celebrated the flowering of Catholic renewal in the mid-seventeenth century but neglected to tell how the roots were established. A kind of self-censorship has continued to operate at least in part because the forms of religious practice that dominate in the late sixteenth century make many historians uncomfortable. The self-mortification practiced by members of new religious orders and lay confraternities is strange and even repellant to modern sensibilities. At the same time, the evolutionary process of Catholic renewal has been obscured by historians studying the politics of the League. It has been more convenient to paint the ultra-Catholic enthusiasm of the League as politically inspired fanaticism, a momentary delusion, than as a disputed but nevertheless essential stage in the evolution of Catholic identity in France.[36]

---

[36]On the *fable royaliste* of the League, see Robert Descimon, *Qui étaient les Seize? Mythes et réalités de la Ligue parisienne (1585–1594)* (Paris: Klincksieck, 1983), 26–34.

On the most elemental level, French Catholics responded to the Protestant challenge by organizing demonstrations of faith and by cultivating among the laity a greater understanding of and appreciation for fundamental doctrines. Both functions were served when they organized public processions to implore divine forgiveness for acts of sacrilege committed by Protestant iconoclasts. Taking to the streets to deplore the breaking of a statue of the Virgin or the desecration of a eucharistic chalice, Catholics publicly displayed their faith but also inculcated a greater respect for Marian piety, the doctrine of the real presence, and other disputed tenets of faith. Religious processions increased in number and in complexity as confessional tensions erupted into war and were clearly intended not to proselytize for conversion but rather to reaffirm Catholic truths and to mobilize energies for the war against heresy.[37] Catholic preachers also took a more directly didactic approach in sermon cycles that, in explaining key doctrines, focused directly on those teachings contested by the Protestants. These sermons were often inflammatory, provoking outrage against the heretics accused of polluting the social body and of threatening, through their abuses, to bring the wrath of God down upon it. They could also be overtly political, even seditious, in their attacks against monarchs perceived as insufficiently militant in their defense of the Catholic faith. But their educative value should not be lost in contemplation of their political message, any more than the publication of catechisms and other educative devotional literature should be lost in the welter of polemics.

Not everyone responded to the religious appeal addressed in sermons and didactic literature to cultivate a more meaningful faith, but for those who did, an increasing number and variety of lay devotional organizations offered new avenues for Catholic practice. Jesuits founded Marian confraternities in their *collèges,* mendicants founded or expanded third order devotions for a newly devout bourgeoisie, and parishes founded new confraternities dedicated to the blessed sacrament.[38] Although they also retained important collective dimensions, these organizations deepened personal piety by introducing such practices as mental prayer, increasing the frequency of communion, and encouraging pious laypeople to seek more and better spiritual direction. The most dramatic innovation was the founding of penitential confraternities beginning in the 1570s in a number of French cities. Defining themselves as "true spiritual soldiers," whose purpose was "combatting the devil, the world, and the flesh," the penitents saw themselves as a

[37]Diefendorf, *Beneath the Cross,* 38–48. See also Moshe Sluhovsky, *Patroness of Paris: Rituals of Devotion in Early Modern France* (Leiden: Brill, 1998), 108–37.

[38]On the former, see Louis Châtellier, *L'Europe des dévots* (Paris: Editions de la Maison des sciences de l'homme, 1987).

spiritual elite.[39] Their processions were intended both to deepen members' own piety and to serve as an example to others.[40]

Sometimes viewed as an atavistic revival of medieval flagellants, the penitential companies should rather be seen as the advance troops of the Catholic Reformation. Their statutes contain explicit references to Tridentine reforms and reflect the intensification of both individual and collective religious practice associated with the seventeenth-century Catholic renewal. On the individual level, examination of conscience, frequent confession and communion, and mental prayer were emphasized. The congregations nurtured a Christocentric devotion, with a special focus on the Passion and the Eucharist. A Tridentine ethic, or attempt to reform personal morality, is evident as well. Penitential congregations had active programs of charity. Members of some brotherhoods visited prisons and accompanied condemned men to their death; others visited the sick in hospitals, distributed aid to the poor, and provided dowries for poor girls.

These confraternities were just one manifestation of a revival within French Catholicism of ascetic and penitential forms of piety in the last decades of the sixteenth century. The rapid spread of the reformed Franciscans known as Capuchins, first introduced into France in 1574, and the stunningly ascetic reform of the Cistercian abbey of Feuillants undertaken by its abbot Jean de la Barrière in 1577 are the first tentative signs of the rigorous austerity that was to be a striking characteristic of the reform of religious life in France during the first decades of the seventeenth century. During the wars of the League, moreover, penitential piety became not just a marginal phenomenon but rather the dominant form of religious expression in French cities. When news arrived that Henri III had ordered the League's leader and hero, Henri, duc de Guise, assassinated at Blois,

[39]This aspect of the confraternities is well developed in Robert Schneider, "Mortification on Parade: Penitential Processions in Sixteenth- and Seventeenth-Century France," *Renaissance and Reformation/Renaissance et réforme*, n.s. 10 (1986): 123–46, esp. 140–41. The growing literature on France's penitential confraternities during the Wars of Religion also includes Andrew E. Barnes, *The Social Dimension of Piety: Associative Life and Devotional Change in the Penitent Confraternities of Marseilles (1499–1792)* (New York: Paulist Press, 1994); Philip Benedict, *Rouen during the Wars of Religion* (Cambridge: Cambridge University Press, 1981), 200–3; Jacqueline Boucher, *Société et mentalités autour de Henri III* (Lille: Presses de l'Université de Lille, 1981), 1357–92; Robert R. Harding, "The Mobilization of Confraternities against the Reformation in France," *Sixteenth Century Journal* 11 (1980): 92–98; Wolfgang Kaiser, *Marseille au temps des troubles, 1559–1596: Morphologie sociale et luttes de factions,* trans. Florence Chaix (Paris: Editions de l'Ecole des hautes etudes en sciences sociales, 1992), 181–92; Marguerite Pecquet, "Des Compagnies de Pénitents à la Compagnie du Saint-Sacrement," *XVIIe siècle* 69 (1965): 6–13; Pecquet, "La Compagnie des Pénitents Blancs de Toulouse," *Annales du Midi* 84 (1972): 213–24; and Robert Schneider, *Public Life in Toulouse, 1463–1789: From Municipal Republic to Cosmopolitan City* (Ithaca: Cornell University Press, 1989), 115–20.

[40]Henri de Calais, *Histoire de la vie, de la mort et des miracles du R. P. Honoré Bochart de Champigny, Capuchin,* new ed. (Paris: Veuve Poussielgue-Rusard, 1864), 35.

the League denounced the king as a murderous tyrant and went into open rebellion against him. At the same time, a powerful wave of penitential devotion—of prayers, fasting, and processions intended to appease the wrath of God—swept over the cities controlled by the League.[41] In Paris, white-robed children from all of the city's parishes paraded to the church of Saint Geneviève on 10 January 1589. Adults took up the pattern, and for nearly three months the processions continued day and night. Despite the dank chill of winter (and as much as a foot of snow), many of the participants walked barefoot, some robed only in a thin shift, as they chanted penitential psalms and prayed ardently for God's mercy. As Easter approached, the processions became even more elaborate. Witnesses describe participants wearing simple loincloths or penitents' hoods and carrying the implements of Christ's Passion. Meanwhile, the city's churches, draped in black, memorialized their murdered hero with endless vigils, funeral masses, and sermons denouncing the king.

Parisians' anguish over the death of the duc de Guise also took the form of a serious, if inconsistent, attempt at moral rearmament. The journal kept by the Parisian known only as "François" notes on 2 January that, from the moment the news of the murders at Blois arrived, "everyone turned to prayer to appease the wrath of God, and some fasted two, three, or four times a week and others all week long—including one or two days on bread and water alone—by order of their preachers and curates."[42] Although the white processions gradually faded from the scene after Easter was celebrated on 2 April, a mood of heightened religious sensibility persisted through at least the first two years of the League, with waves of intense devotion recurring at moments of crisis in the city's defense.

Barbe Acarie, most famous as a founder of the French Discalced Carmelites of Saint Teresa of Avila's reform, but also active in the founding of the French Ursulines and Capuchin nuns, later described the period of the League as "an Age of Gold, when people didn't think about eating or drinking but only about turning to God." Referring specifically to the spring and summer of 1590, when the royal army of Henri de Navarre held Paris under siege, she recalled that "she had never been happier or felt more contentment."[43] Taking part in religious processions

---

[41]The seminal article on this subject is Denis Richet's "Politique et religion: les processions à Paris en 1589," in his *De la Réforme à la Révolution: Études sur la France moderne* (Paris: Aubier, 1991), 69–82, esp. 70–71. See also Denis Crouzet, *Les guerriers de Dieu: la violence au temps des troubles de religion, vers 1525–vers 1610* (Seyssel: Champ Vallon, 1990), 1:379–407.

[42]*Journal de François, bourgeois de Paris. 23 décembre 1588–30 avril 1589,* ed. Eugène Saulnier (Paris: E. Leroux, 1913), 19.

[43]ACP, *Procès apostolique de la bienheureuse soeur Marie de l'Incarnation,* testimony of Sr. Marie du Saint-Sacrement (Valence de Marillac), fol. 644r; also testimony of André Du Val, fol. 322v; Françoise de Jésus (de Fleury), fol. 339v; Jeanne de Jésus (Seguier), fol. 822r; and Marie de Jésus (de Breauté), fol. 619v.

with the other women of her parish, caring for wounded soldiers brought in to the hospitals of the city, or simply giving the food from her own plate to the poor, she experienced in the League a kind of religious exaltation, entranced by what she perceived as a common effort to "appease the wrath of God and avert the great misfortunes with which the state was menaced."[44] After the League was defeated, she continued to serve in hospitals, visit prisons, attempt to convert prostitutes, and engage in other works of charity. She was joined in her efforts by other devout women, some of whom had been ardent Leaguers alongside her. Denis Richet was right in seeing that, alongside the political League but with an even broader appeal, a new circle of devout laypeople—or *dévots*—grew out of the devotions, moral rearmament campaign, and processions of the League. Despite the defeat of the political League, the "League of the Devout was to survive victorious, or at least tolerated, throughout the seventeenth century."[45]

Richet is correct to be wary of postulating a simple and direct continuity between political allegiance to the League and engagement in the Catholic Reformation's "League of the Devout." It is the susceptibility to the rhetoric of penitence marking the League's spiritual side that is the defining element here. When religious vocations began to pick up sharply in the last years of the sixteenth century, after the disruption caused by the wars of the League, by far the strongest pull was to ascetic and penitential orders like the Capuchins and Feuillants. Prior to 1604, the only option for women determined to share the austerities of the male orders was to go to Toulouse, where the Feuillants, yielding to the insistence of female followers that "they too had bodies capable of suffering," had established a sister house of Feuillantines. After this time, the founding of new orders of Carmelites and Capuchin nuns offered an ascetic experience closer to home, but this was just the beginning of the wave. By 1650, some sixty new convents or monastic houses had changed the physical and spiritual landscape of Paris. Other cities witnessed similar revivals, often with only a few years' lag time. A very large proportion of the new houses were not only austere in discipline, but emphatically ascetic in their rule.

Not everyone admired the new spirituality. Pierre de L'Estoile, commenting in 1606 on the "great novelty, in Paris and elsewhere" of the "sons and daughters of good family" who were flocking to join the new congregations of Capuchins, Feuillants, Recollettes, and Carmelites, scornfully derided the spirituality that

[44]ACP, *Procès apostolique*, testimony of Marguerite de Gondi, marquise de Maignelay, fol. 619v. See also Barbara Diefendorf, "An Age of Gold? Parisian Women, the Holy League, and the Roots of Catholic Renewal," in *Changing Identities in Early Modern France*, ed. Michael Wolfe (Durham: Duke University Press, 1997), 169–90, esp. 174–76.
[45]Richet, "Politique et religion," 81. See also Richet's "La contre-réforme catholique en France dans la première moitié du dix-septième siècle," in his *De la réforme à la Revolution*, 83–95.

RELIGIOUS DIFFERENCES IN FRANCE

characterized this revival of religious life. Most who joined the new orders, he claimed, did so out of a "simple and silly devotion," persuaded the last days had arrived. Others were drawn in by personal disappointments, laziness, or cowardice; but all had in common that they "preferred the inventions and traditions of men to the commandments of God."[46] When his niece died in 1610 at the age of twenty-three, he blamed her demise on the "silly devotions now fashionable, with the fasts and austerities of the Carmelite sisters, ... with whom she remained cloistered ten months," and he railed against spiritual directors who advised their penitents that the path to true devotion required the "sacrifice" of the body.[47] And yet, as L'Estoile recognized, his condemnation flew in the face of much popular sentiment, which was inclined to identify as saintly the very practices he abhorred.

By the early seventeenth century, French Catholicism was thus split between ultra-Catholic *dévots* and moderates who, like Pierre de L'Estoile, wanted church reform without dogmatism or extremes. Divisions between them were exacerbated by mutual accusations rooted in the religious wars. Indeed, to a large extent these divisions continued and reproduced the divisions between ultra-Catholic Leaguers and moderate Catholics, or *politiques,* and the memory of these conflicts continued to make compromise difficult. In principle, the League's revolt and all that took place during it were forgotten. Each of the Leaguer cities, in submitting to Henri IV's authority, benefited from the king's clemency in having the veil of oblivion thrown over the past. The edict for the reduction of Paris in 1594 was typical:

> Recognizing that there is nothing that testifies better to our creation in the image of God than clemency and good-nature, candidly forgetting the offenses and faults of the past: [accordingly] we have declared and declare by these present [ordinances] that we have taken and take back into our good graces the citizens and inhabitants of our good city of Paris: we have of our special grace and royal authority abolished and abolish the things that occurred in the aforesaid city during and on account of the current troubles, which we wish and order to remain extinguished, abolished, appeased, and regarded as not having happened....[48]

Like the edicts issued for the pacification of interconfessional quarrels, the ordinances tried to draw a line between acts of war and ordinary criminal behavior. Complaints of the latter sort might still be adjudicated in the courts. For this reason, crimes against those of the same party were excepted, as were complicity in the murder of Henri III and attempted assassinations of Henri IV. The provisions for amnesty were nevertheless generous ones, considering the nature and duration

---

[46]Pierre de L'Estoile, *Journal pour le règne de Henri IV* (Paris: Gallimard, 1948–1960), 2:207.

[47]L'Estoile, *Journal,* 3:54

[48]*Edict et declaration du roy, sur la reduction de la ville de Paris soubs son obeyssance* (Paris, 1594), 11–12.

of the rebellion.[49] And while traditional policy in cases of rebellion required that at least a few of the ringleaders pay with their lives as an example to others (even in the era of the religious wars one thinks of the several hundred men summarily executed for participating in the Conspiracy of Amboise, their bodies left hanging from the castle ramparts as a warning to all who passed), Henri IV had no one sentenced to death and ordered relatively few men into exile. The initial list of those expelled from Paris contained only 118 names, all of them associated with the most active and violent faction within the League. A few more names were added later, but within six months the exiles were seeking and often receiving permission to return.[50]

As with the confessional quarrels, however, the order to forget remained in tension with the will to remember. In compliance with the king's orders, local officials destroyed records, writings, insignia, and mementos associated with the League. Lyon burned "all tangible reminders of the League in the public square"; Paris organized a more limited bonfire of the writings of the League's most rabid propagandists.[51] Consigning the past to the flames could, however, be an act of remembering and not forgetting, as when the most radical leaders of the Paris League were burned in effigy in the courtyard of the Palais de Justice on Saint John's Eve three months after the city's reduction.[52]

Henri's clemency inevitably caused hard feelings among those who had remained faithful to the Crown. They had paid a high price for their loyalty and few could resist the all too human desire to see their sufferings avenged. Even the men responsible for executing Henri's policy were torn by these feelings. The judges of Parlement who had obeyed Henri III's order to reassemble at Tours and Châlons were outraged to learn that the magistrates who had remained in Paris through the League were permitted to keep their offices, with both groups being reintegrated into a single court.[53]

Henri's clemency was no doubt a wise policy—the League's revolt had a very broad popular base. So many people had supported it in one way or another that

[49]*Edict* 1594, 12–17, 22.

[50]L'Estoile, *Journal,* 1:416, 430.

[51]On Lyon, see Michael Wolfe, "Amnesty and *Oubliance* at the End of the French Wars of Religion in "Clémence, oubliance et pardon en Europe, 1520–1620," special issue, *Cahiers d'histoire* 16 (1996), 184. On Paris, see L'Estoile, *Journal,* 1:408. Administrative documents, like the records of Parlement for the period of the League, were more quietly destroyed—to the everlasting regret of historians.

[52]L'Estoile, *Journal,* 1:419.

[53]The judges at Tours and Châlons did, however, score a victory over their fellows in Paris when the first president declared that rank and precedence in the court would be established according to the date of a judge's oath of loyalty to the king. Since the judges at Tours and Châlons had remained loyal to the Crown all along, they did not have to take a new oath of loyalty to Henri IV and therefore automatically acquired precedence over judges who had remained in Paris during the League.

any attempt at a thorough investigation of its activities or purging of adherents would have posed insuperable barriers to peace. Because a thorough purge did not take place, however, the fear that the League had not been vanquished but had merely disappeared underground continued to haunt French magistrates. Attempting to root out hidden remnants of the League, they tended to direct their attacks against religious organizations suspected of harboring pro-League sympathies if not actually fomenting plots against the Crown. In October 1594, the Parlement of Paris outlawed the clandestine assemblies of penitential confraternities said to still be meeting in city chapels as "prejudicial to the king's service and public tranquility."[54] The campaign against the Jesuits that began shortly after Henri IV's entry into Paris and culminated in January 1595 with their expulsion had the same motive of protecting the state from an ultra-Catholic conspiracy. The Capuchins were expelled from Rheims in April 1597 on the charge of factional conspiracy, and Paris's Capuchins were twice threatened with expulsion: first when their superior refused to admit Henri IV to Mass shortly after his entry into Paris, and again in 1598/99, when Capuchin preachers not only led an active preaching campaign against registration of the Edict of Nantes, but also refused to obey Parlement's directives to stop meddling in affairs of the state.[55] These actions were politically motivated, but they carried both explicit and implicit judgments of religious practices as well.

To cite just one example, in December 1598, just as the campaign against registration of the Edict of Nantes was approaching its climax, the Capuchins, along with ultra-Catholic parish clergy, proposed introducing a new custom into the traditional Advent celebrations. They wanted to institute a new form of religious procession in which the consecrated Eucharist would be carried through the streets under an elaborate canopy while church bells chimed to bring parishioners out of their houses to stand with blazing torches and so do homage to it. The new bishop of Paris authorized the ceremony, but Parlement quickly intervened to prohibit it, admonishing the bishop "to content himself with seeing that the ancient traditions and ceremonies of the church were observed with no innovations or changes." Several parishes went ahead with the new practice despite the court's order, with the result that one gentleman—a loyal Catholic, as it turned out—was attacked by a crowd for having merely lifted his hat when the sacrament passed instead of descending from his horse and getting to his knees.[56]

[54]BN, Ms. fr. NA 2266: Tables Le Nain, fols. 227–28.

[55]On the Capuchins' expulsion from Rheims, see L'Estoile, *Journal,* 1:501; on their threatened expulsion from Paris, see BN, Ms. fr. 25046: "Eloges historiques de tous les grands hommes et les illustres religieux Capucins de la Province de Paris…2e tome," 35–36; and Bibliothèque mazarine, ms. 2418: "Annales des Reverends Peres Capucins," 490–512, esp. 506.

[56]L'Estoile, *Journal,* 1:547–48

Pierre de L'Estoile, who recorded the incident in his journal, betrays his own attitude toward the new procession when he first describes it as "a ceremony more of sedition than of devotion." He also describes it as having taken place "in the Spanish fashion," a loaded statement, given Spain's intervention on the ultra-Catholic side in the wars of the League. L'Estoile's denunciation of the new processions is in keeping with his denunciation eight years later of the newly fashionable religious orders of the Catholic Reformation. He cannot contemplate their ascetic piety without being reminded of the League. L'Estoile's judgment accords well with modern sensibilities, disapproving of the new procession because it clearly did serve to fan the fires of religious passions at the very moment they should have been allowed to die down. But this judgment, which seems self-evident to the modern mind, was nevertheless a partisan reaction that many Catholics did not share.

If ex-*politiques* like L'Estoile recalled the religious devotions of the League as seditious and full of superstition, ex-Leaguers and the *dévots* who continued their ultra-Catholic politics remembered the League's revolt in very different terms. Sharing Barbe Acarie's very positive memories of the religious exaltation of the League, they retold its history as an epic defense of the Catholic faith and the French monarchy as well. They played down the League's violence and its resistance to Henri de Navarre, at the same time that they portrayed its adherents as intensely loyal to the fundamental principles of the French monarchy—so intensely loyal, in fact, that they had risked their lives to prevent the Crown of the Most Christian King from falling to a heretic. Crediting the League's partisans with having forced Henri IV to convert to the Catholic faith, they borrowed Henri's own rhetoric of conciliation in blaming the most treacherous policies of the League on a Spanish conspiracy, while blotting from memory the role that ardent Leaguers had played in soliciting Spanish aid and attempting to put a Spanish princess on the French throne.[57]

The *dévot* perspective on the League has disappeared from modern memory; royalist histories celebrating the triumph of Henri IV with the aid of moderate Catholics, or *politiques,* long ago won the day. This makes it hard to remember that ex-Leaguers—and the *dévots* who carried on their ultra-Catholic cause—did not repent the activities of the League. Quite the contrary, they continued to believe that they had fought for a righteous cause, just as they continued to deplore the Edict of Nantes as unduly favorable to the Huguenot minority. Opposed to both the principle and the realities of religious toleration, they supported missionary

[57]This subject is treated in more detail in my "Reconciliation and Remembering: A *Dévot* Writes the History of the Holy League," in "Clémence, oubliance et pardon en Europe, 1520–1620," special issue, *Cahiers d'histoire* 16 (1996), 69–79.

campaigns and public debates aimed at converting the Huguenots, even as they continued to lobby for an end to coexistence and a return of the kingdom to a single faith.[58] The missionary campaigns, which were undertaken largely by Capuchins and Jesuits, aimed to revivify and regenerate the Catholic community as well as to convert Protestants; historians such as Bernard Dompnier and Keith Luria have suggested that their success in the former role was far greater than in the latter. Forging a unified Catholic community, however, "required a rupture with local Protestants, provoked by collective devotions that championed Catholic dogma." In Keith Luria's words, Counter-Reformation missionaries "turned the frontier between [Protestants] and their Catholic neighbors into a strict, sacred boundary."[59] Only by defining their own identity in opposition to the Huguenots could the Catholics see themselves as one.

Philippe Joutard, writing that the Revocation of the Edict of Nantes, like Saint Bartholomew's Day, "was the result of a political miscalculation by the government, and the average Frenchman found it easier to identify with the victims and resistance to misguided policy than with the policy itself," stated a truth that has more validity for 1998 than for 1685 or 1572.[60] The Revocation and even Saint Bartholomew's Day received broad popular support at the time. All of French monarchical tradition supported a policy of *un roi, une foi*, and to many people it was the policy of religious coexistence that appeared a miscalculation. Admittedly, it is difficult today to sympathize with this view. This is why the ultra-Catholic faction that defended *un roi, une foi* even at the price of rebellion against their legitimate king has not fared nearly as well in historical memory as the Huguenots traditionally viewed as their victims.

---

[58]Diefendorf, "Reconciliation and Remembering," 78.
[59]Luria, "Rituals of Conversion," 70–71, 77. See also Dompnier, *Le venin de l'hérésie*, 139–52.
[60]Joutard, "Museum of the Desert," 377.

Sharing Sacred Space

PROTESTANT TEMPLES AND RELIGIOUS COEXISTENCE IN THE SEVENTEENTH CENTURY

Keith P. Luria

THE SIXTEENTH-CENTURY WARS OF RELIGION shattered the French kingdom's political and religious unity. Henri IV (r. 1589–1610) restored the country's political order, but religious uniformity was permanently lost. Roman Catholicism remained the majority, legally dominant church, but the minority Reformed Protestant faith survived and would outlast even Louis XIV's (r. 1643–1715) brutal attempt to repress it. For most of Henri's subjects it was axiomatic that rival religions could not live together peacefully; the lesson seemed obvious after decades of bloody conflict. Not only did the presence of religious heterodoxy in the kingdom insult God and jeopardize salvation, but it also inevitably threatened social order. But if the deep sense of antipathy between the confessional groups could be overcome and a way found of encouraging them to coexist, then peace could be restored even if religious conformity could not. Coexistence did not mean religious toleration in the most positive (and modern) sense of the term. Very few early modern Europeans entertained the notion of toleration as a positive goal.[1] But for a people sick of confessional conflict and political upheaval, coexistence was better than a return to violence.

The Edict of Nantes—the settlement of the religious wars Henri negotiated in 1598—provided the means to achieve coexistence. Admirers of the edict have celebrated its proclamation of "liberty of conscience," seeing it as a signal achievement on the road to modern, tolerant religious pluralism. Critics have long condemned the strict constraints the edict imposed on Protestant religious life in

---

Unless otherwise indicated, all translations from foreign language sources are the author's.

[1]Toleration was most often seen as a necessary evil: a rival group had to be tolerated because it could not be eliminated. See Elisabeth Labrousse, *"Une foi, une loi, un roi?" Essai sur la révocation de l'Édit de Nantes* (Geneva: Labor et Fides, 1985), 95–96; and Guy Saupin, Rémy Fabre, and Marcel Launay, eds., *La tolérance: Colloque international de Nantes (mai 1998)* (Rennes: Presses Universitaires de Rennes, 1999).

the country. For them, Nantes foreshadowed the monarchy's later persecution of the minority.[2] Neither understanding of the edict is entirely satisfactory. The restrictions placed on Protestants were severe—they could practice their faith publicly only in certain places and they had to observe some Catholic obligations, for instance, tithe paying. Yet the edict ordered that their worship not be troubled. Huguenots would have the same access as Catholics to occupations and government positions. And they could bring lawsuits to special Parlement chambers set up to guarantee them fair hearings.

In part, different opinions about the Edict of Nantes stem from its often unclear or even contradictory provisions. But they also result from variations in how the law was applied. Although the edict provided the framework for coexistence, it did not simply create coexistence. Disputes between the confessional groups did not disappear, but after 1598, rather than being fought out on battlefields or in city streets, they were settled in courtrooms, royal councils, and local negotiations between Catholics and Protestants. In these negotiations, Nantes provided the confessional groups with mechanisms for reaching accommodations on a host of potentially explosive issues and, thereby, for constructing coexistence. The government promoted settlements by inserting royal officials into these local negotiations. Provincial magistrates or governors sometimes served as the king's representatives, but most important were the "commissioners of the edict" the government periodically sent into confessionally mixed areas to hear complaints from both sides, resolve disputes, and enforce the king's will.

In the middle and later years of the century, the commissioners used their authority very much to the Huguenots' disadvantage. But in the decades immediately following the edict's promulgation, their efforts were much more equitable. In their pursuit of confessional peace, they impressed both Catholics and Huguenots with the king's authority and with their duty to be obedient. The contracts Catholics and Protestants signed and the oaths they took often spoke of their desire to live peacefully with each other "under the king's edicts" or "because the king commanded it."[3] In promoting an evenhanded policy, the monarchy was departing

---

[2]Criticism started in the seventeenth century, as is apparent in Elie Benoist's *Histoire de l'Édit de Nantes contenant les choses les plus remarquables qui se sont passées en France avant & après sa publication...*, 5 vols. (Delft: A. Beman, 1693–94). For a modern critic, see Janine Garrisson, *L'Édit de Nantes et sa révocation: Histoire d'une intolérance* (Paris: Seuil, 1985). Admirers of the edict include liberal historians such as John Viénot, *Histoire de la réforme française de l'Édit de Nantes à sa révocation* (Paris: Fischbacher, 1926). For an overview of how historians have understood the edict, see Bernard Cottret, *1598, L'Édit de Nantes: Pour en finir avec les guerres de religion* (Paris: Le Grand livre du mois, 1997), 193–98.

[3]On the commissioners, see Francis Garrisson, *Essai sur les commissions d'application de l'Édit de Nantes, première partie: Règne de Henri IV* (Montpellier: P. Déhan, 1964); Elisabeth Rabut, *Le roi, l'église et le temple: L'exécution de l'Édit de Nantes en Dauphiné* (Grenoble: La Pensée sauvage, 1987);

from its traditional role of protecting Catholicism and combating heresy. Instead, it became the arbiter of disputes between the rival faiths. This is not to say the state was a neutral referee. The edict and royal enforcement of it left no doubt that Catholicism was the legally dominant religion. But within Nantes's limitations, Huguenot interests were protected and their requests often granted.

Historians often think of the French monarchy, like other early modern states, as having strengthened itself through a policy of confessionalization in which it enforced religious uniformity not difference. Eventually the early modern French monarchy would pursue such a strategy, only to see it backfire. But in the early decades of the seventeenth century, royal power and authority were increased by encouraging coexistence based on an acknowledgment by all involved that it was the king and his law that ensured peace, social order, and the privileges of both confessional groups.[4]

The three-way encounters between Catholics, Protestants, and representatives of royal authority led to agreements on or arbitrations of a range of matters crucial to constructing local coexistence, including the timing and location of religious observances (for example, Catholic processions and the Reformed *prêche*). But one of the most contentious issues was the location of Huguenot places of worship, or temples. Much was at stake in the negotiations over temples. As the site of public Reformed worship, they were a very visible manifestation of Calvinist belief and its difference from Catholic doctrine. Though the architecture of temples varied, Huguenots avoided the traditional cross-shaped design of Catholic churches in favor of circular, rectangular, octagonal, or oval plans. They thereby rejected Catholic investment in the symbol of the cross (for Calvinists a manifestation of Catholic "idolatry") and also arrayed worshipers as close as possible to the pulpit from which ministers preached the word of God, the main activity of Reformed worship.[5] Reformed Protestantism rejected the Catholic doctrine of the real presence. So within temples, Huguenots sang hymns instead of observing priests performing the Mass. They participated in the Lord's Supper at communion tables instead of taking the Eucharist, which had been transubstantiated on altars. Temples had no side chapels because Calvinists renounced the cult of saints. And they contained no statues or images, which were also considered idolatrous.

---

and Keith P. Luria, *Sacred Boundaries: Religious Coexistence and Conflict in Early-Modern France* (Washington DC: Catholic University of America Press, 2005), 16–17.

[4]Luria, *Sacred Boundaries,* xxi–xxii.

[5]Daniel Ligou, "Un vandalisme oublié: La destruction des temples réformés par l'autorité royale au XVIIe siècle," in *Révolution française et "vandalisme révolutionaire": Actes du colloque international de Clermont-Ferrand, 15–17 décembre 1998,* ed. Simone Bernard-Griffiths, Marie-Claude Chemin, and Jean Ehrard (Paris: Universitas, 1992), 333–41, esp. 335.

In addition, the sites of Reformed worship challenged Catholic notions of sacred space. For Catholics, certain locations were endowed with sacredness, for example, churches on whose altars the miracle of transubstantiation was performed or saints' shrines at which divine power healed the sick. Calvinists rejected the notion that one place was holier than another; indeed, they repudiated the very idea that the spiritual manifested itself in the mundane. Thus temples were not consecrated or sacred; they were, in principle, no holier than any other spot. Because temples stood as a direct and physical denial of Catholic beliefs, during the Wars of Religion they were the targets of much violence, which Catholic propaganda accentuated by spreading rumors of Huguenot misdoings and sexual immorality during worship.[6]

And yet, even if Huguenots did not invest their temples with sacred significance, they still fought hard to maintain them in or near the communities where they lived side by side with Catholics. Temples continued to share with Catholic structures what might be called the sacred space of biconfessional communities, that is, the sites within towns devoted to the worship and other religious activities of both faiths.[7] Of course it was important for Huguenots to have convenient places to assemble and hear the word of God preached, but the presence of a temple in a confessionally mixed community was also an important symbol of their full membership in that community. The destruction of temples or even their removal from biconfessional towns was a potent statement of the Huguenots' exclusion from local society, their marginalization in the country, and the loss of an important part of their French identity.

The Huguenots' collective identity depended on their attachment to the Reformed faith with its particular beliefs and practices. But it also depended on their political situation as subjects of the French monarch, their position within the French social order, and their place in the communities they shared with Catholics. The various elements of this identity could be in conflict, as they were during the Wars of Religion, but they were not necessarily so. The Edict of Nantes outlined the way Huguenots could be loyal subjects of the king, members of social or corporate groups, and neighbors of Catholics and still live according to many, if not all, the dictates of their religion. The stability of that collective identity depended on how

[6]Natalie Zemon Davis, "The Rites of Violence," in *Society and Culture in Early Modern France* (Stanford: Stanford University Press, 1975), 152–87, esp. 158; and Penny Roberts, "The Most Crucial Battle of the Wars of Religion? The Conflict over Sites for Reformed Worship in Sixteenth-Century France," *Archiv für Reformationsgeschichte* 89 (1998): 247–67.

[7]On the issue of religion and space in confessionally mixed communities, see Bernard Dompnier, "La logique d'une destruction: L'église catholique, la royauté et les temples protestants (1680-1685)," in *Révolution française et "vandalisme révolutionnaire,"* 343–51, esp. 346–49. For a somewhat different approach to the issue of Protestant space, see Henry Phillips, *Churches and Culture in Seventeenth-Century France* (Cambridge: Cambridge University Press, 1997), 205–25.

the laws governing Huguenots were interpreted and applied, and in the long run, full participation in the life of their communities and that of the kingdom was denied them. However, in the early decades of the century, it was possible for the complex collective identity of French Protestants to receive official recognition. Maintaining their temples in the sacred space of communities was both a sign of that recognition and a way to achieve it.

THE LOCATIONS OF REFORMED WORSHIP

The Edict of Nantes left no doubt that Catholicism would dominate the kingdom's religious landscape. Catholic worship was permitted everywhere and it was to be restored in places where Huguenots had halted it. Catholic clerics were to suffer no obstruction in the performance of their duties or in the enjoyment of their property and perquisites. All "churches, houses, goods, and revenues" were to be returned to them. Protestants, who had seized many Catholic churches, were no longer allowed to practice their religion in any building or on any property belonging to the Roman Catholic Church.[8] Nonetheless, in confessionally mixed areas, the majority faith would now have to share space with the religion it deemed heretical. Huguenots were permitted "to live and dwell in all the cities and places of [the] kingdom...without being inquired after, vexed, molested, or compelled to do anything in religion, contrary to their conscience."[9] In contrast to Catholics, however, they could not publicly practice their religion everywhere. They were limited to places that met certain requirements. Huguenot noblemen who possessed domains with the feudal privilege of high justice were permitted to establish fief worship on their estates for their families, dependents, and other local coreligionists. Those nobles not entitled to high justice were only allowed private worship for their families and households, with no more than thirty participants.[10]

In towns with established Protestant congregations and temples, the edict authorized Reformed worship either by "possession" or "concession." Huguenots "possessed" a legitimate exercise of their religion in locales where they had regularly exercised their faith in 1596 and 1597. They could also continue in certain other places "conceded" to them in the Peace of Bergerac (1577) and in the conference of Fleix (1580), which is to say that the edict granted Huguenots public worship in the suburbs of one town in each *bailliage* or *sénéchausée* (intermediate level court jurisdictions) where they lived. But they could not choose a place on

[8]Article 3 of the Edict of Nantes as translated by E. Everard in Mousnier, *Assassination of Henri IV*, 316–63, see esp. 319.

[9]Edict of Nantes, article 6 in Mousnier, *Assassination of Henri IV*, 320.

[10]Edict of Nantes, articles 7 and 8 in Mousnier, *Assassination of Henri IV*, 320–21. Generally, nobles with a right to such fief worship did not build separate temples, but instead conducted it in châteaux, chapels, or outbuildings. Ligou, "Vandalisme oublié," 334.

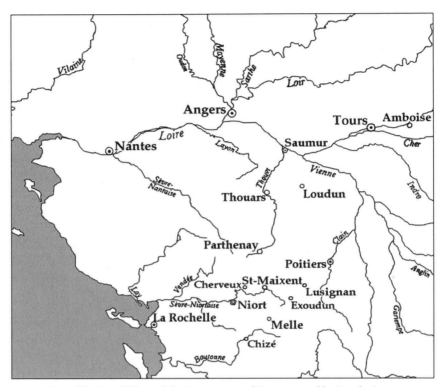

Map of the Loire Valley and the Poitou region of France, created by Douglas Long.

an ecclesiastical fief or in a city that was an episcopal seat. The edict also prohibited Huguenot worship in Paris and a five-league radius around it.[11] Paris was not
only the capital of Catholic France but also the scene of great anti-Huguenot violence during the Wars of Religion.[12] Reformed worship frequently provided the
spark for such violence, and Henri may have agreed to exclude Protestant worship
from Paris as much to preserve public order as to restrict the minority.[13]

[11]Edict of Nantes, articles 10, 11, and 14 in Mousnier, *Assassination of Henri IV,* 321–22. On
Bergerac and Fleix, see Cottret, *L'Édit de Nantes,* 356–57. See also Andrew Spicer, "'Qui est de Dieu oit
la parole de Dieu': The Huguenots and Their Temples," in *Society and Culture in the Huguenot World,
1559-1685,* ed. Raymond A. Mentzer and Andrew Spicer (Cambridge: Cambridge University Press,
2002), 175–92, esp. 180.
   [12]Diefendorf, *Beneath the Cross.*
   [13]As Roberts points out in "Most Crucial Battle," 249.

Despite their apparent precision, the Edict of Nantes's provisions concerning Reformed worship provided grounds for countless disputes. Disagreements between Catholics and Huguenots arose, for instance, over whether individual seigneurs did or did not have the privilege of high justice. And if a Huguenot nobleman converted to Catholicism but his wife did not, Catholics questioned whether Protestants could continue a fief exercise on the seigneurial estate. Catholics also filed lawsuits against temples constructed after 1597, as many were. They challenged Huguenots to produce documents, which were not always clear or had not always survived, proving that their predecessors had publicly practiced their religion in that year.[14] And the choice of *bailliage* locations sparked many quarrels. When royal policy under Louis XIII and Louis XIV began to interpret the edict "à la rigueur," the permissible grounds for legal challenges to temples expanded well beyond what it had explicitly stipulated. Then temples were moved or shut down if they were close enough to a Catholic church that the sound of Reformed worship interfered with the celebration of the Mass. And after 1682, the discovery of any new Catholic convert returning to a Reformed temple condemned it to destruction.

Yet even while forcing the French Protestants to practice their faith under severe constraints, the Edict of Nantes offered them places of worship that were sufficient for their numbers. And Protestant temples were frequently able to withstand the charges Catholics brought against them, either because of the law's ambiguities or because the two groups were willing to reach an agreement. Royal officials were eager to promote these arrangements. It was in the adjudication of disputes and the working out of accommodations that coexistence was constructed. Examining the issue of temples shows these processes at work in shared communal sacred space. It also provides the means to examine the state's impact on these processes through its policies of enforcement and the activities of its representatives. Local Catholics and Protestants did not resolve conflicts in a vacuum. They relied on the king's law, will, and officials to reach settlements. Finally, examining the treatment of temples provides a way to trace the larger history of French Catholic-Protestant relations and to understand both the possibilities and limitations of religious coexistence across the seventeenth century.

TEMPLES AND SACRED SPACE IN BICONFESSIONAL COMMUNITIES
Examples illustrating the disputes and negotiations over temples are drawn primarily from the western province of Poitou. Catholicism here as elsewhere was the dominant religion, but the region had a large and powerful Protestant population.

[14]On temple construction in the seventeenth century, see Spicer, "Huguenots and Their Temples," 185–90.

Some towns had Huguenot majorities and others they controlled politically. A large number of Poitevin nobles also followed the Reformed faith and the Edict of Nantes granted Protestants a number of the province's important towns as *villes de sûreté,* places in which they could maintain military garrisons. Establishing peace and coexistence in this region meant the confessional groups would have to reach agreements on a variety of issues—cemetery arrangements, civic office sharing, scheduling religious observances, as well as temple locations.

In the years following the Edict of Nantes's promulgation, Huguenots could ensure the prominent positioning of temples within communal sacred space in towns where they were politically powerful. Niort and Saint-Maixent, for example, were *places de sûreté* with Huguenot governors who could protect their coreligionists' position and power. Here temples sat squarely inside the town centers, often in close proximity to Catholic churches. The same was true in places where Huguenots were numerically important. At Cherveux, the temple and the parish church were only forty or fifty feet apart. In Melle, only a wall separated the temple from the church of Saint Radegonde.[15]

The temples' locations were powerful statements about the Huguenots' presence and position in these communities they shared with Catholics. There is little indication from the early years of the century that the temples provoked any harsh conflicts. That would change later, when many of these buildings were ordered destroyed precisely because they were near Catholic churches. But the 1599 commissioners of the edict in the region, the Protestant governor of Niort Jean Baudéan de Parabère and a Catholic *conseiller d'état* Martin Langlois, had no disputes over temple locations in these towns to arbitrate. Indeed, though evidence of day-to-day interactions between Catholics and Huguenots is scarce, there is little indication of serious confessional strife at this time in any of these places.

That was not true everywhere, and it may be more revealing of the successes and failures of coexistence under the Edict of Nantes to examine towns where the Protestants were in a weak position numerically and politically. In such places, they generally had to locate their temples outside of town walls, a sign of their weakness and an ominous precedent for the future, when royal policy sought to force all Protestant worship outside of towns, if not to shut it down completely. But if a temple was situated beyond the walls as a result of negotiation rather than by the application of force, then Protestants could still claim a fully recognized

---

[15]For Cherveux, see AN TT 240 (24), 1345. These figures come from the measurement of the distance between the temple and the church in 1683, when legal action was brought against the temple precisely because of its proximity to the church. For details on Melle, see Jean Filleau, *Décisions catholiques ou recueil general des arrests dans toutes les cours souveraines de France en éxécution, ou interpretation, des edits qui concernent l'exercice de la religion pretendue reformée…* (Poitiers: Veuve H. Braud, 1668), 245; and Emilien Traver, *Histoire de Melle* (Melle: n.p., 1938; repr., Marseille: Lafitte, 1980), 125–26.

position in the life of a biconfessional community. Negotiations in and of themselves could ameliorate tensions and promote coexistence.

In Parthenay, the two religious groups negotiated a contract in 1600 by which the Huguenots were able to establish a temple. Here Catholics outnumbered Protestants and dominated local government. Perhaps as a result, the document reveals considerable tensions between the two sides. But it also indicates a recognized need to reach an accommodation to maintain order and obedience to the king's laws. In the contract, the Huguenots claimed the prerogative of exercising their religion in the town, but they acknowledged that their doing so displeased Catholics and "engendered divisions and enmities between them." Hence they agreed to locate their temple outside the town on the estate of their fellow Huguenot Pierre Alloneau, seigneur de Saint Pardoux. He had the privilege of high justice and thus could establish a temple on his fief. The Catholics insisted that the nobleman did not possess high justice and, therefore, the Huguenots could not claim the right of a fief exercise in Parthenay or its suburbs. The Protestants found this opposition "severe and grievous" and complained that they had to travel a considerable distance to worship, which left their "wives, children, and families at the mercy of the weather . . . or deprived of the exercise of their religion and of instruction in piety."[16]

The two groups appeared greatly at odds, but they backed off from the confrontation. The Catholics acknowledged that their opposition to Protestant worship had provoked a "great altercation between the parties, such that each side was close to taking up arms to preserve its rights." So, "to avoid tumult and sedition and to nourish peace between the inhabitants who for the past thirty years have unanimously maintained themselves in the king's service," they consented to public Protestant worship, "providing it was held neither in the town nor the [immediate] suburbs." This compromise would "maintain friendship [between Catholics and Protestants], inasmuch as it is the king's intention that all live in peace under his edicts." The Huguenots responded with a declaration of their desire to remain in friendship with their Catholic neighbors. And "not having great interest in which place they hold their worship," they reached an agreement with the Catholics on a pasture that lay beyond the town's immediate suburbs as a place for their temple.[17] The agreement favored Parthenay's Catholics. Reformed and Catholic

---

[16]The contract was signed 15 December 1600. A copy may be found in the Bibliothèque municipale de Poitiers, *Fonds Fonteneau* 79:303–6, and another in BPF Ms. 869 (1). See also Pierre Dez, *Histoire des protestants et des églises réformées du Poitou* (La Rochelle: Imprimerie de l'Ouest, 1936), 235. The Parthenay situation is discussed in Luria, *Sacred Boundaries,* 23–26.

[17]In 1610 in a similar dispute over the temple in Luçon, the bishop (Richelieu), the cathedral chapter, and the inhabitants of both faiths signed a letter addressed to the provincial lieutenant-general Parabère in which they assured him of their "resolution to live in peace . . . without regard to

worship would not share civic space within Parthenay, but the majority Catholics did not deny their Huguenot neighbors a temple, and thus Protestants did secure a right to practice their faith and live in Parthenay. Despite the apparently tense confessional situation in the town, a common interest in maintaining order in the community enabled each side to accommodate the other.

The task of promoting this interest and of reminding everyone that the king wanted them to live in peace fell to a third party in the negotiations, the Catholic lieutenant-general of Poitiers, Louis de Sainte-Marthe, a magistrate known for his *politique* views. Scholars cannot know the role Sainte-Marthe played behind the scenes or the degree to which he pressured Parthenay's inhabitants to reach an agreement, but it is certain that he endorsed the contract and enjoined all involved to conduct themselves as fellow subjects in the union ordered by the king's edicts. He also warned that anyone obstinate enough to oppose the agreement would be guilty of disturbing the peace and of *lèse-majesté*. The threat was a clear sign of the seriousness with which authorities approached the resolution of confessional conflict in a town like Parthenay and of their worries about just how difficult the task might be. Confessional tensions here did not permanently disappear.[18] But the three-way parley involving the local confessional groups and state authority in the person of Sainte-Marthe did, at least temporarily, ameliorate tensions with its agreed-upon arrangement of the community's sacred space and its allowance of Protestant worship, albeit outside the town. Members of the minority group traded the inconvenience of traveling some distance to their temple for recognition of their right to live in the town peacefully as Protestants under the protection of the king's law.

The settlement of the temple issue in Parthenay helped create a situation in which the two confessional groups could live together. Huguenots were not able to conduct worship in the center of the town's sacred space, as they did in Niort, Cherveux, and other places where they were stronger. Their weakness led to a clear separation between the devotional lives and activities of the two confessional groups. But this separation of the confessions was essentially what the Edict of

---

religion... according to their oath of fidelity to the king and the regent." Copy of "Lettre addressée par le chapitre de Luçon et les habitants..." (24 May 1610), BPF, Ms. 870 (1). See also Auguste-François Lièvre, *Histoire des protestants et des églises réformées du Poitou* (Poitiers: Grassart, J. Cherbuliez, 1856), 1:273–74.

[18]Conflict reemerged on Christmas Eve 1618, when Parthenay narrowly escaped an armed fracas. Catholics heard that Huguenots were arming themselves. Huguenots later told royal investigators of rumors that Catholics were planning to massacre them. The incident occurred during a time of rising political and confessional tension throughout the country, but despite the apparent hostility, no violence was committed. The *procès-verbal* of the investigation is in AN TT 261 (21) (29 December 1618).

Nantes envisioned. It did not require that temples be removed from cities to their suburbs; Protestant and Catholic religious practices could coexist in the sacred space of towns and still be distinct. But a mixing of the religious practices of the two faiths was, in a sense, as contrary to the edict's spirit as would be prohibiting the minority religion altogether. Such a situation might not be considered "tolerant," but it did allow for coexistence. Even if a temple was located outside a town, as in Parthenay, Huguenots and their worship still had, as a result of local negotiations, a publicly acknowledged and legally recognized presence in the biconfessional community.

Elsewhere the process of picking a site for a temple did not have such an effect. In Poitiers, the provincial capital of Poitou, confessional relations were always hostile. Poitiers was a Catholic League stronghold during the late stages of the religious wars, and Henri IV reached an accord with the League in 1594 prohibiting Reformed worship in the city. Furthermore, Poitiers was an episcopal seat; thus no temple could be constructed within its walls. The dispute over the temple's location was particularly aggravated, and Poitiers's confessional groups did not arrive at an agreement through negotiations. Instead, in 1599, commissioners Parabère and Langlois decided the issue by choosing a site at the far end of a suburb.[19] Perhaps the lack of direct negotiations is why locating the structure at a distance from the city did little to decrease tensions. During the temple's construction, Huguenots complained of being insulted and attacked while traveling between the city and the building site. Their Catholic assailants had reportedly referred to the temple as a pigsty, and when one Protestant objected that such speech was contrary to the king's law, he was punched and thrown into a pond.[20] Indeed, situating Protestant worship at a distance from the town may actually have increased the opportunities for suspicion and conflict. On 20 July 1606, the city's Huguenots celebrated a fast day during which they remained at the temple from 6:00 in the morning until 5:00 in the afternoon. A rumor spread that they were planning to take over the city. The mayor deployed the militia, which only increased the panic. Eventually, civic magistrates gained control over the situation, but similar incidents occurred later in the decade.[21]

[19]F. Garrisson, *Essai sur les commissions,* 97; Lièvre, *Histoire des protestants,* 1:265; and Luria, *Sacred Boundaries,* 21–22, 28.

[20]Dez, *Histoire des protestants,* 239n3.

[21]In 1609, Protestants complained that their pastor was being subjected to insults and that troublemakers threw stones at his windows on Catholic festivals. Local magistrates did not intervene and it required direct orders from the royal court to put an end to the problem. Lièvre, *Histoire des protestants,* 1:271–72, 274–75; Dez, *Histoire des protestants,* 240. After Henri IV's assassination in 1610, the city government refused to publish Marie de Médicis's confirmation of the Edict of Nantes. On the night of 30 June Catholics raised barricades on city streets, which they maintained for several days. Fearful Protestants mostly remained indoors. Lièvre, *Histoire des protestants,* 1:275–76.

Various reasons account for the ongoing confessional hostility in Poitiers: the city's history of bloodshed during the religious wars; its past as a Catholic League stronghold; the militant anti-Protestantism of its bishop, Henri Chasteigner de La Rocheposay; and its Catholic municipal government's unwillingness to prevent street violence against Huguenots. Given this situation, the commissioners may have despaired of encouraging an accommodation over the temple; they simply dictated a solution in keeping with the Edict of Nantes's provisions. In a sense, however, their answer to the problem worked. Huguenots in Poitiers remained beleaguered. In the 1620s, their cemetery was attacked, they were prohibited from joining guilds, and they were deprived of posts in the university. They were also excluded from the city's guard corps and obliged to pay a special tax to cover the cost of their replacements.[22] But Huguenots maintained their temple and their right to worship until 1685, long after many of the province's other temples had disappeared.[23]

The monarchy's policy of intervening as a third party in these temple disputes was crucial, whether successful, as in Parthenay, or not, as in Poitiers. When that changed and government orders or court decisions forced Reformed worship out of communities, coexistence was threatened. After the fall of La Rochelle in 1628, Louis XIII announced in the Peace of Alais his commitment to the Edict of Nantes. But now that Huguenots were shorn of their military power, the monarchy's attitude toward them took a harsher turn.[24] In 1634, the government convened a Grands Jours court in Poitiers. Grands Jours consisted of parlementary magistrates temporarily assigned to particular regions to repress lawlessness and impose royal will.[25] One of the judges' chief tasks in Poitiers was to consider accusations that Protestants were contravening the laws governing their religious life. Temples were a major target of complaints.[26] Catholic officials filed suits against temples located throughout the western provinces, and the judges condemned half a dozen of them in Poitou alone.[27] The charges against them varied. In certain

---

[22]Dez, *Histoire des protestants,* 265, 268; and Yves Krumenacker, *Les protestants du Poitou au XVIIIe siècle (1681–1789)* (Paris: H. Champion, 1998), 40–41. The decade of the 1620s was a time of renewed religious civil wars.

[23]Lièvre, *Histoire des protestants,* 2:147.

[24]On the Peace of Alais, see Holt, *French Wars of Religion,* 186–87.

[25]Marcel Marion, *Dictionnaire des institutions de la France aux XVIIe et XVIIIe siècles* (New York: B. Franklin, 1968), 268.

[26]So, too, were Huguenot schools and cemeteries. On cemeteries, see Keith P. Luria, "Separated by Death? Burials, Cemeteries, Confessional Boundaries in Seventeenth-Century France," *French Historical Studies* 24, no. 2 (Spring 2001): 185–222.

[27]The most important was that of Saint-Maixent. Lièvre, *Histoire des protestants,* 2:12–16; and Krumenacker, *Protestants du Poitou,* 41. One Poitevin magistrate and active anti-Protestant campaigner who was involved in these cases was Jean Filleau. He later reproduced many of the court decisions in his massive compilation of anti-Protestant laws, regulations, and court decisions: *Décisions catholiques,*

places, temples were challenged because Protestants could not produce documents proving they had worshiped in these locations in 1596 and 1597, as the Edict of Nantes stipulated. Some were condemned because, like that of Saint-Maixent, they were constructed on fiefs held by ecclesiastics or because they were located in former church buildings. Yet others were built after 1598 or did not have explicit royal permission to operate as places of "concession" in a *bailliage*. Protestants also lost the right to worship when the court decided that Huguenot seigneurs did not have the privilege of high justice and thus could not offer places for worship to anyone outside their immediate households.

Plaintiffs also employed a new legal strategy. They objected to temples located close to Catholic churches, chapels, or religious houses because the sound of Reformed worship disturbed that of the Catholics. As Jean Filleau, Poitevin magistrate and anti-Protestant campaigner, put it: "the religionnaires have used force in locating the places they exercise their worship (which by abuse they call temples) too close to our churches." The sound of their voices "resembles more the clamor of an insensible multitude than an assembly of people praying."[28] The accusations cited article 3 of the Edict of Nantes, which ordered that Catholicism could be "peaceably and freely exercised" everywhere without "any trouble or impediment." No one could "trouble, molest, or disquiet" ecclesiastics in their "celebration of the divine service."[29] Previously this article had provided the legal means for reestablishing Catholic worship in places where it had ceased and for returning the Catholic clergy's property to them. Henceforth it would be a potent weapon against the presence of Reformed worship within the sacred space of biconfessional communities.

In response to the accusations and court decisions, Protestants insisted that the laws governing them be interpreted as they had been previously.[30] They protested the charge that they worshiped in places that the edict did not permit and pointed out that royal commissioners had been through the region several times since 1599 without raising the issue of temple locations.[31] Huguenots also objected to the Catholic complaint that they had constructed temples after 1598. Of course they had: "Almost all of [the temples had] been built after the edict, some earlier and some later depending on when those of the said religion had the

---

26, 30, 163, 365, 439, 444.

[28]Filleau, *Décisions catholiques,* 241. For the citing of article 3 in arguments for condemning temples too close to churches, see ibid., 26.

[29]Mousnier, *Assassination of Henri IV,* 319.

[30]The Huguenots' response is contained in Archives Départmentales de Vienne C 49 "Sommaire des raisons que ceux qui font profession de la religion refformée ont de se plaindre de l'arrest du seiziesme septembre 1634 donné par nos seigneurs de parlement tenants les grands jours en la ville de Poictiers."

[31]"Sommaire des raisons," 4–4v.

means to do so." Nothing in the law prevented them from doing so. "Of what use would it be to give them the right to preach and exercise their religion if they were not also given the right to build a place to do it?"[32] But Huguenots knew that they argued from a position weaker than the one they had held in earlier years, and so they added a conciliatory note to their complaint. They had done nothing contrary to the edict and nothing to obstruct the reestablishment of Catholicism.[33] But given that they never had any intention of troubling Catholics, "if it is determined that their temples are close enough to churches to cause some inconvenience, they are willing to cease worship in them, providing they are allowed to build new ones elsewhere."[34]

That is what happened, for instance, in Chizé, whose temple the Grands Jours condemned. Huguenots were given permission to choose a place in the suburbs to build another. At first, this arrangement might appear the same as that established in Parthenay in 1600—and in spatial terms it was. But there is a significant difference between the two. Confessional relations in Parthenay were tense, but the town's inhabitants, with the active participation of a royal official, negotiated an agreement. In Chizé, the decisions of a royal court dictated the removal of the temple to a new location and the re-Catholicization of the town's sacred space.[35]

Conceding to Catholics a means of attacking temples based on their proximity to churches would come back to haunt Huguenots in later decades, but they had little choice. The increasing hostility they faced in royal courts made it difficult for them to mount successful defenses of temples. A more successful strategy was simply to drag their feet, sometimes for decades, in complying with court orders. In Thouars, despite the protection of the local seigneurs (the powerful ducal La Trémoïlle family), the temple was condemned in 1634 because it was too close to a church. But Thouars's Huguenots delayed destruction of their temple until the 1640s, when they exhausted their legal appeals. Then duc Henri de La Trémoïlle granted them a new place near the wall of the city in what had been the Protestant cemetery. In doing so, he made clear his desire to prevent confessional conflict. He wished to avoid "any pretexts of division" between the two groups and "maintain them in peace." The new temple would not be in the center of Thouars like the old one. It was pushed to the town's edge, and with it the Huguenots were symbolically displaced as well. But the duc de La Trémoïlle allowed their worship to continue in the community's sacred space.[36]

[32]"Sommaire des raisons," 3v–4.
[33]"Sommaire des raisons,"1–1v.
[34]"Sommaire des raisons," 3v.
[35]"Registre de baptêmes et mariages et du consistoire de l'église de Chizé," AN TT 241 (2), 201, 215–16.
[36]AN 1AP 428, 8–9; Louis, duc de La Trémoïlle, *Les La Trémoïlles pendant cinq siècles* (Nantes: E. Grimaud, 1895), 4:88–90; Hugues Imbert, *Histoire de Thouars* (Niort: Clouzot, 1871), 298–300; and

In Melle, a town Protestants dominated, they actually managed to build a new temple in 1634, adjacent to the Saint Radegonde church—indeed, separated from it only by a wall. In 1643 the Parlement of Paris ordered it closed on the grounds that Melle was not a "conceded" place in its *bailliage*. The decision provoked resistance; local Huguenot nobles barricaded the town's gates against the official sent to carry out the order. They quickly backed off this show of defiance, but still managed through legal appeals to delay demolition for another three years.[37] As the cases of Thouars and Melle indicate, despite the intentions of the anti-Protestant campaigners of the 1630s, the condemnation of temples did not necessarily mean the immediate end of Reformed worship in those edifices or its expulsion from the sacred space of biconfessional communities.

In the middle years of the century, the state relaxed its policy toward the religious minority. The regent, Anne of Austria, and Cardinal Mazarin had too much need of Huguenot loyalty during the Fronde to pursue a policy of persecution. Instead, the government issued confirmations of Huguenot privileges and legal protections. Catholics accused Protestants of taking advantage of the situation to regain lost ground, for example, by rebuilding more than sixty temples.[38] But the respite was brief. Throughout the late 1650s and on into the next decade, the Catholic clergy actively lobbied for a more restrictive policy; and their complaints found sympathetic ears in the royal administration. In 1661, after Louis XIV's assumption of power, his finance minister, Jean-Baptiste Colbert, sent new commissioners to Poitou to regulate the confessional situation. He appointed his brother, Charles Colbert de Croissy, as the Catholic commissioner and the local Poitevin nobleman Claude de La Noue as the Protestant commissioner. Over the next six years, with Colbert de Croissy outmaneuvering La Noue, the commission outlawed temples and Protestant worship in thirty-six communities.[39]

Huguenots could no longer hope for legal redress. Instead, pastors reportedly urged resistance in their sermons. The provincial synod meeting at Lusignan in 1666 included ministers from prohibited temples despite orders not to do so. The

---

Luria, *Sacred Boundaries,* 173–76. The duke had converted to Catholicism in 1628, but his wife, Marie de La Tour d'Auvergne, remained a staunch Protestant. The family continued to offer its protection to the community's Huguenots until her death in the 1660s.

[37]Lièvre, *Histoire des protestants,* 2:32–34; and Traver, *Histoire de Melle,* 125–26.

[38]Solange Deyon, *Du loyalisme au refus: Les protestants français et leur député-général entre la Fronde et la Révocation* (Villeneuve-d'Ascq: Université de Lille, 1976), 37–44. Deyon provides a detailed discussion of the government's relations with Protestants during this period.

[39]Only thirteen were confirmed. Another eight were left undecided but placed in jeopardy. Six fief exercises were also condemned. For a discussion of this campaign, see Lièvre, *Histoire des protestants,* 2:71–80; Dez, *Histoire des protestants,* 325–41; and Krumenacker, *Protestants du Poitou,* 48–49. Deyon (*Du loyalisme,* 87–88) provides a different tally. According to her, in 1665, the royal council condemned twenty-seven temples and maintained twenty-three.

synod urged the ministers to continue preaching in the ruins of temples already destroyed or in nearby fields, a provocative act that foreshadowed later resistance efforts in the 1680s and Protestant preaching in the Desert after the Revocation.[40] And in Exoudun, the attempt to tear down the temple led to an armed confrontation. When the demolition team arrived, they found that two local noblewomen had gathered some two to three thousand armed people to protect the temple.[41] The women were quickly imprisoned and the temple was demolished.

The assault on temples in the 1660s in Poitou was severe. It reveals the government's increasing determination to restrict Reformed worship. It might well be assumed that with Catholic authorities tearing down temples and desperate Protestants responding with provocative preaching and even armed resistance, relations between the two groups in biconfessional communities were completely breaking down. Unfortunately, the state of such matters inside Poitevin communities during these years is not well known; however, Protestant worship in the province did not cease and coexistence did not disappear. Some of the factors that had shaped local confessional relations earlier in the century still existed. Huguenot numbers remained strong; relatively few converted to Catholicism.[42] In certain towns, like Niort and Melle, Huguenots remained politically powerful, as they also did in some rural areas where many of the lower-ranking nobles stayed within the faith. Evidence from certain localities indicates that people of the two religions continued to marry each other frequently, a sign that both groups were willing to ignore their clergies' denunciation of mixed marriages as a means for families to make advantageous matches across the confessional divide.[43]

Despite the impact of this assault on Reformed worship, there was still in some places little or no change at all. In Cherveux, where temple and church stood near each other, the king permitted the Protestant place of worship to survive despite the Grands Jours order of 1634 against it. He did the same in Niort, where Catholics had charged that the temple was built on former ecclesiastical property and was located too close to a Catholic almshouse where the celebration

---

[40]On the resistance movement in southern France in 1684, see Elisabeth Labrousse, ed., *Avertissement aux protestans [sic] des provinces (1684)* (Paris: Presses Universitaires de France, 1986).

[41]On the two women, Marguerite de Saint-Georges (widow of Exoudun's seigneur) and her daughter Louise Forain (widow of the seigneur of Regny), see the comments of Alfred Richard in Jean Babu, *Poésies de Jean Babu, curé de Soudan, sur les ruines des temples protestants de Champdeniers, d'Exoudun, de La Mothe-Sainte-Héraye (1663–1682)*, ed. A. Richard (Poitiers: P. Blanchier, 1896), 78–79. The Exoudun temple had already suffered condemnation in 1634 because of its proximity to a church. But as in other places of Huguenot strength, the order had not been carried out. Lièvre, *Histoire des protestants,* 2:13; and Luria, *Sacred Boundaries,* 215–17.

[42]Krumenacker, *Protestants du Poitou,* 43.

[43]Consistory records of Melle reveal numerous mixed marriages between 1660 and 1669. Archives départmentales des Deux-Sèvres 2J 35 (1).

of the Mass in the chapel was disturbed.[44] But in those communities where temples were successfully condemned, the reorganization of sacred space likely had a large impact on interconfessional relations. Catholics marching in processions would no longer encounter their Protestant neighbors singing psalms on their way to the *prêche*. Huguenots now had to troop off to surviving temples in nearby towns to worship. Indeed, the size of the remaining Reformed congregations swelled considerably in these years as they absorbed coreligionists from nearby communities where temples had been demolished. In the province of Aunis, neighboring Poitou, the Huguenots of Mauzé sparked Catholic protests because their temple became a center of Reformed worship after those in La Rochelle and other communities in the region were closed down.[45]

Huguenots also found refuge on the estates of nobles. A 1681 *memoire* to the government on fief exercises in Poitou complained that "many gentlemen had begun worship in their homes on their own authority [between 1665 and 1668] and in the following years. They pretended to be in no way subjected to the rulings [of the 1660s]."[46] It is unlikely that many Huguenot nobles were able to establish worship on estates where no one had practiced it before. But given the pressures on the Reformed Church in these years, it is entirely possible that nobles were bending the rules that restricted the numbers of worshipers in their homes if they did not have the right of high justice.

By 1680 only about half the temples that had existed in France in 1598 were still in operation.[47] In the early years of that decade, the monarchy began an attempt to eliminate Protestantism in France through a campaign of conversions—if necessary, forced conversions. Poitou in 1681 was the first region to experience the infamous *dragonnades,* the quartering of troops in Protestant homes and their use in terrorizing Huguenots into abjuring.[48] But sending in troops was only one way to gain conversions; attacking temples was another. It had long been a contention of Catholic polemics against Protestantism that Huguenots could not find their way to the Catholic Church because they were in thrall to ministers who preached lies about Catholicism; if they could only hear the simple truth of the Catholic faith, they would be sure to embrace it. Temples provided the setting in which they imbibed their ministers' falsehoods. As an official of the Poitiers diocese explained in 1681, "destroying temples will contribute to conversions because

[44]AN TT 240 (24), 1339–40 (Cherveux); and AN TT 260 (10), 1122 (Niort).

[45]The complaints date from 1682. AN TT 252 (Mauzé), 836.

[46]"Memoire pour monseigneur le chancelier touchant les exercises de fief en Poictou" (1681), AN TT 262, 245–51, see esp. 249 (Poitou).

[47]Elisabeth Labrousse, *"Une foi, une loi, un roi?"* 168.

[48]For a recent assessment of the 1681 *dragonnade,* including a discussion of Huguenot resistance, see Krumenacker, *Protestants du Poitou,* 62–83.

the people themselves say when they can no longer go to the *prêche*, they will go to the Mass."[49] Or, as the 1682 Catholic complaint about Mauzé's temple put it, "the demolition and interdiction [of the temple] is very necessary to bring about conversions because the *religionnaires* will not want to hear anything that proves the truth of our religion until that building is torn down."[50]

Destroying temples would gain converts, but gaining converts would also destroy temples. Those bent on closing down Reformed worship in the 1680s had tried and true legal means at their disposal; for instance, courts continued to condemn temples for being too close to Catholic places of worship. But now Catholics had a new weapon: a 1663 law that prohibited Protestants who had converted to Catholicism from relapsing to their former faith.[51] A royal council decision in June 1682 ordered that not only would new Catholic converts caught returning to the *prêche* be arrested, the temples to which they returned would be destroyed, their ministers removed, and Reformed worship in the community outlawed.[52] A temple's proximity to a church could lead to its closing while still leaving its congregants the possibility of seeking a location for a new one in their city's suburbs. By contrast, if a *nouveau converti* was apprehended in a temple, the result could be the end of Protestant religious life in the community altogether.

Throughout France both strategies were deployed with increasing ferocity against temples. In the last seven months of 1681, only one temple in the country suffered condemnation. In the next year, twenty-eight were closed. In 1682 the tally jumped to forty-eight, with a similar number the following year. In 1684 the total soared to sixty-five.[53] In Poitou, temples like those of Niort and Cherveux, which had survived previous assaults, were now targeted. In July 1683, the intendant (and Catholic commissioner of the edict) Lamoignon de Basville ordered the destruction of Niort's temple because of its closeness to an almshouse where a priest celebrated Mass in a chapel. The Niort temple was also on land that the Catholic Church claimed, but Basville allowed that the temple could be "translated" to a place in the suburbs, where the city's churches "would receive no incommodity."[54] The Huguenots dragged their heels in complying with the intendant's

[49]"Requeste et pieces pour le sindic du clergé de Poitiers," AN TT 262, 131–35, see esp. 133 (Poitiers).

[50]AN TT 252, 836 (Mauzé).

[51]The law was reinforced in 1665 and 1679 after which those convicted of relapse could be banished and their property confiscated. Labrousse, *"Une foi, une loi, un roi?"* 167.

[52]A 1680 royal declaration prohibited all Catholics whether *anciens* or *nouveaux* from becoming Protestants. Labrousse, *"Une foi, une loi, un roi?"* 168. On the 1682 decision, see Dez, *Histoire des protestants,* 389.

[53]Deyon, *Du loyalisme,* 150–51.

[54]"Proces-verbal de M. de Basville et de M. de Jaucourt touchant la proximité du temple de Niort 17 juillet 1683," AN TT 260 (10), 1158–69. Catholics also claimed to be worried about the temple as a security threat, since it had large and rather mysterious underground chambers.

orders. On 19 April 1684 in the early afternoon, a crowd of Catholics reportedly numbering around ten thousand gathered in front of the temple. Among them were about 120 Catholic priests and monks and the children of the *hôpital général,* who had marched there in procession. The city's magistrates unlocked the temple's doors and six or seven thousand people rushed in. The clergymen opened the doors and windows and began to chant as loudly as they could ("in voices screaming like thunder" according to the Huguenot complaint). They blew horns and trumpets to accompany their chanting. The rest of the crowd set about sacking the temple. They destroyed Bibles and psalters, broke benches, tore up seat cushions, and defecated in the pulpit.[55]

This act of aggression, so reminiscent of popular violence during the Wars of Religion, was not aimed just at desecrating the temple. It was also intended to demonstrate beyond a shadow of a doubt that the temple's location interfered with Catholic worship. Basville positioned himself in the nearby almshouse chapel; the Protestant commissioner, the Marquis de Villarnoul, had absented himself from the proceedings. The intendant had no trouble confirming that he could hear chanting from the temple. Niort's Huguenots objected to the procedure: they certainly did not scream at the top of their voices when singing psalms; they did not open all the windows; they did not blow horns and trumpets. Protestants complained that Catholics resorted to such "artifice" because they knew the *prêche* did not really disturb their worship.[56] After all, as Niort's Huguenots pointed out, "in the past when they were much more numerous, Catholics were not bothered. So how could they be now when their number was so diminished?" Even the chapel's priest, they insisted, had recently testified that Protestant worship did not hinder his performance of the Mass.

Cherveux's temple suffered a similar invasion. In 1683 the intendant had ordered an official survey of the distance from it to the parish church. "How could it be," Basville asked, "that this place should be alone in maintaining the right to a temple such a small distance from a church in which Catholics are being disturbed, when throughout the kingdom temples built too close to churches are being demolished."[57] The Protestants tried to delay the inevitable, but after an order of

[55]This account comes from the complaint Niort's Huguenots sent to the king's minister Louvois, a copy of which was inserted into their consistory record. See "Consistoire de Niort," BMP Fonds Fonteneau 37:261–63. See also Lièvre, *Histoire des protestants,* 2:141–43; and Krumenacker, *Protestants du Poitou,* 88–89.

[56]"Niort, au sujet de la demolition du temple, 1684," AN TT 260 (10), 1204–5; and "Memoire pour les temples de Niort et de Cherveux" (ibid., 1198–99).

[57]"Pièces concernant les contestations relatives à la démolition de temple dudit lieu (Cherveux)" and "Proces-verbal de Messieurs de Basville et de Jaucourt touchant la proximité du temple de Cherveux a l'eglise parroisialle, 17 juillet et 3 aoust 1689," AN TT 240 (24), 1339–46, 1356–78, quote at 1359.

the royal council, the intendant arranged for the measurement on 20 April 1684. According to the Huguenots present, before the surveyors could begin, twenty-five or thirty priests "chosen for having the strongest possible voices," accompanied by others with "strong and penetrating voices," stormed into the temple. Some mounted the pulpit, others climbed onto the benches, and all started singing as loudly as they could. As in Niort, Basville positioned himself in the nearby church and readily testified to hearing the sound of chanting from the temple; indeed it could be heard "a quarter league away."[58]

Nonetheless, while the temples in Niort and Cherveux were ordered closed, Reformed worship was not completely prohibited. To accomplish that goal Catholics resorted to the law against relapses. Of the thirty-four Poitevin temples prohibited in the early 1680s, at least twenty-two were targeted because *nouveaux convertis* had reentered them.[59] In Cherveux, the temple was still standing in 1685 when authorities found in it children who had converted. Reformed worship in the community was now banned.[60]

Niort's Huguenots had suffered that fate only eleven days after the temple was sacked. The consistory had been zealously guarding the temple's doors to make certain no apostate slipped in. But their vigilance did not work. On 30 April the Catholic mayor accosted the minister, Pierre Bossatran, and produced a young man, recently converted to Catholicism, whom he claimed to have found at the *prêche*. "Say goodbye to your temple," he told the Protestants. The Huguenots insisted that the discovery of the convert was a long-planned trap and that the man had been found in the street, not in the temple. Elders had carefully watched everyone attending the service and the doors were locked immediately after they had all exited. Bossatran reported to the consistory that a few days earlier he had encountered the mayor, who told the minister that he would do everything he could and look for all possible occasions to defeat the Protestants. And his associate pastor, Jacques Misson, added that earlier on 30 April he had encountered the mayor, who had repeated to him several times that if he could not get a *nouveau converti* into the temple by the doors he would do so by the windows.[61]

Of course, disputes over closing temples or over discovering converts in them became moot with the Revocation of the Edict of Nantes on 18 October 1685. But even before this final prohibition of Reformed worship in the kingdom, the formerly shared sacred space of biconfessional communities was becoming almost

[58]"Proces-verbal de la descente faitte par...Basville...au bourg de Cherveux, 20 avril 1684," AN TT 260 (10), 1196–97.
[59]Krumenacker (*Protestants du Poitou,* 87) refers to the law against relapses as a "veritable war machine" against Protestant temples.
[60]Lièvre, *Histoire des protestants,* 2:147.
[61]"Consistoire de Niort," BMP Fonds Fonteneau 37:134–35; and Lièvre, *Histoire des protestants,* 2:144.

entirely Catholicized and the possibility of coexistence was disappearing. This is not to say that good personal relations between Catholics and Protestants vanished. Stories that emerged from the horrors of the post-Revocation *dragonnades* suggest that individuals of the two faiths could remain friendly and that Catholics were often willing to aid their Huguenot neighbors.[62] But the conditions necessary for creating communal coexistence had vanished. State policy had long since turned against the idea of encouraging it and, as the actions of Niort's mayor suggest, local Catholic leaders would no longer willingly participate with their Huguenot counterparts in the negotiations that led to accommodations. Indeed, in Niort and Cherveux, they were prepared to whip up crowd actions against their Protestant neighbors.

The persecution French Protestants suffered in the second half of the seventeenth century crystallized a sense of their collective identity as a beleaguered minority living in a hostile society and beset by an intolerant state. It is difficult to take issue with such a characterization given a history from the 1680s that details discriminatory legislation, social exclusion, forced conversions, and clandestine religious life. The memory of persecution has not disappeared and, to a degree, the sense of Protestant separateness in French society endures today, more than two centuries after Huguenots gained full citizenship rights. But early in the seventeenth century, a lack of tolerance did not preclude the possibility of coexistence; finding a means for Catholics and Protestants to live together was possible.

The Edict of Nantes provided the framework for coexistence. But it is important to recognize both the possibilities it created and the limitations it imposed. The edict did not envision a religiously pluralistic society; all French subjects were members either of the Catholic or Reformed Church. Other religious groups, for instance, Lutherans or Jews, had no legal standing in the country. Nor did the edict seek to establish a secularized society in which religious belief was privatized and confessional allegiance was de-emphasized in public life. Affiliation with one of the two permissible churches still determined one's place in society. Hence confessional identity was concretized not blurred, but the minority was not excluded from a legally recognized place in French society.

Coexistence was frequently tenuous. While relations between Catholic and Protestant neighbors might be—and often were—good, they could not ensure local confessional harmony when the two groups came into conflict. Then they had to

---

[62]See the account of the Huguenot refugee published in Jean Migault, *Les dragonnades en Poitou et Saintonge: Le journal de Jean Migault* (Le Poiré sur Vie: Imprimerie graphique de l'ouest, 1988).

negotiate their differences and, to promote peace, the state had to encourage them to reach accommodations. In the early decades of the century, the monarchy was interested in doing so—a testament to its desire for order, though admittedly, also to its awareness of continuing Huguenot strength. This situation allowed members of the minority faith to maintain a dual collective identity; they were both Protestants and loyal subjects of the Catholic monarch. The positioning of their temples in the center of communal sacred space symbolized the state's acceptance of this identity. As the monarchy's attitude changed and as temples were forced out of towns or closed down, Huguenots' identity changed. From fully recognized subjects of the king, they became a persecuted minority who, in defiance of their monarch, now worshiped in the ruins of their former temples or in fields and woods far from their former confessionally mixed communities.

Religion and Politics in France during the Period of the Edict of Nantes (1598–1685)

Christian Jouhaud

THIS ESSAY WILL EXAMINE briefly the connection between politics and religion in France during the period of the Edict of Nantes (1598–1685), that is to say, during the century of absolutist rule, focusing on attitudes and behavior both of those in power and of their detractors, at the intersection between the political and the religious. First this essay will review some of the political ramifications of the application of the Edict of Nantes, then attempt to define the contours of the political theology of those in power in the absolutist system, as developed by the cardinal-ministers Richelieu and Mazarin. Finally, this essay will consider some of the political stakes of Catholic spiritual radicalism as manifested in the Counter-Reformation (a much debated notion) of this "century of saints" (a famous historiographic designation, which is also very debatable).

POLITICS AND RELIGION UNDER THE EDICT OF NANTES—A NEW
POLITICO-RELIGIOUS ORDER
On 13 April 1598, Henri IV signed and sealed the Edict of Nantes. The edict offered Protestants liberty of conscience and a certain number of guarantees for the exercise of such liberty, referred to at the time as "privileges." The document proscribes any discrimination against adherents of the Reformed religion (excluding access to certain public offices), but, needless to say, was not prompted by any modern version of tolerance. The edict did not establish the equality of both religions. It accorded some religious liberties to the adherents of the Reformed religion, comprising roughly 5 percent of a population of eighteen million people, liberties that gave Protestantism the status of an *autonomous body,*

This essay was translated from the French by Duane Rudolph.

that is, "the so-called Reformed religion" (*la religion prétendue réformée*). Those who claimed to be adherents of it could now avoid the discipline of the Roman Catholic Church and practice their religion, albeit with certain restrictions.[1]

For the great majority of political figures—from the most to the least powerful, the aristocracy to the lesser officers—the accession and subsequent political success of Henri IV was generally a welcome break and a return to lost unity. Catholics, however, were obliged to live with the sanctioned and protected presence of heretics, just as Protestants had to accept the constraints and limits of their own status as a tolerated minority. It is difficult to imagine nowadays the extent to which such an arrangement would have seemed unusual or even repugnant at the time to militants from both sides. Nondiscriminatory access of the Reformed to most public offices seemed particularly scandalous to Catholic officers. Such a policy, nevertheless, was one of the keystones of Henri IV's plans. Henri IV was to state before the Parlement of Toulouse, "I want those of the (Reformed) religion to live in peace in my kingdom and I want them to be able to enter into office, not because they are of a religion, but because they are loyal servants to me and to the Crown of France."[2] By so doing, Henri IV affirmed the primacy of political loyalty over religious affiliation and took the opposite course of action to the Catholic League, which had argued in favor of the interests of the Catholic religion over those of the nation. But Henri's statement also confirmed the abandonment of Christianity as an ideal expressed by the dictum "une foi."

The collapse of the notion of a unified Christianity, eroded from within by conflicts on a national level, and the effacing of the notion of a city of God on earth (a goal of all Christian politics) in the course of the horrors of the civil wars, slowly gave rise to the idea of an autonomous realm of action for the state, answering only to its own rationale. This is the famous reason of state (*raison d'état*). The subjects of the king of France were certainly responsible for their own personal salvation, but the connection between politics and communal salvation was now beyond their control. Its interpretation had now become the domain, almost the reserved territory, of those in power, with a fundamental political consequence: the recognition of royal power as the only guarantor of civil peace.

On the one hand, it soon appeared that the power relations of the Catholic majority and the Huguenot minority placed the latter on the defensive. The edict ordered that in the regions controlled by the Reformed, Catholicism would be

[1]See Jean-Pierre Babelon, *Henri IV* (Paris: Fayard, 1982); David Parker, "Sovereignty, Absolutism, and the Function of the Law in Seventeenth-Century France," *Past and Present* 122 (1989); 36–74; and Keith Cameron, ed., *From Valois to Bourbon: Dynasty, State, and Society in Early Modern France* (Exeter: University of Exeter Press, 1989).

[2]Robert Descimon and Christian Jouhaud, *La France du premier XVIII siècle* (Paris: Belin, 1996), 45.

reinstated everywhere and the church would regain possession of the property and possessions it had lost during the period of unrest. Thanks to this provision, a rather wide field was opened to Catholic zealots to undertake missionary work and to arouse dispute and conflict in the application of the edict, dispute that was left to the courts to resolve.

On the other hand, if Protestants practiced collective debate and governance by consensus at all levels, they left military matters to party leaders. Such leaders were professional fighters whose religious militancy was joined to values, behavior, and familial and social solidarity particular to the French military nobility at the time. An uncompromising policy could only link the fate of Protestantism with the interests of its bellicose aristocracy and lead it to a series of dangerous confrontations in which its survival would depend only on military force. In this regard, Protestantism appeared to hold the upper hand vis-à-vis the royal armies, at least in its strongholds. It could quickly mobilize well-equipped, determined troops who were well commanded and benefited from foreign support.

The seizures of arms between 1614 and 1616 clearly demonstrated the efficiency of such military organization, though from 1620 onwards, Protestant determination was to face new governmental determination. Royal armies sent to fight against the Protestants were stronger by the year until the political misjudgment of the latter in making a pact with England increased tenfold the resolve of the king's council, now headed by the Cardinal de Richelieu, to take measures that would guarantee absolute victory. La Rochelle was the true capital of the Huguenot party and it seemed impregnable. If there was going to be a decisive battle, it would take place there. It was one of the largest cities in the kingdom and one of the most prosperous. It was solidly fortified, surrounded by marshes on the mainland side, sustained by a dense network of the small Protestant towns of Aunis, and opened onto the sea through a well-protected harbor. Twice during previous decades, the siege had to be raised (the most considerable attempt occurring in 1572). The enterprise seemed destined for failure. The inhabitants of La Rochelle approached the matter with great confidence and expected a compromise. Nonetheless, thirty thousand men were mobilized, thousands of workers from the region (right up to Poitou and Limousin) were conscripted to dig trenches, make entrenchments and small forts, and then construct the famous wall designed to stop all access from the sea.

The siege, supposed to last for more than a year, soon took on an emblematic aspect, as if two utopian cities had risen up against each other.[3] On the one hand, there was the Huguenot capital, its resistance galvanized by the sermons of

[3]Christian Jouhaud, *La Main de Richelieu ou le pouvoir cardinal* (Paris: Gallimard, 1991); and "Imprimer l'événement: La Rochelle à Paris," in *Les Usages de l'Imprimé (XVe-XIXe siècles)*, ed. Roger Chartier (Paris: Fayard, 1987), 381–438.

preachers and the dictatorship of its mayor, Jean Guiton. On the other was the immense enemy camp with its besieging troops, accompanying shops, warehouses, and trades put together in haste, and its strict discipline, which was rare for the period. Soldiers who stole or raped were hanged immediately. An army of Capuchin monks patrolled the camp, preaching, converting, ministering, and hearing confession. Richelieu said Mass for the highest-ranking officers, and officers and soldiers were regularly paid. The enterprise was supposed to be edifying from beginning to end.

The outcome is known. After two unsuccessful English attempts at lifting the blockade, La Rochelle, reduced to famine, was forced to surrender unconditionally. The city had lost more than three-quarters of its population—between ten and fifteen thousand people. Royal troops entered the city in time for All Saints Day in 1628. Catholicism was immediately reestablished. But there was neither pillage nor excess of any kind; the city's submission was carried out according to a meticulous plan. The city walls were completely demolished and urban privileges were suppressed. Care was taken, however, to maintain liberty of religious conscience and practice. The king's victory and indulgence were celebrated in stories, poems, and engravings in hundreds of broadsides. They caused an extraordinary stir in public opinion both abroad and at home. The following summer, the surrender of the remaining Protestant troops and the Edict of Alès (also known as the Peace of Alais) brought to light the extent of the military, moral, political, and even religious defeat.

Thirty years before, when Henri IV's victory had become inevitable, the main rift in the Catholic camp was between the radical members of the League and those who had more or less recently been won over by the converted monarch, known as the *politiques.* It could be asked to what extent such a division persisted. It is certain that at first the most radical members of the League—who advocated the murder of the king to eliminate a heretical monarch or one who made pacts with heresy, and believed that only a revocable contract unified him and his subjects—did not collect a following. Though their theories continued to circulate secretly, they only had currency among very few people.[4] Nevertheless, it is clear that the *noblesse de robe,* the upper bourgeoisie and the families who had once supported the League, now participated in a Catholic militancy from which political opposition was able to reestablish itself; and thus *le parti dévot* (the devout party) was created. Of course, it was not a party in the modern political sense of the term, but a network of relatives, allies, friends, and colleagues who alternated, depending on the circumstances, between a vague special interest group and an

---

[4]Frederic J. Baumgartner, *Radical Reactionaries: The Political Thought of the French Catholic League* (Geneva: Droz, 1976).

active secret society. The *parti dévot* in no way contested the validity of an absolute monarch, but rejected any policy that would privilege national interests over religious ones and thereby abandon the dream of a Christian faith united behind its natural leader. Above all, the party rejected the consequences of such a policy, such as the tolerance of heresy and hostile relations with Spain, itself the champion of an intransigent Catholicism. Because of its attachment to the papacy and acceptance of the pope's preeminence in national matters, the party was referred to as *ultramontane*.

In the other camp, from the same milieu, and well established in the Parlement of Paris, was the party of the "good Frenchmen." Its stance can be categorized as Gallican in that it advanced the importance of the national traditions of the Catholic Church of France (called the liberties of the Gallican Church). Such Gallicanism had a particularly incendiary political aspect, as it denounced Rome's claims that it could, at the very least, indirectly exercise power over Christian monarchs and, therefore, over the king of France.

The assassination of Henri III by a monk, the accession of Henri de Navarre to the throne, and his death at the hands of Ravaillac in 1610 conferred an extreme virulence upon the question of indirect papal rule. To fight such a doctrine, at the opening of the Estates General in 1614 the Third Estate proposed in the first article of its register of grievances that the proposition be passed into the *fundamental law* of the kingdom, that "there is no power on earth whatever, spiritual or temporal, that has any authority over this kingdom to take away the sacred nature of our kings or to dispense [or absolve] their subjects of the fidelity and obedience that they owe him for any cause or pretext whatsoever."[5] The proposition was finally rejected by an alliance of the nobility and the clergy.[6]

Article 1 of the register of grievances of the Third Estate proposed the most striking definition of the principle of the divine right of kings; in answer to such militant zeal, the French monarchy offered ambiguous responses between 1610 and 1660. On the one hand, the monarchy could only be delighted in seeing its legitimacy, sovereignty, and independence celebrated so forcefully. The king, his principal ministers, and the two regent queens were always grateful for so monarchist a doctrine. Yet, on the other hand, the French monarchy needed the papacy. Sometimes the monarchy was even tempted to request papal intervention. Was the pope not himself an absolute monarch ruling by divine right with whom it was rather convenient to resolve ecclesiastical matters directly, between two powers,

[5]Quoted in Alexander Sedgwick, *The Travails of Conscience: The Arnauld Family and the Ancien Régime* (Cambridge: Harvard University Press, 1998), 22–23; and by J. Michael Hayden, *France and the Estates General of 1614* (Cambridge: Cambridge University Press, 1974), 131.

[6]Victor Martin, *Le gallicanisme et la réforme catholique: Essai historique sur l'introduction en France des décrets du concile de Trente (1563–1615)* (Paris: Picard, 1929).

without having to resort to reason or to the deliberative practices of the customary institutions such as parlements and provincial synods, or even an assembly of the clergy? However, that was not the crux of the matter. Papal intervention could put an end to dangerous debate, stay the circulation of suspicious doctrine and, above all, consolidate the legitimacy of a dynasty. For example, the pope granted the dissolution of Henri IV's first marriage; had the matter been in the power of the national clergy to resolve, it is possible that this situation would have led to undesirable discussions. Louis XIII retrospectively assessed the situation quite well when he stated that the king's own legitimacy was in question if he disputed the pope's power to dissolve dynastic alliances.

In fact, the political authorities took great care to maintain a solid position from which they could arbitrate the predominant currents of thought and action that divided Catholicism. A lot of evidence even suggests that the authorities stirred dissension amongst the Gallican and the ultramontane camps so that the two would neutralize each other (for example, by encouraging both sides to prepare polemical works). Indeed, each camp developed strong political perspectives that opened up choices regarding both internal and external politics, choices that were coherent yet exclusive of each other, choices not consonant with those of the king's council.

POLITICS AND RELIGION—THE POLITICAL THEOLOGY
OF THE SYSTEM OF THE *EXTRAORDINARY*

In seventeenth-century France, the king was Catholic and so, therefore, was the state (according to Melanchthon's formulation, "cuius regio, eius religio," by which the religion of the ruler was to be that of the people). Richelieu and Mazarin, both Roman Catholic cardinals, were living examples of the interpenetration of the church and the state and were at the forefront of French politics for more than forty years. In no way did they renounce their position in the church by maintaining positions of political power. They had the most lucrative benefices in the kingdom and oversaw the most powerful abbeys, whose revenue thus constituted a significant part of their fortunes.[7] Yet, their ecclesiastical positions also permitted them to govern. Their ecclesiastical authority and wealth allowed them to consolidate their power and intervene in doctrinal decisions, in matters regarding ecclesiastical discipline, and the management of public charity. For Richelieu and Mazarin, there existed no contradiction between reformed religious discipline and the political use of church funds. Nor did they see any contradiction between their status as Roman prelates and their refusal to swear political allegiance to the pope.

---

[7]Joseph Bergin, *Pouvoir et fortune de Richelieu* (Paris: R. Laffont, 1987); see also Claude Dulong, *La Fortune de Mazarin* (Paris: Perrin, 1990).

RELIGIOUS DIFFERENCES IN FRANCE

Portrait of the Cardinal de Richelieu, from *Letters of the Cardinal-Duke de Richelieu, great minister of state to Lewis XIII of France. Faithfully translated from the original by T. B.* (London: Printed for A. Ropel, R. Clavel, J. Sturton, and A. Bosvile, 1697). Reprinted with the kind permission of the Cornell University Library, Rare Book and Manuscript Division.

It is therefore useful to examine the relationship between theology and the exercise of power in the seventeenth century in light of the position of cardinal-ministers in the workings of the state. Richelieu said, "States do not have any subsistence after this life; their salvation is present or nonexistent," and, "Reason and experience show us that there ought to be a balance between the worldly princes for the good of the [Catholic] Church, so that in their equality the [Catholic] Church might subsist and continue its work and its splendor. ..."[8] The second quotation proposes a rather spectacular reversal that is not entirely devoid of irony. It suggests nothing less than regarding Christianity and its head from the perspective of the political compromise established in France by the Edict of Nantes and the development of what is referred to for convenience as Bourbon absolutism.[9] The French monarchy, which knew how to salvage and adapt the model of sovereignty perfected by the pope's spiritual monarchy, returned to it, as if through a distorting mirror, the image of rule founded on the arbitration between dissenting forces, which, in France, was the political means of ending the crisis of the Wars of Religion. Pacification was effected through the secularization (laïcisation) of the state, clearly a model quite in opposition to that of a papal monarchy.

Richelieu's belief that the salvation of the state was either present or nonexistent would mean that the security, the preservation of the state, and the fulfillment of its power in the service of the public were born of the temporal sphere and refer to it. Significantly, what remained was a theological vision of ultimate political goals founded on the belief that the purely temporal salvation of the state must guarantee the existence of order, which would favor its subjects' own search for salvation. The state could no longer claim the power to establish a city of God on earth that would guarantee the salvation of the political community, but it could create conditions that were favorable for the salvation of souls. The unrest and civil problems that thrive when the state is unable to guarantee and demonstrate its temporal salvation present numerous opportunities for the perdition of those subjects who would participate in the destruction or the destabilization of the state as a temporal force. These subjects reject the purely temporal dimension of

---

[8] "Advis donné au Roy après la prise de la Rochelle pour le bien des ses afaires," 13 January 1629, in Les Papiers de Richelieu, ed. Pierre Grillon (Paris: A. Pedone, 1980), 4:35:"Les Etats n'ont pas de subsistance après ce monde, leur salut est présent ou nul"; and Mémoires du Cardial de Richelieu, ed. Roger Gaucheron and Emile Dermenghem (Paris: H. Laurens, 1921), 5:293: "La raison et l'expérience nous montrent qu'il faut pour le bien de l'Eglise qu'il y ait balance entre les princes temporels, en sorte que dans leur égalité l'Eglise puisse subsister et se maintenir en ses fonctions et en sa splendeur. ..." See Christian Jouhaud, "La tactique du lierre: Sur 'L'Etat au miroir de la raison d'Etat' de Marcel Gauchet," Miroirs de la raison d'Etat, Cahiers du Centre de Recherches Historiques 20 (April 1998): 39–47.

[9]William Church, Richelieu and Reason of State (Princeton: Princeton University Press, 1972); and "The Decline of French Jurists as Political Theorists," French Historical Studies 5 (1967): 1–40.

the salvation of the state in the name of the spiritual salvation of the political community; but, after the Wars of Religion, this model could not maintain its hold.

There is therefore a collective political salvation that paves the way for the individual salvation of souls. Yet, it could be asked, even if this collective temporal salvation, which is the present salvation of the state and is conceived as charity that a king owes his subjects, eventually aligned itself with one political strategy that was practiced by Richelieu, could it have conceivably led to other very different strategies? The difference between two notions, the *ordinary* and the *extraordinary,* is examined in the short study entitled *La France du premier XVIIe siècle.* These two terms refer to a fundamental choice between two policies that both postulated and aimed at an expansion of the reason of the state.[10] The ordinary refers to the customary perception of the exercise of power in which different political institutions would exercise and develop their administrative role and their duty to counsel the monarch. This concept may include an administrative rationalization of the state's power, the expansion of its prerogatives, or the reinforcement and extolling of its authority. The extraordinary advances the development of the state's power over innovations frequently appropriated from other spheres—the invention and control of mostly financial expedients that would make it possible to run a wartime policy. While the former assumes the development of a "rational bureaucracy" of officers, the latter assumes the power of the king's favorite and of the clients and other dependents that he could mobilize and control.

The victory of the system of the extraordinary under Richelieu had many consequences. The first consequence was a rerouting of the transfer of sacredness from the church to the state. This was due, for the most part, to Richelieu's particular situation and to the mechanism of power that this situation allowed him to implement. Richelieu was a Roman Catholic cardinal, a priest, bishop, theologian, chancellor of the Sorbonne, and abbot of many abbeys. His status authorized him to interpret and define, with more legitimacy and authority than anyone else, the reformulated link between the absolute power of the state and the divine. This transfer of control was achieved at precisely the time that the connection between these two was being reformulated and applied. As a priest, Richelieu was careful to ask the necessary dispensations of the pope, dispensations relative to the daily execution of his work as prime minister. Richelieu was also very careful to monitor closely the public expression of things spiritual and miraculous and he kept watch over theological debate. The Santarelli affair, the possession of Loudon, and the imprisonment of the abbot of Saint-Cyran are indeed manifestations of his power. His association with the famous Father Joseph, a wily and unscrupulous diplomat who was also head of a strictly controlled religious order in which the

---

[10]Descimon and Jouhaud, *La France du premier XVII siècle.*

signs of a connection maintained with the divine were appealed to, interpreted, and praised, was an important part of the power structure he elaborated. Thus a truly religious rationale (and no longer merely a theological interpretation of the political) was reinstituted at the heart of the power apparatus, in the very framework of a political strategy that elsewhere completed the rupture with Christian ideals. It could be said that a sacredness transferred to the state or mediated by it was thus made holy again by its return to the religious domain.[11]

Such an undertaking supports the power structure that the cardinal put into place, not only because of the belief system produced, but also because it defines the central role of the king's favorite (and imposes the centrality of the role) through a position assumed with regard to the king on the one hand and officers of the state on the other. Without clear institutional limitations, the cardinal-minister's power allowed him to act as a mediator between the king and officers of the state by proposing an efficacious interpretation of the relationship between the divine and the absolute power of the king and therefore of the state. The cardinal-minister's power protected those who held delegated powers from the obsessive fear of sin in the exercise of their offices while they worked for the state. In this way, this power guaranteed the present salvation of the state while liberating it from the threat of sin in order that it might act. For the king, the role of the cardinal-minister assigned to itself the sin of state violence, a result of the choice of the extraordinary as a policy.[12]

Such a role was crucial as regards officers of the state and those whose charge it was to apply its policies and impose its constraints throughout the country. The cardinal-minister offered something resembling a pact to the officers of the state. They were to abandon any attempt to uncover the ulterior motives behind the policies they were to enforce if they wished to be exonerated of all possible culpability that might arise in the exercise of their functions. Underlying the pact was the belief that the king's favorite had in his possession a double secret. The first secret that he possessed, which could be qualified as a secret of affairs, was that of the aims of state politics (and thus the appropriate means); the second was the nature of the connection maintained with a now invisible divine. In the system of power that Richelieu instituted, one secret never existed without the other. Such a double-faced state secret, whose duplicity was functional, was forceful only because state policies had been displaced by political choice from the foreseeable, customary, and logical

---

[11]The term "sacredness" is used here out of convenience without taking a stand on what it includes, more so from an anthropological standpoint than from a religious one. Evidently, this is all rather controversial. Cf. Alphonse Dupront, *Du Sacré: Croisades et pèlerinages. Images et langages* (Paris: Gallimard, 1990).

[12]In principle, the king's position could not be contaminated by such a policy; evidence of this can be found in the constant appeals made to him against such a policy.

reasons of the ordinary management of affairs. The mutually convenient (to the king, his minister, and his officers) concept of a "secret place" gained significance only when the evidence of the effects of secret diplomacy, the hardship of arbitrary financial practices, and the dissolution of opposition through recourse to special tribunals became inescapable.

The effect of the political practice of holding sacredness in a secret place, capturing, cultivating, and reserving it (as in a reserved judgment) was possibly the momentary hold on the long-term transfer of religious sacredness to the state as an entity, embodied in the monarchy but undergoing abstraction. This process of abstraction is often referred to as the secularization of the political. This hold would therefore delay the completion of the process, all for the benefit of a particular system of political domination.

Thus it can be said that even if the theologico-political individual was successfully kept at a distance by the French monarchy after the League's demise (with the active help of Gallican jurisconsults), the goal of theology was still the return to the political terrain through the implementation of practices of the extraordinary as well as the reinforcement of the reason of state and the power structures elaborated by the cardinal-ministers. During Louis XIV's personal reign, the reorienting of the extraordinary to the person of the king made it possible to take drastic action against the political return of theology by the elimination of the Compagnie du Saint-Sacrement and of Jansenism and Protestantism, and the designation of the prophetic movement of the *camisards* as "fanatical." However, this was only possible at the price of the absorption of the royal function into the *raison d'état* in the context of the extraordinary with detrimental long-term consequences for the monarchy. Therefore it seems that the *désacralisation* (desacralizing) of the state was not univocal and regular. The process probably went through a *resacralisation* (resacralizing) phase in which religious motivations reentered the sphere of power, a phase associated with the development of the *raison d'état* defined by the extraordinary (as opposed to a *raison d'état* defined by rational bureaucracy) that ruptured the process of rationalizing state practices begun in the previous century. This is quite possibly one reason for the impossibility of the evolution of the French monarchy toward a constitutional government. In any case, as it expanded, the state, defined from the perspective of the concept of the *raison d'état*, found itself confronted with the dilemma of a choice between conflicting policies corresponding to different interests. It was not known in advance that politics of the extraordinary would be the only possibility in the modernization of the French state. It was its choice that inflected government practices, not toward absolutism strictly speaking (in a sense Cardinal de Bérulle, Louis Marillac, the keeper of the seals, the duc d'Orléans, and even the Parlement of Paris were as absolutist as Richelieu), but toward a political culture of secrecy, of expediency, seconded by a brief period of intense confusion of the relationship between the divine and the absolute nature of state power whose "salvation is present or nonexistent."

POLITICS AND RELIGION—THE QUESTION OF SPIRITUAL RADICALISM

Control over the transfer of the sacred to the mechanisms of absolute power that then use it to the fullest extent possible requires a theological system that both favors and facilitates such a transfer. Such were the stakes of some debates that took place during the course of the first half of the seventeenth century, for example, the debate on penance. It is known that Richelieu was in favor of attrition while his devout detractors favored contrition.[13] The debate is not without fundamental political implications. For the small group of people in the service of the state, the important choice between the end of the Wars of Religion and the personal reign of Louis XIV could be summarized as the possibility or the impossibility, the necessity or lack thereof, of reconciling political action and religious obligation. If the officers of the state came to believe that they could only be saved by a positive movement of contrition and not solely by the careful avoidance of damnation, their public work would inevitably be submitted to self-examination. These were the political stakes of the first Jansenist movement, which preferred both the abandonment of state employment and the development of self-examination among those whose vocation was to serve the state, a lethal association for the efficacious application of policies of the extraordinary.

It was important for the state that the religious zeal of its officers cause them to call into question neither the policies they were ordered to enforce nor the raison d'être of their offices. Yet, in Paris and in certain other cities of the kingdom, Catholic militancy that characterized the beginning of the seventeenth century had initially recruited its most determined and brilliant protagonists, such as Pierre de Bérulle or Madame Acarie (also known as Marie de l'Incarnation), founders of the Carmelite order in France, from among the families of old *ligueurs*.[14] Compared to the period of the Wars of Religion, the actual relationship between politics and religion had changed and had calmed, though it remained a subject of speculation. The actual force and fluidity of political relationships in this particular context remains to be studied.

The compromise the state offered its officers often clashed with the surge of Catholic zeal, but the success, both of the Counter-Reformation and of royal policies, appeared to many as evidence of its validity and of the divine approval that such a pact was receiving. During Cardinal Richelieu's time, the authorities made a point of silencing any opposition. On the one hand, they suppressed without

---

[13]The debate between attrition and contrition had not been resolved by the Council of Trent.

[14]Richet, "La Contre-Réforme catholique en France dans la première moitié du XVIIe siècle," in *De la Réforme à la Révolution*, 83–95.

hesitation any movements inspired by uncontrolled spiritual radicalism that could have been of political consequence. Such was the fate, for example, of the Illuminés of Picardy, a mystical sect with origins in Spain whose adherents refused the sacraments. This group was destroyed in 1635. The political danger of such groups was their emphasis on individual spirituality rather than the authority of the church. By extension, this brought into question the authority of the state.[15] On the other hand, the authorities made a point of making the signs of divine presence in those closest to the seat of power known, including the most extraordinary ones such as miracles and visions. At Richelieu's side was Father Joseph, a Capuchin monk charged with many diplomatic tasks after having militated quite a while for a crusade against the Ottoman Empire. Father Joseph was to become the principal figure of a foreign policy very strongly opposed by the *parti dévot,* while continuing to run the Calvairiennes, an order that he founded, and to make their convent a kind of observatory of the presence of God, from which came accounts of certain visions and miracles widely circulated in printed form.

The compromise gave expression to a delicate balance. The momentum of reform, having returned with exactitude to old rules, caused customary practices to be called into question, as well as denouncing a loss of direction in many religious institutions. Jesuits, for example, had to confront a series of mystical manifestations in 1630 that gave rise to a rejection of common discipline.[16] For these spiritual men, the return to former discipline proved the necessity of a rupture with everyday reality so that they could give themselves over entirely to the daily practices of devotion. Nothing, in the opinion of the Jesuits, should have impeded such a systematic reexamination. Many religious institutions were affected by such radicalism. Most often, however, such radicalism concerned isolated individuals who had no interest in commanding a following and had very few direct ties with the world. In one case, however, the ties established between the laity and the religious, between theology and practices of religious devotion, between action in the world and spiritual engagement resulted in a matter of great consequence: Jansenism. Granted, Jansenism was then a movement of the "solitary," with its ties to the two houses of Port-Royal (Paris and des-Champs). The latter convent, which depended on the Cistercian order, had practiced a spectacular reform based on austerity, conducted under the aegis of Mother Angélique Arnauld. The Arnaulds, a powerful patrician family, and their relatives and allies, played a dominant role at Port-Royal and in the history of Jansenism until the 1660s. A former friend of Jansenius, Jean Duvergier de Hauranne, abbot of Saint-Cyran, also played a significant role there. A theologian and polemicist (he had distinguished himself in 1626

---

[15]For a history of the Illuminés, see Henri Brémond, *Le procès des mystiques* (Paris: A. Colin, 1968).

[16]Certeau, *La fable mystique.*

with his writings against the Jesuit, François Garasse), Duvergier de Hauranne was the influential spiritual director of some well-known penitents. Many such penitents, though secular, began to question their own participation in worldly circles as they were won over by spiritual radicalism. The first great manifestation of such fervor occurred in 1637 when Antoine Le Maistre, a brilliant lawyer, a senior member of the Council of State, close to Chancellor Séguier, and, it appears, destined for the highest offices in the kingdom, decided to renounce all public life and isolate himself. This disciple of the abbot of Saint-Cyran was an Arnauld through his mother, who was herself leading a retired life at Port-Royal. He took up residence in a small house adjoining the Paris convent. His decision was made public by two letters widely circulated afterwards—one addressed to his father and the other to Chancellor Séguier. Moreover, he made it known that he did not want to enter any religious order and that he did not aspire to any ecclesiastical office. He simply intended to live as layman who had withdrawn from the world. A few weeks later, his brother, who had withdrawn from the army while France was at war with Spain, joined him.[17]

Such decisions to live in seclusion in the middle of a large city without applying for any ecclesiastical office, without taking any monastic vows, only affected a few individuals who were referred to as *les solitaires*. The decisions, however, had considerable repercussions and appeared to some to call the fundamental principles of life in society into question. They also seemed to threaten the bases of the political-religious system put into place by Cardinal Richelieu. In 1630, the *parti dévot* had been defeated and now, only a few years later, a dangerous movement was on the rise, no longer an organized opposition to a policy but something much more elusive: a withdrawal from all action among those whose vocation was to govern as officers of the state. It is easy to imagine what the consequences would have been had this movement made its mark among officers.

Duvergier de Hauranne had many times refused the bishopric offered him. Far from being considered a sign of humility and modesty, such refusals were perceived

---

[17]Sedgwick (*The Travails of Conscience,* 84–85) quotes Le Maistre's letter, originally quoted in Nicolas Fontaine, *Mémoires pour servir à l'histoire de Port-Royal* (Utrecht: au dépens de la Compagnie, 1736), 36–37: "I would be lacking in the respect that I owe you and I would be guilty of ingratitude if, having received from you so many extraordinary favors, I carried out a decision of such importance without informing you. I am abandoning, my Lord, a career that you have been very helpful in promoting, as well as everything that I might hope for or desire in this world. I am withdrawing into a life of solitude in order to do penance and to serve God the rest of my days.... I do not feel obliged to justify this action, which requires no justification. However, I think that I must let you know my most secret intentions so that you may not be misled by rumors that may be circulated against me. You should know that I renounce forever all ecclesiastical as well as civil offices and that I am not simply motivated by a change in ambition; I have no ambition at all. I am even less inclined to enter the clergy and to receive benefices than I am to resume the career that I am renouncing."

as challenges. Further, Duvergier de Hauranne was the supporter of a demanding theology of repentance that was not without links to the radical decision of the *solitaires* and that, in itself, had significant political ramifications.

The movement founded by Port-Royal continued, though without taking as much hold among the laity as the authorities had feared. Antoine Arnauld took over from the abbot of Saint-Cyran as the theologian and polemicist, and people began to speak of the "Jansenist party." The theological and doctrinal implications of this movement became evident, divided the Sorbonne, and provoked Rome to condemn Jansenism with increasing vigor. During the regency and the Fronde, civil authorities hid behind the decisions of Rome. In 1656 and 1657, Blaise Pascal published eighteen letters, handed down to posterity under the title of *Provinciales*.[18] The success of such pamphlets written against the enemies of Jansenism, their literary brilliance, and their clandestine circulation seemed to prolong the flood of pamphlets published against Mazarin, known as *mazarinades,* during the Fronde. Discussion was leaving the arid, in any case academic, territory of theology as a university discipline and was reaching the reading public, giving birth to a kind of literary theology—a sardonic popularization founded on common sense. Thus, this theological debate quite remarkably inundated the public sphere of fashions as well as the legal and illegal circulation of printed mass-market articles.

Jansenism suffered a serious blow under Louis XIV but continued to exist, and also played a determining role in the articulation of politics and religion until the French Revolution. In December 1660, Louis XIV declared his will to put an end to Jansenism in an address to the representatives of the Assembly of the Clergy. At the same time, the king had the Compagnie du Saint-Sacrement banned, another institution founded by Catholic zeal. Louis XIV was thus interested in eradicating any indication of religious dissension, indeed, of eradicating any gathering of the faithful outside of the traditional structures of the Catholic Church. Yet the activities of the Compagnie du Saint-Sacrement did not present any theological-political threat; adherents wanted to think of themselves as perfectly orthodox. Still, their regulations prescribed a strict code of secrecy in both their actions and discussions. From this emerged the threat of a secret society or cabal as it is often called,[19] capable of imposing itself as a secret pressure group, firmly rooted in the kingdom, a rich breeding ground of members constituting a very wide network.

[18]Blaise Pascal's *Provinciales* were published as pamphlets between 1656 and 1657. They were later published in English as *The mystery of Jesuitism: Discovered in certain letters written upon occasion of the present differences at Sorbonne between the Jansenists and the Molinists: Displaying the pernicious maximes of the late Casuists: With additionals,* 3rd ed. (London: Printed for Richard Royston..., 1679).

[19]See Raoul Allier, *La cabale des dévots* (Paris: A. Colin, 1902).

The Compagnie du Saint-Sacrement was founded between 1627 and 1629 on the initiative of both lay aristocrats (the duke of Ventadour and the baron of Renty) and prominent clerics, some close to Cardinal Richelieu (Charles Noailles, bishop of Saint-Flour, Antoine Godeau, and Philippe Cospeau). It was inspired by brotherhoods of penitents and, by focusing its devotional practices on the Eucharist, it placed itself at the heart of Tridentine spirituality, willingly surpassing the divisions of the Catholic world—divisions separating competing institutions and theological or disciplinary differences. In it, men close to the Jesuits or close to the Oratoire were to be found, some inspired by Port-Royal. The Oratoire, introduced in France in 1611 by Cardinal Pierre de Bérulle and based on an association of the same name in Italy in which men gathered to pray, sing, and read texts together, was instrumental in the reform of the French clergy over the course of the seventeenth century. The Compagnie du Saint-Sacrement wanted to guarantee spiritual cooperation between adherents and take care of the souls of the dead; to practice charity to its fullest extent and with all of its demands; to pursue atheists, the blasphemous, deviant practices, and the unholy artisan guilds; to fight against duels; and to contain Protestantism by monitoring the behavior and actions of the Reformed. It hoped to do all this without breaking the laws of the kingdom and, more specifically, the Edict of Nantes.

Many brotherhoods practiced secrecy, but the Compagnie du Saint-Sacrement placed secrecy at the center of its work. Acts of charity were kept secret out of a desire for humility, so that no earthly repayment might be received for its work. Secrecy also protected the equality of its members. Social divisions, hierarchies, and precedence of one person over another were absent from the Compagnie. It did not want its members to be bothered by such classifications in the world, a world in which such realities continued to classify men and to frame their behavior.

All this leads us to the most important point, that the Compagnie du Saint-Sacrement perceived itself somewhat differently from other religious groups. To enter it and be militant did not mean the same thing as for the solitary men of Port-Royal who broke away from the world. In the Compagnie du Saint-Sacrement, it meant investing one's life on two levels, the first being earthly activity and the second the Christian city, as adherents withdrew into the Compagnie. The questions that arose were therefore those concerning the ties and the communication between the two levels.[20]

The reconstitution of the career of René de Voyer, comte d'Argenson—one of the founders and most active members of the Compagnie du Saint-Sacrement until his death in 1651—and the study of his writings have placed us in a better

---

[20] Alain Tallon, *La Compagnie du Saint-Sacrement (1629–1667)* (Paris: Cerf, 1990).

position to understand the question. Argenson was the sort of man who would become a great servant of the state. First he was a member of the Paris Parlement, then *maître des requêtes,* member of the Council of State, and intendant many times over. He was the intendant of Dauphiné in 1630; of Limousin in 1632; of Saintonge and Poitou in 1633; and of Auvergne in 1634. After 1635, Argenson was many times quartermaster of the army, then *surintendant* and ambassador pleni-potentiary. He became a prisoner of the Spanish in Italy in 1640. He then wrote a *Traité de la sagesse chrétienne ou de la riche science de l'uniformité aux volontés de Dieu*[21] that could be classified as a book dealing with mysticism. He had himself been ordained as a priest before his death during his ambassadorship to Venice.

Argenson's career took him to the very heart of the most controversial aspects of Louis XIII and Richelieu's politics. This career broadened in scope, without changing direction, on either side of the split between Richelieu and the *parti dévot.* His life was divided between two registers of activity and engagement, experienced as tension but without rupture. The common ground of these two registers—which, according to Michel de Certeau, a historian of Argenson, would bring together the zealous service of policies of the State and the service of God— is to be located in support of the sovereign's good pleasure, that of God and king, in a shared position of obedience and humility.[22]

Argenson's attitude to the state is therefore poles apart from that of Antoine Le Maistre, beginning, however, with a spiritual engagement that underscores their shared traits and in great part draws from the same source. Moreover, before Louis XIV's reign, the authorities did not exhibit any hostility to the Compagnie du Saint-Sacrement. In this way as in others, the Sun King destroyed a compromise that was beneficial to the state, a compromise between the service of God and men, which allowed the officers of the state to employ the greatest efficacy in both domains without contradiction. However, this compromise was perhaps no longer as necessary as it had been in the time of Louis XIII and Richelieu, as the spiritual crisis that had affected the *noblesse de robe* and the *haute bourgeoisie* more than other crises had disappeared. Louis XIV treated the Jansenists in an ill-advised manner, as Catherine Maire shows,[23] and the *parti dévot* despotically, essentially adopting the negative view of that party presented in Molière's *Tartuffe.* Rather than follow Argenson's model of balancing the interests of the state with those of

---

[21] *Treatise on Christian Wisdom or the Rich Science of Conformity to the Wills of God* (Paris: S. Hurè, 1651).

[22] Michel de Certeau, "Politique et mystique: René d'Argenson (1596–1651)," *Revue d'ascétique et mystique* 39 (1963): 45–82.

[23] Catherine Maire, *De la cause de Dieu à la cause de la nation: Le jansénisme au XVIII siècle* (Paris: Gallimard, 1998).

personal spirituality, Louis XIV demanded loyalty to the state first and foremost and he demanded that religious practices demonstrate loyalty in their uniformity, thereby creating divisions that would have far more serious consequences in the next century.

Catholic Conciliar Reform in an Age of Anti-Catholic Revolution

Dale K. Van Kley

IN 1795, JUST AFTER THE TERROR and the campaign to "dechristianize" France, the ragged ranks of the constitutional Catholic clergy who had accepted the French Revolution and initially served it as salaried priests tried to make the best of their situation of enforced independence by reconstituting themselves as a new national Catholic Church. This enforced independence was of two kinds: from the revolutionary state that officially cut its ties with the constitutional clergy in 1795 after closing just about all Catholic churches during the Terror of 1793–94, but also from the papacy and Rome, which had all but excommunicated this clergy for its loyalty to France and its new constitution as early as 1791.

Defiantly regarding itself as both Catholic despite papal anathematization and patriotic despite continuing hostility by the national state, the leadership of this clergy—the abbé Grégoire and the so-called united bishops—convened something the Catholic world had not seen since the late Middle Ages: two national church councils, which met in Paris in 1797 and 1801. These councils called for and enacted an ambitious array of forward-looking reforms, among them the election of the clergy by their parishioners, the establishment of deliberative structures from local synods to the national council, a purged devotional style that stressed reasoned belief over ritual conformity, and the accommodation of national differences in liturgical styles, including the use of vernacular languages in the administration of the sacraments. The councils even called for

Unless otherwise indicated, all translations from foreign language sources are the author's.

A version of this piece was originally published as "Catholic Conciliar Reform in the Age of Anti-Catholic Revolution: France, Italy and the Netherlands, 1758–1801" in *Religion and Politics in Enlightenment Europe*, ed. James E. Bradley and Dale Van Kley, 46–118 (Notre Dame, IN: University of Notre Dame Press, 2001).

renewed efforts to resolve the Protestant schism as well as the Catholic Church's
earlier break with the Eastern Orthodox Church. Failing, however, to obtain any
sign either of recognition from the papacy or of reconciliation with the "refractory" French clergy who had originally joined Rome in condemning the French
Revolution, both councils appealed to a general or ecumenical council of all Catholic churches as the only legitimate judge of the French constitutional church's differences with Rome.

This extraordinary conciliar moment was a uniquely French by-product of
the French Revolution's unsuccessful attempt at integrating the French Catholic
(or Gallican) Church into the new constitutional order it set up in 1789. For far
from formally separating the new state from any ecclesiastical establishment on
the American model, the French Revolution's first instinct was to try to transform
the French Catholic Church from a branch of an international institution deriving
its authority from on high into a national church almost entirely subordinate to a
state deriving its legitimacy from the will of its citizens below.[1] Without altering
the substance of Catholic doctrine, the revolutionary National Assembly unilaterally abolished the tithe, nationalized the church's property, loosened its ties with
Rome, redrew its diocesan and parochial boundaries, dissolved most of its
monastic clergy, and reformed the secular clergy into salaried civil servants
elected by the citizens in their secular capacity as citizens alone. Known as the
Civil Constitution of the Clergy, this legislation gave the Gallican Church all the
disadvantages of a state church without any of its advantages. For while the Revolution restricted its salaries to members of the Catholic constitutional clergy
alone, it refused to accord Catholicism the status of a state religion and with it
exclusive rights to public worship, which that clergy had to share with Protestants,
Jews, to say nothing of those numerous dissident Catholics and their refractory
clergy who refused to accept the Civil Constitution at all.[2]

Numerous enough as a result of the revolutionary requirement that all bene-
ficed clergy swear an oath of loyalty to the state, the dissident or refractory clergy
enrolled many more recruits after the papacy's condemnation of the Civil Constitution became known in the spring of 1791, provoking a full-scale schism
between those French Catholics who accepted the papacy's condemnation of the
French Revolution and those who followed the constitutional clergy, who wanted
to have their Catholicism and their Revolution too. That schism began a polarizing cycle of action and reaction that radicalized the Revolution against religious

[1]In the immense literature on the Catholic Church and French Revolution, the work to begin
with is André Latreille, *L'église catholique et la Révolution française*, 2 vols. (Paris: Hachette, 1946–50).
[2]On the history of the Civil Constitution, Ludovic Sciout's work remains indispensable. See his
Histoire de la Constitution civile du clergé et de la persécution révolutionnaire (1790–1801), 4 vols.
(Paris, 1872–1881). On the constitutional clergy that accepted it, see Dom Henri Leclercq, *L'église constitutionnelle, juillet 1790–avril 1791* (Paris, 1934).

fanaticism and charlatanism, enlisted French Catholicism in the ideology of the counterrevolution, and exposed the constitutional clergy ever more directly to the cross fire between these contending forces. By the time the remains of this church were formally disinherited by the revolutionary state in the wake of the Terror in 1795, the relative freedom of movement with which it organized its national councils was the only compensation for its isolated and shriveled estate.

That independence, the conciliar reforms, and the hopes these engendered proved ephemeral enough and fragile even while they lasted, casualties of the concordat Napoleon Bonaparte negotiated with the papacy in 1801. Although that concordat restored the French Catholic Church to the position of subsidized appanage of the state for the duration of the nineteenth century, this restoration was unable to arrest, and in fact did much to accelerate, the putatively progressive parting of the paths between French Catholicism and the political and other aspects of modernity inaugurated by the revolutionary experience. By the time all the revolutionary dust had settled, French Catholicism had been purged of most of its reformist elements and redefined in militantly traditionalist fashion while revolutionary republicanism had developed a tradition of its own that voluntarily relinquished any connection to the nineteenth-century Catholic conscience. Although the French Revolution was, in the last analysis, a uniquely French affair, its armed export to most of the rest of Europe ensured that the conflict between republicanism and Catholicism would become a European experience as well.

The story of Catholicism's falling out with the French Revolution and all that followed is usually explained as the institutional consequence of the secularization of thought in the form of the Enlightenment and the resistance of retrograde religious forms of thought as embodied in the Catholic Church. Although this familiar version of events is not without elements of truth, it has about it an aura of inevitability belied by the possibilities of radical liturgical, ecclesiastical, and theological reform from within eighteenth-century Catholicism, which were briefly realized by the two national councils of Paris that, had they found more durable institutional expression, might have given this story a significantly different outcome. For while these two national councils undoubtedly drew inspiration from the French Catholic Church's peculiar tradition of independence from Rome, they were also hardly unique to France, and represented the culmination of reformist impulses and conciliar precedents that had found earlier institutional expression in the Provincial Council of Utrecht in 1763 and the Synod of Pistoia in Tuscany on the eve of the French Revolution in 1786. The full story culminating in the two national councils of Paris cannot therefore be told without reference to these earlier precedents.

Since the prospect for liturgical or theological reform ultimately depended on the possibility of some institutional means or agency other than the papal curia or the state's authority as well as on some margin for maneuver between these two, it is the efforts directed toward ecclesiastical reform (in particular, those giving the Catholic Church a more deliberative and conciliar structure) that are the primary focus of this analysis. Although the cause of church councils is in principle separable from any particular theology or religious sensibility, this cause was in fact locked in a fatal embrace with Jansenism during most of the century, making it impossible to tell one story without recounting elements of the other.

THE DIOCESE OF UTRECHT AND THE PROVINCIAL COUNCIL OF 1763— MODELS FOR THE ARTICULATION OF CATHOLIC INSTITUTIONS IN A NON-CATHOLIC NATION

Among the precedents available for the Civil Constitution, the most obvious was the ecclesiastical legislation of the Habsburg emperor Joseph II, who during the 1780s had abolished contemplative monastic orders, redrawn diocesan boundaries, secularized much church property, and tried to sever communications between Austrian bishops and the papacy, all on his secular authority alone. In part because he had managed to do all this without incurring formal papal condemnation, the National Assembly thought that it could do as much. One important difference between the two situations was that while Joseph II acted as a divine-right sovereign without a conciliar, much less a democratic, bone in his body, the France that the National Assembly was remaking in 1790 was already a republic with only a monarchical facade and so provided that the constitutional clergy be elected by lay citizens, as its legislators were to be.

A more pertinent precedent for the National Assembly was the situation of the Dutch Protestant Republic where two Catholic churches, a larger one obedient to Rome and a smaller one without formal relations with the papacy, had uneasily coexisted while enjoying toleration by a non-Catholic republic since 1723. This situation has some resemblance to that of the French Republic between 1795 and 1801 after it formally ceased to pay salaries to the constitutional clergy which, still condemned by the papacy, then tried to reconstitute itself as a Gallican Catholic Church in competition with a propapal missionary church under a government that was not Catholic at all. The similarity of these situations thus poses the question of why the Revolution could not simply have begun at that point—why, as Edgar Quinet asked, did the Revolution not immediately declare the separation of church and state? Or, having arrived at that point, why did it not stay there much longer?[3] The question is all the more pertinent in that the smaller of the two churches, the one in Utrecht, had long taken its theological and canonical cues from French Catholics, many of whom had left France to live there. It was also a

---

[3]Edgar Quinet, *La révolution* (Alençon: Belin, 1987), 150.

French Catholic bishop, Dominique Varlet, who had consecrated the first four archbishops of Utrecht, thereby enabling the diocese to maintain Catholic episcopal succession despite papal condemnation and furnishing the model whereby, sixty-six years later, the clergy loyal to the Revolution and its Civil Constitution also maintained themselves as Catholic in the face of papal condemnation.

The origins of an independent Catholic archdiocese in Utrecht lie in the conflicts between the indigenous Dutch secular clergy and regular orders, especially the Jesuits, in the wake of the Calvinist conquest of the northern Netherlandish provinces and the creation of an independent Protestant Republic in the sixteenth century. While what remained of a native Catholic clergy tried to preserve itself as an ordinary hierarchy despite the loss of its property and the secularization of its chapters, the papacy tended to see the northern Dutch provinces as mission territories, subjecting them to its direct spiritual governance by Jesuits and other Counter-Reformation orders that undermined the authority of ordinary priests and bishops. From the very outset, the "apostolic vicars" of Utrecht, as they were officially called, found themselves in conflict with the papal curia not only over the number and behavior of the Jesuits but also over the nature of their own authority, whether they administered the diocese as bishops in their own right or only as papal delegates, as the title of "apostolic vicar" implied. For if they exercised episcopal authority not as archbishops of Utrecht but as bishops of some formerly Catholic territory (bishop *in partibus infidelium*, as the phrase went), this was not only at the insistence of Rome but was also the doing of the States General of the Netherlands, which then forbade the use of the title of Archbishop of Utrecht. Usually more latent than overt, this conflict between Utrecht and Rome came to the fore especially on the occasion of episcopal succession when the local vicariate with which the first apostolic vicar had replaced the cathedral chapter tried to assert its rights to elect a successor against Rome's insistence on naming him.[4]

By the end of the century, this conflict had become further complicated by the Jansenist controversy which, after originating in the Spanish Netherlands where the Louvain theologian Cornelius Jansen had given his name to the movement, had spread south to France and north to the archdiocese of Utrecht. From the beginning, this controversy was most explosive in France where Jansen's attempt to restate Saint Augustine's theology of predestination and unmerited grace in his *Augustinus* was translated by his friend Duvergier de Hauranne, abbot of Saint-Cyran, for use as a rigorous penitential discipline for the convent of Port-Royal. It also provoked the hostility of the Jesuits and their partisans seconded by the absolute monarchy, whose renewed persecution of the movement in the 1680s added a rivulet of Jansenists to the stream of Huguenots fleeing Louis

---

[4]M. G. Spiertz, *Eglise catholique des Provinces-Unies et la Saint-Siège pendant la deuxième moitié du XVIIe siècle* (Louvain: Publications Universitaires de Louvain, 1975).

XIV's *toute catholique* France for the more tolerant Netherlands. French Jansenists were well received by Utrecht's apostolic vicar Jan van Neercassel who found himself drawn to a Catholic Augustinianism more intelligible to a surrounding Calvinist population that his church was trying to reclaim. So it was only natural that Jesuit missionaries who were already in jurisdictional conflict with the secular clergy in Utrecht should have tried to further undermine the authority of this clergy by accusing them of the heresy of Jansenism. These accusations were plausible, as Neercassel had befriended such well-known Jansenists as Sorbonne theologian Antoine Arnauld and Pasquier Quesnel, and had associated himself with the convent of Port-Royal des Champs, visiting it several times. Neercassel's principal book, *Amor poenitens,* seemed sufficiently inspired by Arnauld's *La fréquente communion* to warrant charges of Jansenist sacramental rigorism as early as in the 1680s, while his successor, Pieter Codde, although Rome's own choice as apostolic vicar, went to Rome in 1700 to face similar accusations against his pastoral theology and choice of liturgical books and catechisms.[5]

Codde was perhaps the last apostolic vicar to enjoy immediate communion with the papacy. Although he was retained in Rome for three years, only from the vicariate in Utrecht did he learn of his deposition as apostolic vicar and only at the insistence of the States General of the Republic was he finally able to regain his homeland. Meanwhile, in Utrecht, the vicariate refused to acknowledge the authority of Rome's replacement for Codde while Rome persisted in trying to govern the diocese directly through the nuncios in Cologne and Brussels in defiance of both the vicariate and the States General, which sided with the more national of the rival Catholic clergies. The result was a twenty-year interregnum during which the local clergy, without a bishop who could celebrate ordinations, was unable to replace itself and found itself reduced to inactivity as numerous priests defected from its ranks and missionary priests obedient to Rome seized control of local churches when incumbent *curés* died. The only factors preventing the elimination of Utrecht's clergy were occasional ordinations by sympathetic bishops from Ireland and Gallican France supplemented by influxes of French Jansenist clerics dislodged by a new round of persecution in the wake of the French monarchy's determination to enforce the last of the papal condemnations, the bull *Unigenitus,* as a law of church and state. With Utrecht dependent on these sources of survival, it was only natural that its clergy prevailed upon Varlet, in Amsterdam on his way to Persia as missionary bishop *in partibus infidelium* of Babylon, to ordain six hundred priests in 1719; or that the Utrecht vicariate should have decided that year to

[5]For this and the following account, see Bastien Abraham van Kleef, *Geschiedenis van de Oud-Katholieke Kerk van Nederland,* 2nd ed. (Assen: Gorkum, 1953), as well as Dupac de Bellegarde, *Histoire abrégée de l'église métropolitaine d'Utrecht, principalement depuis la révolution arrivée dans les 7 provinces unies des Pays-Bas, sous Philippe II, jusqu'à présent* (Utrecht: J. Schelling, 1784).

join the appeal of the bull *Unigenitus* to a general council interjected by four French Jansenist bishops in 1717.

These developments led to Utrecht's definitive union with the Jansenist cause, its perennial entanglement in the affairs of France, and its eventual break with Rome. For it represented only a logical step from surreptitious ordinations of priests by bishops outside their own dioceses when, back in Holland after having been interdicted by Rome, the same Varlet in 1724 consecrated Cornelis Steenhoven as Archbishop of Utrecht, a title unused since 1572. Rome was only extending its previous condemnation of the appeal of *Unigenitus* when it responded to this consecration with anathemas and a formal sentence of excommunication of the whole Utrecht clergy. The result in this Protestant republic was a Catholic Church containing only a small percentage of a Catholic minority, which, opposed to episcopal as well as papal "despotism" and committed to conciliar forms, found itself vulnerable to Protestant-like discussion and chronic dissension within its own diminished ranks. At least this church boasted its own ecclesiastical hierarchy which, later reinforced by the erection of bishoprics in Deventer and Haarlem, was able to administer the sacraments of confirmation and ordination without waiting for itinerant bishops. The church of Utrecht also enjoyed the de facto favor of the Dutch Republican government, which, while still denying basic civic rights or *burgherrechten* like guild membership to old Catholics, allowed this church a public role that came closer than any other in eighteenth-century Europe to realizing a separation of church from state.

The public presence enjoyed by this conciliar Catholic Church in a non-Catholic state is unique in ancien régime Europe, and never more so than on the occasion of the meeting of a provincial council in Utrecht during the week of 13–21 September 1763. The purpose of this council, which was called for, planned, and dominated by the French, was first to demonstrate the diocese of Utrecht's catholicity by condemning the errors of a certain Pierre le Clerc, a French Jansenist in exile in the Netherlands since the mid-1750s, who had progressively taken his opposition to Rome's anti-Jansenist pronouncements to the Protestant point of denying the primacy of the papal see, the divine basis of the episcopacy, and finally the validity of anything not spelled out in scripture.[6] Against Le Clerc, the council affirmed its adherence to the doctrine of papal primacy, the divine institution of bishops, and the validity of tradition, and solemnly reaffirmed its Catholic faith as expressed in the profession of Pius IV.[7] Situating itself in the orthodox middle, the

[6]See B. A. van Kleef, "Das Utrechter Provinzialkonzil vom Jahre 1763" in *Internationale kirchliche Zeitschrift*; "Die Zeit vor dem Konzil" 49 (1959): 197–228; and "Das Konzil" 49 (1960): 65–91, esp. 222–27.

[7]Pierre Le Clerc's errors and heresies are analyzed and condemned in reports 1–7 by François Meganck, dean of the metropolitan church of Utrecht, in *Actes et décrets du IIe Concile provincial*

council condemned the equally "pernicious" but opposite "errors" of the French Jesuits Jean Hardouin and Isaac Berruyer who, in an attempt to magnify reliance on the papal *magisterium*, had similarly undermined the scriptural and patristic basis of central dogmas like the Trinity as well as, more predictably, the Augustinian doctrines of grace and predestination. Along with Jean Pichon, whose "lax" defense of the practice of frequent communion was also condemned, Jesuits had long functioned as *bêtes noires* for the Jansenists.[8] But for this council to condemn them in 1763 was politically opportune, as the Jesuits had been expelled from Portugal in 1759 and had just been condemned to dissolution by the Parlement of Paris. In a tenth and eleventh report condemning sundry "errors" by "new casuists" (all Jesuits) the Council of Utrecht furnished a needed ecclesiastical sanction for the Parlement of Paris's earlier condemnation of the same assertions. By including in this condemnation Jesuits who defended the papacy's "indirect authority" to sanction resistance to "tyrannical" (that is, heretical) princes, the council found a convenient occasion to affirm the principle of obedience to secular authorities, including the Protestant Republic that had allowed it to convene.[9]

But holding a council was also its own justification, an occasion to vindicate Utrecht's conciliar conception of the ecclesiastical hierarchy: for that hierarchy "to practice," as Archbishop Meindarts stated, "the form of governance established by Jesus Christ himself, and since then constantly observed in all Catholic churches."[10] However loudly the Council of Utrecht may have trumpeted its catholicity and its commitment to the doctrine of papal primacy, the holding of such a council to judge doctrine apart from Rome was a rebuke to papal claims to infallibility or the rights of "a universal and ecumenical bishop" who might "despotically order other bishops about." The council had not very clearly distinguished these qualities from the pope's legitimate role as "visible and ministerial head by divine right."[11]

In addition to so dramatically witnessing to its orthodoxy, the abbé Augustin Clément, one of the council's French architects, wrote in a letter to the archbishop of Utrecht in the following year, "we cannot doubt that the *éclat* of the [conciliar]

---

d'Utrecht, tenu le 13 septembre MDCCLXIII dans la chapelle de l'Eglise provinciale de Sainte Gertrude, à Utrecht (Utrecht: Au dépens de la compagnie, 1764), 108–231.

[8]The errors of Hardouin, Berruyer, and Pichon are analyzed and condemned in reports 8–9 in *Actes et décrets du IIe Concile provincial d'Utrecht*, 236–376. For an example of the treatment of Hardouin and Berruyer in the Jansenist press, see *Nouvelles ecclésiastiques, ou Mémoires pour servir à l'histoire de la constitution Unigenitus* (Utrecht, 1728–1803), 19 March 1760, 49–64.

[9]*Actes et décrets du IIe Concile provincial d'Utrecht*, 376–94.

[10]"Discours de M. l'Illustrissime et Révérendissime Archevêque d'Utrecht, président, au Concile provincial," in *Actes et décrets du IIe Concile provincial d'Utrecht*, 10.

[11]"IIIe rapport: De la primauté du pape, par François Meganck," in *Actes et décrets du IIe Concile provincial d'Utrecht*, 142–43, 171–73.

canonical forms, equally applauded by the whole church, will bear its own fruit, and that sooner or later it will contribute to the reestablishment of so salutary and holy a practice."[12] These canonical forms were given a new twist by the council's inclusion of ten priests as voting members and designation of two of them as reporters for congregations, an act that spoke louder than the council's condemnation of Pierre le Clerc's conflation of bishop and priest and constituted an implicit challenge even to orthodox notions of councils, which reserved for bishops alone the right to judge doctrine. Lest any of this ecclesiological meaning remain merely implicit, the Jansenist weekly *Nouvelles ecclésiastiques* (Ecclesiastical News) further radicalized it in an account of the council, noting how the Dutch bishops subscribed to the judgments of the council "along with the pastors of the second order who," stressed the weekly, "had exercised a deliberative voice in the synod following the usage commonly observed since the Council of Jerusalem (the model for all others) where priests judged with the apostles."[13] Glossing over the extent of the real disagreements in the council regarding the subscription to the profession of Pius IV and judging Le Clerc without hearing him, *Nouvelles ecclésiastiques* underscored the unanimity of the council followed by the unanimous acceptance of its decrees by "the entire clergy of Holland."[14] The French rushed to publish the council's acts, commissioning the comte Dupac de Bellegarde's French translation and soliciting testimonies of adherence from as many Catholic quarters as possible.[15]

Failing to reunite the church with the papacy, Utrecht's tactic of soliciting adherence to these acts was to establish a state of direct communion with enough other Catholic churches supported by their sovereigns to surround the Holy See. The intent was to force the papacy to the conclusion that it and not Utrecht was isolated, forcing it to conform to a fait accompli and thereby alter the structure of the Catholic Church. The model for this tactic was the action whereby the overwhelming majority of the French parlements had taken the initiative against the Jesuit order, eventually forcing the monarchy either to acknowledge that they could undertake so important a measure without royal authority or to give their action its belated imprimatur.[16] Failing any such happy ending, the publication

[12]Het Utrechts Archief (hereafter HUA), Inventaire des pièces d'archives françaises se rapportant à l'Abbaye de Port-Royal des Champs et son cercle et à la résistance contre la bulle Unigenitus et à l'appel (hereafter 215), Ms 2767, Clément to Pierre-Jean Meindaerts, archbishop of Utrecht, 13 September 1764.

[13]The Council of Jerusalem refers to the meeting in Acts 6:1–7 where the twelve apostles and the disciples chose seven deacons.

[14]*Nouvelles ecclésiastiques* (28 May and 11 June 1764): 85, 93.

[15]Van Kleef, "Das Utrechter Provinzialkonzil vom Jahre 1763: Das Konzil," 91.

[16]This tactic is spelled out in manuscript notes from a conference of "friends" in Vienna, 27 December 1767, in HUA, 215, Ms 2630. On the example of the parlements in the case of the Jesuits,

and selective sending of the council's *Actes* not only produced a thousand or more signatures of adherence on individual and collective letters to the archbishop of Utrecht, especially in France in the years immediately following the council, but it also lent contemporary substance to the half mythical image of a precurial apostolic church in which everything had been decided on collegially and in council.

That these acts never saw publication in Dutch is evidence of the limits of the Protestant Republic's policy of de facto toleration, as was later in the same decade the States General's refusal to grant passports to delegates from the archdiocese of Utrecht to the Rome of Pope Clement XIV to participate in the century's most serious negotiations toward reunion with the papacy.[17] But the presence of a Jansenist Catholic hierarchy, even one both backed and bedeviled by a cadre of querulous French exiles, did not constitute a major affair of state for the Dutch Republic, which absorbed it into the landscape of its own constitutional particularism.

JANSENISM, THE GALLICAN CHURCH, AND THE MONARCHY IN ANCIEN REGIME FRANCE

The contrast could not be more complete than with Catholic and monarchical France where from the very outset the Jansenist movement carried a political charge peculiar to that time and place. That was perhaps the crucial difference between a state like the Dutch Republic where, since the Reformation, the victorious Reformed Church became not a state church but merely the only public church, and a state like France where, the Reformation having been defeated, religion remained inseparable from royalty. A religious movement whose profoundest tendency was to regard fallen creation as totally concupiscent and utterly incommensurate with the order of charity sat uneasily with a sacral monarchy that had long justified its domination of the Gallican Church by virtue of its mediating place in the cosmic hierarchy. The French monarchy had just survived the challenge of Calvinism in the sixteenth-century Wars of Religion, and while Jansenism's elimination of faith as a means of assurance deprived it of Calvinism's activism, it was easy to misread the movement as Calvinism in Catholic clothing. At the same time, Jansenism's origins in the ultra-Catholic *parti dévot*, and initial interest in the reform of the church clashed with the monarchy's need to maintain control over the Gallican Church and with Louis XIV's project of using the bishops as partners in the construction of absolutism. The monarchy had also survived the Catholic League (la Ligue, an ultra-Catholic group revived by Henri de Guise in the 1580s with a strong propapal, antimonarchy stance)

---

see Jean Egret, "Le procès des jésuites devant les parlements de France," *Revue historique*, 204 (July–Dec.): 1–27.

[17] HUA, 215, Ms 2439, Archbishop van Nieuwenhuizen to Dupac de Bellegarde, 22 April 1770.

that had seized and held onto Paris against two French kings at the end of the Wars of Religion.[18]

It was effective control over the Gallican Church by an absolute but also sacral monarchy, and not that church's liberty, that was most at stake for the monarchy in the so-called liberties of the Gallican Church that its General Assembly solemnly proclaimed at Louis XIV's behest in an extraordinary assembly in 1682. In an era of growing absolutism, a lessening of papal power necessarily translated into an increase in royal control. That was the main meaning of this declaration's first article, which, crucial to royal absolutism and new to the seventeenth century, proclaimed the king of France to be independent of the papacy in temporal affairs and answerable for them to God alone. This article disallowed any disobedience to the king as temporal sovereign by virtue of any connection to spiritual affairs, even in cases of excommunication. Although the same assembly also reasserted the Gallican Church's right to judge doctrine concurrently with Rome as well as reiterating its adherence to the Council of Constance's proclamation of the ultimate authority of general councils over the papacy in the church, the monarchy of Louis XIV had a declining stake in these traditional tenets.[19] They merely stood in the way of the papacy's help in the monarchy's effort to suppress Jansenism in France. In contrast to the Protestant Netherlands, there were no Catholic councils in the one Catholic realm where the supremacy of the council was formal law.

Whether or not the papacy would have on its own initiative so single-mindedly condemned Jansenism is an open question, since the initiative was taken by the French monarchy from the start. Both the bull *Cum occasione*, which condemned the five heretical propositions supposedly extracted from Jansen's *Augustinus* in 1653, and Alexander VII's *Ad sacram*, which attributed these propositions to Jansen in 1665, came at the behest of France as represented by Cardinal Mazarin acting for the minor king in the first instance and by Louis XIV in person in the second. After the reprieve of the so-called Peace of Clement IX from 1668 to 1679, during which Louis XIV fought his Dutch wars and for a time restored Catholicism to dominance in the province of Utrecht, again the Sun King demanded and got Clement XI's bull *Vineam domini*, which disallowed any distinction between Jansen's text and the condemned propositions, followed by the same pope's bull *Unigenitus* in 1713. These pronouncements facilitated new acts of persecution in France: *Cum occasione*, Arnauld's expulsion from the Sorbonne; *Ad sacram*, the dispersion of the sisters of Port-Royal; *Vineam domini*, the physical destruction of Port-Royal; and *Unigenitus*, the lion's share of the persecution in the eighteenth century. With the condemnation of LeMothe Fénelon's quietism in

---

[18]See Dale K. Van Kley, *The Religious Origins of the French Revolution: From Calvin to the Civil Constitution, 1560–1791* (New Haven: Yale University Press, 1996), 15–74.

[19]Aimé-Georges Martimort, *Le gallicanisme de Bossuet* (Paris: Editions du Cerf, 1953), 70.

1699, also at Louis XIV's initiative, the impression is hard to avoid of a papacy doctrinally dominated by French religious and political divisions from the onset of the Jansenist controversy to the condemnation of Lamennais's liberal Catholicism in 1834.[20]

The most divisive of the papal pronouncements solicited by France was incontestably the bull *Unigenitus*, and while the papacy itself and most of Catholic Europe remained relatively unaffected by its fallout until the 1760s or so, it dominated the scene in France until that decade. This is so very much the case that, in the reputed capital of the Enlightenment, the eighteenth century may be as plausibly christened the century of *Unigenitus* as of *lumières*. The result there was virtually a full-scale religious conflict played out on political and social as well as theological and ecclesiastical registers, one that in fact replayed the religious civil wars of the sixteenth century, if not in physical violence, at least in polemics. The conflict also relived the sixteenth-century religious civil wars, since defenders of papal and royal authority, symbolized by the bull *Unigenitus,* never ceased to regard Jansenists as rewarmed Calvinists while Jansenists were no less certain of descrying a reborn Catholic League in the rhetoric and comportment of their Jesuitical and episcopal persecutors.[21] Forty or fifty thousand *lettres de cachet* and several major political crises later, the French clergy and the religious orders found themselves largely purged of Jansenists who had replaced Protestants as the most numerous category of residents of the Bastille while Jansenists in revenge had exploited every possible form of resistance to absolutism short of armed rebellion, recalling and recirculating much of the literature of both the Huguenot and Leaguer revolts.[22] No other religious conflict in eighteenth-century Europe presents anything comparable to the French case in duration or intensity.

So ardently did the French protagonists in these conflicts nurse the memories of the Wars of Religion that they transformed eighteenth-century reality in this image. Jansenists obliged those who persistently accused them of covert Calvinism by becoming a little more Protestant. While continuing and updating Port-Royal's project of translating scripture into the vernacular, Quesnel and his successors enjoined the regular reading of scripture on all the laypeople, including women, and encouraged vernacular translation and explanation to the Catholic liturgy and Mass in an effort to involve laypeople in public worship.[23] The negative side of the

[20]On the condemnation of Fénelon, see Denis Richet, "Fénelon contre Bossuet: La querelle du quiétisme," in *De la réforme à la Révolution: Etudes sur la France moderne* 119–39 (Paris: Aubier, 1991).
[21]See Van Kley, *Religious Origins of the French Revolution*, 100, 160–70.
[22]On Jansenists in the Bastille, see Monique Cottret, *La Bastille à prendre: Histoire et mythe de la forteresse royale* (Paris: Presses Universitaires de France, 1986), 35–73. On their tactics of resistance, see Cottret, *Jansénisme et lumières: Pour un autre dix-huitième siècle* (Paris: Albin Michel, 1998), 270–301.
[23]On Quesnel's injunction to read scripture, see *Unigenitus*'s condemnation in Augustin Gazier, *Histoire générale du mouvement janséniste depuis ses origines jusqu'à nos jours*, 2 vols. (Paris: Honoré

importance attached by Jansenism to knowing the sources of Catholicism and understanding its doctrines was a steady hardening of its attitude against the sensual side of baroque Catholicism symbolized for Jansenists by the Jesuit-sponsored devotion to the sacred heart as well as the ritualistic aspects of baroque devotion like novenas, rosaries, and the veneration of saints, regarded as ignorant, superstitious, and mechanical.[24] Giving significance to these developments was a Jansenist campaign on behalf of civil toleration of Protestants that, beginning midcentury, culminated with significant Jansenist support for Louis XVI's Edict of Toleration in 1788.[25] Meanwhile, a few French Jesuits like Berruyer, Hardouin, and Jean Pichon exaggerated the doctrinally latitudinarian and penitentially lax tendencies associated with their "Molinist" theology, while others connived at the League-like vilification of Louis XV after royal religious policy began to deviate from their desires during the tempestuous 1750s.[26]

But when all is said and done, the French eighteenth century was not the sixteenth century, nor was it any less the century of Enlightenment for being that of *Unigenitus*. That is to say that the religious conflict born of the condemnation of Jansenism in France took place during a period of rising literacy, rapidly expanding print culture, and in the wake of geographical discoveries and scientific revolutions that had created conceptual possibilities unavailable to the sixteenth century. While elsewhere in Europe the Enlightenment took shape in reaction against the memory of the Reformation's religious bloodbaths, for French philosophes this conflict was an ongoing and oppressively present reality, as the many Jansenists and Jesuits in Voltaire's philosophical stories attest. When Voltaire quipped that there were "no sects among geometricians," he made a point polemically that would not have had the same effect outside of France.[27] Although the Jansenist controversy is not the only factor in the making of the anticlerical character of the French Enlightenment, it is not the least, either. The result was an enlightenment that Jean Le Rond d'Alembert, author of the *Encyclopédie*'s famous

Champion, 1924), 2:326. On Jansenist translations after Sacy's in the course of the eighteenth century, see Bernard Chédozeau, "Les traductions de la Bible, le jansénisme, et la Révolution," in *Jansénisme et Révolution*, ed. Catherine Maire, 219–39, *Chroniques de Port-Royal* 39 (Paris: S.A.P.R., 1990). And on Jubé's innovations, see Cottret, *Jansénisme et lumières*, 250–53.

[24]Michel Albaric, "Regard des jansénistes sur l'église de France de 1780 à 1789," *Jansénisme et Révolution*, 72.

[25]On Jansenists and toleration, see Jeffrey Merrick, *The Desacralization of the French Monarchy in the Eighteenth Century* (Baton Rouge: University of Louisiana Press, 1990); and articles by Charles O'Brien, summed up in his "Jansénisme et tolérance civile à la veille de la Révolution," in *Jansénisme et Révolution*, 131–45.

[26]Van Kley, *Religious Origins of the French Revolution*, 180–90.

[27]Voltaire, "Secte," in *Dictionnaire philosophique, comprenant les 118 articles parus sous ce titre du vivant de Voltaire avec leurs suppléments parus dans les Questions sur l'Encyclopédie*, ed. Raymond Naves, 385 (Paris: Garnier Frères, 1967).

"preliminary discourse," self-consciously defined as a "third party" of "philoso-phy" on the occasion of the dissolution of the Jesuits in France, a party productive of a militantly anti-Christian form of incredulity that, whether atheistic or deistic, surfaced as the Voltairian campaign against the "infamous thing" in the declining ancien régime. And of course it arose even more spectacularly as dechristianiza-tion during the French Revolution.[28] The role of the monarchy in the controversy also gave rise to calls for a state so adamantly secular as to be as intolerant in this sense as sacral absolutism had ever been in a confessional sense, a potential that similarly surfaced as the French Revolution's quest for ideological orthodoxy with all of its attendant secular schisms, to say nothing of its sponsorship of the cult of theophilanthropy.[29]

This brand of Enlightenment was also peculiar to France, for not even in the England of John Toland and David Hume did Edmund Burke, reacting to the French Revolution in 1790, have any trouble distinguishing the local Enlighten-ment from the French variant.[30] By the time of the demise of the Jesuits in the 1760s, militant unbelief had attracted enough alarmed attention in France to pro-duce calls for a common Catholic front against unbelief from Jansenists if not from their adversaries, and from institutions formerly so much at odds in the Jan-senist controversy as the General Assembly of France in 1775 and the Parlement of Paris in 1776.[31] Although such a common Catholic front never became a real-ity, the decades after the demise of the Jesuits witnessed the formation of a Catho-lic counter-Enlightenment in France that—exemplified by ex-Jesuits such as the abbé Lenfant or, in a more secular vein, journalists like Elie-Catherine Fréron—subordinated Jansenism along with Protestantism to auxiliary roles in what it saw as a multipronged "philosophic" plot to destroy papal altars, to undermine abso-lute thrones, and to replace both with anarchy and unbelief.[32] A counterrevolu-tionary religious right of sorts tended to displace the Jansenist-devout division with a Catholic-philosophy one as the dominant polemical opposition in France, just when the international campaign against the Jesuits was bringing the hitherto French Jansenist-*zelanti* standoff to the rest of Catholic Europe.

[28]Jean Le Rond d'Alembert, *Sur la destruction des jésuites en France, par un auteur désintéressé* (n.p., 1765), 103.

[29]A homology nowhere more brilliantly suggested than in Edgar Quinet's *Le christianisme et la Révolution française* (Paris: Fayard, 1984), 229–45, esp. 240–41.

[30]Edmund Burke, *Reflections on the Revolution in France* (Indianapolis: Bobbs-Merrill, 1955), 95–102.

[31]For an example of such a call, see the anonymous *Lettre à M. xxx, chevalier de l'ordre de Malte, touchant en écrit 'Sur la destruction des jésuites en France'* ("en France," 1765), 26.

[32]The full lineaments of this counter-Enlightenment have now been ably sketched out by Darrin McMahon in "Enemies of the Enlightenment: Anti-Philosophes and the Birth of the French Far Right, 1778–1830" (PhD diss., Yale University, 1997).

What remained unique to the Jansenist controversy in France, at least until the end of the French Revolution, is that it subjected Jansenism to a process of politicization that extended to absolute monarchy itself, arguably giving the movement a more pronounced antiabsolutist political point than the *philosophes* as late as on the eve of the Revolution. Whether such a pessimistic religious sensibility as Jansenism's would ever have developed in the direction of active opposition had French absolutism known how to leave well enough alone is also an open question, since persecution of the movement based on the assumption of its subversive potential actualized that assumption in the long run. To be sure, the two elements of Gallicanism and parliamentary constitutionalism that were to coalesce with Jansenism and bring out its political potential while attenuating its otherworldliness were already at hand in the seventeenth century, even during the Fronde. But this midcentury and partly Parlement-led uprising did not yet cause them to coalesce, while in the short run it worsened Jansenism's image in the eyes of the monarchy by associating it with the memory of French Huguenot resistance and both of these with the Puritanism that had played so rambunctious a role in the English Civil War.[33]

A half century of condemnation and persecution culminating in the papal bull *Unigenitus* in 1713 effected a synthesis of the elements in question. Although the book anathematized by this bull, namely Pasquier Quesnel's *Réflexions morales sur le Nouveau testament* (Moral Reflections on the New Testament), already contained a radically Gallican conception of the Catholic Church as the "assembly of all the faithful," the condemnation of such Gallican propositions along with classically Jansenist ones linked the cause of Jansenism with conciliar Gallicanism. The adoption of this Gallicanism by Jansenists culminated in the appeal of *Unigenitus* to a general council by four bishops in the Sorbonne in 1717, an appeal initially supported by three quarters of the Parisian clergy with whom the diocese of Utrecht associated itself two years later.[34] By forcing a reluctant Parlement of Paris to register this anti-Gallican bull as a law of state, the bull also confirmed an alliance between Jansenists and the Parlement of Paris, which in the absence of the Estates General had intermittently claimed to "represent" the nation by means of its rights to register and remonstrate against new royal legislation, most notably during the Fronde. These Frondish claims acquired new life when, soon after the Sun King's death in 1715, the Parlement regained the right to remonstrate against royal edicts and declarations prior to registering them as law, a right withdrawn by Louis XIV in 1672.

[33]Elisabeth Labrousse, "'Une foi, une loi, un roi?': Essai sur la révocation de l'Edit de Nantes," *Histoire et société* 7 (Geneva: Labor et Fides, 1985), 39–44.
[34]Marie-José Michel, "Clergé et pastorale janséniste à Paris, 1669–1730," *Revue de l'histoire moderne et contemporaine* 27 (April–June 1979): 177–97.

As the century progressed and persecution continued, the conciliar Gallican element in this synthesis underwent a process of radicalization and democratization in the hands of Jansenist canonists. With conceptual help from the Gallican tradition of conciliar thought going back to the works of John Major, Jean Gerson, and Edmond Richer, syndic of the Sorbonne in the early seventeenth century, Jansenist canonists developed an ecclesiology that vested supreme spiritual authority in the whole church, or "assembly of the faithful," including the parish priests touted by the Jansenist press on the occasion of their participation in the Provincial Council of Utrecht. This brand of Gallicanism or "Richerism" hence defined itself against the Gallican bishops themselves, the majority of whom accepted *Unigenitus*, holding that parish priests derived their sacerdotal mission directly or "radically" from Christ rather than indirectly through bishops and that, though subordinate to bishops, they had a right to attend both synodical and general councils as "judges of the faith."[35]

Further democratizing this ecclesiology was the influence of the eschatological theology and biblical hermeneutic called figurism which, developed by Jansenist theologians at the Oratorian seminary of Saint-Magloire in the wake of *Unigenitus*, offered an active role even to the laity as "witnesses" if not judges of the faith, competent to raise a "cry of conscience" amidst the prophesied "obscurity" caused by a largely apostate hierarchy.[36] In the most radical statement of this ecclesiology—radical in the literal sense of appealing to the root of spiritual power in Christ's gift of it to the whole believing community—even general councils were infallible only to the extent that they were free, observed canonical forms, and genuinely represented the entire church.[37] As secularized and applied to the state by the abbé Claude Mey and Gabriel-Nicolas Maultrot in their *Maximes du droit public françois* (Maxims of French Public Law), published in defense of the French "constitution" against Chancellor René-Nicolas de Maupeou's suppression and "reform" of the French parlements in 1775, this line of argument produced a sort of conciliar constitutionalism that located legislative sovereignty in the whole nation as represented in the Estates General, which "has the right to change the

[35]On Richerism, see Edmond Préclin, *Les jansénistes et la Constitution civile du clergé: Le développement du richérisme, sa propagation dans le bas clergé* (Paris: Librairie universitaire J. Gamber, 1929).

[36]"Decreto della fede e della chiesa," sessione III, in *Atti e decretti del concilio diocesano di Pistoia dell'anno 1786*, ed. Pietro Stella (Florence: Olschi, 1986), 1:77. See also Stella's "L'oscurimento delle verità nella chiesa dal sinodo di Pistoia alla bolla 'Auctorem fidei' (1786–1794)," *Salesianum rivista trimestrale di cultura ecclesiastica* 43 (1981): 731–56. On figurism in general, see Catherine L. Maire, *La cause de Dieu à la cause de la nation: Le jansénisme au dix-huitième siècle* (Paris: Gallimard, 1998), 163–234.

[37][Abbé Claude Mey and Gabriel-Nicolas Maultrot], *Apologie de tous les jugemens rendus par les tribunaux séculiers en France contre le schisme*, 2 vols. ("en France": 1752).

form of its government, when it has good reasons for doing so."[38] The culmination of this argument was the Parlement of Paris's appeal to the Estates General in 1787, which resulted in the meeting of the Estates two years later.

In the absence of any Estates General the only laymen whose "witness" or "cry of conscience" was of any consequence for Jansenism were the magistrates and barristers in the parlements of France, especially the Parlement of Paris, which, aside from occasional sympathetic bishops, afforded the only institutional protection that Jansenists ever enjoyed from public refusals of sacraments or interdiction from sacerdotal functions. Hence the second element of symbiosis, that between Jansenism and that constitutionalism in terms of which the Parlement claimed the right to oppose the religious policies of both monarchy and church. Conciliar constitutionalism as articulated by a Mey or Maultrot ran entwined through most of the century with another form, which substituted the Parlement of Paris for the defunct Estates General as the secular counterpart, not to the general council, but rather to the faithful lay remnant in the church. In what in contrast to the conciliar variety might be called "judicial constitutionalism," the proper role of the Parlement and its remonstrances were to testify to antique constitutional truth in the face of royal despotism, much as a faithful lay remnant might also witness to patristic truth amidst the obscurity of episcopal and papal apostasy. Most influentially articulated by the Jansenist barrister Louis-Adrien Le Paige, this constitutionalism rooted the Parlement's rights of registration and remonstrance in the mythical memory of Merovingian national assemblies to which the Parlement stood as legitimate successor and thus bound, in that capacity, to suffer passively in defense of the repository of fundamental law.[39] Although eclipsed after Chancellor Maupeou brutally revealed the fragility of the parlements as constitutional bulwarks in 1771, when he dissolved all of them and exiled the magistrates from Paris, substituting this judicial body with courts to which he named all the members, this judicial constitutionalism remained viable enough to have produced a still distinct strain in the pro-parliamentary pamphlet literature on the eve of the Revolution.[40]

But although judicial constitutionalism surely embraced the conciliar tenets of the Gallican tradition, it also committed Jansenism to the defense of royal Gallicanism, or at least of the parliamentary version of it. For, as the realm's chief royal

[38][Abbé Claude Mey and Gabriel-Nicolas Maultrot] et al., *Maximes du droit public françois*, 2 vols. (Amsterdam: Marc-Michel Rey, 1775), 1:269.

[39][Louis-Adrien Le Paige], *Lettres historiques sur les fonctions essentielles du parlement, sur le droit des pairs, et sur les loix fondamentaux du royaume*, 2 vols. (Amsterdam, 1753–54).

[40]For example, *La conférence entre un ministre d'état et un conseiller au parlement* (n.p., n.d.); and *Suite de la conférence…*, Bibliothèque de Port-Royal (BPR), Collection Le Paige, Ms 915, no. 6. Le Paige himself probably still had a hand in these pamphlets, judging from his handwritten corrections in his copies of them in this collection.

court claiming also to be the Court of Peers, the Parlement of Paris arrogated to itself the right to speak in the name of the king to the nation as well as in the name of the nation to the king, and to vindicate regalian rights even against the king and his ministers should they compromise such a national heritage. Since these regalian rights included the king's prerogative both as quasi-sacral "exterior bishop" and secular magistrate to a certain purview and control over the Gallican Church, the Parlement naturally defended these rights as well. It was in the name of these rights that the Parlement intervened against the bishops—and the king so long as he supported them—to protect Jansenists in such apparently spiritual affairs as the refusal of sacraments to appellants in the 1750s or, again, to prosecute their enemies, as in dissolution of the Jesuits in the 1760s.

In the hands of Jansenist canonists in the heat of battle against the independence of ultramontane bishops, the justification for extending the jurisdiction of the *regnum* at the expense of the *sacerdotum* went very far. Beginning with a conception of the church as purely spiritual, and prepared to give the state power over everything external, the Jansenist canonists could think of few if any things so spiritual that they did not include some admixture of the external that would justify state intervention. The same Maultrot who so radicalized and laicized the conciliar legacy also maintained that the "prince," by which he meant the Parlement, had the right to prevent unjust public refusals of sacrament to appellants because he was duty bound to protect any citizen's public reputation and therefore these citizens' access to the sacraments, as the "legal possession of even spiritual things is a purely profane matter."[41] This jurisprudence impinged on the autonomy of even general councils, seeing that whether they were ecumenical or not depended on the observance of all the canonical forms of which, external as these were, the prince was a valid judge.[42] So far was this line of argument taken that by the end of the 1760s it had produced a level of intellectual and spiritual confusion such that typically judicial Jansenist appeals to canon law and early church precedents jostle for position with rousseauian states of nature and social contracts in the same texts, and where moderate conclusions justifying parliamentary intervention to prevent abuses in ecclesiastical justice approach much more radical ones calling for the nationalization of church property. This polemical literary genre makes it hard to say exactly where judicial Jansenist "discourse" fades away and enlightened discourse dawns.[43] Just as conciliar constitutionalism led to the Parlement's appeal

[41][Gabriel-Nicolas Maultrot], *Les droits de la puissance temporelle, défendue contre la seconde partie des Actes de l'Assemblée du clergé de 1765 concernant la religion* (Amsterdam, 1777), 82.
[42][Mey and Maultrot], *Apologie de tous les jugemens*, 1:348.
[43]See Dale K. Van Kley, "Church, State, and the Ideological Origins of the French Revolution," *Journal of Modern History* 51 (Dec. 1979): 629–66.

to the Estates General in 1787, so judicial constitutionalism pointed the way toward the Civil Constitution of 1790.

Judicial constitutionalism existed in tension with the commitment to councils and conciliar procedures as well as with the ecclesiastical independence that these presupposed. Yet eighteenth-century French Jansenists were only imperfectly aware of these tensions, as the chief architects of conciliar constitutionalism like Mey and Maultrot often lent their weighty authority to justifications for judicial intervention in spiritual affairs, while the high priest of judicial constitutionalism, Adrien Le Paige, wielded the language of conciliarism when it suited his purposes.[44] With no prospect of holding councils in their own country, French Jansenists showed their good faith by staging them elsewhere, as in Utrecht in 1763, or by applauding them elsewhere, as in Pistoia in 1786. Moreover, the same reasoning used to justify judicial intervention at the expense of ecclesiastical jurisdiction, that the state might enforce Gallican canon law against bishops acting in contempt of it, could also be used on behalf of the rights of bishops, as when the Dutch States General permitted the election and consecration of an archbishop of Utrecht in defiance of papal disapproval. It was not until the revolutionary National Assembly, assuming all of the old monarchy's Crown rights in its turn, used the same lines of argument in arranging for episcopal succession to legitimate a constitutional church that it had almost entirely subjected to a national state, that the latent tension between judicial and conciliar constitutionalism broke into open conflict.

ITALY AND THE JANSENIST INTERNATIONAL—THE CONFLICTS
WITH JESUITS OUTSIDE OF FRANCE

To be sure, the controvery over the refusal of sacraments did produce some pro-Jansenist and anticlerical popular disturbances, particularly in Paris. There, as in other northern French cities like Troyes and Orléans, a socially judicial public opinion most surely took shape and sided with Jansenists against sacrament-refusing priests and the Jesuits.[45] But it is hard to assign causal weight to crowd action or public opinion as factors in the two most signal Jansenist successes in France: the de facto fall of the bull *Unigenitus* from its status as a law of state in 1757 followed by the trial and dissolution of the Society of Jesus by the parlements led by the Paris Parlement in 1762 and confirmed by royal declaration in 1764. For by the early 1760s, when the Council of Utrecht also added its voice to the

[44]For example, in Le Paige's anonymously published *Lettres adressées à mm. les commissaires nommés par le roi pour délibérer sur l'affaire présente du parlement au sujet du refus de sacrements, ou Lettres pacifiques au sujet des contestations présentes* (n.p., 1753).

[45]Dale Van Kley, *The Damiens Affair and the Unraveling of the Old Regime, 1757–1770* (Princeton: Princeton University Press, 1984), 13–55, 226–65.

anti-Jesuit chorus, the campaign against the papal curia and the Jesuits as its chief symbols was not the work of French Jansenists alone or even limited to France alone. For by that time Jansenism had become an international cause.

The decisive event in the internationalization of Jansenism and the successful offensive against the Jesuits was the sojourn in Rome in 1758–59 by the abbé Augustin-Charles-Jean Clément de Bizon, a French Jansenist canon in Auxerre and brother of several influential magistrates. His purposes were first to help negotiate a doctrinal statement from Benedict XIV favorable to French appellants, and then, after Benedict's untimely death in 1758, to observe and if possible influence the outcome of the papal conclave.[46] By themselves, the election of Carlo Rezzonico as Clement XIII followed by the death of the well-disposed secretary of state Cardinal Alberico Archinto and his replacement by Torrigiani may not have been the pro-Jesuitical catastrophes calling for a counteroffensive that Clément and his Italian friends deemed them to be. But they did deem it so, with self-confirming effects for Catholic Europe as a whole.

One all but invisible but important result was the institutionalization of what had been an occasional correspondence between Clément and some Italian Augustinians—Giovanni Gaetano Bottari, for example, first guardian of the Vatican Library and confidant of Cardinal Neri Corsini; or Carlo Armano, comte di Gros, one of Italian Jansenism's rare lay adepts. Italian Augustinians and anti-Jesuits, they now entered a kind of Jansenist International. This International remained primarily a correspondence concerned with the publication and dissemination of approved books on behalf of solid doctrine as well as the circulation of news and ecclesiastical news sheets like the *Nouvelles ecclésiastiques* throughout Catholic Europe. As a historical record of dedication to the cause, this correspondence was precious enough to Clément that he thought of sending it to Utrecht for safekeeping on the eve of the Terror in January 1793.[47] But its purpose was also to establish and nourish contacts near the centers of power in the papal curia and in the various princely courts of Catholic Europe with a view toward influencing the course of events in favor of the status of the diocese of Utrecht and the situation of appellants in France. The international's one major accomplishment was the suppression of the Jesuits in France and elsewhere, culminating in their abolition by the papacy in 1773.

The first of the Jesuit dominoes to fall was in Portugal, where Sebastian Carvalho e Melho, the marquis de Pombal and chief minister to José I, alleged the complicity of the Jesuits in an attempt on the king's life in order to expel them

---

[46]Abbé Augustin-Charles-Jean Clément de Bizon, *Journal de correspondances et voyages d'Italie et d'Espagne pour la paix de l'église en 1758, 1768 et 1769 par M. Clément, alors trésorier de l'église d'Auxerre, et depuis évêque de Versailles*, vol. 1(Paris: Longuet, 1802).

[47]HUA, 215, Ms 3441, Clément to Mouton, 3 January 1793.

from both the metropolis and the American colonies. Besides causing a crisis in relations between Lisbon and the papacy, this literal expulsion revealed that the deed could be done, no doubt encouraging the French to try to do as much.[48] Yet even more crucial for France was the advice that Clément, Le Paige, and their cohorts received in late 1758 and 1759 from their Italian friends, notably Bottari, that because the papacy would never disavow *Unigenitus*, the French "friends of the truth" should "attack the Jesuits from whatever angle does not concern the bull or unites their cause with the court of Rome." Once rid of the Jesuits, "all the rest will be easy."[49] To be sure, neither the Italian nor French Jansenists could have created the right circumstances—the bankruptcy of the French Jesuits' mission in Martinique in 1759, the favorable disposition of the duc de Choiseul—but their close connections to the Parlement of Paris through Le Paige and Clément's brother Clément de Feillet are enough to account for the parlementary *parti janséniste*'s determination to profit from such circumstances as arose.[50]

The fall of the Jesuits in France was also much more decisive than in Portugal— as decisive as the Italian Jansenists had predicted it would be. Being an international state within many states, the Jesuits suffered the adverse consequences of the dynastic alliance negotiated by Choiseul between the Bourbon rulers of France, Spain, Naples, and Parma in 1761, just as the Parlement of Paris was striking the first decisive blow against the Jesuits in France. Even if less directly, the Jesuits were also the victims of the diplomatic revolution of 1756 which, by realigning Habsburg Austria with her erstwhile enemy Bourbon France until the French Revolution, deprived the Jesuits of any support from Austria where Jansenists had become sufficiently influential in the ministry by the late 1760s to interest Empress Maria Theresa in Utrecht's case against Rome.[51] Thus, when the government of Carlos III of Spain alleged Jesuit complicity in a popular riot in Madrid a year earlier in order to motivate an edict expelling Spanish Jesuits and confiscating their property on 2 April 1767, the Bourbon rulers of Naples and Parma felt free to follow suit without fear of local Habsburg disapproval in Lombardy and Tuscany.

[48]Samuel J. Miller, *Portugal and Rome, c. 1748–1830: An Aspect of the Catholic Enlightenment* (Rome: Università Gregoriana, 1978).

[49]For Bottari's advice, see Archives de la Bastille, Bibliothèque de l'Arsenal, Ms 12883, fols. 152, 157. For Clément's summary, see HUA, 215, Ms 2676, Clément to Rivière, 31 January 1761.

[50]Dale K. Van Kley, *The Jansenists and the Expulsion of the Jesuits from France, 1757–65* (New Haven: Yale University Press, 1975), 37–136.

[51]See Anton de Haen's "Résultat de la conférence tenue à Vienne le 27 décembre 1767 fête de Saint-Jean," HUA, 215, Ms 2630. On Maria Theresa and Austrian Jansenism, see Reginald Ward, "Late Jansenism and the Habsburgs," in *Religion and Politics in Enlightenment Europe*, ed. Bradley and Van Kley. On De Haen, see J. Broersma, *Antonius de Haen, 1704–1776: Leven en werk* (Assen: Vrije Universiteit van Amsterdam, 1963).

RELIGIOUS DIFFERENCES IN FRANCE

But when the duke of tiny Parma tried to emulate France and Spain by asserting control over ecclesiastical appointments and banning all papal briefs and bulls
that did not carry the duke's permission, a humiliated Clement XIII struck back,
issuing a brief annulling Ferdinand's edict as well as a fulminating bull of excommunication—events recalling the specter of *Unam Sanctam* and medieval papal
claims to temporal power. Now it was the turn of the Bourbons and their sympa-
thizers in Italy to be outraged, as Naples seized the papal enclaves of Benevento
and Portecorvo while French troops occupied Avignon.[52] This sequence of
actions and reactions was repeated with even more polarizing effect from 1769 to
1774 when Ganganelli emerged from the papal conclave as Clement XIV with
both Bourbon and Habsburg support on the implicit condition, most insisted
upon by Spain, that he dissolve the Jesuits. Again, Italian and especially Roman
friends advised their French and Dutch cobelligerents that if, in the words of Pier
Francesco Foggini, all other causes "do not wait until after the suppression of the
Jesuits, nothing fundamental can ... be hoped for"; while once again, as in 1759,
an apparently amenable pope died an untimely death, not long after fulminating
the bull dissolving the Jesuits but only a day before Dupac de Bellegarde was to
see him on behalf of Utrecht. Thus were Jansenists once again left empty-handed
as an even deeper curial reaction than under Clement XIII set in under Pius VI.[53]

But it should not have taken until 1775 for the partisans of Rome to have
realized that as soon as the offensive against the Jesuits reached Italy it was no
longer possible to effect a clean separation between the cause of the Jesuits on the
one hand and that of the papacy on the other. The papacy was after all among the
few genuinely indigenous institutions in an Italy which, except for old aristocratic
republics of Genoa and Venice, had become a patchwork of Bourbon and Habsburg territories. Italians of diverse stripes were thus bound to feel a sense of
humiliation to see these hitherto rival Catholic dynasties of Europe all but broker
their differences at the expense of the papacy to which, in the person of Clement
XIV, they virtually dictated the brief dissolving the Jesuits in 1773. So while in the
mid-1770s the archbishop of Siena had been almost persuaded to make a public
profession of communion with the appellant diocese of Utrecht, "he has changed
so much since the time of the expulsion of the Jesuits," according to Jansenist professor Paolo Marcello Del Mare, "that no one can now remove from his head the

[52]Owen Chadwick, *The Popes and the European Revolution* (Oxford: Clarendon Press, 1981),
364–68. *Unam Sanctam* was issued by Boniface VIII in 1302 and represented the apogee of papal
imperial claims.

[53]On Foggini's advice, see HUA, 215, Ms 2207-2, Foggini to Clément, 13 November 1771. On
Dupac de Bellegarde's trip to Rome, see his manuscript "Journal du voyage de Dupac d'Utrecht à
Rome et de son séjour à cette ville, 1774 juin 19–oct. 2," HUA, 215, Ms 2619. See also Pontien Polman,
OFM, *Katholieke Nederland in de Achttiende Eeuw* (Hilversum: Paul Brand, 1968), 2:157–59.

idea that the Jansenists are out to destroy religion."[54] In Rome, the 1770s also witnessed the dispersion of what remained of Bottari's Jansenist group called the *Archetto* that had met in Cardinal Corsini's palace, along with several newer conventicles including one clustered around the theologian Pietro Tamburini headquartered in the library of Cardinal Mario Marefoschi and still another centered in the Oratorian seminary of the *Chiesa Nuova*.[55]

The dissolution of the Company of Jesus created a host of angry ex-Jesuits, many of them in the papal states where Gianvincenzo Bolgeni and Francescantonio Zaccaria emerged as the most prolific polemicists. When under Pius VI they became objects not only of pity but of favor, they came to constitute a kind of ex-Jesuit International corresponding and opposed to the Jansenist one with representatives and journals scattered throughout Catholic Europe. For every Jansenist periodical modeled on the *Nouvelles ecclésiastiques*,[56] there came to correspond an ex-Jesuit one: Feller's *Journal politique et littéraire* in Luxembourg, Goldhagen and his *Religionsjournal* in Mainz, and of course Barruel's *Journal ecclésiastique* in France. Furthermore, these ex-Jesuits enjoyed the support of all manner of Catholic allies whom they would have been hard-pressed to enlist in their cause before the dissolution of their order. When Rome itself came to have a journal comparable to many ex-Jesuit ones, the *Giornale ecclesiastico di Roma*, founded in 1785, the ex-Jesuit Zaccaria was joined by the Dominican Maria Tomasso Mamachi and even an Augustinian, Luigi Cuccagni, as editors.[57]

While this militant ex-Jesuit International took shape in defense of papal authority on the ecclesiastical "right," Dupac de Bellegarde's abortive journey to Rome followed by the reactionary pontificate of Pius VI prompted a fresh contingent of Italian Augustinians and moral rigorists to become regular correspondents with the church of Utrecht, which increasingly took the place of Paris as the capitol of the Jansenist International. Even more than for the previous generation, this affiliation tended to remake them into Jansenists in the full French sense of the term. That is to say that, in addition to a commitment to theological Augustinianism and moral rigorism, Italian philo-Jansenists began to adopt the polemical party tone and antipapal Gallican ecclesiology as radicalized by French Jansenists

[54]HUA, 215, Ms 2557, De Vecchi to Dupac de Bellegarde, 25 January 1775; and Ms 2153, Del Mare to Dupac de Bellegarde, 23 March 1787.

[55]Enrico Dammig, *Il movimento giansenista a Roma nella seconda meta del secolo XVIII* (Cita del Vaticana: Biblioteca Apostolica, 1945), 207–12.

[56]For example, Follini's *Annali ecclesiastici* in Florence, Scheidel's *Mainzer Monatschriften von geistlichen Sachen* [Mainz's Monthly Reports on Spiritual Matters] in Mainz, Wittola's *Wienerische Kirchenzeitung* [Viennese Church Newspaper] in Vienna, and Grégoire's *Annales de la religion* in post-Thermidorian Paris.

[57]Giuseppe Pignatelli, *Aspetti della propaganda cattolica a Roma da Pio VI a Leone XII* (Rome: Istituto per la Storia del Risorgimento Italiano, 1974).

in alliance with the parlements in the course of the earlier *Unigenitus*-related controversies. This development transformed some Italians from would-be Catholic reformers into anticurial rebels.[58] As to the ecclesiology, not all may have gone so far as Scipione de' Ricci, bishop of Pistoia and Prato in Tuscany, who held the Gallican articles of 1682 to be articles of faith and who, writing in French, excoriated the curia for its ultramontane pretensions, clearly forgetting on which side of the Alps he himself resided.[59]

What slipped out of the Gallican baggage in its journey over the Alps was the conciliar tenets. While eighteenth-century Frenchmen witnessed a formal appeal to a general council, Italians no more contemplated such an eventuality than they did the rebirth of an Ostrogothic kingdom in Rome. A general council was the best remedy for the ills of the church, conceded the Paduan professor Giuseppe Pujati to the abbé Clement in 1786, "but this just and pious desire is not at all understood by our princes and is little understood by our bishops, while in the center of Catholic unity it is condemned as an attempt to break it."[60] Given papal hostility and in the absence of anything like French parlements, Italian Jansenists' only recourse was to Italy's secular sovereigns whose divine right to undertake ecclesiastical reform without the concurrence of either papacy or councils they tended accordingly to magnify. By the eve of the French Revolution, Jansenists in Italy as everywhere else in Catholic Europe had come to stand for the right of secular authority not only to defend local episcopal authority against the papal curia in such matters as the right to grant dispensations from the canonical laws prohibiting marriage within degrees of familial relatedness, but also to change those laws, revise seminary curricula, dictate the content of theological education, and reform or suppress monastic orders, as well as the right to limit and tax ecclesiastical property. Only in the language of French Jansenists did the secular authority thus aggrandized mean anything other than royal or ducal authority.

Precisely when and why in the 1760s Italian Augustinians began to give up on the papacy is less germane than to see that, even if radical Jansenist or Gallican ecclesiology was supposed to be subordinate to theology, it was the ecclesiology that made the difference. Writing from the University of Siena, the theologian Fabio de Vecchi came to think that it was "from the false notions of the church that the great [doctrinal] errors have been born," rather than the other way around.[61]

---

[58]Mario Rosa, *Riformatori e ribelli nel '700 religioso italiano* (Bari: Dedalo, 1969).

[59]HUA, 215, Ms 2489, Ricci to Dupac de Bellegarde, 6 January 1782 and 2 February 1783.

[60]Bibliothèque de Saint-Sulpice (BSS), Collection Clément (CC), Ms 1291, no. 761, Pujati to Clément, 24 January 1786. Pujati's correspondence with Clément has been published by Maurice Vaussard, *L'epistolario di G. M. Pujati col canonico Clément di 7 di ottobre 1776–19 di dicembre 1786* (Venice: Fondazione Giorgio Cini, 1964).

[61]HUA, 215, Ms 2557, De Vecchi to Dupac, 30 June 1783.

The conviction gained ground that if the unredeemed human will had come to play a prominent role in Catholic theology, the root cause was the play of despotic will in the structure of the church. Augustinian orthodoxy would arise naturally from the practice of correct or conciliar canonical forms, even if these could be implemented only at the synodical level.

The presence of consensus and the absence of *Unigenitus* as an issue had made possible the so-called Catholic Enlightenment in Italy, as well as the place of Augustinianism in it. A movement displaying much more continuity with the Christian humanism of Erasmus or Lorenzo Valla than the French Enlightenment, the Catholic Enlightenment had flourished just about everywhere in Catholic Europe before the 1760s outside France although its Catholic character was perhaps most salient in Italy where it enjoyed the patronage of a pope, Benedict XIV, and personification by a priest, Antonio Ludovico Muratori. Described by Bernard Plongeron as a new "religious anthropology" open to the rights of reason within a more christological faith as well as to the prospect of secular amelioration with some help from a less hierarchical church, the Catholic Enlightenment endorsed textual and historical criticism of the scriptures and the dissemination of the Bible in the vernacular, called for more honest, less partisan church histories and what Muratori called a "moderate devotion" purged of baroque excesses and superstitious accretions, and opposed both Aristotle and scholasticism, in the one case in favor of newer sciences and in the other in favor of older patristic sources.[62] But it is obvious from even this thumbnail description that the existence of such a movement presupposed a modicum of consensus between moderates from both Augustinian and Molinistic camps, a consensus made possible in turn by the fact that *Unigenitus* and papal authority were not issues.

The "gallicization" of Italian Augustinianism undermined the doctrinal consensus on which the Catholic Enlightenment rested because Gallican ecclesiology exacerbated the issues, relating them as it did to so much else. With the once powerful Jesuits extinct but the pro-Jesuitical Pius VI as new pope, Dominicans and Augustinians allowed themselves the luxury of a great falling out, Dominicans making common cause with the fallen ex-Jesuits and the papal curia against the Augustinians who responded not only with a neo-Gallican ecclesiology but with a hardening of their theology of grace. The result of this fratricide was what Emile Appolis has called "the fragmentation of the third party" or theological center which gave way to the extremes on either side.[63] While theological reflection on

[62]Bernard Plongeron, "Recherches sur l' 'Aufklärung' catholique en Europe occidentale, 1770–1830," *Revue d'histoire moderne et contemporaine* 16 (1969): 555–605.
[63]Emile Appolis, *Le "tiers parti" catholique au dix-huitième siècle* (Paris: Picard, 1960), 369–512. For firsthand evidence of this falling out, see the Augustinian General Francisco-Xavier Vasquez's letter to Dupac in HUA, 215, Ms 2556, 28 May 1775.

the Molinist side of the debate in Italy was perhaps only a little more prolific than in France, it attracted some of the best talent including the ex-Jesuit Giovan Vincenzo Bolgeni who quite simply eliminated contrition or disinterested love for God from his confessional theology, arguing that attrition or expanded self-love was the only legitimate means of relating to God.[64] While in the second half of the century French Jansenists all but abandoned theology in favor of canon and public law, the end of the century in Italy was one of prolific Jansenist theological production. Natali, Georgi, De Vecchi, Palmieri, Tamburini, Zola: this "who's who" of Augustinian theological eminences at the end of the *Settecento* is also a list of those who produced multivolume works on grace, predestination, and confession, among other characteristically Jansenist subjects, all the while holding or hardening the Augustinian position on such edifying subjects as the damnation of infants who died without baptism.[65] While the French Jansenist theologian Etienne Gourlin's treatise on grace fell on stony ground in France when posthumously published there in 1781, it was avidly read and much appreciated by all Italian Jansenists except perhaps for Carlo di Gros who thought it too Thomist.[66] This fin-de-siècle's widening of the theological fault lines contributed to the collapse of Italy's Catholic Enlightenment, a fragile combination of incompatibles held together by a common faith and certain "enlightened" assumptions that fell prey to polarization. The result was that the Jansenists and *zelanti* divided up the Catholic Enlightenment's harvest between them, appropriating those parts that seemed most compatible with very partial confessional agendas. To the *zelanti* went the Enlightenment's sensate epistemology, rehabilitation of will and self-interest, optimistic estimate of human nature, and openness to the prospect of progress; in short, all the real compatibilities between ethical and theological Molinism and the Enlightenment that Jansenists in Italy as well as in France never tired of denouncing. To Jansenists went an antischolastic rationalism, the Renaissance quest for pristine origins, the reformational rehabilitation of secular government, an anticlerical campaign against the regular clergy and the papal curia, and the Muratorian project for a better "regulated devotion."[67] In Jansenist hands, this project took the form of a catechetical campaign to stamp out popular ignorance and superstition with solid doctrine and reasoned conviction based on the

[64]Giovan Vincenzo Bolgeni, *Della carita o Amor di Dio Dissertazione* (Roma: Stampiera Salomini, 1788).

[65]Alberto Aquarone, "Giansenismo italiano e rivoluzione francese prima del Triennio giacobino," *Rassegna storica del Risorgimento: organo della Società nazionale per la storia del Risorgimento italiano* 39 (1962): 559–624.

[66]Maire, *De la cause de Dieu à la cause de la nation*, 363; and HUA, 215, Ms 2551, no. 100, Di Gros to Dupac de Bellegarde, 28 March 1783.

[67]Lodovico Antonio Muratori, *Della regolata divozione de' Christiani, trattato di Lamindo Pritanio* [pseud.] (Trent: Monauni, 1766).

doctrine that ignorance, being one of the chief consequences of the fall, was itself a sin and so excused no other sins.[68]

For Roman Jansenists in particular the result was ironic indeed. On the one hand, the stated purpose and expected result of the advice to French Jansenists to put the campaign against the Jesuits ahead of that against *Unigenitus* was to take the sharp edges off the religious and political divisions in France. By both discrediting religious disputes and depriving French Jansenists of their preferred scapegoats, their victory over the Jesuits seems to have had that effect, creating the possibility of something like an autumnal Catholic Enlightenment there. But the effect of the same campaign in Italy was the reverse, bringing the French political, ecclesiastical, and even religious divisions there in its train. The French thereby contrived to pass their polarized ecclesiastical situation on to Italy, ironically by Italian invitation, as the abbé Clément and Dupac de Bellegarde replied to requests for good books and solid doctrine by engineering an avalanche of French Jansenist publications from over the Alps onto the Italies.[69]

THE ERA AND END OF JANSENIST ABSOLUTISM

One of the chief differences between France and the Italies is that whereas the supposed capital of the Enlightenment produced no enlightened or Jansenist rulers, the Habsburg principalities of late eighteenth-century Italy produced at least one of each in the persons of Joseph II, who directly ruled Lombardy as a province of the Empire, and his brother Peter Leopold, grand duke of Tuscany. This remarkable contrast reflects an anterior difference between the French and Italian situations: whereas the French monarchy had long vindicated its Gallican liberties vis-à-vis the papacy, Italian princes and potentates had yet to gain them, and could only do so with the aid of Catholics and a theology that, although Catholic, was also antipapal. Hence the late-eighteenth-century alliance between absolutists in need of clerical help in aggrandizing the secular jurisdiction's control over people as subjects at the expense of the church's control of them as the faithful, and Jansenists, who looked to secular rulers to help them undertake the reform of the church. So typical is this alliance in prerevolutionary Catholic Europe outside of France—Jovellanos or Roda and Carlos III of Spain, Simioli or Sarao and Don Carlos of Naples, Blarer or De Haën and both Maria Theresa and Joseph II in Austria, Nény and Le Plat and the same sovereigns in the Austrian Netherlands—

---

[68]See Acquarone, "Giansenismo italiano e rivoluzione francese prima del Triennio giacobino," 613–14. On a clear statement of the doctrinal basis of this campaign, see "Decreto delle grazia, della predestinazione, e dei fondamenti della morale," in *Atti e decreti del concilio diocesano di Pistoia dell'anno 1786*, ed. Pietro Stella (Florence: Olschki, 1986), 1:90.

[69]For an idea of the extent of this exportation, see Maurice Vaussard, *Jansénisme et gallicanisme aux origines religieuses du Risorgimento* (Paris: Letouzey et Ané, 1959).

RELIGIOUS DIFFERENCES IN FRANCE

that the period might as plausibly be dubbed that of Jansenist despotism as of enlightened despotism.

Nowhere did the concept of Jansenist absolutism come nearer to being a reality than in the Tuscany of Grand Duke Peter Leopold whose favorite reading included Jacques Duguet's *L'institution d'un prince* (*The Education of a Prince*). Thus the grand duke's "fifty-seven points," his blueprint for ecclesiastical reform sent to Tuscan bishops and others, were largely oriented toward producing the *buon paroco* or good pastor as the model for all clergy at the expense of the regular clergy and priests holding benefices without cure of souls, as well as toward making the parish church the center of worship at the expense of confraternal chapels, public oratories, and other loci of devotion. But Leopold's chief theological inspiration came not from books but from a resident Tuscan Jansenist theologian and churchman, Scipione de' Ricci, whom Leopold had promoted from being grand vicar in Florence to the bishopric of Pistoia and Prato in 1780.

The most spectacular result of this Tuscan edition of the Jansenist-absolutist entente was the Synod of Pistoia in 1786. Convened by Ricci but presided over by the synod's chief theologian, Pietro Tamburini of the University of Pavia, the synod included almost every *curé* and curate in the diocese, which was canonical enough for a diocesan synod in contrast to a provincial council.[70] The particular significance of this synod was Leopold's plan to have it be the first in a series of synods leading to a national council. Ricci assured the *curés* and curates that they were to be voting with their bishop as "judges of the faith."[71] The agenda entrusted to these judges was also universal—that is, conciliar—in scope, as Ricci and Tamburini persuaded them to subscribe to a series of decrees articulating an unmistakably Jansenist theology of grace, predestination, and penitence, enjoining the reading of Quesnel's *Réflexions morales* and proclaiming the four Gallican articles of 1682 to contain the true doctrine of the church and the pope to be only its "ministerial head."[72] Four references to "times of obscurity" suggested that Pistoia's Gallicanism had not failed to keep up with French figurism, and that the visible magistracy, even with a majority of bishops and not the papacy alone, was not always to be trusted.[73] Nor did Ricci and the synod fail to go on record, as had the

[70]The synod's published acts and decrees contain a detailed account of participants of which *parochi* is no. 171. See *Atti e decreti del concilio diocesano di Pistoia*, 18–27.

[71]"Scipione de' Ricci per la misericordia di Dio vescovo di Pistoia e Prato, ai venerabili fratelli consacerdoti e cooperatori suoi della citta, e diocesi di Pistoia," in *Atti e decreti del concilio diocesano di Pistoia*, 1–8.

[72]"Decreto della grazia, della predestinazione, e dei fondamenti della morale," 84–96; "Decreto della penitenza," 141–57; and "Decreto della fede e della chiesa," 75–83, esp. 78, 81–82; and "Decreto della preghiera," 209–10, in *Atti e decreti del concilio diocesano di Pistoia*.

[73]References to the occasional "obscurity" of the truth are to be found in *Atti e decreti del concilio diocesano di Pistoia*, 5, 32, 77, 84, 216. On this point see Pietro Stella, "L'oscurimento della verità nella

council of Utrecht, in favor of councils and conciliar forms, opposed as these were to the "spirit of domination" or any hint of "monarchy and despotism" in the church.[74] Indeed, the church of Utrecht was never far from Pistoia's agenda, as many priests wanted the synod to avow its communion with that church, which itself adhered to the *Acts* of the Synod of Pistoia in 1789.[75]

In sharp contrast to Utrecht's provincial council of 1763, however, which had downplayed its differences with Rome in an effort to give public proof of its orthodoxy, the Synod of Pistoia bore a frankly reformist and anticurial stamp. For it not only staked out controversial doctrinal and ecclesiastical positions, but also deduced from these positions a program of liturgical and pastoral reform that at once ratified and radicalized the assault on "baroque piety" that Ricci, with Leopold's support, had been visiting on unreceptive parishioners ever since his episcopate began in 1780. On the grounds that the clergy's only purpose was "the sanctification of the faithful," the synod praised the grand duke's attempts to reallocate church resources to the service of the parish and its clergy at the expense of the monastic clergy, which it all but urged him to destroy.[76] From the premise that the Eucharistic sacrifice was spiritual and not material, the synod concurred with Ricci's campaign against visual and auditory distractions like loud organ music and the display of relics in favor of instructional books and vernacular translations whereby the laity might "even participate in the sacrifice."[77] On the principle that Christ and not "created things" was the only cause of true prayer, the synod endorsed Ricci's crusade against repeated novenas and numbered recitations, and called upon the grand duke to restrict the number of religious feast days and required oaths. This bookish offensive against devotional practices considered exterior, material, or smacking of superstition deepened the gulf between Jansenist and indigenous popular religious sensibility and proved to be the synod's undoing.[78] For unlike Jansenism in the more text-oriented north, Italian Jansenism was

chiesa dal sinodo di Pistoia alla bolla 'Auctorem fidei' (1786–1794)," *Salesianum rivista trimestrale di cultura ecclesiastica* 43 (1981): 731–56.

[74]Scipione de' Ricci's letter of convocation dated 31 July 1786 and printed as part of *Atti e decreti del concilio diocesano di Pistoia*, 1–8.

[75]HUA, R86–1, Ms. 170, "Scipione de' Ricci, met minute van akte, waarbij van Nieuwenhuizen, Broekman en Nobelman hun adhsesie betuigen aan het concilie van Pistoia 1789." For Dutch reaction to the Synod of Pistoia, see Peter J. van Lessel, "Il Paesi Bassi e il sinodo di Pistoia," in *Il sinodo di Pistoia del 1786: Atti del Convegno per il secondo centenario Pistoia-Prato, 25–27 settembre 1986*, ed. Claudio Lamioni (Rome: Herder, 1991), 401–9.

[76]"Decreto dell'ordine" in *Atti e decreti del concilio diocesano di Pistoia*, 163–80, esp.165–66, 171–79; and "promemoria riguardante la riforma dei regolari," 235–39.

[77]"Decreto della eucharistia," in *Atti e decreti del concilio diocesano di Pistoia*, 123–33, quotes at 125, 130.

[78]"Decreto della preghiera" and "della preghiera pubblica," in *Atti e decreti del concilio diocesano di Pistoia*, 196–211; and "promenoria circa la riforma dei giuramenti" and "sulla riforma delle feste,"

fated to remain a clerical and professorial phenomenon, never acquiring much of a popular lay constituency.

Another contrast to the church in Utrecht is of course that the Tuscan Jansenists answered to an absolute Catholic sovereign. Yet a remarkable feature of Peter Leopold's rule in Tuscany is that, until the going got rough and in the sharpest contrast to the more autocratic style of his brother in Vienna, he was willing to experiment with conciliar forms instead of promulgating reforms without the church's concurrence. Even though the Synod of Pistoia was the only one of Peter Leopold's planned synods to actually meet, it was the example of the conciliar form as well as the synod's doctrinal pronouncements that resonated and ricocheted so widely in Catholic Europe. Like the unanimity of Utrecht earlier touted by the Jansenist press, it was as much the uniformity of more than two hundred priests despite their nearness to the papal curia and its "lackeys" as it was the synod's "plan of doctrine and ecclesiastical discipline" that gave its promoter Pietro Tamburini "reason to hope for a felicitous revolution in the church of Italy."[79] The hope thus inspired extended well beyond the Italies, especially after the belated publication of the council's *Acts* in 1789. As far away as Mainz, Professor Scheidel of the archiepiscopal university there tried to arrange for a German translation of "such a celebrated assembly," hoping that it would help unite the German suffragans behind their archbishops in a statement against "Roman pretensions" that the congress of the four Rhenish prince-archbishops in Ems, also in 1786, had failed to fulfill.[80] Reacting to the Synod's Acts in Paris in 1789, the abbé Clément had never dared hope to see anything so good, especially the parts on history and penitence, and called for a speedy French translation in the hopes that the synod might serve as a model for ecclesiastical reform in the upcoming meeting of the Estates General.[81] Back in Utrecht, Dupac de Bellegarde shared Clément's enthusiasm and produced the desired translation.

It was also all too good to be true, because the revolution that overtook Tuscany was neither the felicitous revolution that Tamburini hoped for nor the one that soon transformed the awaited Estates General into the National Assembly in France. For the revolution in Tuscany took a conservative, even pointedly anti-Jansenist direction, as those segments of the clergy alienated by Ricci's reforms allied

---

225–33. For critique against superstition in the name of a regulated devotion, see 200, 202.

[79]HUA, 215, Ms 3603, no. 64, Tamburini to Zola, 18 December 1786.

[80]HUA, Ms 2518, Scheidel to Dupac, 7 March 1789. On the Congress of Ems, see Timothy C. W. Blanning, *Reform and Revolution in Mainz, 1743–1803* (Cambridge: Cambridge University Press, 1974), 177–79, 220–28. On the general reaction to the Synod of Pistoia in the Germanic world, see Peter Hersche, "Eco del sinodo di Pistoia nel mondo germanico," in *Il sinodo di Pistoia del 1786*, 393–95.

[81]HUA, 215, Ms 2207–2, Clément to Dupac, 11 January 1789; Ms 3441, Clément to Mouton, 3 September 1790; and Ms 2489, Dupac de Bellegarde to Ricci, 5 January 1789.

themselves with elements of the lay population that perceived these reforms as an attack on religion as such. This coalition of anti-Riccian forces first reared its revolutionary head in May of 1787 when popular riots erupted in Pistoia and Prato at the very moment that Ricci and his allies in the Tuscan episcopacy sustained decisive defeat at the hands of a majority of Tuscan bishops in an assembly convened by Leopold in Florence as a shortcut to the convocation of the desired national council. Never to meet, the council was the main casualty of these events. Even more disastrous for Ricci and the Synod of Pistoia was the riot in Florence itself three years later on 9 June 1790. In the absence of Peter Leopold, who had left Florence for Vienna to take the place of his deceased brother, a regency council reacted to the riot by abandoning almost all of the reforms the grand duke had sponsored.

While in prerevolutionary France, popular hostility already often made scapegoats of Catholic clergymen without distinguishing among them, the Tuscan riots, preceded and accompanied by clerical pamphlets against Ricci and the Synod of Pistoia, sought to undo the ecclesiastical and liturgical reforms promoted by them in defense of other priests or the regular clergy and a more traditional Catholicism. The immediate occasion of the uprisings of May 1787 was the rumor of the impending removal of the altar dedicated to the relic of the Virgin's garter, while the riots of June 1790 demanded and to a degree obtained the restoration of sundry altars, oratories, images, and even of abolished monasteries to their monks—all objects of the synod's decrees. They also drove Ricci out of Pistoia and Prato, and his friend and ecclesiastical provost Antonio Baldovinetti out of Leghorn, and Ricci and Baldovinetti submitted their resignations within the year.[82] From the perspective of these Jansenist victims, the riots were directed principally against them and were clearly orchestrated by Rome.[83] Viewing the same events from Rome, Joseph II's Jansenist imperial postal agent there, Girolamo Astorri, went so far as to advance a complex conspiracy theory to show how "emissaries of the court of Rome," aware of time spent by Tuscan peasants as farmhands in the papal states each winter, "took advantage of this time to instruct them, to turn them against the reforms, and to embolden them for the explosion which has just gone off."[84]

Astorri's conspiracy theory is symptomatic of how, by raising the stakes in the debate, the coming of the era of revolutions and the end of the European Old Order would further exacerbate relations between Italian Jansenists and their

[82]On the riots in the spring of 1790, see Eric Cochrane, *Florence in the Forgotten Centuries, 1527–1800: A History of Florence and the Florentines in the Age of the Grand Dukes* (Chicago: University of Chicago Press, 1973), 399–418. On the riot in Pistoia and Prato of 20–21 May 1787, see Carlo Fantappiè, *Riforme ecclesiastiche e resistenze sociali* (Bologna: Mulino, 1986).

[83]HUA, 215, Ms 3397, Baldovinetti to Mouton, 2 November 1790; and Ms 2489, fol. 277, Ricci to Dupac de Bellegarde, 12 August 1787.

[84]HUA, Ms 3394, Astorri to Mouton, 29 May 1790.

zelanti opponents. In the competition between rival conspiracy theories, the *zelanti* were bound to prevail to the precise degree that the French Revolution came to overshadow the Catholic and conservative revolutions in Tuscany and the Austrian Netherlands that preceded it. For while it seemed plausible to traumatized Jansenists that the papacy and its agents would have fomented the popular revolts directed against Jansenist-like ecclesiastical, liturgical, and devotional reforms, it also seemed plausible to defenders of orthodoxy and papal primacy that Jansenists might have been in league with philosophes in the making of a revolution that promulgated anything like the Civil Constitution of the Clergy. Among the authors of the French Revolution the Jansenists were the most dangerous, in the opinion of one pro-papal pamphleteer, in that, unlike philosophes or Protestants, they passed as Catholics. Taken in by Jansenism's "appearance of moral severity, cultic purity, disciplinary reform, and dogmatic antiquity," adepts of this sect came to challenge first sacerdotal, then royal authority, thereby planting a "mine under the throne of France."[85] While the further evolution of the debate subordinated Jansenists to philosophes in the French counterrevolutionary rendition of this plot, the Jansenist in the role of chief plotter remained much more pronounced in the counterrevolutionary imagination in Italy than in France.[86]

Italian Jansenists did not readily recognize themselves in the role of proto-Jacobins. Had it not been they who had been the mainstays of secular authority and absolutism in late settecento Italy? Reading the *Nouvelles ecclésiastiques* with mixed chagrin and disbelief in Rome in 1791, Astorri could not "understand how the admirers of Arnauld, Nicole, etc. can accept the principles being erected about obedience and the nature and power of the authority of princes," thus lending credence to the thesis that Jansenists were just as subversive in the eighteenth century as Protestants had been in the sixteenth.[87] The most memorable Jansenist utterance to emerge from this Italian situation was Pietro Tamburini's *Lettere theologico-politiche sullo presente situazione della cosa ecclesiastica* (Theological-Political Letters on the Present-Day State of Ecclesiastical Matters), which, coming to the defense of secular authority, and Jansenism, against Spedalieri's *De' diritti dell'uomo* (On the Rights of Man), perforce also distanced itself from Gabriel-Nicolas Maultrot and the editors and authors of *Nouvelles ecclésiastiques*, who had

---

[85]*Dal "problema se i giansenisti siano giacobini"* (Rome: Luigi Perego Salvioni, 1794), as reprinted in Vittorio E. Giuntella, *Le dolci catene, testi della contro-rivoluzione cattolica in Italia* (Rome: Istituto per la Storia del Risorgimento Italiano, 1988), 298, 300, 306.

[86]For examples of Jansenism in French counterrevolutionary literature, see Emmanuel-Louis-Henri, comte d'Antraigues, *Dénonciation aux Français catholiques, des moyens employés par l'Assemblée nationale, pour détruire en France, la religion catholique* (London: Edward Pall-Mall, 1791), 5–6; and Joseph de Maistre, *De l'église gallicane dans son rapport avec le souverain pontif* (Lyon: J.-B. Pélagaud, 1862), 106–8.

[87]HUA, 215, Ms 3394–2, Astorri to Mouton, 13 July and 19 August 1791.

indeed put the absolutism of their seventeenth-century predecessors behind them. The situation was very particular, as Tamburini's colleague Zola apologetically explained in 1795 to the abbé Jean-Baptiste Mouton, who had become an editor of the *Nouvelles ecclésiastiques*.[88] But it was also general enough inasmuch as just about all Italian Jansenists reacted negatively to the Revolution, seeing Carlo di Gros as a divine punishment on a country that, "instead of profiting from the great lights that God had spread there for over a century... had visited persecution on those who had disseminated them."[89]

Occupation by French revolutionary armies forcefully imposed republics on Italy in which Jansenists, to the extent they were visible as a group, delineated a collective profile as defenders of a moderate constitutional and officially Catholic republicanism where religious dissent was accorded civil toleration but not rights to a public presence. That is to say that, minus the formally republican component, Italian Jansenists had found their way to positions not very far from their prerevolutionary French counterparts who had similarly come to stand for a kind of consultative constitutionalism in both church and state and a tie between the two that at least allowed for the rights of citizenship for religious dissenters.

If there was one aspect of the early French Revolution to which Italian Jansenists tended to react favorably, it was the Civil Constitution of the Clergy. Although promulgated by the French people as represented by the National Assembly over the obvious reservations of their king, the Civil Constitution bore a close enough resemblance to the antipapal legislation that Italian Jansenists had been supporting to receive their cautious approval. While worried about the French Revolution's reactionary effect on the project of absolutist ecclesiastical reform, Astorri as late as September 1791 called the papal examination of the Civil Constitution a farce, hoping that the French National Assembly would go as far as to secure the abolition of the Formulary. "If this moment escapes us it is not likely that another so propitious will come around again."[90] As in the offensive against the Jesuits by the parlements thirty years earlier, Italian Jansenists lifted their eyes beyond the Alps, hoping the National Assembly's ecclesiastical legislation would score the decisive blow against the papal curia.

FROM THE CIVIL CONSTITUTION TO THE CONCORDAT
Meanwhile, the abbé Clément had also been turning his eyes toward the Alps, but from the French side of them, hoping that Dupac's French translation of the Acts

---

[88]HUA, Ms 3606, fols. 30–32, Zola to Mouton, undated (but written in spring or late winter of 1794). On Tamburini's *Lettere teologico-politiche* as a defense of secular authority, see Luigi Salvatorelli, *Il pensiero politico italiano dal 1700 al 1870* (n.p.: Giulio Einaudi, 1949), 113–18.

[89]HUA, 215, Ms 3441, Di Gros to Mouton, 26 May 1791.

[90]HUA, Ms 3394–1, Astorri to Mouton, 22 September 1790.

of the Synod of Pistoia would inspire the National Assembly to sponsor similar reforms for the French Catholic Church, long convinced as he had been that the torch of truth had passed from France into the more enlightened monarchies of Italy and Spain.[91] That the National Assembly did no such thing is the understatement of the French Revolution. Jansenists were nonetheless conspicuous in the debates that led to what was called the Civil Constitution of the Clergy, which restored diocesan synods and subjected bishops to the advice of a council; instituted the consecration of bishops by their metropolitans and all but bypassed the papal curia; gave *curés* independence from bishops and subjected both to election by the people; and forbade the sorts of oaths and formulas that had tormented Jansenist consciences for more than a century.

The trouble was that, unlike the Synod of Pistoia, the National Assembly was not a church council despite some efforts to feature it as such by virtue of the presence of nearly three hundred clergymen in its midst. The National Assembly therefore imposed its reform on the Gallican Church in its purely secular capacity as a constituent power, without recourse to the spiritual power of the Catholic Church in conciliar or papal form. Hence the care taken by the National Assembly to make it clear that its reform was purely secular or civil, affecting only what was external about the church, leaving the substance of Catholic belief alone. While that line of argument bothered many French Jansenists more than it initially did Italian ones, the National Assembly derived it from a largely Jansenist body of jurisprudence previously used to justify the intervention of the Parlement of Paris in the controversy over the refusal of sacraments and in the suppression of the Jesuits: these secular initiatives either only implemented or enforced Gallican canon law or they concerned only the external aspects of church organization over which secular courts exercised a legitimate purview. As no one could make these arguments better than Jansenist jurists themselves, Jansenists again were among the Civil Constitution's most outspoken apologists, led by canon lawyer and Third-Estate deputy Armand-Gaston Camus.

If the National Assembly's reform of the Gallican Church had not gone beyond measures that bore the imprimatur of Christian antiquity or the Gallican past, these arguments would no doubt have been more persuasive and the issue of the National Assembly's authority in spiritual matters would never have provoked the crisis of conscience that it did. But a National Assembly that prided itself on breaking new ground was no more likely to content itself with hoary precedents in this than in any other domain, and in fact burdened its legislation with several provisions quite alien to any ecclesiastical past. For Catholic consciences, two such measures stood out like the planks of a cross: first, the unilateral reduction in

[91]HUA, Ms 3441, Clément to Mouton, 3 September 1790.

dioceses from about 135 to 82, thus severing the tie of more than fifty bishops from their former dioceses; and, second, the replacement of royal or other forms of nomination of clergy with popular election by active citizens in their purely secular capacity, depriving the clergy of any corporate role in its own recruitment. Combined with the National Assembly's abolition of the tithe, nationalization of church property, and refusal to allow the church any corporate identity beyond the diocesan level, these provisions had the effect of stripping the Gallican Church of all autonomy in relation to the state, as though in compensation for its almost complete independence from the papacy, and thereby seeming to vindicate Pius VI's harsh judgment of the Gallican liberties as the slavery of the French clergy to the state in lieu of obedience to the papacy.[92]

Not surprisingly, the National Assembly's ecclesiastical legislation confirmed the devout opinion's most apocalyptic prophecies of a coming godless revolution, and helped transform this Catholic counter-Enlightenment into a counterrevolution. In the Civil Constitution in particular, the devout imagination also saw the nightmare of Jansenist ecclesiology come true.[93] Nor is it surprising that this opposition to the Revolution came to include most bishops, stripped as they were by the Civil Constitution of much of their own jurisdiction. Initially finding its voice in the works of an abbé Augustin Barruel, a Jean-Baptiste Duvoisin, or a Capmartin de Chaupy, this religious right gave the counterrevolution a cause more exalted than the interested defense of aristocratic privilege or even royal prerogative. It also gave the cause of counterrevolution a full-blown ideology derived from the premise of the ultimate sovereignty of God.[94]

More surprising is that the Civil Constitution of the Clergy also split what remained of the French Jansenist community, the Catholic constituency most eager for ecclesiastical reform. While most Jansenists were able to set aside their qualms about the reduction of dioceses and mode of clerical election and defend the Ecclesiastical Committee's whole proposal as more beneficial than harmful, a hard core of critics led by the veterans Mey, Maultrot, and the abbé Henri Jabineau

---

[92]Words attributed to Pius VI by the Neapolitan diplomat L. A. Ferdinandi in correspondence with the archbishop of Utrecht in HUA, R86–1, Ms 65, Ferdinandi to van Niewenhuizen, 5 December 1779.

[93][Jacques-Julien Bonnaud], *Découverte importante sur le vrai système de la Constitution du clergé, décrétée par l'Assemblée nationale* (Paris, n.d.), 9–10. This pamphlet has also been attributed to the abbé Barruel.

[94]For example, Abbé Augustin Barruel, *Question nationale sur l'autorité et sur les droits du peuple dans le gouvernement, par M l'abbé Barruel* (Paris: Crapart, 1791); Bertrand Capmartin de Chaupy, *Philosophie des lettres qui auroit pu tout sauver. Misosophie: Votairienne qui n'a que tout perdre. Ouvrage inutile à la présente tenue des Etats, pour laquelle il avoit été entrepris, mais qui pourra servir à celle qui pourra lui succéder*, 2 vols. (Paris: J. Beuchot, 1789–90); and Jean-Baptiste Duvoisin, *La France chrétienne et vraiment libre* (n.p., 1789). On the formation of this religious right, see J. M. Roberts, "The French Origins of the 'Right,'" *Transactions from the Royal Historical Society* 23 (1973): 27–53.

took the field against these measures, pointing to their clear lack of canonical precedents and announcing them as unacceptable so long as they remained unsanc-
tioned by the spiritual power deliberating as a Gallican National Council. In
taking this position, they laid bare and widened the issue of lay versus ecclesiastical authority, or of judicial versus conciliar constitutionalism, that had run like a
fault line through Jansenist political and ecclesiological thought throughout the
whole eighteenth century.[95] They also made it clear that part of the issue was the
absolutist quality of the National Assembly's ecclesiastical legislation.

For what was objectionable to the majority of the National Assembly about
the prospect of a church council deliberating on the merits of its ecclesiastical legislation was not necessarily that such a council represented the church, but that it
represented anything other than the nation, thus dividing the sovereignty that
Jean Bodin had taught them was indivisible. Presiding over the National Assembly's abolition of the church's corporate property, separate organization, and general assemblies was the same bias against all partial associations that caused it to
abolish separate orders, privileged provinces, municipal guilds, and to disallow
workers' associations, a bias arguably inherited from the ideology of absolutism.
Although judicial Jansenists like Camus proved willing to extend the logic of
ancien régime argumentation to defend this aspect of the Civil Constitution, it is
most improbable that they would ever have eliminated the independence of the
church so totally had they been left to their own devices. Although there is nothing specifically anticlerical much less anti-Catholic about this bias, it was in fact
those deputies most marked by the century's philosophic spirit who, at crucial
points in the debate, most strongly brought this absolutist logic to bear. Arguing
against giving the clergy any separate voice in the election of its own ranks,
Robespierre held that to do so was "to reconstitute a solitary corps."[96]

So it is perhaps not accidental that the Jansenists most adamant in opposing
this absolutist aspect of the National Assembly's ecclesiastical legislation had also
been among those first in the field with a thesis of national sovereignty in opposition to royal absolutism before the onset of the Revolution. Published as early as
1775 as an addition to his and Mey's monumental *Maximes du droit public
françois*, Maultrot's *Dissertation sur le droit de convoquer les Etats généraux* (Dissertation on the Right to Convoke the Estates General) circulated separately as
one of the more politically radical pamphlets in 1787, while his three-volume
Origines et justes bornes de la puissance temporelle (Origins and Rightful Limits of

---

[95]See Monique Cottret, "Les jansénistes juges de Jean-Jacques," in *Jansénisme et Révolution*, 81–
102; and Yann Fauchois, "Les jansénistes et la Constitution civile du clergé: Aux marges du débat,
débats dans le débat," in *Jansénisme et Révolution*, 195–209.

[96]*Archives parlementaires de 1787–1860, première partie (1787–1799)*, 94 vols., ed. M.-J. Madival
and M.-E. Laurent (Paris, 1867–), 9 June 1790, 16:154–56.

Temporal Authority), published in 1789, was a target of Tamburini's apology for enlightened absolutism in an Italian context in 1794.[97]

It was this absolutist aspect of revolutionary ideology that prevented the National Assembly from playing the conciliar card: of allowing the Gallican Clergy to be Gallican enough to convene in a national council to deliberate on the Civil Constitution of the Clergy. This denial is tragic not only because it split the core constituency in favor of radical ecclesiastical reform, but because it also split Gallican sentiment as a whole, dividing it into its political and ecclesiastical halves. This painful choice was imposed upon the Gallican episcopacy at a time when, with the Jansenist controversy largely behind it, the Gallican cause had begun to lose its association with heresy, arguably making the episcopacy more Gallican than at any point in the eighteenth century since the advent of *Unigenitus*. Speaking for his fellow bishops, Boisgelin de Cucé, archbishop of Aix, virtually offered clergy's acceptance of the Civil Constitution to the National Assembly on 29 May, new dioceses, lay elections, and all, if only the Gallican Clergy were allowed to convene itself as a national church council in order to formalize its acceptance.[98]

By splitting the Gallican community, this denial of a national council also split whatever France had by way of a Catholic Enlightenment. For in sharp contrast to what happened in Italy where the suppression of the Jesuits had ended the Catholic Enlightenment, in France it had made one possible. While in Italy the import of Gallican ecclesiology had envenomed the doctrinal debate, in France it was the diminution of the theological controversy that tamed Gallicanism and made it available for other causes. Wedded to Jansenism ever since the appeal of *Unigenitus* to a general council, Gallicanism had to transcend that exclusive association before being able to become an essential element in the creation of a uniquely French Catholic Enlightenment. During the ancien régime's last decades, future patriotic priests like Claude Fauchet, Adrien Lamourette, and Henri Grégoire were able to put together the political theologies representing such a synthesis, which enabled them to travel so many miles with the Revolution.[99]

The result of the refusal to exercise the conciliar option was ironically to make the approval or disapproval of these communities dependent on the decision of the

---

[97]Gabriel-Nicolas Maultrot, *Origines et justes bornes de la puissance temporelle suivant les livres saints et la tradition sainte*, 3 vols. (Paris: Le Clère, 1789). On the *Dissertation sur le droit de convoquer les Etats-Généraux, tirée des capitulaires, des ordonnances, et les autres monumens de l'histoire de France* (n.p., 1787), see Dale Van Kley, "The Estates General as Ecumenical Council: The Constitutionalism of Corporate Consensus and the Parlement's Ruling of September 25, 1788," *Journal of Modern History* 61 (March 1989): 1–52.

[98]On Le Clerc de Juigné, see *Archives parlementaires* (10 August 1789), 8:394. On Boisgelin, 29 May 1790, see ibid., 15:724–31.

[99]See Rita Hermon-Belot, *L'abbé Grégoire: La politique et la vérité* (Paris: Seuil, 2000), 63–129, 183–226.

international Catholic Church in the only form in which it then existed, namely the papal curia. The threat of papal disapproval threw many Catholic communities into the curial camp, thereby disrupting the formation of a clear Gallican-ultramontane or reformist-traditionalist division that might have reinforced the identity of the constitutional church as a national church and an ally of the Revolution. Since the crisis of conscience posed by papal disapproval in the absence of conciliar approval was far from unique to the episcopacy or monastic clergy, the resultant schism also prevented a clear hierarchical split between privileged and unprivileged clergy that might have diluted the Revolution's anticlericalism in the larger pool of hostility to privilege and aristocracy. Clerical opposition to the Revolution was hence representative enough of the clergy as a whole to make the whole clergy into targets of revolutionary anticlericalism. These targets soon came to include the constitutional clergy as well, which, being more vulnerable precisely because more visible, bore the brunt of the revolutionary hostility to the clergy provoked by the refractory clergy's contribution to the counterrevolution.[100]

Whether without these circumstances the French Enlightenment's peculiar distillation of militant anti-Catholicism would have come to play the spectacular role in the Revolution that it did is open to question. Suggesting that it would not have is the evidence of the *cahiers de doléances*, which called for the reform but certainly not the destruction of the Gallican Church as a corps, or even the much more radical prerevolutionary literature where pamphlets written in the vulgar Voltairian mode surface as no more than trace elements in the whole.[101] What was quite predictable from either source is that the monastic clergy might very well be eliminated, that the parish clergy would improve their status in relation to the regular clergy and their bishops, even that the clergy as a whole might lose its status as a privileged constitutional order and a good deal of its wealth, but not that Catholicism itself would come under attack. Pointing in the opposite direction is the growing polarization between the cause of religion championed by a proto-right and the cause of an anti-Catholic philosophy on the left visible in a sizable body of literature, as well as evidence of popular hostility to the clergy as a whole in the cities, particularly Paris.[102] Paris witnessed a full-scale anticlerical

[100]Michel Vovelle, *La Révolution contre l'église: De la raison à l'Etre suprême* (Paris: Editions complexes, 1988), esp. 101–54.

[101]On the unanticipated novelty of the provisions of the Civil Constitution, see Timothy Tackett, *Religion, Revolution, and Regional Culture in Eighteenth-Century France: The Ecclesiastical Oath of 1791* (Princeton: Princeton University Press, 1986), 6–16; and Dale K. Van Kley, "The Debate over the Gallican Clergy on the Eve of the French Revolution: A Supplementary Introduction to Section III of the Pre-Revolutionary Debate," in *The Pre-Revolutionary Debate*, ed. Jeremy Popkin and Dale Van Kley, The French Revolution Research Collection 5, ed. Colin Lucas (Oxford: Pergamon Press, 1989), 19–22.

[102]See McMahon, "Enemies of Enlightenment," esp. ch. 1.

riot on 29–30 September in the wake of a *curé's* reluctance to bury the body of a journeyman carpenter for less than twenty-three *livres*. Since the parishes where the riot took place had been ones repeatedly purged of their clergy and traumatized by public refusals of sacraments in the course of the Jansenist controversy, this evidence suggests the role of this controversy in the popular anticlericalism where Jansenism had put down roots.[103]

But whatever the potential for something like revolutionary dechristianization in 1789, it was certainly increased by the Civil Constitution of the Clergy which, by alienating and ultramontanizing half the clergy, placed the remaining clergy in the cross fire between counterrevolutionary right and revolutionary left. Once the Catholic clergy as a whole had become a symbol of counterrevolution, revolutionaries were bound to have recourse to the heaviest anticlerical artillery available.[104] Hence the Revolution's campaign against Catholicism stretching from the beginnings of dechristianization in the fall of 1793 to the directorial Terror following the coup of 18–19 Fructidor 1797, a campaign that put a permanent rift between the republican principle and Catholicism well into the twentieth century. Nor were the consequences confined to France alone, since French revolutionary armies and the Convention's "representatives on mission" crossed French borders into the Austrian Netherlands, the Catholic Germanies, and of course Northern Italy, bringing parts of the Revolution's ecclesiastical legislation with them. Thus did France impose its divisions on the rest of Europe a second time, replacing the rift between Jansenism and Jesuitism with that of Catholic conservatism and militant unbelief, as the Revolution spawned imitators on the one hand while reform-minded Catholics and Jansenists found themselves labeled as Jacobins by conservative *zelanti* on the other.

A last chance for a more complicated and Catholic outcome to a century of Enlightenment came in the form of the remnants of the constitutional church that had survived the Terror and regrouped under the leadership of the abbé Henri Grégoire, constitutional bishop of Blois and deputy to the Convention and then to the Council of 500 until Bonaparte dismissed it in 1799.[105] Formally cut off from all state support by the Convention on 18 September 1794—a measure that only legalized a situation that had existed since 1793—this church at least regained a

---

[103]Siméon-Prosper Hardy, "Mes loisirs, ou Journal d'événemens tels qu'ils parviennent à ma connoissance," 8 vols., Bibliothèque Nationale (BN), Nouvelles acquisitions (henceforth Nouv. Acq.), Manuscrits Français (Mss Fr) 6687 (29–30 September 1789), 493–94, 497. The parishes in question are Saint-Jacques de la Boucherie and Saint-Nicolas-des-Champs.

[104]See Claude Langlois, "La rupture entre l'Eglise catholique et la Révolution," in *The Transformation of Political Culture, 1789–1848*, ed. François Furet and Mona Ozouf, The French Revolution and the Creation of Modern Political Culture 3 (Oxford: Pergamon Press, 1989), 375–90.

[105]The most authoritative history of this final phase of the constitutional church's history is Rodney Dean, *L'Eglise Constitutionnelle, Napoléon et le Concordat de 1801* (Paris: R. J. Dean, 2004).

small margin for maneuver after Grégoire, exploiting his access to the national podium and invoking the principle of religious toleration, called for the liberty of worship in a speech drowned out by the cries of still hostile colleagues on 21 December 1794.[106] The Convention did not remain indefinitely insensitive to the current of opinion released by the printed distribution of Grégoire's speech, and responded with decrees that, tantamount to the formal separation of church and state, declared that the freedom to worship might "not be disturbed" and even allowed for the limited use of nationalized church buildings.[107] Using this opening to good advantage, a small group of united bishops—Grégoire and four other formerly constitutional bishops in Paris—took it upon themselves to address an encyclical letter to the remaining bishops and vacant churches, beginning the task of reconstituting what remained of the constitutional church and giving it a new reason for existence.[108]

The task was staggering. As it emerged from the trial of the Terror, this church counted at most twenty active bishops of its original contingent of eighty-two, the others having died natural deaths, perished during the Terror, or in one way or another renounced their episcopate whether from fatigue or under pressure from the Terror. The percentage of survivors from the priesthood was no better and possibly worse, for the same reasons. Whole dioceses, even areas, found themselves with virtually no constitutional clergy.[109] This vacuum was easily occupied by the refractory clergy, which, in circumstances not entirely dissimilar to those in the Netherlands in the first quarter of the century, was better able to take advantage of the regime of semiliberty after 1795 than was the constitutional clergy and may have won a majority of Catholics to its side by the time of the Napoleonic Concordat of 1801. While the refractory clergy may have also been the preferred target of state-sponsored persecution because of its continued reluctance to swear loyalty to a republican government, the constitutional clergy hardly benefited from the protection of a regime that remained hostile to Catholicism, and it remained bedeviled by Pius VI's condemnation of the constitution of 1791 and their oaths of loyalty to it.

So just as the Provincial Council of Utrecht had proclaimed the duty of obedience to temporal authorities including the Protestant republic that allowed it to convene, so too did this Gallican Church—as the constitutional church rechristened itself in 1795—declare its "entire submission to the laws of the [Directorial

[106]Henri Grégoire, *Discours de Grégoire à la Convention sur la liberté des cultes*, in Augustin Gazier, *Etudes sur l'histoire religieuse de la Révolution française, d'après des documents originaux et inédits* (Paris: Armand Colin, 1887), 346–47.

[107]Joseph Lacouture, *La politique religieuse de la Révolution* (Paris: Picard, 1940), 106–8.

[108]"Lettre encyclique de plusieurs évêques de France à leurs frères les autres évêques et aux églises vacantes," in Gazier, *Etudes sur l'histoire religieuse*, 390–411.

[109]John McManners, *The French Revolution and the Church* (New York: Harper & Row, 1969), 121.

French] republic" as soon as it convened in a national council with that government's permission on 14 August 1797,[110] a gesture reiterated by swearing the oath of "hatred for royalty and anarchy" imposed on all Catholic clerics in the wake of the Directory's antiroyal and anticlerical coup d'état of 18–19 Fructidor just a few weeks later.[111] This declaration represented the Gallican Church's dogged commitment to the principle of obedience to secular authority, that is, to the first or royal of the four Gallican articles of 1682, which it regarded as "founded on the holy canons and the tradition of the [church] fathers."[112] Obedience to secular authority in all matters within its temporal competence was of course this clergy's foundational act in the form of its constitutional oath of 1791, a stance that also continued to distinguish that clergy from the refractory priests who challenged the legitimacy of the republic and much that it had done.

In contrast to its stand of 1791, but like the Church of Utrecht, this church's self-proclaimed Gallicanism finally included a real commitment to the conciliar tenets of the Gallican tradition, convening two national councils in the space of its short six-year life. The first of these councils in 1797 took advantage of the abrogation of the Civil Constitution of the Clergy to create deliberative and electoral procedures and structures at every level of the clerical hierarchy through a nexus of metropolitan councils, diocesan presbyteries, diocesan and rural synods, and ecclesiastical conferences that required collegial consultation and bound bishops to the counsel of their parish clergy and both to election by a combination of clergy and laity.[113] With Utrecht's pending appeal to a general council in mind, the same council submitted its case to the "legal and canonical judgment of the universal church" in the form of an ecumenical council if the pope consented to convene it or in the form of other national churches and Catholic universities if he refused.[114] As in the case of Utrecht, but more explicitly so, this conciliar stance and structure

[110]See René Taveneaux, "Les anciens constitutionnels et l'église d'Utrecht: À propos de quelques inédits d'Henri Grégoire et de Joseph Monin," in *Jansénisme et réforme catholique* (Nancy: Presses Universitaires de Nancy, 1993), 177–93.

[111]"Recueil des délibérations du Concile national du clergé de France en 1797," in BN, Nouv. acq., Mss Fr. 2779, sessions on 14 August and 7 September, fols. 8–12, 34–35.

[112]*Decret de pacification proclamé par le Concile national de France, dans l'église métropolitaine de Notre Dame de Paris, le dimanche 24 septembre 1797*, in *Collection des pièces imprimées par ordre du Concile national de France* (Paris: Imprimerie-Librairie Chrétienne, 1797), no. 5, p. 14.

[113]*Decret du Concile national de France [de 1797] sur les élections* in *Collection des pièces*, no. 15; and *Seconde lettre encyclique de plusieurs évêques de France, réunis à Paris, à leurs frères les autres évêques et aux églises veuves, concernant un règlement pour servir au rétablissement de la discipline de l'église gallicane* (Paris: Imprimerie-Librairie Chrétienne, 1795), 64–120. See also Bernard Plongeron, *L'abbé Grégoire ou L'arche de la fraternité, 1750–1831* (Paris: Letouzey et Ané, 1989), 73–78.

[114]*Quatrième lettre syndique du Concile national de France, aux pasteurs et aux fidèles, pour leur annoncer la fin de sa session* (Paris: Imprimerie-Librairie Chrétienne, 1797), in *Collection des pièces*, no. 12, p. 8; and *L'église gallicane, assemblée en concile national à Paris, à Sa Sainteté le pape Pie VI*, in *Collection des pièces*, no. 13, pp. 10–11.

Portrait of Henri Grégoire, from the *Mémoires de Grégoire:.Ancien évêque de Blois* (Paris: J. Yonet, 1840). Reprinted with the kind permission of the Cornell University Library, Rare Book and Manuscript Division.

also enabled the Gallican Church's first National Council of 1797 to be Catholic in spite of its rupture with the papacy because, while confessing with the same formula as Utrecht's Provincial Council that the pope was "by divine right the ministerial and visible head of the universal church" enjoying a "primacy of honor and jurisdiction," the United Bishops' *Seconde lettre encyclique* (Second Encyclical Letter) convoking this council also specified that "he would exceed the powers given to the first of the Apostles of whom he is the successor were he to arrogate to himself an authority superior or even equal to the Church's, and were he to govern without the concourse of other bishops." This was enough to enable this church to reject Pius VI's condemnations of the Civil Constitution as a "usurpation violating the rights and majesty of the universal church," seeing that "it was in the power of no church, not even of Rome, either to separate another church from universal communion or to declare it schismatic short of a declaration of separation by that church itself or unless it were summoned, heard, and judged following canonical forms."[115] Placing the onus of schism on their enemies, the delegates of the National Council of 1801 challenged the ultramontanist dissidents to show them "a single error proscribed by that same church to which we do not say anathema."[116]

Still, lack of legitimation as a Catholic Church by the papacy made it imperative for the Gallican Church to replace it, as had Utrecht, in the form of public testimonies to its Catholicity from as many other Catholic churches as possible. The subject of such relations with other churches already occupied pride of place in Grégoire's report to the National Council of 1797 on the work of the "united bishops," and this council wasted no time in imitating the Provincial Council of Utrecht by addressing its decrees to as many foreign churches as would receive them as well as by establishing a bureau of international correspondence, which was really an extension of Grégoire's own.[117] Although Grégoire bore the burden of this correspondence, the aged abbé Clément remained on duty at the crossroads of the Jansenist International and most certainly rerouted its traffic to take in Grégoire, whose epistolary traces first show up in Utrecht in 1795.[118] In using this correspondence to elicit letters of communion, Grégoire was most successful in Italy, which sent the only genuine foreign delegates to the National Council of 1801 in the persons of Giovanni Francesco Bergancini and Eustachio Degola

---

[115]*Décret de pacification*, in *Collection des pièces*, no. 5, 2–13, 18; and *Seconde lettre encyclique*, 19, 24.

[116]"Lettre synodique au clergé incommuniquant," in *Actes du second concile national de France, tenu l'an 1801 de J[ésus] C[hrist] (an 9 de la République française) dans l'église métropolitaine de Paris* (Paris: Imprimerie Chrétienne, 1801), 1:241.

[117]"Recueil des délibérations," BN, Nouv. acq., Mss Fr 2779, sessions of 17 and 19 August, 16 September, and 2 and 24 October 1797, fols. 20–21, 40–41, 60–61, 83.

[118]HUA, 215, Ms 3458, Grégoire to Mouton, 23 Frimaire IV (1795).

from Casal and Genoa.[119] To veterans of the Italian Jansenist International, the sight of these quasi-independent Gallican councils stirred all but extinguished ashes of hope for one last time. "The National Council of France now interests me for the sake of the church," wrote Pujati to Mouton in Utrecht of the first of these councils in 1798. "While the French [armies] are now taking away [territory] from Rome that their ancestors once gave her, perhaps God can yet reform the church in head and members by means of a French clergy that the supercilious Romans regard as schismatic."[120]

Reliance on the Jansenist International and relative independence from the state gave the post-Thermidorian constitutional church a somewhat more Jansenist cast than was the case at its beginning in 1790.[121] The overwhelming bulk of lay donations for the support of the impoverished delegates to the National Council of 1797 meeting in Paris came from the traditionally most Jansenist parishes of Paris, with Saint-Médard in the lead followed by Saint-Etienne-du-Mont and Saint-André-des-Arts.[122] Among bishops, such Jansenists as Clément and Jean-Baptiste Saurine were more influential in the leadership of the church than before, as were Paul Baillet and Paul Brugière among priests and Pierre-Jean Agier and Charles-Jacques Saillant among lay consultants. Although he had not clearly been a Jansenist in a strictly theological sense before 1795, Grégoire himself became more of one after that date. He penned the first edition of his *Ruines de Port-Royal* (*The Ruins of Port-Royal*) in 1801. As one of the founders of the Gallican Church's periodical mouthpiece, the *Annales de la religion*, Grégoire availed himself of the editorial assistance of Jansenists Noël de Larrière and Guénin de Saint-Marc, also the principal editor of the *Nouvelles ecclésiastiques*.[123] If neither of the councils produced an Augustinian doctrinal statement comparable to that of Utrecht in 1763 and or the Synod of Pistoia in 1786, this was not for want of good intentions, as the abbé Clément drafted a statement of doctrine condemning such post-Tridentine errors as Molinism and ultramontanism, and had submitted his report to the Council of 1801 on 4 July, a month or so before it came to a premature conclusion at Bonaparte's command.[124]

[119]BPR, Collection Grégoire (GR), correspondance étrangère, bishop of Noli to Grégoire, 22 Dec. 1800; and *Actes du second concile national de France*, 3:21–54.

[120]HUA, 215, Ms 3546, Pujati to Mouton, 23 February 1798.

[121]Hermon-Belot, *L'abbé Grégoire*, 427–61.

[122]A summary count based on the manuscript *procès-verbal* of the National Council of 1797, "Recueil des délibérations," BN, Mss Fr, 2779, sessions of 5, 11, 13, 18, 22, and 29 September; 3, 5, 8, 10, 20, and 23 October; and 11 November.

[123]Maire, *De la cause de Dieu à la cause de la nation*, 577.

[124]*Recherches historiques et dogmatiques, de ce qui a interessé la doctrine chrétienne depuis le Concile de Trente*, in BPR, RV 108–38 (8292), no. 23, 3–21, a doctrinal statement repeated in Clément's published *Lettre de M. l'évêque de Versailles à S. S. le Pape Pie VII* (n.p., 1801) in BPR, RV 108–38

This short-lived Gallican Church can no more be simply categorized as Jansenist than its two councils as simple replays of the provincial council of Utrecht or the Synod of Pistoia. To be sure, the Gallican church fathers were well aware of the precedents of 1763 and 1786, to which Grégoire referred in his inaugural address to the second National Council of Paris in 1801.[125] But while Utrecht and Pistoia had opposed a factitious unanimity to papal infallibility, the two councils of Paris, with the legislative experience of the whole French Revolution behind them, shelved the desideratum of moral unanimity each time it was invoked, contenting themselves with simple majorities and making no effort to conceal the extent or subject of the divisions in their ranks. The council of 1797 featured spirited debates on the use of vernacular languages in the liturgy, the relation of the civil contract to the sacrament in marriage, and the respective roles of the laity and clergy in the election of the clergy. The large number of cures delegated by the presbyteries of vacant dioceses outnumbering the bishops in both national councils (in 1797, by as many as fifty-seven to thirty-one) produced procedural tensions that erupted in a battle in the Council of 1801 between the bishops of Auch and Saint-Claude on the one hand, partisans of a purely episcopal Gallicanism, and on the other hand the cures François Detorcy and Augustin Frappier—the latter a veteran signer of circular letters of communion to Utrecht—who defended the rights of cures as voting members along with bishops in national and general councils. In this debate delegates heard the names of Maultrot and Mey not only reverentially cited but also vitriolically taken in vain.[126] While Jansenism clearly related to such projects as the purification of Roman ritual, the vernacular translation of the scriptures and liturgy, the campaign against the "ignorant piety of scapulars and rosaries," and ecumenical conversation with Protestant and Orthodox churches (all initiatives undertaken by the two national councils), these were causes that also linked the Gallican Church to projects of the Catholic Enlightenment of the earlier eighteenth century.[127]

(8292), no. 38, 1–11. For its place on the agenda of the Council of 1801, see the Actes du second concile national de France, tenu en 1801, 1:68, 463.

[125]Henri Grégoire, "Discours pour l'ouverture du concile," in Actes du second Concile national de France, tenu l'an 1801, 1:130–31.

[126]On the mode of election, see "Recueil des délibérations," BN, Mss Fr 2779, sessions of 25, 27, 28, and 29 September. On the liturgy, see sessions of 2, 6, 7, 8, and 9 November. For the debate between proponents of episcopal and parochial Gallicanism, see Actes du second concile national de France, tenu l'an 1801, 1: 161–425.

[127]See Grégoire, Réclamation des fidèles Catholiques de France au prochain concile national, en faveur de l'usage primitif de la langue vulgaire dans l'administration des sacrements et la célébration de l'office divine (Paris: Brajeux, 1801); Traité de l'uniformité et de l'amélioration de la liturgie, présenté au concile national de 1801 par le citoyen Grégoire (Paris: Imprimerie-Librairie, an X), 67, 102–21; and Compte rendu par le citoyen Grégoire au concile national, des travaux des évêques réunis à Paris (Paris: Imprimerie-Librairie Chrétienne, 1797), 65.

Here, in these two councils in Paris, all the conciliar possibilities of eighteenth-century European Catholicism were finally if only fleetingly realized: a conciliar Catholic church enjoying a modicum of independence from a constitutional state that, since the extension of French borders since 1794, intermittently included both Utrecht and Pistoia. Indelibly associated with Jansenism throughout the century, the conciliar cause here also had a prospect of including Jansenism without being dominated by it, and of acquiring a momentum of its own.

From the perspective of the Directorial Republic of 1795–99, it would seem to have made good sense to maintain toward this church a policy of benevolent neutrality. After all, the Gallican Church was republican both in its internal structure and external stance toward the state, going well beyond Utrecht's acceptance of the Dutch Republic's legitimate authority as a temporal state by proclaiming in the Council of 1797 that "republican government is that which most closely conforms to the principles of the gospel," founded as it was on principles recalling "the very order that Jesus Christ came to restore on earth."[128] It appears that Grégoire sincerely accepted the principle of separation from the state and the freedom of religion it entailed, even if nobody in the constitutional clergy entirely broke with the notion of Christendom and separation was seen as a means for the revival of Catholicism in France.[129] The capacity of this church to survive under a republic was assured by the existence of enough Frenchmen who wished "to be republicans while never ceasing to be Christians," in the words of a petition sent by communes in the Drôme to the Convention just as dechristianization was getting under way in 1793.[130] All the Gallican Church asked of the state was to be spared the obligation of active compliance with laws that tormented Catholic consciences, such as the *décadi*, and an end to persecution.

That is what it never obtained from the Directorial Republic. Indeed, the persecution that befell the Gallican clergy after the coup of 18–19 Fructidor by reason of noncompliance in the enforcement of the *décadi* was more purely governmental than that of the dechristianization of the year II and the Terror. The government's conceptual incapacity to come to terms with the postconstitutional church ought to be seen as one of the causes of its failure, along with its inability to put up with the results of its own elections or the formation of political parties.[131]

---

[128]*Lettre syndique du Concile national de France, aux pasteurs et aux fidèles, sur les moyens de rétablir la paix religieuse*, in *Collection des pièces*, no. 6, 12. See also *Actes du second concile national de France, tenu l'an 1801*, 2:283–84.

[129]Bernard Plongeron, *Théologie et politique au siècle des lumières, 1770–1820* (Geneva: Droz, 1973), 149–82.

[130]BPR, RV 35. See also Suzanne Desan, *Reclaiming the Sacred: Lay Religion and Popular Politics in Revolutionary France* (Ithaca: Cornell University Press, 1990), 135–58. For a recent example of a hostile treatment of the postconstitutionalist church as non-Catholic, see Jean de La Viguerie, *Christianisme et révolution: Cinq leçons d'histoire de la Révolution française* (Paris: Nel, 1986), 197–203.

[131]Lynn Hunt, David Lansky, and Paul Hanson, "The Failure of the Liberal Republic in France,

Only after Napoleon Bonaparte's coup d'état of 18–19 Brumaire and the formation of the consulate did this church enjoy a reprieve from persecution, holding the Council of 1801 with the government's permission. "At the epoch in question, that is to say in 1800 or 1801," wrote Grégoire eight years later, "nothing was easier than to maintain this constitutional clergy in place."[132] It is plausible to imagine this church continuing to exist and negotiating with the papacy and refractory clergy, even if the schism had never come to an end and the republic, as in the Netherlands, had had to contend with two Catholic churches instead of one. To the formerly refractory clergy, the two national councils proposed conciliatory conferences and offered bishoprics and even mass resignations in their favor on condition of their accepting the republican government and the formerly constitutional clergy as Catholic. To these overtures the refractory clergy responded with hostile pamphlets and often baptizing and remarrying the constitutional clergy's former parishioners, something that the Catholic Church had not even demanded of converted Protestants in the worst days of the Wars of Religion. Still, it is possible to imagine the refractory clergy settling down, becoming a missionary clergy under the authority of the papacy, and even accepting the republic, as Pius VI himself finally recommended that they do in the brief *Pastoralis Sollicitudo* issued in 1796.[133]

Vis-à-vis the papacy, the Gallican Church would at the minimum have held out for what it considered the canonical mode of election of the clergy by clergy and laity, for the right of metropolitan bishops to confirm their newly elected suffragans, and for the right of both the clergy and the government to approve or reject new papal bulls and briefs.[134] It is of course unlikely that the Gallican Church would have obtained these conditions even with the support of the government, whereupon it would have probably convened the general council that the second National Council in 1801 had included in its agenda.[135] As late as April 1802, just as the provisions of the Napoleonic concordat were being revealed, one of Ricci's old allies, Bishop Pannili of Chiusi and Pienza in Tuscany, still dared to nurture the "hope … that this quarrel [between the Gallican Church and the papacy] would

---

1795–1799: The Road to Brumaire," *Journal of Modern History* 51 (Dec. 1979): 734–59.

[132]Henri Grégoire, *Mémoires de Grégoire, ancien évêque de Blois, député à l'Assemblée Constituente et à la Convention Nationale, Sénateur, membre de l'Institut, suivies de la Notice historique sur Grégoire d'Hippolyte Carnot*, ed. Jean-Michel Leniaud (Paris: Editions de Santé, 1989), 155.

[133]The reference is to Pius VI's brief, *Pastoralis Sollicitudo*, on which subject, see Plongeron, *Théologie et politique au siècle des lumières*, 131–32, 141–42. La Viguerie, in *Christianisme et révolution*, 200, persists in raising the question of its authenticity.

[134]BPR, GR, Ms 2405, doc. 9, "Observations au citoyen consul," 28 August 1801, by Le Coz, bishop of Rennes; Dufraisse, bishop of Bourges; Grégoire; Moyse, bishop of Saint-Claude; and Perier, bishop of Clermont.

[135]*Actes du second Concile national de France, tenu l'an 1801*, session of 7 August, 2:471.

create the need for a general council in which, besides this affair, other matters would be resolved, such as the recognition of our union with Utrecht ... as well as the annulment of the bull [*Unigenitus*] that serves as such an obstacle for the weak-minded, persuading them to condemn precious propositions from the sacred scriptures and holy fathers." But failing this council, he hoped that a Bonaparte advised by Grégoire would insist on "at least a little compassion for the poor Utrechters and get the four Gallican articles recognized by all...as Catholic not only in France but by the whole church."[136]

But all that supposed the continued existence of the French Republic whereas Napoleon's concordat with the papacy, which put an end to the Gallican Church, was already negotiated as though by a monarchy. That Napoleon Bonaparte was more of a *philosophe* than a Catholic was already evident in 1801, but what was perhaps not understood by most of the Gallican clergy in 1801 was that he was not a very fervent republican either. Arguably, he was a better Catholic than he was a republican because he at least appreciated the force of a hierarchical and authoritarian ecclesiastical structure that commanded obedience, and which, if he could control it, would enable him better to command in France. Years later, while on visit to Holland, he spoke disparagingly of the so-called archbishop of Utrecht and the so-called bishops of Deventer and Haarlem.[137]

Negotiated on high and above the heads of all concerned, the concordat gave Bonaparte the power enjoyed by kings to nominate all of France's bishops while his unilaterally added organic articles gave these bishops a power never enjoyed by their predecessors: that of naming their parish *curés*. The only Gallican feature of these provisions was of state control of the church: the papal acceptance of the Revolution's nationalization of church property, the inclusion of twelve formerly constitutional bishops in the new episcopacy, and of course the state's right to inspect and reject all papal bulls and briefs destined for France. So the concordat made short shrift of the Gallican Church's experimentation with synods, presbyteries, metropolitan and national councils—and with them, a half century's hopes for conciliar ecclesiastical reform and the limited independence that formal separation from the state had finally promised. Such liberties as were to be had vis-à-vis the state could therefore only be sought by means of the total sacrifice of the Gallican liberties in relation to the papacy, whose power over the Gallican clergy the concordat enormously enhanced. Not only did the papacy regain the power to consecrate bishops at the expense of their immediate metropolitan superiors, but it was by virtue of papal authority that the entire episcopacy was abolished and

---

[136]BPR, GR, Correspondance étrangère, Italy I, Pannili to Degola, 1 April 1802.
[137]L. J. Rogier, "Henri Grégoire en de Katholieken van Nederland," in *Terugblik en Uitzicht: Verspreide Opstellen van L. J. Rogier* (Hilversum and Anterwerp: Paul Bland, 1964), 1:198–99.

reconstituted *de novo*. In order to effect this canonical revolution, the pope obtained the resignations of just about all the formerly constitutional bishops and most of the formerly refractory ones, dismissing the thirty who resisted. Those formerly constitutional bishops who were reappointed squared this unprecedented procedure with their Gallican consciences by submitting their resignations in what they deemed a canonical way, most of them to their metropolitans, and by signing a letter to the papacy that fell short of retracting their oath to the Civil Constitution. But they were joined by formerly refractory bishops who, armed with papal briefs, were soon demanding such retractions from the *curés* who fell under their authority.

Neither the influence of the formerly refractory clergy in the Gallican Church nor the future increase in papal power were widely foreseen in 1801, and Grégoire could legitimately congratulate himself in negotiating a discharge for the constitutional clergy far more honorable than it would have obtained from a Bonaparte left to his own authoritarian instincts. Yet the long-term implications of the concordat did not go unperceived by worldly-wise Italians or a seasoned observer of curial diplomacy like the abbé Clément, who excoriated the concordat even before he knew its chief provisions.[138] Getting wind of the concordat's chief provisions, Vincenzo Palmieri wrote to Degola from Genoa in August 1801 that although the plan of resignations by both clergies "did not displease" him, he would have liked to see it paired with "an authentic and solemn act acknowledging the reason and zeal of the constitutional bishops." Otherwise, he warned, the papal briefs against the constitutional clergy of 1791 and the bull *Auctorem Fidei* condemning the Synod of Pistoia of 1794 were so many means for the papacy to validate its interpretation of events in due course.[139] Degola, who attended the Second National Council, was even more prescient, warning the council on 15 July 1801 that any mass resignations of the constitutional clergy would mean "the most complete victory of ultramontane maxims."[140]

Thus ended a half-century's efforts to reform the Catholic Church. Whether it be called reform Catholicism, enlightened Catholicism, or Jansenism, the general drift of these efforts tended toward a more deliberative and decentralized ecclesiastical structure better able to accommodate national liturgical differences and forms of lay initiative as well as a church more open to renewed conversation with Protestants and Orthodox and some of the coming century's profounder movements, most notably the people's political coming-of-age. The greatest risk

[138]HUA, 215, Ms 3441, letters from Clément to Mouton from 28 September 1801 to 31 January 1803.

[139]BPR, GR, Correspondance étrangère, lettres rendues par Mlle Pernaud le 16 février 1950, Palmieri to Degola, 10 August 1801.

[140]*Actes du second concile national de France, tenu l'an 1801*, 2:87.

in attempting to dismantle papal centralization was of course the division of the Catholic Church into so many national churches and the subjection of each to a state. It is in the light of that risk that the Provincial Council of Utrecht, the Synod of Pistoia, and the two French national councils of 1797 and 1801 constitute such special, if fragile, moments. The chances of success for this reformist endeavor were slim enough and are perhaps of interest only to devotees of lost causes. What is certain is that these efforts, having everywhere sustained a rude blow by the French Revolution from the left, were then dealt the *coup de grâce* by the concordat from the right. The Napoleonic concordat is as good a candidate as any for marking the end of the French Revolution. For while the constitutional clergy knew very well that they could not survive the demise of the Republic, the republicans never understood that the Republic could not survive the demise of the constitutional Gallican Church.

French Protestants, Laicization, and the Separation of the Churches and the State, 1802–1905

Steven C. Hause

ON 18 GERMINAL AN X (8 April 1802),[1] the Corps Législatif voted, and the First Consul promulgated, the Law Relative to the Organization of the Churches and the Organic Articles on the Protestant Churches.[2] For the next century, the Napoleonic Organic Articles of 1802 served as a Protestant concordat and closely bound the Calvinist Reformed Church and the Lutheran Church to the government of France. Although a concordat is technically a treaty between a sovereign power and the Vatican, the term *système concordataire* has been applied to minority religions as well as to Catholicism for the period following the concordat of 1801.[3]

Under this arrangement, Protestant temples and associated structures (such as residences for pastors) were the property of the state, sustained by an appropriation in the national budget. By article 7, pastors and auxiliary ministers became

---

Unless otherwise indicated, all translations from foreign language sources are the author's.

[1] In 1793, the Convention adopted a calendar that started at 22 September 1792 and divided the year into twelve months of thirty days each: Vendemiaire, Brumaire, Frimaire (autumn), Nivose, Pluviose, Ventose (winter), Germinal, Floreal, Prairial (spring), Messidor, Thermidor, Fructidor (summer), with five or six days left over at the end of the year.

[2] The best source for documents relative to the status of Protestantism in nineteenth-century France is Armand Lods, ed., *La Législation des cultes protestantes, 1787–1887* (Paris: Grassart, 1887), see esp. 34–38 (Loi relative à l'organisation des cultes), and 48–55 (Articles organiques des cultes protestantes). The Organic Articles are reprinted in many modern sources, such as Alfred Fierro, André Palluel-Guillard, and Jean Tulard, eds., *Histoire et dictionnaire du consulat et de l'empire* (Paris: Laffont, 1995), 495–504. For an explication of such texts, see Armand Lods, *Traité de l'administration des cultes protestantes* (Paris: Grasset, 1896).

[3] See, for example, the use of the term in Jean Baubérot, *Le Retour des Huguenots: La Vitalité protestante, XIXe–XXe siècle* (Paris: Cerf, 1985), 16n2.

employees of the state, like any other civil servant, with an annual salary voted by the legislature. The training of these pastors was specified by law and provided in state institutions, the faculties of theology, variously located at Geneva (until detached from France in 1814), Strasbourg (until detached from France in 1871), Montauban, and Paris (after 1871, as a replacement for Strasbourg); and they were also funded by the legislature. The organization and governance of the churches was specified by law and a Ministry of Religion[4] administered, inspected, and regulated the application of the Organic Articles of 1802. A lengthy series of decrees covered the details of linking the churches to the state, such as the decrees of 1804–5 that established the consistories of the Reformed Church and named pastors for each parish, or the decree of 1805 that established the pay scale for pastors in the Lutheran Church.

The nineteenth-century debate over the separation of church and state (usually known to Protestants as the separation of the churches and the state) concerned the abrogation of the Organic Articles of 1802, the abolition of the Ministry of Religion, the suppression of the state budget for religion, and the independent self-government of the churches. Insofar as they are considered in general histories, French Protestants are usually depicted as natural and strong supporters of separation—Calvin, after all, preached the doctrine of the total sovereignty of God, which dictated the complete separation of the church from control by the state. There is significant truth in this generalization, but it must be limited and nuanced because not all Protestants welcomed separation, much less worked for it.[5] This essay explores the roots of nineteenth-century Protestant attitudes toward separation of the churches and the state (and, to a lesser degree, to the parallel question of secularization of the state, or laicization), considers the variety of Protestant responses to the nineteenth-century debate, and examines the role of Protestants at the time of separation.

In a simple statistical sense, Protestantism prospered under the Organic Articles of 1802, as each of the regimes of the nineteenth century increased its funding.

---

[4]The Ministry of Religion was initially an independent ministry headed by Jean-Etienne-Marie Portalis (1746–1807), one of the authors of the civil code and one of the negotiators of the concordat between France and the Vatican in 1801. In later years, the ministry was often combined with the portfolios for public instruction and fine arts depending upon the politics of the moment, but a Protestant premier, William Waddington, restored a full ministry. On the eve of the separation of the churches and the state, the portfolio for religion was combined with the more important post of Minister of the Interior. Both of the premiers during the great debate over separation from 1899 to 1905, René Waldeck-Rousseau and Emile Combes, held the combined portfolio of Minister of the Interior and Religion.

[5]Jean Baubérot also presents this division of Protestant opinion: "Chez les évangéliques comme chez les libéraux, certains sont partisans de cette mesure, d'autres extrêmement réservés à son égard" (Among the evangelists as among the liberals, some are in favor of this measure, others are very hesitant concerning it). *Le Retour des Huguenots*, 85.

The Reformed Church had survived in France throughout the persecution of the eighteenth century, when it was a capital crime to preach in a Protestant service. Not surprisingly, the number of pastors had fallen sharply, reaching a nadir of forty-eight in 1750. When the church was legally established at Paris in 1802, Napoleon immediately created two temples with three pastors; when the reestablishment was complete in 1804, there were 120 pastors on the new emperor's payroll. The presidents of twenty-seven Calvinist consistories attended his coronation. Napoleon added two more pastors each year, bringing his total to 137.[6]

Napoleon, who had no great fondness for any religion, recognized the benefits of binding the Protestant minority to his regime and welcomed the service of a Protestant president of the Corps Législatif, Pierre-Antoine Rabaut-Dupuy (the son of a celebrated Nîmes pastor, Paul Rabaut), and several Protestant generals, such as Baron de Chabaud-Latour (also a Nîmois Protestant) and Comte Walther (who became the commander of Napoleon's Garde Impériale and whose daughter Napoleon took as his goddaughter).[7] The first Minister of Religion, Jean-Etienne-Marie Pontalis (a devout Gallican Catholic), recalled Martin Luther and underscored Napoleon's instinct to welcome Protestants to imperial service in a memorandum for the emperor entitled *Observations sur les protestants de France:* "The Protestant religion has characteristics that render it particularly commendable to the governors of peoples—the first article of its discipline is an absolute submission to temporal power."[8]

Despite the closer ties of the Bourbon monarchs to the Roman Catholic Church, the restoration saw a steady growth of state support for Protestantism: Louis XVIII named thirty new pastors and Charles X appointed eighteen—an average of three per year. The churches prospered most dramatically during the reign of Louis Philippe, who allowed 168 additional appointments, making a total of 390 state-salaried pastors when Napoleon III proclaimed the Second Empire. By the early years of the Third Republic, the Reformed Church had grown to 101 consistories with 532 parishes, 920 temples and oratories, and 638 state-supported pastors. It is noteworthy, however, that the estimated number of Calvinist pastors in France in 1561 had been 2,500.[9]

---

[6]These data are combined from a variety of sources; the fullest survey is in Henry Dartigue, ed., *Annuaire protestant: Année 1937* (Paris: Fischbacher, 1937), 137. There is also a historical survey in *Le Protestant libéral,* 9 January 1886; and Armand Lods, "De la Réorganisation de l'Eglise Réforme," *Revue de droit et de jurisprudence à l'usage des églises de France et d'Algérie* (January 1889): 320.

[7]For biographical information on such prominent Protestant figures, see: André Encrevé, ed., *Les Protestants,* vol. 5 of *Dictionnaire du monde religieux dans la France contemporaine,* ed. Jean-Marie Mayeur and Yves-Marie Hilaire (Paris: Beauchesne, 1993), 120 (Chabaud-Latour), 402–3 (Rabaut, also known as Rabaut-Dupui and Rabaut "Le Jeune"), 506 (Walther).

[8]"Observations sur les protestants de France," reprinted in *Revue de droit et de jurisprudence à l'usage des églises protestantes de France,* January 1887, 297.

Many French Protestants felt comfortable with the July monarchy and many served the regime of 1830–48. Approximately 5 percent of the Orleanist legislature were professing Protestants (compared to 2 percent of the population), three of whom served as vice president (Antoine Odier, Benjamin Delessert, and François Delessert). Louis Philippe named a Protestant premier (François Guizot), four Protestant ministers of the interior (Guizot, François de Maleville, and Comte Adrien de Gasparin twice), plus a fifth Protestant who sat in the cabinet as under-secretary of state for the interior (François Passy), two Protestant Ministers of Finances (Claramond Pelet de la Lozère and Hippolyte Passy), repeated Protestant ministers of public instruction (Guizot in four cabinets and Pelet de la Lozère in one), and Protestants in the ministries of agriculture, commerce, and foreign affairs.[10]

Yet, at the same moment that some Protestants were beginning to feel comfortable with the monarchy, Protestant support for the separation of church and state began to grow. A nucleus of separationist thought naturally existed with Protestant republicanism as a legacy of the French Revolution—for many republicans, the secular state (with freedom of religion), created in the early stages of revolution, remained the model for church-state relations. It was a Protestant member of the Committee of Public Safety, François-Antoine de Boissy d'Anglas, who had established the revolutionary system of freedom of religion in churches separated from the state by the decree of 3 Ventose year III (21 February 1795). This legacy in French republicanism ("The French Revolution in its full reality," Jules Ferry would later say) would, of course, be a central fact of the political campaign to separate church and state in the late nineteenth and early twentieth centuries.[11] But the response of French Protestantism to separation had more complex origins.

The origins of a Protestant argument for separation came from the Protestant awakening, known in France as le Réveil.[12] The Réveil was an evangelical

<hr />

[9]Dartigue, *Annuaire protestant: Année 1937*, 137; *Le Protestant libéral*, 9 January 1886; and *Revue de droit et de jurisprudence à l'usage des églises de France et d'Algérie*, January 1889, 320.

[10]A convenient record of nineteenth-century ministries and biographical sketches of those who served in ministries can be found in Benoît Yvert, ed., *Dictionnaire des ministres de 1789 à 1989* (Paris: Perrin, 1990). On the July Monarchy, see ibid., 93–200.

[11]For a good illustration of the republican attitude, see Jules Ferry's speech to the Chamber of Deputies on 3 June 1876. The quotation in context is: "To have built this secular state, to have taken away from the clergy its political organization and role as a cadre within the state—that, precisely, is the French Revolution in its full reality." The full text of this speech is in the *Journal officiel, Débats*, for 3 June 1876. A translation is available in Jan Goldstein and John W. Boyer, eds., *Nineteenth-Century Europe: Liberalism and Its Critics* (Chicago: University of Chicago Press, 1988), 358.

[12]For the Réveil, see Alice Wemyss, *Histoire du Réveil, 1790–1849* (Paris: Les Bergers et Les Mages, 1977); Daniel Robert, *Les Eglises Réformées en France, 1800–1830* (Paris: Presses Universitaires de France, 1961), 418–60; André Encrevé, *Les Protestants en France de 1800 à nos jours: Histoire d'une réintégration* (Paris: Stock, 1985), 59–66; Henri Dubief, "Réflexions sur quelques aspects du premier

movement that sought to reawaken a devout and orthodox faith of the past. Although influenced by a variety of religious forces, such as the Moravian Pietist movements in Germany and Switzerland (and *les frères moraves* in France), the primary source of the Réveil was an Anglo-Dutch missionary effort, which consisted chiefly of Methodist missionaries from England.

The congregations formed by foreign missionaries existed outside the *système concordataire,* but the principle of freedom of religion (which was essential to the working of the *système*) meant that the state could not deny the right of French citizens to form an *église non-concordataire*. Missionaries, who were often called *séparatistes,* encouraged French Protestants to consider such independent churches.[13] The impact of the missionaries of the Réveil should not be measured in numbers of churches established or converts won. During the nineteenth century, missionaries established a few scattered Methodist churches (chiefly in the Protestant regions of the south) and even Baptist churches; by the 1850s, there was even a Methodist newspaper published in France.[14] But the total number of Methodists, Baptists, and Moravian Brothers at the end of the nineteenth century was perhaps two thousand.[15]

Simultaneously, French Protestants were exposed to the idea of separating church and state through the teaching and writings of one of the most influential theologians of the nineteenth century, Alexandre Vinet (1797–1847).[16] Vinet was

---

réveil et sur le milieu où il se forma," *Bulletin de la Société du protestantisme français* (BSHPF) 114 (1968): 373–402; and Léon Maury, *Le Réveil religieux dans l'Eglise Réformée à Genève et en France, 1810–1850* (Paris, 1892).

   [13]For the work of missionaries during the Réveil, see Wemyss, "Les séparatistes en France," in *Histoire du Réveil,* 158–60.

   [14]*L'Evangéliste* (subtitled *Journal du Méthodisme*) was published biweekly from 1858 until 1939; the Bibliothèque nationale holds an almost complete run. At the time of the debates on the separation of church and state in the early twentieth century, there were actually two Methodist papers in France with the founding of *Le Lien* at Nîmes in 1903. There were also two Baptist newspapers: *La Cloche d'alarme* (published at Paris, 1893–1919) and *L'Echo de la vérité* (published initially at Lyon and later at Nîmes, 1879–1911).

   [15]The leading Protestant newspaper of the Third Republic, *Le Signal,* reported that the Methodist church (of France and Switzerland combined) claimed a total membership of 1,877 in 1884. *Le Signal,* 19 July 1884.

   [16]The most up-to-date work on Alexandre Vinet is Ellen A. Koehler, "Religious Liberty and Civisme moral: Alexandre Vinet, French Protestantism, and the Shaping of Civic Culture in 19th Century France" (PhD diss., University of California–Davis, 2002). The previous standard work in English was Paul T. Fuhrmann, *Extraordinary Christianity: The Life and Thought of Alexander Vinet* (Philadelphia: Westminster, 1964). There are many French studies of Vinet, chiefly written by admiring French Protestants. The briefest is Philippe Bridel, *Alexandre Vinet: Sa personne et ses idées* (Paris: La Cause, 1912); the closest to Parisian Protestants is Edmond Scherer, *Alexandre Vinet: Notice sur sa vie et ses écrits* (Paris: Ducloux, 1853). The most detailed is Eugène Rambert, *Alexandre Vinet: Histoire de sa vie et de ses ouvrages,* 5th ed. (Lausanne: Payot, 1930). The newest is Bernard Reymond, *A la redécouverte d'Alexandre Vinet* (Lausanne: L'Age d'homme, 1990).

a Swiss educator, ordained in the Reformed Church, who made his initial reputation as a literary critic. As a theologian, Vinet became one of the thinkers most responsible for the nineteenth-century emphasis on individualism within Protestantism. He constructed this argument by his emphasis on the individual conscience and the consequent direct moral relationship of the individual with God.[17] Vinet used the argument of moral individualism to champion freedom of belief; that, in turn, led him to conclude that such freedom must include freedom of the church from the state. He developed his theory of the separation of church and state in *Mémoire en faveur de la liberté des cultes* (1826) and built upon it for the remainder of his life.[18] These ideas soon led Vinet into conflict with the Swiss government. In 1845, when he considered that the civil government had intervened unacceptably in his church, Vinet personally led a secession from the state church to form an independent church, which he termed the *église libre*—the free church.

The evangelical fervor of the Réveil and the theology of Vinet came together in Paris in the mid-nineteenth century to produce the first strong voice for separation of church and state within French Protestantism, the Eglise Taitbout. The Eglise Taitbout was the first important *église non-concordataire* founded in France and it became a center of separationist opinion. The origins of the church are in the Réveil and its founding is sometimes called the *le Réveil parisien*.[19] Stimulated by the enthusiasm of an English missionary, Mark Wilks, a group of well-to-do Parisian-Protestant families (of *haute société protestante*—the H.S.P.) decided in 1828 to hold weekly religious meetings, every Thursday evening, in their residences. Wilks had been a preacher in London when the White Terror of 1816 inspired him to rush to the side of Protestants in France.[20]

The founding families of this circle were a prominent group chiefly composed of foreign-born Protestants who were the descendants of French Huguenot refugees. They included: [21]

[17]See Alexandre Vinet, *Essai sur la conscience et sur la liberté religieuse* (Paris and Geneva: Henry Servier, 1829).

[18]Alexandre Vinet, *Mémoire en faveur de la liberté des cultes* (Paris: Servier, 1826). This is not a brief pamphlet, but a 340 page book thoroughly arguing the case; it was reprinted throughout the nineteenth century and as recently as 1944. Vinet then followed it with an even longer argument for separation of church and state, *La Liberté des cultes,* 2nd ed. (Paris: Chez les éditeurs, 1852). Many of his writings on separation were published posthumously. See especially Alexandre Vinet, *Liberté religieuse et questions ecclésiastiques* (Paris: Chez les éditeurs, 1854).

[19]The expression is from Wemyss, *Histoire du Réveil,* 185.

[20]On Wilks, see Encrevé, *Les Protestants,* 514–15. Wilks is discussed at length in Wemyss, *Histoire du Réveil,* where he is depicted as the moving force in the founding of the Eglise Taitbout; see esp. 174–79 ("Le Parti de M. Wilks") and 185–96 ("Le Réveil parisien").

[21]Biographies of the founders of the Eglise Taitbout can be found in Encrevé, *Les Protestants,* 164–65 (Delaborde), 254–55 (Hollard), 304–6 (Lutteroth), 346–47 (Monod), 396–97 (Pressensé). Obituaries exist in the Protestant press and especially in the *BSHPF.* Delaborde received a sketch in the

(1) Henri Lutteroth, a German-born descendant of Huguenot refugees. His father had returned to Bonaparte's Paris as a rich banker and endowed Henri with the wealth to devote himself to the faith; Henri Lutteroth became one of the founders of a society to distribute religious tracts, a Société des Missions (and an editor of its Journal), a weekly Protestant newspaper *Le Semeur* (which he edited at Paris, 1833–50), and a biblical society—clearly the record of someone devoted to the Réveil.

(2) Thomas Waddington, an English-born industrialist who founded one of the most important textile mills of Normandy and whose son, William Waddington, would become premier (president of the council) in 1879 and marry Mathilde Lutteroth, Henri Lutteroth's daughter.

(3) Victor de Pressensé, the son of a *payeur général* in the Ministry of Finances and descendant of an old Huguenot family that converted to Catholicism after the Edict of Nantes; his marriage to Victoire Hollard led to his reconversion to the Protestant faith of his mother.

(4) Henri Hollard, a Swiss-born descendant of Huguenot refugees; returned to Paris to be a physician at the Faculté de Médecine; he was also an evangelical missionary and his sister, Victoire, married Victor de Pressensé and became the mother of Senator Edmond de Pressensé and grandmother of a deputy, Francis de Pressensé.

(5) Comte Jules Delaborde, the son of one of Napoleon's generals, a lawyer at the Cour de cassation who would be especially known for defending Protestant pastors who had angered the authorities.

(6) Frédéric Monod, the Swiss-born son (one of twelve children) of Pastor Jean Monod, who arrived in Paris in 1808 and established the most remarkable pastoral dynasty of French Protestantism—Frédéric Monod was one of five of his sons who also became pastors.

In several cases, the wives of these founders were among the strongest founders of the Eglise Taitbout, such as Victoire Hollard, the wife of Victor de Pressensé, who played an important role in his conversion to Protestantism.[22] The founders also included two strong women who were not wives of the men who

---

Dictionnaire de bilgraphie française and Hollard in *Vapereau*. For information on Henri Hollard, see the biography of his son, Pastor Roger Hollard: Philippe Bridel, *Roger Hollard* (Lausanne, 1902). On Monod, see Henri Monod, *La Famille Monod* (Lyon, 1909); and on Pressensé, see Henri Cordey, *Edmond de Pressensé et son temps* (Lausanne, 1916).

[22]The church kept records of membership by gender and some of those accounts have survived. The congregation was not disproportionately masculine, nor was it typical of the feminization of Christianity. According to the accounts given by Edmond de Pressensé, the mid-nineteenth century membership ranged from 58 percent male in 1849 to 58 percent female in 1854: Pressensé, *Une église séparée de l'état: Notice historique sur l'Eglise Taitbout à Paris, et discours pronouncés à l'occasion du cinquantenaire de sa chapelle le 6 mai 1890* (Paris, 1890), 35.

founded the church: Suzanne Marie-Anne de Chabaud-Latour, the daughter of
Baron Antoine de Chabaud-Latour, who served in the legislature of three different
regimes and used his influence to protect threatened Protestants, and Elisabeth
Sophie Bonicel Guizot, the mother of François Guizot, who had taken the future
premier to Geneva after her Girondist husband was guillotined at Nîmes.[23]

This group of Protestant notables was encouraged by the revolution of 1830 to
believe that a more sympathetic era for Protestantism was beginning in France. In
the hope that the new regime would be tolerant and accept religious liberty, they
discussed founding their own chapel. This led in October 1830 to their rental of a
hall on rue Taitbout in the ninth arrondissement, near the future home of the
Opéra, suitable for use as a school during the week. By 1839, the Eglise Taitbout
was on a sufficiently sound basis that the founders drafted a more permanent *acte
constitutif* and invested in a larger meeting hall on rue Taitbout. The new church
building opened in May 1840 and gave the devout founders an especial pleasure:
the previous tenants had been a Saint-Simonian group who, in the words of one
gleeful Protestant, "had weekly pronounced there the funeral oration of Christianity."[24] True to the roots of the church in the Réveil, one of the pastors most frequently invited to speak at rue Taitbout was Jean-Henri Grandpierre, the leader of
the missionary society of Paris, who subsequently became pastor at the church.[25]

As the first successful *non-concordataire* church, the Eglise Taitbout was an
outstanding illustration of the principle of the separation of church and state. And
the founders, steeped in the enthusiasm of the Réveil, worked to spread their
example. They soon founded a second chapel in a working class district for
"l'évangélisation populaire." Indeed, the membership of the Eglise Taitbout never
grew to large numbers in the nineteenth century, partly because it became the
mother church as other congregations were formed out of it. At the celebrations
of the fiftieth anniversary of the Eglise Taitbout in 1890, pastors from three other
églises libres in Paris joined in recognizing the Eglise Taitbout's role in creating a
church outside the *système concordataire*.[26]

The role of the Eglise Taitbout in the history of the separation of the churches
and the state went much deeper than serving as a role model and leader of the

[23]See Wemyss, *Histoire du Réveil,* 186.
[24]Pressensé et al., *Une église séparée de l'état,* 5–9, quote at 13; "Le Cinquantenaire de la Chapelle
Taitbout," *Le Protestant,* 17 May 1890; *Le Protestant,* 8 March 1890; and Wemyss, *Histoire du Réveil,*
185–96.
[25]On Pastor Grandpierre, see Encrevé, *Les Protestants,* 230–31.
[26]The size of the congregation had grown to 77 in 1849, 119 in 1851, and 206 in 1854, indicating
the appeal of the church; by 1877, however, the congregation stood at 132 (following the creation of
another *église libre*) and in 1880 at 69 (again following the creation of a new congregation); by 1886,
however, it had grown back to 112 and there was again talk of creating a new church. Pressensé et al.,
Une église séparée de l'état, 35–38, 62.

églises libres. From the start, the church maintained a close connection with Alexandre Vinet and the theological principle (and the political ambition) of the complete separation of church and state. Henri Lutteroth established contact with Vinet and maintained a long correspondence with him. Lutteroth invited Vinet to write for *Le Semeur,* and from 1833 until his death in 1847 Vinet was the most important voice of the newspaper.[27] An even more important link between the Eglise Taitbout and Vinet's separationism was formed in the 1840s when Victor and Victoire de Pressensé sent their son, Edmond, to study with Vinet.

Edmond de Pressensé (1824–91) studied theology with Vinet at the Académie de Lausanne in 1842–46 and for the rest of his accomplished life, Pressensé described himself as "a disciple of Vinet," the greatest of his masters. As a student at Lausanne, Pressensé witnessed firsthand the struggle to establish the *église libre* of the canton of Vaud and became even more attached to the principle of the separation of church and state. At the end of his studies, Edmond de Pressensé married a young Swiss woman who redoubled his religious and political ideas. Elise du Plessis-Gouret was the daughter of a family of aristocratic Huguenots who had fled to Switzerland and whose faith had been rekindled by the Swiss Réveil. When Pressensé met her, Elise du Plessis had become a Methodist (variously described as "a little rigid" or "revivalist"), a devoted student of Vinet, and an outspoken supporter of leftist political causes.[28]

After a brief trial appointment as an auxiliary pastor at one of the Eglise Taitbout's subsidiary chapels in 1847, Pressensé quickly became auxiliary pastor (*suffragant*) at the Eglise Taitbout and at age twenty-three became the pastor to his parents' distinguished congregation. Pressensé remained a pastor at the Eglise Taitbout for over twenty years. In addition to the pulpit there, his voice was heard through the monthly *La Revue chrétienne* (which he founded in 1854 and edited until 1884) and more than a dozen books (including books on Vinet, on religion and the French Revolution, and on the freedom of religion)—and that voice consistently called for the separation of church and state. In July 1871, Pressensé took that separationist voice to Parlement when he was elected as a center-left deputy; his parliamentary influence reached its peak during the 1880s as a life

[27]Encrevé, *Les Protestants,* 304–5. For more details on this relationship, see Alexandre Vinet et al., *Alexandre Vinet d'après sa correspondence inédite avec Henri Lutteroth* (Paris: Fischbacher, 1891); and Alexandre Vinet, *Lettres de Alexandre Vinet et de quelques-uns de ses correspondants* (Lausanne: Bridel, 1882).

[28]There is a detailed sketch of both Edmond and Elise de Pressensé in Encrevé, *Les Protestants,* 393–96. A slightly more detailed portrait can be found in Steven C. Hause, "A Pastoral Family in French Politics: Edmond, Elise, and Francis de Pressensé," *Proceedings of the Western Society for French History* 18 (1990): 383–91. The most detailed source for Edmond de Pressensé is Cordey, *Edmond de Pressensé.* On Elise de Pressensé, see Marie Dutoit, *Mme. Edmond de Pressensé, sa vie d'après sa correspondance et son oeuvre* (Paris: Fischbacher, 1904); and Mme. Suchard de Pressensé, *L'Oeuvre de Mme. de Pressensé* (Paris: Fischbacher, 1903).

senator. Pressensé's election in 1871 was appropriately saluted by another Protestant pastor, Eugène Bersier (an editor of *La Revue chrétienne* and a former pastor *suffragant* at the Eglise Taitbout); Bersier told the leaders of the church that the election of Pressensé "attests to the progress made in Paris toward separation of church and state, of which our brother is the best known champion in France."[29]

The Eglise Taitbout was not alone as an *église libre* voice of separation. A second powerful voice came from the strict orthodoxy of the Pastors Monod, especially the brothers Adolphe Monod (1802–56) at Lyon and Frédéric Monod (1794–1863) at Paris. Pastor Adolphe Monod was one of the most celebrated preachers of the nineteenth century and has been called "the voice of French evangelical Christianity."[30] Monod had begun his career as a liberal, but the Réveil (especially his contact with Pietism) produced a severe crisis of faith, from which he emerged an ardent and uncompromising champion of strict orthodoxy. Barely a year after his arrival at his first post, as pastor to the Reformed Church at Lyon, he had fallen into a battle with his colleagues and the elders of the church over the strictness of his views; this battle came to a head in 1831 when he refused Easter Communion to parishioners with "a profane and unbelieving mouth." Within a year, Adolphe Monod had been stripped of his post. He opened his own independent church *non-concordataire,* not so much because he shared Pressensé's separatist sentiments, but because he was determined to teach the true faith.[31]

Adolphe Monod might have remained pastor to a small, independent church, but he had a very important supporter. François Guizot, a Protestant minister, shared the orthodoxy of Adolphe Monod, and he urged Pelet de la Lozère to name Monod to a professorship at the Protestant Faculté de Théologie at Montauban when a vacancy occurred in 1836. Monod thus shaped the thinking of a generation of Protestant pastors.

At the end of the 1840s, Adolphe Monod returned to Paris where his elder brother Frédéric was already a noted and controversial leader. The Réveil had given him a rigorous, orthodox faith, and even his exceptionally devout family recognized him as "one of the most firm."[32] When the revolution of 1848 made it possible for Protestants to hold a synod (the traditional governing body of the church, but not a part of Napoleon's system), Frédéric Monod spoke as a leader of the evangelical wing of the church. Frédéric Monod and Agenor de Gasparin

[29]Bersier as quoted in Pressensé et al., *Une église séparée de l'état,* 56. On Bersier, see Encrevé, *Les Protestants,* 67–69.

[30]See James L. Osen, *Prophet and Peacemaker: The Life of Adolphe Monod* (Lanham, MD: University Press of America, 1984), quote at 1. For a brief biography, see Encrevé, *Les Protestants,* 345–46.

[31]Encrevé, *Les Protestants,* 346.

[32]The best source for the Monod family in the nineteenth century was written by Gustave Monod, the younger brother of Adolphe and Frédéric: *La Famille Monod: Portraits et souvenirs* (Paris, 1890). On Frédéric, see 161–74, quote at 163.

led a minority that insisted upon the adoption of a *confession de foi* (such as the profession adopted at La Rochelle in 1559–71) to state the essential credo of the Reformed Church. Liberal Protestants, favoring a more flexible faith, carried the day, and the Synod of 1848 did not adopt a confession. Frédéric Monod concluded that the church had fallen into a "faithless condition" (un état infidèle) and led an 1849 schism. He resigned as *pasteur titulaire* of the Reformed Church and founded the Union des églises évangéliques de France, as a national organization to link the *églises libres,* such as his Chapelle du Nord (a converted *atelier* on Chabrol street) in Paris. Frédéric Monod became the first president of the governing "synodal commission" of the *église libre.*[33]

The *église libre* did not become a large part of French Protestantism in numbers, but it exercised a disproportionate influence on Protestant thought—much of the Protestant population collectively did not become a large part of French society in numbers but also exercised a disproportionate influence. The Synod of 1881 of the *églises libres* reported a total membership of 3,139—less than 1 percent of the Protestant population. But the combination of their newspaper, *L'église libre* (published 1869–1928), the influential pulpits of the Eglise Taitbout and of Frédéric Monod, the role of Adolphe Monod at the Faculté de théologie, and the political role of Edmond de Pressensé gave the *églises libres* a loud voice in advocating the separation of church and state. As a Lutheran observer commented in 1870, "The *église libre* never ceases to be persuaded that the union with the state is the source and the cause of all our troubles."[34]

Even in silence, the *églises libres* played an essential role in persuading Protestants to accept separation: they were living proof that the church could flourish without the financial support of the state. The economics of separation would become one of the great debates of the late nineteenth and early twentieth centuries; champions of separation simply pointed to the non-concordat churches that somehow survived—Methodist and Baptist as well as the *église libre.* This was cold comfort for some because the finances of the *églises libres* were known to be precarious. The Synod of 1881 found that all of the churches combined were operating at a deficit of 28,000 francs in 1880, although foreign contributions balanced the books.[35]

[33]Monod, *La Famille Monod.* See also the shorter sketch in Encrevé, *Les Protestants,* 346–47.

[34]*Le Témoignage: Journal de l'église de la Confession d'Augsbourg,* 9 April 1870. The observation is probably from the editor, Pastor Félix Kuhn, who was unconvinced of the need for separation.

[35]For a detailed report on the synod, see *Le Journal du protestantisme français,* 25 November 1881.

The Calvinist tradition, the heritage of the French Revolution, the impact of the Réveil, the influence of Alexandre Vinet and separationist theology, and the establishment of successful *églises non-concordataires* meant that there was already a strong current of separationism within French Protestantism when the establishment of the Third Republic reopened the republican debate on separation of the churches and the state. That debate existed from the founding of the republic. Separation had been one of the demands of Gambetta's "Belleville Manifesto" of 1869 ("la suppression du budget des cultes et la séparation des églises et de l'état") and it remained at the core of French republicanism, although some Gambettists later wavered.[36] Separation was so intertwined with the republican agenda that even moderates such as Jules Ferry embraced it, as he explained to the Chamber of Deputies in 1876:

> I maintain that the state must be secular, that the totality of society is necessarily represented by secular organizations. What, exactly, is this principle? It is the doctrine that [the church] prides itself on having introduced to the world: the doctrine of the separation of temporal and spiritual power. … After taking four centuries to introduce this doctrine, the church has then spent seven or eight centuries vehemently attacking it. Gentlemen, what was the key accomplishment, the major concern, the great passion and service of the French Revolution? To have built this secular state, to have taken away from the clergy its political organization and role as a cadre within the state—that, precisely, is the French Revolution in its full reality.[37]

Despite such sentiments, republicans could not build a majority in favor of separation during the first generation of the Third Republic. As one distinguished historian of religion has put it, French republicans enjoyed combining "the luxury of violent words with the security of moderate politics."[38]

Republicans raised the question of separation repeatedly during the 1880s era of republicanizing France, but the idea did not have enough support to come to a full debate and vote in the Chamber of Deputies. Consequently, late-nineteenth-century separationists devoted their efforts to two parallel efforts: the creation of secular laws and institutions—the program of laicization—and partial separation of the churches and the state by the steady reduction of the budget for the Ministry of Religion. French Protestants were divided in their reaction to these alternatives

---

[36]The text of the Belleville Manifesto is reproduced in many places. See J. P. T. Bury, *Gambetta and the National Defense* (London: Longman, 1936), 285–85, app. 2 (text), 16–19 (discussion). On Gambetta's later uncertainties, see Bury, *Gambetta's Final Years: "The Era of Difficulties," 1877–1882* (London: Longman, 1982), 3:157, esp. n59.

[37]The full text of this speech is in the *Journal official, Débats,* for 3 June 1876. A translation is available in Goldstein and Boyer, *Nineteenth-Century Europe,* 358.

[38]John McManners, *Church and State in France, 1870–1914* (New York: Harper, 1972), 140.

to separation. In general, Protestants strongly supported laicization but opposed the reduction of the state budget for Protestant interests.

The Protestant support for laicization is best known in the context of the historic effort to create the French public school system in the legislation of 1879–85, typically known as the Ferry Laws. Protestants had a long tradition of supporting education because literacy was required for a religion that placed so much stress on reading the Bible. (In contrast, the Catholic bishops of France had condemned the translation, distribution, and reading of the Bible as recently as 1827.) This had led to a network of Protestant schools and to the prominence of Protestants in the Ministry of Public Instruction. François Guizot had laid the foundation of a modern school system with the Education Law of 1833. Protestants provided much of the membership, financing, and leadership of the French pressure group seeking a universal, compulsory, free, and laic school system, the Ligue de l'enseignement. The league took root first in Alsace under the patronage of the Protestant industrial patriarchate—the Dollfus, Kestner, Koechlin, Thierry-Mieg, and Engel-Dollfus families; and its president in the 1880s was a Protestant, Charles Robert.[39]

The generation of talents that Jules Ferry drew to the Ministry of Public Instruction to create the French secular (*laïc*) school system was filled with Protestants—many of the most able Catholic educators were, after all, concerned with the preservation of the Catholic school system and the teaching posts of thousands of priests and nuns. Ferry was not a Protestant himself (he was a lapsed Catholic) although he had married into a prominent Protestant family, the Rislers. But the Protestants around him included Ferdinand Buisson, who served as the *inspecteur général* for French primary education from 1879 to 1896 (and who had grown up attending the Eglise Taitbout with his mother and uncles, but soon found himself too liberal for their beliefs); Félix Pécaut, a former pastor, who served as an *inspecteur général* and was the founder of the Ecole normale supérieure for women in primary education at Fontenay-aux-Roses (under the direction of Madame de Friedberg, another Protestant); Julie Favre (née Velten), the first *directrice* of the Ecole normale supérieure for women in secondary education at Sèvres; Jules Steeg,

---

[39]For the best overview of the league, see Katherine Auspitz, *The Radical Bourgeoisie: The Ligue de l'enseignement and the Origins of the Third Republic, 1866–1885* (Cambridge: Cambridge University Press, 1982). Auspitz recognizes the Protestant role in the early history of the league (see, e.g., 72), but does not emphasize the importance of Protestants. See also Gabriel Compayre, *Jean Macé et l'instruction obligatoire* (Paris: Delaplane, n.d.); Prosper Alfaric, *Jean Macé, fondateur de la Ligue française de l'enseignement* (Paris: Ligue française de l'enseignement, 1955); Arthur Dessoye, *Jean Macé et la fondation de la ligue de l'enseignement* (Paris: Marpon et Flammarion, 1883); and Charles Robert, *De l'Instruction obligatoire* (Paris: Hachette, 1871). For a concise history of the Ligue de l'enseignement, see Ferdinand Buisson, ed., *Nouveau dictionnaire de pédagogie et d'instruction publique* (Paris: Hachette, 1911), 1039–41.

another former pastor who became an *inspecteur général* after leaving the Chamber of Deputies and replaced Pécaut as the *inspecteur* for Fontenay-aux-Roses; Pauline Kergomard (née Reclus), the niece of a famous pastor, who became the role model for influential women in educational administration, serving as *inspectrice générale* between 1881 and 1910 and becoming the first woman to sit on the Conseil supérieur de l'enseignement in 1886; Louis Liard, the director of higher education between 1884 and 1902; Gabriel Compayré, one of the architects of the Ecole normale supérieure system and the author of many of the secular system's manuals before becoming the *inspecteur général* for secondary education in 1908.[40]

As with the question of the separation of the churches and the state, it is an oversimplification to portray Protestants as favoring the secular school system and Catholic as opposing it. A nuanced view of Protestant opinion must consider the serious reservations that some prominent Protestants held. Pastor Benjamin Couve provides a good illustration. Couve served as an auxiliary pastor in Paris from 1868 to 1874 before being called to one of the most prominent pulpits of the Reformed Church at Pentemont (Paris). Pastor Couve also contributed regular articles to the voice of orthodoxy within the Reformed Church, *Le Christianisme au XIXe siècle,* and he became the director of the newspaper in 1880 when Pastor Emile Doumergue left to assume a professorship at the Faculté de Théologie at Montauban.[41]

Couve expressed the concerns of many conservatives in an article entitled "L'Instruction laïque" in *Le Christianisme* in 1872. He worried that the idea of secular education was being pressed by anticlerical republicans as a convenient way of attacking the Catholic Church, and he argued that Protestants should not participate in such fights: "Let us content ourselves with asking for complete liberty; let us not dishonor the holy cause of Protestantism by an alliance with priest haters [*prêtophobes*]." But that was not Couve's greatest concern. He spoke for many on the Orthodox side of the Reformed Church (Buisson and most the architects of the secular school system were liberals or lapsed Protestants) when he worried about the fate of religious instruction if it disappeared from the schools and about the nature of secular education if religion were removed from it. In a secular system, he said, "The state cannot teach religion. But can it teach without religion? For some Christians, to pose this question is to answer it negatively." Turning to the idea that the state would replace religious instruction with *morale laïque,* the pastor asked simply, "How can one separate morality from religion? Can one have

---

[40]The literature of these educators and their role in creating the secular school system is enormous. Brief biographical sketches can be found in Claude Lelièvre and Christian Nique, eds., *Bâtisseurs d'école: Histoire biographique de l'enseignement en France* (Paris: Nathan, 1994); and Encrevé, *Les Protestants.* For an introduction to the secular system, see Buisson, *Nouveau dictionnaire de pédagogie.*

[41]A biography of Couve can be found in Encrevé, *Les Protestants,* 150–51.

a morality without God?" The result, he feared, would be an anti-Christian school system teaching "the religion of the state."[42] *Le Christianisme au XIXe siècle* continued to express such concerns throughout the debates on the Ferry Laws, which the paper called (in 1881) "an innovation full of the unknown." Couve noted, with horror, the closing of Protestant schools as the state subventions disappeared. As the secular schools were opening in France, Couve, one of the most influential voices of orthodox Protestantism, remained critical: the secular school was "an outrage to God in the systematic suppression of his presence."[43]

The concerns of orthodox conservatives about secular schools were minor compared to the Protestant concerns about the other alternative to separation, the gradual elimination of the budget for the Ministry of Religion by annual reductions. Paul Bert, a distinguished scientist and a Gambettist deputy who was one of the leading non-Protestant architects of the secular school system, explained this policy quite bluntly. Separation was the unquestioned goal, but the hesitancy of the majority meant "we must march toward this destination by little steps, as rapidly as prudence allows."[44]

Under the policy of separation by budget cuts, the support for Protestant churches steadily declined in the late nineteenth century. The monarchist assembly of the 1870s had increased the budget for religious institutions, and they were generous with the Protestant budget as well as the Catholic budget. Thereafter, budgets were cut regularly. The allocation for the pastoral corps was cut from 1,589,100 francs per annum in 1880–83 to 1,533,400 francs in 1884 (a 3.5 percent cut), then to 1,520,100 francs (a 0.9 percent cut); by 1895, it stood at 1,281,000 francs (a cut of 19.4 percent in fifteen years). Other sectors of the budget were cut more: the allocation for church buildings was cut (in several slices) from 150,000 francs in 1871 to 40,000 francs in 1884 (a 73.3 percent cut for this budget). Scholarships for Protestant theology students were suppressed entirely in 1885. The three cuts combine to a 13.1 percent cut in the budget for Protestantism.[45]

In June 1886, the Budget Commission of the Chamber of Deputies voted to carry this policy to its logical conclusion and simply suppress the entire budget for the Ministry of Religion, although the full chamber refused to adopt this policy.

[42]Benjamin Couve, "L'Instruction Laïque," *Le Christianisme au XIXe siècle*, 5 January 1872.

[43]*Le Christianisme au XIXe siècle*, 28 January 1881 and 4 February 1881.

[44]Paul Bert, as quoted by Eugène Réveillaud, the strongly pro-separation editor of the largest circulation Protestant newspaper, *Le Signal*. See Eugène Réveillaud, "L'Agonie du budget des cultes," *Le Signal*, 1 December 1883.

[45]For the 1870s, see *Le Christianisme au XIXe siècle*, 14 August 1874; and *La Renaissance*, 9 June 1876. The figures for the 1880s were compiled by Armand Lods, the foremost nineteenth-century Protestant scholar of separation. See his data in many issues of *Le Protestant; Le Christianisme au XIXe siècle;* and *La Revue de droit et de jurisprudence à l'usage des églises protestantes de France et d'Algérie*. A good set of basic tables is available in *Le Protestant*, 3 September 1887; and *La Revue de droit*, August 1887.

When the Budget Commission agreed to reinstate the budget, it introduced cuts
that horrified many Protestants, including the suppression of the budget for the
facultés de théologie. Le Protestant, a separationist newspaper in principle, a voice
of liberal Protestantism, was horrified. This form of partial separation "would
have incalculable consequences.... It would, in a single stroke, cut off an entire
branch of scientific high culture in France." The budget was restored when four
members of the Budget Commission abstained from a final vote after great political pressure. The government supported the budget on the argument that the law
required all pastors to be the graduates of a *faculté de théologie.* Two years later,
the Budget Commission came back with an even bigger cut that affected the *facultés de théologie* and the seminaries attached to them—and once again, the cabinet had to fight to reinstate the cuts. This time a compromise resulted in cutting
the budget line for Protestant chaplains in the prisons; pastors could now hold the
post at one-third of the previous salary. Subsequent budgets cut chaplains in
schools and hospitals, then all funding for churches in the colonies.[46]

Numerous municipal and departmental governments, acting with a complex
mixture of motives, seized the opportunity to try to reduce or eliminate financial
assistance given to churches. The Municipal Laws of 1884 allowed municipal
councils to eliminate funding for repairs to church buildings and that immediately became the policy. The Lutheran Church reported that it had prepared for
this eventuality, yet found itself with a budget deficit of 12,000 francs in 1885 due
to the new costs of repairs; in a year this grew to 60,000 francs. In 1886, the
Municipal Council of Val-les-Bains (an important center of Protestantism in
Ardèche) voted to eliminate their annual subvention for housing a pastor and the
prefect supported this policy.[47]

How did Protestant opinion, especially separationist opinion, react to the program of gradual separation by budget cuts? According to the Protestant press,
opinion was unanimously opposed. (They were wrong: *La Revue de droit* was
pleased that separation was making progress.) Several consistories petitioned the
government to reverse the changes, citing a variety of catastrophic consequences—
starting with Lyon, a bastion of the *église libre.* Some churches went to court, citing
a Napoleon decree of 1806 promising housing ("un logement et un jardin") for
each pastor. The press was not calm in fighting against gradual separation by budget cuts. According to *Le Protestant,* the Chamber of Deputies' plan would destroy
the remnants of the Faculté de Théologie of Strasbourg, which had been reestablished at Paris; this meant that the separationists in the chamber wanted "to com-

---

[46]*Le Protestant,* 12 June 1886, 25 September 1886 (quoted), 17 March 1888, 5 May 1888; *Le
Christianisme au XIXe siècle,* 19 March 1885; and *La Revue de droit,* January 1887, February 1888,
March 1888, June 1894.

[47]*Le Protestant,* 9 October 1886; and *La Revue de droit,* June 1886.

plete the work of the Prussians who have ravished Alsace." The Protestants in the French senate who organized to revise the budget and restore money to the faculties were led by the great champion of separation, Edmond de Pressensé.[48]

The most important Protestant reaction to this stage of the separation debate, however, was to learn. By the early 1890s, many Protestants had concluded that they must begin to prepare for the inevitable financial problems of losing state aid. An 1889 campaign to develop funding for the *faculté de théologie* and scholarships for theology students served as a model. It brought together the two wings of the Reformed Church, as liberals and the orthodox worked together. As usual, this meant appeals to the leaders of the *haute société protestante*, especially the industrial and banking families. The first subscribers were a Dollfus and a Steiner. When the chamber and senate agreed on a large cut in the budget for Protestant churches in 1893, the Protestant protest was minor; Protestant politicians such as Jules Siegfried chiefly used their influence to shift the funding to places where it was most needed. When the chamber cut the 1894 budget by another 14.2 percent, the Protestant press scarcely complained.[49]

By the end of the nineteenth century, therefore, Protestant attitudes toward the separation of the churches and the state contained many complexities.[50] The majority of the politically active Protestant community favored separation in some form. Support was drawn chiefly from the *églises libres,* the *églises non-reconnues* (such as Methodists), liberal Protestants (such as the Coquerels), and lapsed Protestants who remained Protestant in a cultural sense (such as ex-pastor Senator Dide). The orthodox wing of the Reformed Church remained more cautious. Some important orthodox voices, such as Eugène Réveillaud and *Le Signal,* supported it; others, such as *Le Christianisme au XIXe siècle,* hesitated. The hesitant also included a significant portion of French Lutherans. The Lutheran population, chiefly concentrated in the Franche-Comté region known as the pays de Montbéliard, had been shaped more by the Peace of Westphalia (and its necessity of Protestant-Catholic coexistence) than by the revocation of the Edict of Nantes (and its legacy of Protestant-Catholic hostility). Thus Lutherans, while sharing the concern of Catholic predominance, lacked the instinctive opposition to church and state ties that activated many Calvinists. Lutheran voices such as *Le Témoignage* even suggested that the *système concordataire* might provide the best security that Protestants could obtain.[51]

[48]*Le Protestant,* 17 March 1888 (quoted), 24 March 1888; and *La Revue de droit,* June 1886.

[49]*Le Protestant,* 21 and 28 September 1889, 4 February 1893, 24 June 1893.

[50]For a discussion of Protestant sentiments in 1903–5, see Baubérot, *Le Retour des Huguenots,* 85–90.

[51]For an illustration of evangelical Calvinist thinking, see Réveillaud's "Une grande question toujours en suspens," *Le Signal,* 10 April 1886. For Lutheran thinking, see *Le Témoignage,* 21 September 1872.

When separation finally won a political majority in France in the aftermath of the Dreyfus affair, several Protestants played prominent roles in achieving the historic reform of 1905. Some of the names reveal the long tradition of Protestant separationism: the author of the bill for the separation of the churches and the state, deposited in the Chamber of Deputies in April 1903 and finally adopted (in a much revised form) in December 1905, was Francis de Pressensé, the son of Edmond and Elise de Pressensé and grandson of Victor de Pressensé, the founder of the Eglise Taitbout. The similar *proposition de loi* in the Senate was deposited by François Boissy d'Anglas, a senator of the Ardèche and the direct descendant of the François Boissy d'Anglas who sat on the Committee of Public Safety, establishing a family tradition for the separation of the churches and state combined with freedom of religion. The *rapporteur* for the Commission on Separation who shepherded the bill into law was not a Protestant—it was Aristide Briand. Briand, at the time a member of the Chamber of Deputies and later prime minister of France and Nobel laureate, in 1906 accepted the role of minister of public instruction and worship so that he could put the separation of the churches and the state into effect. Briand's secretary and *conseiller,* who joined him in editing the changing drafts of the bill, however, was Louis Méjean, a devout Protestant from the Gard, the son and brother of pastors. The *chef de cabinet* to Emile Combes (the prime minister who carried separation to completion) and thus the man charged with all of the paperwork of organizing the political struggle was Jean Réveillaud, the son of Eugène Réveillaud, the editor of *Le Signal* who had led much orthodox Calvinist opinion to the cause of separation; Eugène Réveillaud was himself a deputy from Charente-Inférieure during the debates of 1903–5 and the author of the motion to establish a commission on separation in 1902.[52]

Protestants discussed the subject of separation at great length in the first years of the twentieth century. While many parts of the Protestant community in France welcomed separation and most parts accepted it, there remained reservations—chiefly concerns about how disadvantageous separation would be for Protestant churches. This concern was widely articulated by Raoul Allier, a professor at the Faculté de Théologie at Paris who was active in many evangelical circles. Allier used the columns of *Le Siècle,* where he had written regularly after using

[52]Francis de Pressensé was not active in the church of his forebearers and does not figure in Encrevé's dictionary. He was, however, a deputy from 1902 until 1910, so there is a biographical sketch in Jean Jolly, ed., *Dictionnaire des parlementaires français... 1889–1940* (Paris: Presses Universitaires de France, 1960–77), 7:2753–54. On his role in the separation debate, see H. Kuntz, "La Séparation des églises et de l'état et la proposition de Francis de Pressensé," *Revue chrétienne* 3 (1903): 450–73. On Boissy d'Anglas, see Jolly, *Dictionnaire des parlementaires français,* 2:646. On the first Boissy d'Anglas, see Claude Manceron, ed., *La Révolution française: Dictionnaire biographique* (Paris: Renaudot, 1989), 86–87. On Méjean (elected to Senate in 1920s), see Jolly, *Dictionnaire des parlementaires français,* 7:2423–24. On Réveillaud, see Jolly, *Dictionnaire des parlementaires français,* 8:2827–29.

them to defend Dreyfus, and later to argue that the conditions of separation made a great deal of difference to Protestantism and show that significant problems remained.[53]

Separation, voted with the support of Protestant deputies in December 1905, did cause the anticipated financial problems. Almost all church budgets were in deficit in the years before World War I. A careful church study of financial data for 1911 showed that the liberal Calvinist churches,[54] which had long supported separation, were well prepared and experienced a deficit of 0.1 percent of their collective budgets. Evangelical churches, whose budget was fifteen times the size of the liberal churches, faced a deficit of 11.5 percent (a total of over 200,000 francs). All Lutheran churches combined had a deficit of 7.8 percent, but there was a great difference between the more prosperous synod of Paris (0.4 percent deficit) and the poorer and more rural synod of Montbéliard (15.5 percent deficit). The Faculté de Théologie of Paris, which had learned to prepare in the 1880s, nonetheless had a deficit of 2.5 percent.

Such aspects of separation were obviously a matter of concern to French Protestants, but they did not join in the protest and outrage of many Catholics. Ferdinand Buisson, who had been a deacon in the Eglise Taitbout at age twenty-two, one of the fathers of the secular laws of the 1880s, and a lifelong champion of separation, explained his acceptance in an essay in *Le Radical* in October 1906, hailing the age of a "new social principle" that would guarantee both liberty and public order. "Henceforth, religion in France is no longer considered as a public thing but as a private thing. It is an act of the individual conscience…."[55]

[53]For a brief biography of Allier, see Encrevé, *Les Protestants,* 41–43; for a full study, see Gaston Richard, *La Vie et l'oeuvre de Raoul Allier* (Paris: Berger-Levrault, 1948). For Allier's concerns, see his *Le Bilan de la séparation pour les églises protestantes* (Paris, n.d.). For other voices in this discussion, see Philippe Jalabert, *De la séparation des églises et de l'état au point de vue du Protestantisme français* (Dole, 1903); and Pastor Louis Trial, *La séparation des églises et de l'état* (Paris, 1905). On the problems confronting Protestantism, see Jean Baubérot, "Problèmes du Protestantisme français face à la séparation des églises et de l'état," *Etudes théologiques et religieuses* 47 (1972): 271–312. For an immediate reaction to separation and the controversial issue of the Associations culturelles, see Auguste Decoppet, *Nos libertés: Sermon…à l'occasion de la fondation de l'Association culturelle de l'Oratoire…* (Paris, 1906). For a pastor's long-term perspective on the success of separation, see Marc Boegner, *Un demi-siècle de séparation des églises et de l'état: Essai de bilan* (Paris, 1955). For local case studies of separation, see Severine de Luze Pacteau, "L'église réformée de Bordeaux et la séparation des églises et de l'état," *Annales du midi: Anthologie du centenaire* 2 (1989): 755–71.

[54]Data collected by Armand Lods for *La Revue de droit*. See especially Lods, "Situation financière des églises protestantes pendant l'exercise 1911," *La Revue* 29 (1912): 193–98.

[55]Ferdinand Buisson, "L'Application de la loi de séparation de l'église et de l'état," *Le Radical,* 16 October 1906. This article, along with many other excerpts from Buisson's writings, is reprinted in Pierre Hayat, ed., *Ferdinand Buisson: Education et république* (Paris: Kime, 2003), 195–96.

Totems, Taboos, and Jews

SALOMON REINACH AND THE POLITICS OF
SCHOLARSHIP IN FIN-DE-SIÈCLE FRANCE

Aron Rodrigue

SALOMON REINACH (1858–1932) was one of the leading figures of the Franco-Jewish establishment at the end of the nineteenth and early twentieth centuries. He was vice president of the most important Jewish organization of the time, the Alliance Israélite Universelle, was a cofounder of the Jewish Colonization Association, the institution established to help Jews leaving Russia to settle on the land in various parts of the world, and was very active in the Société des Etudes Juives, the famous French society of scholarship on Jews and Judaism founded in 1880. He was also a good friend of Zadoc Kahn, the chief rabbi of France. Together with his brothers, the deputy Joseph Reinach and the scholar and later deputy Théodore Reinach, he was also one of the earliest of the Dreyfusards, working indefatigably for the exoneration of Captain Alfred Dreyfus.

This very Jewishly involved personality was at the same time a fixture in the Parisian intellectual scene, penning numerous works on the classics, Greek archaeology, philology, and ancient religions. A member of a prestigious academy, the Institut, professor of the history of art and archaeology at the Ecole du Louvre, director of the Museum of National Antiquities at St.-Germain-en-Laye, and director of the journal *Revue Archéologique,* he was to leave his mark as the major contributor to and propagator of the totem and taboo school of British anthropology in France, applying its findings relentlessly in hundreds of articles to Greek and Roman religion and mythology as well as to Judaism and Christianity, raising the ire of many in the latter two camps.[1]

This essay will analyze the complex trajectory of Salomon Reinach's Jewish and scholarly engagements, try to read one side with the light thrown by the

---

Unless otherwise indicated, all translations from foreign language sources are the author's.

[1] For the most recent overview of Reinach's life and work, see Hervé Duchêne, "Préface," in Salomon Reinach, *Cultes, mythes, religions,* ed. Hervé Duchêne (Paris: R. Laffont, 1996), v–lxxxi.

other, and explore the dialectics of identity, politics, and scholarship. How did the
scholar who came to think that the interdiction on the eating of pork is a vestige
of a distant past—when the ancestors of the earliest Hebrews worshiped the wild
boar as a totem—function as an engagé Jew in the Jewish politics of his time, and
what were the constraints on this involvement? And what does the configuration
of the scholar and the Jew in Reinach reveal about the French Jewish world of the
turn of the twentieth century?

Reinach came of age at the same time that the dominant ideology of Franco-
Judaism that was to mark French Jewry for much of the Third Republic was
receiving its full formulation. Throughout the nineteenth century, thinkers such
as Joseph Salvador, Léon Halévy, Elie-Aristide Astruc, and, most important,
James Darmesteter and Salomon Reinach's own brother Théodore had developed
in their works on Judaism a particular discourse that saw a symbiosis between it
and the post-1789 France of the modern period. According to this worldview,
Jews, first through the Mosaic legislation and then through the message of the
prophets, had created the foundations of universal morality and justice. In spite of
constant persecution through the ages, the Jewish spirit had survived, propagat-
ing this message throughout the world. Although Jewish creativity had suffered
and deteriorated as a result of the Jews' having been turned into pariahs at the
hand of Christian clerics, the evolution of civilization had begun to defeat obscu-
rantism and bigotry, and this was first and foremost as the result of the Revolution
of 1789. After this momentous event, modern civilization was destined to triumph everywhere, as it was doing in France. The identity between the principles
of 1789 and of purified Judaism shorn of the superstitions it had acquired during
the centuries of oppression meant that Jews could now partake as full-fledged citizens in the onward path of civilization.[2]

The Alliance, which had created a vast network of French Jewish schools
around the Mediterranean basin, was the very incarnation of the message of
Franco-Judaism. Its efforts on behalf of Jewish emancipation throughout the
world and its spreading the message of modernity through its schools were
designed to remake Jews everywhere in the image of the emancipated French Jew,
and they represented a self-imposed civilizing mission that was emblematic of the
belief in the normative nature of the French Jewish path of emancipation.[3]

[2]For the ideology of Franco-Judaism, see Michel Marrus, *The Politics of Assimilation: A Study of
the French Jewish Community at the Time of the Dreyfus Affair* (Oxford: Oxford University Press,
1971). For an analysis of the beginnings of this worldview, see Aron Rodrigue, "Léon Halévy and
Modern French Jewish Historiography," in *Jewish History and Jewish Memory: Essays in Honor of Yosef
Hayim Yerushalmi,* ed. Elisheva Carlebach, John Efron, and David Myers (Hanover, NH: University
Press of New England, 1998), 413–27.

[3]On the Alliance and its work, see the following works by Aron Rodrigue: "Les enfants de Crémieux: Devenir de l'Alliance Israélite Universelle," *Les Cahiers du Judaïsme* 1 (1998): 94–100; *Images of*

Socialized with the perspectives of Franco-Judaism, and eventually rising to the leadership of the Alliance, Reinach was also an integral part of the elite of Parisian Jewish scholars. Within the framework of the development of meritocratic universalistic institutions in France, Jews had achieved positions of prominence in academia much earlier than elsewhere in Europe, without giving up their Jewish affiliations; this paralleled the Jews in state service studied by Pierre Birnbaum.[4] For example, Adolphe Franck, the first Jew to pass the *agrégation* examination in philosophy in France (1832), was elected to the Académie des Sciences Morales et Politiques in 1844 and became the first Jewish professor at the Collège de France when he was appointed to the chair of philosophy of law in 1856. He was at the same time vice president of the Jewish Consistoire and wrote many works on Jewish studies. Indeed, it was in France that the first secular academic position in the world was created for the study of rabbinic culture, with Joseph Derenbourg appointed to the newly created post of rabbinical Hebrew at the Ecole Pratique des Hautes Etudes in Paris in 1877. The same institution also created the first chair in rabbinics in France in 1896, appointing Israël Lévi, who was eventually to become the chief rabbi of France. Apart from the case of Franck mentioned above, Jewish scholars such as Arsène and James Darmesteter, Joseph and Hartwig Derenbourg, Théodore and Salomon Reinach, Jules Oppert, and others, though appointed to positions in non-Jewish subjects in the humanities in various institutions of higher education, all wrote extensively on Judaica and made important contributions to the field. The Société des Etudes Juives and its journal, *Revue des Etudes Juives,* brought together many of these scholars and provided an important forum for French Jewish scholarship. These communally identified Jewish academics, most though not all associated with the field of Oriental studies, produced works of decisive significance in the general fields of comparative linguistics, mythology, and ancient religions.[5] Indeed, these French Jewish scholars made a major contribution to the study of the phenomenon of religion, laying some of the groundwork in France for the modern discipline of religious studies (*science des religions*). Their field of cultural production was eventually transformed and transcended by other Jewish figures, such as Emile

---

Sephardi and Eastern Jewries in Transition, 1860–1939: The Teachers of the Alliance Israélite Universelle (Seattle: University of Washington Press, 1993); and *French Jews, Turkish Jews: The Alliance Israélite Universelle and the Politics of Jewish Schooling in Turkey, 1860–1925* (Bloomington: University of Indiana Press, 1990).

[4]Pierre Birnbaum, *The Jews of the Republic: A Political History of State Jews in France from Gambetta to Vichy* (Stanford: Stanford University Press, 1996).

[5]For Jewish studies in France in the nineteenth century, see Perrine Simon-Nahum, *La cité investie: La "science du judaïsme" français et la République* (Paris: Editions du Cerf, 1991). See also Jay Berkovitz, "Jewish Scholarship and Identity in Nineteenth Century France," *Modern Judaism* 18 (1998): 1–33.

Durkheim and Marcel Mauss, who came from the same milieu and whose fame was to eclipse them all.[6]

The uniquely French conjunction of academic careers and Jewish communal and social activism led to a particular universalist political and cultural stance, and at the same time it produced a distinctive type of knowledge about Jews, one that diverges from the German Wissenschaft des Judentums model of the scientific study of Judaism that has been at the center of attention of scholarship until recently. Most studies of these French Jewish scholars have stressed the influence of the Wissenschaft des Judentums (produced by Jewish scholars in Germany barred from teaching in German universities) on them, characterizing their work as derivative of scholarship across the Rhine. However, in a social, political, cultural, and institutional context that differed substantially from Germany, the influence of German ideas and methods led to very different formulations and conclusions, most notably in the foregrounding of universalism as a guiding principle, stressing the comparative and the global.

The scholarly study of Judaism in France was deeply marked by the distinctive and unique process of the emancipation of French Jewry during the French Revolution, which gave the individual Jew legal equality in return for the community's divesting itself of its former corporate autonomous existence. The rise and eventual victory of republicanism as a secularist and militantly anticlerical ideology with which the Jews were deeply engaged, the impetus given to the secular study of religion by Ernest Renan in his treatment of the life of Jesus in the 1860s, and the politics of the strongly interventionist French state that controlled academic departments where such a study could be undertaken all left their mark. At the same time, the legitimation given by the state to the formal organization of French Jewry in consistories, and other strongly institutionalized forms of Jewish political and cultural activism in the shape of the Alliance, also provided the more socially inclined of these scholars the possibility of becoming deeply involved in the reform of French and international Jewish life and an opportunity to move between the worlds of scholarship and Jewish politics. Universalist scholarship and ideals could and did coexist with strong communal engagement. Salomon Reinach provides a perfect example of this stance, its complexities, and its eventual contradictions and limits.

A specific key influence on Reinach was his upbringing and his class background. A son of the German Jewish banker Hermann Reinach, who had immigrated to France in the 1840s, Salomon, born in 1858, grew up in a luxurious villa at St.-Germain-en-Laye just outside Paris and was tutored privately at home until

---

[6]Ivan Strenski's deeply flawed book, *Durkheim and the Jews of France* (Chicago: University of Chicago Press, 1997), deals with some of these themes.

well into his teens. Hermann Reinach, who was to leave the sixth-largest fortune in France at his death, was a great admirer of Voltaire and the *philosophes* as well as a firm proponent of learning languages. Consequently, Salomon acquired a perfect mastery of Greek, Latin, German, and English, though significantly not of Hebrew, his knowledge of which he qualified as elementary later on. There is no evidence that the three brothers were brought up as practicing Jews, but, like most French Jews of their station at the time, all three married Jews in religious ceremonies and remained committed to the Jewish cause all their lives. Like many in the Franco-Jewish upper class, a strong dosage of noblesse oblige toward Jews in distress at home and abroad appears to have been the starting point of their Jewish engagement.[7]

The Reinach brothers shone in all the national examinations, systematically obtaining first prizes in most fields and creating a sensation in the press, which called them "les frères Je-Sais-Tout."[8] Salomon obtained the number-one position in the admission examination to the elite Ecole Normale Supérieure and graduated from there obtaining first place in the national *agrégation* examination of grammar.[9] At the age of eighteen, he had already translated Schopenhauer's *Essay on Free Will,* embarking on a publishing career that would produce hundreds of works until his death in 1932. The bibliography of his publications is a book of 262 pages.[10] Interested in classical philology and trained by the father of French semantics, Michel Bréal, himself of German Jewish background, Reinach soon turned to archaeology after compiling a manual of classical philology that was a work of popularization designed to introduce the new discipline to the educated masses. Reinach would alternate in his work between erudite scholarship addressed to his peers and popular books designed to educate and edify the uninitiated. There, too, the noblesse oblige tradition remained paramount, with the conviction of the imperative necessity of educating and improving the masses that was such a hallmark of the Third Republic.

For almost two decades after his university years, Reinach's principal scholarly preoccupation would remain archaeology. Conducting research in Greece and Asia Minor and also in Tunisia in the 1880s, Reinach produced scores of works describing and analyzing Greek and Roman antiquities in those areas as well as in Gaul. His institutional rise was rapid. He was appointed to a curatorship at the Museum of Antiquities at St.-Germain, becoming its vice director in 1893

[7]Duchêne, "Préface," ix–xiii.

[8]Julien Benda, in his famous *La Jeunesse d'un clerc* (Paris: Gallimard, 1936), 43–44, discusses this sort of Jewish visibility as a cause of anti-Semitism.

[9]Duchêne, "Préface," xv–xvi. An account of his experiences in this institution was published in Emile Zola, Ernest Bersot, and Salomon Reinach, *Notre Ecole Normale,* ed. Hervé Duchêne (Paris: Les Belles lettres, 1994).

[10]*Bibliographie de Salomon Reinach* (Paris: Les Belles lettres, 1936).

and its director in 1902, occupying that position until his death in 1932. It was under his directorship that the museum would be transformed to the Musée des Antiquités Nationales, becoming the prime institution holding antiquities from Celtic and Roman Gaul. He was elected in 1896 to the Institut, the major honorific academy in France, and began to teach art history and archaeology at the Ecole du Louvre in the 1890s, becoming a professor there in 1902.[11]

His public Jewish involvement had begun during his research years in Greece and Tunisia. After visiting the Alliance school in Salonica in 1882, he published in a Parisian newspaper a glowing account approving of the progress made in French by the Jewish population of the city.[12] The spread of the French language was for him, like so many of his contemporaries, the sine qua non of becoming civilized, and it was the duty of French Jews to help their coreligionists advance in this path. It was in this period that he entered into direct professional contact with the Alliance leadership whom he knew socially, sending them long letters bemoaning the situation of the Jews in Tunisia that he had observed while conducting archaeological research there. These letters, redolent of stereotypes, focused on the backwardness of the local Jews, the ridiculousness of the clothes worn by the Jewish women, and the need to transform these "obscurantist" populations into modern civilized beings, approving of the work done by the Alliance schools in this direction.[13] This identity of views with the Alliance and Reinach's social eminence soon led to his election to the Central Committee of the organization in 1887. In 1891 he was, together with Narcisse Leven, the president of the Alliance, one of the close collaborators of Baron Maurice de Hirsch in the foundation of the Jewish Colonization Association, established to coordinate the settlement of Russian Jews in agricultural colonies in their new countries. The aim was both to regenerate the Jewish masses by encouraging the adoption of agriculture as a way of life and to prevent a flare-up of anti-Semitism by diverting them from concentrating in large numbers in urban centers. In 1898 Reinach became vice president of the Alliance, working closely with its executive secretary Jacques Bigart in setting the general agenda of the organization in the Jewish politics of the period.

The most significant crisis for Franco-Judaism, and one that affected Reinach profoundly, came at the time of the extraordinary recrudescence of anti-Semitism in France in the 1890s that saw its apotheosis during the Dreyfus affair. Even more significant than the evolution of the affair itself was the crisis of French universalism it brought to the surface. The republicanism of the tradition of 1789

---

[11]Duchêne, "Préface," xix–xliii.

[12]See the discussion in Paul Dumont, "Le français d'abord," in *Salonique 1850–1918, la ville des juifs et le réveil des Balkans,* ed. Gilles Veinstein (Paris: Autrement, 1993), 208–25.

[13]Archives of the *Alliance Israélite Universelle,* France VII.A. 56; esp. letters from Sfax dated 26 Dec. 1883, and from Djerba dated 3 Feb. 1884.

came under increasing attack by new right-wing forces that posed a serious challenge to Jacobin patriotism. A new nationalism, that of Auguste Barrès's *la terre et
les morts,* grounded and relativized "truth" in the organic "national" as a product
of the determinism of history.

This new nationalism had no place for the Jew, the archetypical alien. Anti-
Semitism, increasingly racialized, moved from the left to become a new fixture of
the nationalist right. Most French Jews reacted to the new political landscape and
to the new anti-Semitism by renewing their universalist and republican zeal and
by redoubling their efforts to preserve and strengthen the principles of 1789 and
the Republic that they incarnated. Franco-Judaism could and did continue as the
official ideology of the community, with few feasible alternatives presenting
themselves.[14] Given the creation of a Jewish sense of self that was predicated on
its transparence with the universalism of the Republic, it was understandable that
the leaders of French Jewry did not become involved with the process of revision
during the Dreyfus affair in the name of a particularist collectivity as Jews, but as
French citizens. Universalism for Jews did not necessarily entail passivity. Recent
research has revised considerably the perception of inaction among French Jews
in this episode.[15] Many Jewish leaders were very active in the Dreyfusard ranks.
However, those Jews who took part in the battle did so in the name of universal
human rights and justice, and indeed many were to be among the leaders of the
organization that came into being to defend these rights, the Ligue des Droits de
l'Homme.[16] Both the internal dynamics of Franco-Judaism and the dominant
political vocabulary and discourse of the Republic pointed inevitably to a strategy
of universalist defense by Jews in the face of anti-Semitism.

Salomon Reinach, like his brother Joseph, was among the ranks of the first
Dreyfusards, convinced together with Bernard Lazare of the innocence of the captain. He was one of the principal leaders of a small group of Jewish notables that
came together in 1894 to form the Comité de Défense contre l'Antisémitisme to
concert efforts to fight attacks against the Jews in the press and public opinion and
to use their influence among their friends and colleagues in public life to defeat the
growing threat.[17] Salomon Reinach proved indefatigable in this task. He was active
behind the scenes, at one stage even passing information gathered through his
international contacts showing the hand of someone other than Dreyfus in spying

---

[14]See the discussion in Aron Rodrigue, "Rearticulations of French Jewish Identities after the
Dreyfus Affair," *Jewish Social Studies: History, Culture, Society,* n.s. 2, no. 3 (1996): 1–24.

[15]See, e.g., Birnbaum, *The Jews of the Republic.*

[16]One of the founders and presidents of this organization has been studied by Françoise Basch,
Victor Basch ou la passion de la justice: De l'affaire Dreyfus au crime de la milice (Paris: Plon, 1994).

[17]See the discussion of this group in Pierre Birnbaum, "La citoyenneté en péril: Les juifs entre
intégration et résistance," in *La France de l'affaire Dreyfus,* ed. Pierre Birnbaum (Paris: Gallimard,
1994), 526–27.

for the Germans.[18] At the time of the reopening of the case in 1898, he also published—under the pseudonym l'Archiviste—a detailed textual study of the anti-Semitic newspaper of Edouard Drumont, *La Libre Parole,* in the years 1894–95. In this book, entitled *Drumont et Dreyfus,* he tried to show how the case against the captain was the result of the machinations of anti-Semites and Jesuits who now threatened all of France.[19] He translated the *History of the Inquisition in the Middle Ages* (1900–1903) by the American historian Henry Charles Lea in order to show the depths of clerical bigotry and the damage that it could cause. He remained among the leading public Dreyfusards throughout the affair, drawing upon himself extraordinarily virulent anti-Semitic attacks.

But the crisis of universalism also had its counterpart in the world of scholarship. In this respect, in order to understand Reinach's intellectual trajectory, it is important to grasp the transformation that had taken place in the academic study of non-Western religions and cultures in the course of the nineteenth century. The ambitious project of the eighteenth-century *science de l'homme* had developed several fields of cultural production, ranging from philology to Oriental studies to anthropology. The universalistic aspiration of *science de l'homme,* while producing knowledge about universals, had to account for the particular, which in its most extreme manifestation could be achieved through full-fledged differentialist, racialized science. However, for much of the nineteenth century, race was a remarkably fluid and polysemic concept, full of ambivalences, contradictions, and slippages. It was, above all, an unstable category that could encompass meanings ranging from people or group to nation to deterministic essence rooted in the physical and physiological. The field of Oriental studies of which Renan is perhaps the most paradigmatic example took as its task the study of the non-European, and therefore by definition was engaged in the production of differentialist knowledge and hence deeply imbricated with various usages of race as a concept. Renan's popularization of the central tenet of this field, the distinction between the Indo-European and the Semite, already sweeping all before it in the world of scholarship since the end of the eighteenth century, was an important milestone in the evolution of the category of race toward an immutable essence.[20]

[18]See the file in Archives Nationales, BB 19/95. This has been published in Robert J. Maguire and France Beck, "Un document inédit de l'affaire Dreyfus," *Les Cahiers Naturalistes* (1993): 326–34.

[19]L'Archiviste, *Drumont et Dreyfus: Etudes sur la "Libre Parole" de 1894 à 1895* (Paris: V.-L. Stock, 1898).

[20]Among the many studies of this development, see Léon Poliakov, *The Aryan Myth: A History of Racist and Nationalist Ideas in Europe* (London: Basic Books, 1974); and Maurice Olender, *Les langues du paradis: Aryens et sémites, un couple providentiel* (Paris: Seuil, 1989). For a history of the term "anti-Semitism," see Reinhard Rürup and Thomas Nipperdey, "Antisemitismus—Entstehung, Funktion und Geschichte eines Begriffs," in *Emanzipation und Antisemitismus: Studien zur "Judenfrage" der bürgerlichen Gesellschaft,* ed. Reinhard Rürup (Göttingen: Vandenhoeck & Ruprecht, 1975), 95–114.

Renan played a decisive role in the wide dissemination of this idea in scholarly circles and beyond. In work after work, this most prolific of rhetoricians had argued that the Semites, with their special gift for religion, and the Aryans, with their gift for art and science, were the two currents that by fusing into Christianity had created modern civilization.[21] According to Renan, the Jews had provided the worldview and forces that had seen the emergence of Jesus, who then transcended the Jewish Semitic message, leaving it behind. Once the Indo-Europeans converted to Christianity, all the constituent elements came into place to create the modern, superior European civilization. Although Renan was frequently quite harsh on Jews and Judaism in his writings, he nevertheless placed them at the heart of history and of civilization. His was a mixed message for the Jews. Much more than Arthur de Gobineau, Renan popularized the Aryan versus Semite distinction in France. And yet, unlike Gobineau, he did not hold race to be important in the modern period; he saw in the evolution of civilization the transcending of race with the triumph of the liberal spirit.[22] And he gave Jews a certain primacy in the making of civilization, stressing their continuing role in the prophetic message for the future. By secularizing the study of Jesus, he also secularized the study of religion as a phenomenon, enabling many Jewish scholars to embark on its study.

His views were received with ambivalence by French Jewish academics of the time, many of whom were his friends whose careers Renan was very active in promoting (most notably James Darmesteter). After all, Renan had once again put the Hebrews at the center of history from which they had been displaced by the Indo-Europeans, who were supposed to be the ancestors of Western, civilized peoples; he had secularized the study of the founder of Christianity, stressing his Hebraic origins, and shared in these scholars' belief in the eventual triumph of liberal ideas. Still, there was much in the writings of Renan that could be (and was) interpreted in an overtly racialist manner. Never a systematic thinker, and given to categorical statements with rhetorical flourish, Renan was perceived as positing an indomitable opposition between the Aryan and the Semite.[23] It was in this way that he was quoted profusely by Edouard Drumont, the leading French anti-Semitic

[21]Ernest Renan, *Oeuvres complètes*, ed. Henriette Psichari (Paris: Calmann-Lévy, 1947–61), 7:86.

[22]See, e.g., Renan's letter to Gobineau in 1856, in Renan, *Oeuvres complètes*, 10:204: "I could not tell you that I am of the same opinion as you on all the points. The fact of race is immense in origins; but it always loses its importance, and sometimes, as in France, it fades away altogether. Is this, strictly speaking, decadence?"

[23]Both Tzevan Todorov and Edward Said interpret him this way. See Todorov, *On Human Diversity: Nationalism, Racism and Exoticism in French Thought* (Cambridge: Harvard University Press, 1993); and Said, *Orientalism* (New York: Vintage, 1978). See also Shmuel Almog, "The Racial Motif in Renan's Attitude to Jews and Judaism," in his *Antisemitism through the Ages* (Oxford: Pergamon Press, 1998).

propagandist of the time, who, however, did not hesitate to criticize him when Renan made statements that appeared to be favorable to the Jews.

French Jewish scholars, though themselves using loosely the term "race" in the sense of "people," soon became deeply concerned with the misuse of this concept. Many of them, such as Franck and Darmesteter, explicitly and implicitly challenged race as a category. Newly admitted to the rank of Europeans and for the first time admitted to the university as participants in European scholarship, and yet inheritors of the archetypical category of the "other" or "different" in the West's sense of self, these scholars, while accepting the Indo-European/Semite distinction, contested the binary categorization and systematically complicated the story. They put the stress on mutual influences, interferences, and hybrid and syncretistic trends in the development of language and religion. Above all, they emphasized the universal and the universalistic, rereading both Judaism and modernity as represented by the France of 1789 in this light. Some Jewish intellectuals, such as Halévy and Hippolyte and Olinde Rodrigues in the first generation after emancipation, before they were able to enter academia, had already made the first steps in this super-universalistic turn with their participation in the St. Simonian movement.[24] French Jewish scholars in the field of Oriental studies, such as James Darmesteter and Sylvain Levi, as well as in fields like anthropology, in the case of Salomon Reinach, continued this tradition in their scholarship and indeed in their activities inside and outside academia. Their scholarly preoccupation—reinserting Judaism into a constitutive element in the making of the West and of modernity, and at the same time complicating the essentialist category of Judaism by emphasizing the comparative and the universal—became the hallmark of much of the Franco-Jewish academic public sphere. And indeed, Durkheim, coming from the same milieu, would consecrate this emphasis on the comparative and the universal into one of the fixtures of French social science.

The evolution of Reinach's intellectual production itself becomes intelligible with this context. Always interested in the religious aspects of existence in antiquity, he had started out sharing many of the current views on the Indo-European world. At the beginning of his career, he was quite influenced by the ideas of Friedrich Max Müller, the leading scholar of comparative mythology at the time, whose Lectures on the Science of Language (1864) focused on the linguistic study of texts of mythology. And since, linguistically, Greek myths seemed to point to Indo-Aryan origins, the Aryans were seen by Müller as the genealogical ancestors of Western culture identified with the Greeks. Reinach's views on myth, which

[24]On Halévy, see Rodrigue, "Léon Halévy." On St. Simonianism and the Jews, see Michael Graetz, The Jews in Nineteenth Century France: From the French Revolution to the Alliance Israélite Universelle (Stanford: Stanford University Press, 1996).

had accepted Müller's perspectives, underwent a dramatic change by the 1890s. With the rising utilization of the category of race in anti-Semitic language and discourse, and in the face of Drumont's growing popularity, Reinach became a passionate foe of the Indo-European origins theory and its racial implications. In this he was following James Darmesteter, the famous Jewish scholar of Zend religion, a Renan protégé, and the leading theoretician of Franco-Judaism.[25] In an article entitled "Le mirage oriental" that Reinach published in the periodical *L'Anthropologie* in 1893, he launched a fierce attack on those who were creating genealogical links between the Aryans and ancient Western religions.[26] Significantly, in the same period he also published a book criticizing theories on Aryans as a race, maintaining that "it is a futile hypothesis to speak of an Aryan race of three thousand years ago; to speak of it as if it still exists is simply an absurdity."[27] He questioned the existence of a Jewish race, attacking the jump made from linguistic groupings to race in social thought. As he put it, "It is madness to determine from the language spoken by a man his physical ancestry," and he concluded that "there has never existed a Jewish race: there never will."[28]

It is also in this same period in the mid-1890s, and broadly coinciding with the period of the Dreyfus affair (which he blamed on the clerical party), that Reinach came to adopt the method and orientation of the British anthropological approaches such as those of E. B. Taylor, W. Robertson Smith, and Sir James George Frazer to myth and religion.[29] Putting his encyclopedic knowledge of the ancient world to good use, he transformed himself into a comparativist anthropological theorist, comparing the ever increasing knowledge about the belief system of the contemporary "primitives" with ancient religions and reaching conclusions about the nature of religion in general. In article after article, which he collected into five long volumes entitled *Cultes, mythes et religions* beginning in 1905 and in a major popular work of a general history of religions entitled *Orpheus* that saw thirty editions from its first publication in 1909 until 1921, Reinach applied the new anthropological theories to ancient and modern religions, including Judaism and Christianity.

Reinach was quite critical of Enlightenment views of religion, such as those of Voltaire, that thought of it as an imposture, an instrumental creation by the powerful and the priests to dupe the masses.[30] He was also hostile to interpretations of

[25]See Darmesteter's critique in *Revue Bleue,* 14 Oct. 1893.

[26]Published separately as *Le mirage oriental* (Paris: G. Masson, 1893).

[27]Salomon Reinach, *L'Origine des Aryens: Histoire d'une controverse* (Paris: E. Leroux, 1892), 90.

[28]Salomon Reinach, "La prétendue race juive," in *Cultes, mythes et religions* (Paris: E. Leroux, 1905–23), 3:461, 471.

[29]For a discussion of this school of anthropology, see Robert Ackerman, *The Myth and Ritual School: J. G. Frazer and the Cambridge Ritualists* (New York: Garland, 1991).

[30]Salomon Reinach, *Orpheus: Histoire générale des religions* (Paris: Picard, 1909), 13–15.

religious interdicts as expressing some early hygienic and medical understanding.[31] Instead, for him, the religious instinct was natural, primarily a sentiment of the individual and its expression in rites. Hence, man created religion and the gods. However, as a strict evolutionist, Reinach was a firm believer that the phenomenon of religion had evolved over time from primitive man, and that the key to understanding it was to study contemporary primitive people who were in many ways living fossils. And, most important, religious ideas had not sprung up in one specific place in the world and were not the product of one people but had occurred everywhere. In this respect, religion had started as a question of individual psychology and had then become socialized.

Reinach was singularly uninterested in issues of faith. For him, religion was primarily the "sum of scruples that impede the free exercise of our faculties and prevent our excesses that can easily degenerate into unbridled barbarism."[32] At its source was animism, the investing of the surroundings with spirits and the projection of power onto objects known as fetishes. The earliest of the scruples manifested themselves as arbitrary interdicts known as taboos, which first evolved from the interdicts around blood and the killing and eating of humans. Eventually, some of the taboos, being invested with social ties in tribes and becoming objects of worship, turned into totems, representing a "hypertrophying of the social instinct."[33]

Following Robertson Smith, Reinach believed that totemism came accompanied with the institution of sacrifice. In exceptional circumstances, the totem vested with power is put to death and eaten, imparting its power to the tribe. Through the institutionalization of the sacrifice, a priestly class emerged that then acquired magical powers. Obliged to produce some results, magic gave rise to art and to empirical observation, leading slowly to the emergence of science and to civilization. It was, therefore, totemism that lies at the core of religion. According to an overall evolutionary pattern but at different rhythms, societies abandoned polytheism for monotheism but also carried vestiges of the distant totemic past. Religion—before it becomes stultifying as orthodoxy—in principle accompanied progress. As shown by the expressions "religion of the fatherland" and "religion of the family," it eventually fuses with morality, which assumes its most purified version in the principles of modern secular society. "The transition from the taboo to the reasoned and reasonable interdict is almost a history of the intellectual progress of man."[34]

[31]Reinach, *Cultes*, 2:2.
[32]Reinach, *Cultes*, 1:27; and *Orpheus*, 3.
[33]Reinach, *Orpheus*, 22.
[34]Reinach, *Orpheus*, 6. *Orpheus* popularizes the general schema of the evolution of religion outlined by Reinach in the first volume of *Cultes, myths, et religions*.

There is much in Reinach's writings on these subjects that is close to Durkheim's views of religion, which received systematic exposition in his *Elementary Forms of the Religious Life* (1912). Here, too, totem and taboo play important roles in the genesis of the phenomenon of religion. However, Durkheim and his followers, such as Mauss and Henri Hubert, put the emphasis on what later would be called the "functional" place of totem and taboo in creating collective solidarity in "primitive" societies. Religion for the Durkheimians was constituted not only by a complex of negative "scruples" but also by positive commands and guidelines, together composing a positive sacred. For the Durkheimians, religion was first and foremost the expression of the social, of the collective, whereas for Reinach it was primarily an outgrowth of individual psychology.[35]

Reinach was firm in his belief that the task of the scholar was to analyze the survival of these primitive religious phenomena among the peoples of the world and, using all the skills at the disposal of modern scholarship, to unearth the different layers that made up the religions and mythologies of all peoples. In the preface of *Orpheus,* Reinach makes it clear that this applies to all religions, including Christianity and Judaism, and assumes the moral responsibility "of giving for the first time a picture of religion in general considered as natural phenomena and nothing more." The times were ripe for this, and "secular reason must exercise its rights" against all zealots.[36] By showing that prejudices are old, "one can change men when one proves that they still think like savages, and that their prejudices and taboos, today imperative and irrational, were once the result of works of primitive logic that would make a child of six blush."[37]

The times were indeed ripe. *Orpheus,* dedicated to all the martyrs, appeared in 1909, four years after the separation of church and state, at the height of a nationalist and Catholic revival in France. It was in many ways an anticlerical manifesto, and Reinach had high hopes that it would be adopted as a textbook in the state schools. A popularized summary of many of the ideas he published in article form, it represented the high point of Reinach's efforts to educate the public and shape opinion. It seems quite clear that Reinach's views on religion and current theories on race were radicalized by the rise in anti-Semitism and the Catholic reaction he witnessed in the last decade of the nineteenth century and the early twentieth century. Very much the *engagé* intellectual, fighting for the rehabilitation of Dreyfus, his scholarship on religion was transformed in this period. Co-opting the ideas of

---

[35]See Henri Hubert's critiques in his book reviews, published in *Anthropologie* 20 (1909): 594–96 and in *Année Sociologique* 11 (1906–9), 72–73. The literature on Durkheim and religion is enormous. See, e.g., Donald A. Nielsen, *Three Faces of God: Society, Religion, and the Category of Totality in the Philosophy of Emile Durkheim* (Albany: State University of New York Press, 1999); and W. S. F. Pickering, *Durkheim's Sociology of Religion: Themes and Theories* (London: Routledge & Kegan Paul, 1984).

[36]Reinach, *Orpheus,* x.

[37]Reinach, *Cultes,* 1:85.

the British anthropologists, he embarked on a corrosive critique of all religion, giving it a central place in the making of civilization but showing its primitive origins and its outdated nature in the modern world, which had taken its loftiest ideals and emancipated them from the dross of the primitives. In the process he was intent on humbling the claims to uniqueness of monotheistic religions and on demoting Christianity from its position of teleological accomplishment by putting it on the same level as the totems of the primitives. What better coup de grâce than to claim that the idea of a killed and resurrected God met a receptive audience because of the familiarity of the peoples of the Hellenic world with the myth that the god Dionysus Zagreus was killed by the Titans, from whom man is supposed to be descended, only to be resurrected again by Zeus?[38] And to link the Christian communion and the Eucharist to the sacrificed and eaten totems of the primitives? This was indeed, as one of the hostile Catholic reviewers of *Orpheus* claimed, "the revenge of Dreyfus."[39]

Reinach's reactions in the face of the crisis of universalism in France took the universalism of Franco-Judaism a step further and eroded all claims of uniqueness by the monotheist religions and all races who shared the good and the bad with the others. Since they were the same, one could not claim to be superior to the other and, as a result, could not attack another. Lofty ethical ideas were present in all religious traditions that evolved gradually toward modern civilization. Although it was an article of faith for Franco-Judaism that the Jewish religion was the purest expression of monotheism and that the ideals of justice and ethics were first launched by the prophets, Reinach was not prepared to privilege Judaism by assigning to it a special role, and he was determined to treat it like all other religions. Hence, mixed with its highest achievements were remnants of a distant totemic past. The non-pronounceability of the name of God was the same as a taboo of contemporary primitive people.[40] The ark of the covenant could not be touched (a taboo) because it contained fetishes.[41] The idea of a special covenant with God was one that Jews shared with primitive tribes and clans who had covenants with a special animal.[42] The Sabbath was, in its origins, an unlucky, taboo day.[43] "The Jehovah of the rocks and clouds of Sinai is a product of animism; the Decalogue is a revision of an old code of taboos."[44]

---

[38]Reinach, *Cultes,* 1:12.

[39]Reinach, *Cultes,* 4:353.

[40]Reinach, *Orpheus,* 5.

[41]Reinach, *Orpheus,* 264.

[42]Reinach, *Orpheus,* 267.

[43]Reinach, *Cultes,* 2:428.

[44]Reinach, *Orpheus,* 10. Duchêne discusses Reinach's influence on Freud's interpretation of totem and taboo in his "Préface," lxxvi–lxxxi.

Reinach drew concrete conclusions from these points. He wanted above all "an inner emancipation of Judaism" that would leave behind the flotsam and jetsam of past taboos and totems, such as giving up the necessity of eating only kosher food, which cost the poor in Eastern Europe money they could ill afford. The idea of the Sabbath, while wrapped in superstition, corresponded to the need for rest in the modern world and could be preserved, but there was no reason why it could not be moved from Saturday to Sunday. This would help the poor Jews of Eastern Europe to get employment and would remove barriers between Jews and others.[45] Although the genealogy of these customs and interdicts has special interpretation for Reinach, his goals were, in the end, not fundamentally different from most of the Jewish reformers of the time: to reform Judaism so that its essence (which corresponded with that of reason and justice) could be preserved while the unnecessary accretions of the past could be thrown overboard. But this aim operated for Reinach in a radical universalist worldview that had removed from Judaism and Jews any privileged, unique role that was the main focus of much of reformist Jewish thought and Franco-Judaism in the nineteenth century.

Unlike their counterparts in Germany, where many Jewish social scientists and other scholars had begun to adopt and adapt the rapidly spreading category of race as an analytical tool to analyze the Jewish past and present,[46] French Jewish scholars, deeply embedded in the institutions of the Republic, proved to be largely resistant to the siren call of racial discourse. In keeping with the stance of the community as a whole in the face of anti-Semitism, they remained firmly committed to the universalism that remained in the foreground of the official ideology of French republicanism.

Reinach took this stance to its logical conclusion, positing a universal evolution from the primitive to the civilized, hence eroding notions of blood-based racial hierarchies as well as religious ones. He applied this perspective with corrosive effectiveness to the study of all religions and peoples, including Judaism and Jews, in the process removing from them all distinctiveness. That was the price he was prepared to pay for the stance he adopted in the face of the emerging racialist anti-Semitism and clericalism. His theories removed the bases of bigotry by leveling distinctions between religions and peoples through the argument for one universal human nature and one human path of progress.

And pay a price he did. Not only was Reinach attacked ferociously by the anti-Semitic and Catholic press, but he also became caught in the new Jewish politics in

---

[45]Reinach, *Cultes,* 2:418–28.

[46]This has been the subject of much study in recent years. See, e.g., John Efron, *Defenders of the Race: Jewish Doctors and Race Science in Fin-de-Siècle Europe* (New Haven, CT: Yale University Press, 1994). See also Mitchell Hart, "Racial Science, Social Science, and the Politics of Jewish Assimilation," *Isis* 90 (1999): 268–97.

the first decades of the twentieth century. Somewhat critical reviews of his works
had been appearing periodically in the French Jewish press in 1900. But that was
nothing compared to the tempest he encountered during the 1911 elections to the
Central Committee of the Alliance. In many ways he became a pretext for a power
struggle for the soul of this first international Jewish organization. The Alliance
leadership, predominantly French, had begun to have increasing problems with
the Deutschen Conferenz Gemeinschaft (DCG), which had come into being to
rationalize fund-raising among the Alliance membership in Germany—a third of
the total Alliance membership of 35,000. As of 1909, tensions over the autonomy
of the DCG had grown considerably, and Zionists had begun to exploit this in
order to attack the Alliance as a French assimilationist institution and gain power
within the DCG.[47] Zionism represented a dramatically different worldview from
Franco-Judaism, attacking its belief in the centrality of individual emancipation
and calling for a nationalist regeneration of the Jews as a collectivity.[48] In response
to a German Jewish newspaper's critique of his work, Reinach sent a summary of
his views about the need to reform Judaism, and this led to an outcry among all
those who were chafing at the place enjoyed by the Alliance in the Jewish world.
His words could be used to mobilize a lot of people:

> The Judaism of today is neither a religion, nor a race, nor a people, nor even,
> as Heine called it, a misfortune. Judaism is a tradition, a very glorious tradi-
> tion, the tradition of martyrs, and of obstinate heroes who were the only
> ones in Europe who refused to believe in appalling rubbish during a thou-
> sand years of shadows in Europe.... Hence it is a tradition of free thinking,
> of horror in the face of polytheism and idolatry, of healthy reason insurgent
> against ridiculous fables and stupid rites. Why has Judaism itself not, as of
> the nineteenth century, shrugged off from its shoulders its own ritualism,
> stupid par excellence, in order to become a purely human and moral belief, a
> friend of progress? It is because I have not given up the hope that this can
> happen one day, because I feel myself authorized with all my heart...as a
> good Jew to work for this end that I will not be turned away by insults and
> calumnies. I work for the inner emancipation of Judaism, to free it from
> intolerance, ignorance, and falsehood. The worst enemies of Judaism are not
> the anti-Semites, who—at least in France—have preserved it, but the fanat-
> ics, the Hasidim, the miracle-working rabbis, the Halukkists,[49] the partisans
> of Hebrew as a living language, and other individuals of that ilk. The words

[47]Volumes 9 and 10 of *Ost und West,* the publication of the DCG, reflects the extent of the conflict. The extensive correspondence that this conflict generated is to be found in Archives of the
Alliance Israélite Universelle, Allemagne IV.A. 4 and Allemagne IV.A. 5.

[48]See the discussion in Rodrigue, *French Jews, Turkish Jews;* and Esther Benbassa, *Une diaspora
sépharade en transition: Istanbul, XIXe–XXe siècle* (Paris: Cerf, 1993).

[49]Those who contributed to the Halukah, the collection of funds to support the Orthodox Jewish
presence in Ottoman Palestine.

of Voltaire, "Ecrasons l'infâme" [Let us crush infamy], apply against all that offends reason.[50]

The fact that Reinach had criticized Zionism even more explicitly in encounters with Ottoman leaders made the matters worse:

> I feared that they would take seriously a reactionary and insane movement that, in a country like present-day Turkey, is incompatible [not only] with the loyalty [of its citizens] but also with common sense.... I see two elements in Zionism. One is without doubt appealing: the misery of the Jews of Russia and Romania who, fleeing a reality that crushes them, find refuge in the kingdom of dreams. The other element, hardly respectable in my view, is the ambition, the thirst for publicity of agitators. In countries where Jews are persecuted, Zionism can be a comforting phantom; in Turkey it is nothing but foolishness.[51]

This stance united the traditionalists and the Zionists, who mounted a campaign against Reinach to prevent his reelection to the Alliance Central Committee, which would have disqualified him from the vice presidency of the organization. It was only with Herculean effort by the leadership of the Alliance, which gave firm directives about how to vote to thousands of members, especially among the Sephardim of the Ottoman Empire, that Reinach was reelected.[52] But he had finished last in terms of votes and he resigned discreetly a year later, in 1912.

The crisis of universalism had begun to reach the Jewish world. In response to the new anti-Semitism, disaffection with the liberal synthesis of the mid-nineteenth century had grown considerably in Central and Eastern Europe. Although Franco-Judaism could maintain itself, albeit with increasing defections, in the interwar period, the ultra-universalist stance of a Reinach could no longer be accommodated in a leadership position in its ranks when Jewish nationalism began to make dramatic headway in the international Jewish arena. The very crisis that had decisively marked Reinach's scholarship and radicalized it had also transformed the Jewish political landscape, making it impossible for him to continue his public Jewish engagement. He could now continue to intervene only as a scholar, the way that he had started his adult years.

[50]Quoted in Archives of the Alliance Israélite Universelle, Allemagne V.A. 8, DCG circular to its members, 9 Apr. 1911. Reproduced in Reinach, *Cultes,* 5:450. The response of his opponents was swift: "A man who makes such declarations cannot be at the head of a Jewish Alliance, not only in the eyes of an Orthodox Jew but also for each liberal Jew. Even if his theories were right, it is impossible to overlook the fact that these kinds of attacks hurt most profoundly the sensibilities of a large number of members of the Alliance and of the great majority of the Jews of the world who are represented as an inferior element" (Archives of the Alliance Israélite Universelle, Allemagne V.A. 8).

[51]From a letter by Reinach to David Fresco, the editor of the Ladino newspaper *El Tiempo* in Istanbul; cited by David Wolffsohn, president of the Zionist Action Committee, and sent to the Alliance Central Committee. Archives of the Alliance Israélite Universelle, Allemagne V.A. 8, 9 Apr. 1911.

[52]See the extensive documentation on this affair in Archives of the Alliance Israélite Universelle, Allemagne V.A. 8.

Catholic Culture
in Interwar France

Philip Nord

THE INTERWAR YEARS have been characterized as a watershed in the history of French Catholicism,[1] and it is not hard to see why. The Roman Catholic Church had experienced the first decades of the Third Republic as a time of trial and persecution. The First World War, however, gave believers reason to look forward to a brighter future. The republican establishment had welcomed the political representatives of Catholic opinion into the Union sacrée. The distress of soldiers and war widows had nourished a revival of popular faith.[2] And with the return of peace, the Catholic laity plunged into an associational activism of unprecedented proportions. The vaulting edifice of voluntary bodies they constructed reenergized the faith and at the same time articulated a Catholic countervision of the proper constitution of *la cité*.

The Catholic community no longer stood on the defensive but carved out for itself a vast, new civic domain. The phrase "ghetto Catholicism"[3] has been invoked to describe the phenomenon, and the term will serve insofar as much of the activism of the interwar years styled itself as apolitical and inward-looking. There should be no mistaking, however, just how innovative the new-style Catholicism was, nor the degree to which its creative impulses had an impact on the wider public arena, all claims to nonpartisanship notwithstanding. The nature of that impact may well be debated. Anglo-American historians have been inclined to highlight the authoritarian leanings of interwar Catholicism, its predilection for dictatorial regimes with a confessional bias like Portugal's Antonio Salazar or Austria's Engelbert Dollfuss.[4] From this angle of vision, the Catholic

---

[1] James F. McMillan, "France," in *Political Catholicism in Europe, 1918–1965,* ed. Tom Buchanan and Martin Conway (Oxford: Oxford University Press, 1996), 34.

[2] Annette Becker, *La Guerre et la foi, de la mort à la mémoire 1914–1930* (Paris: A. Colin, 1994).

[3] Martin Conway, *Catholic Politics in Europe, 1918–1945* (London: Routledge, 1997), 18.

[4] Robert O. Paxton, "France: The Church, the Republic, and the Fascist Temptation, 1922–1945," in

Church hierarchy's deep involvement in the affairs of the Vichy government (1940–44) appears all too predictable. French historians, however, have preferred a more benign interpretation. All sorts of compromises were made at Vichy, but for many militants, the object was not to serve the National Revolution (a conservative movement fueled by the early Vichy government and focused on returning France to its pre-revolutionary glory), but to make it serve the cause of a *redressement national*.[5] When that failed, they poured into the Resistance, finding there a hard core of Christian Democrats who had stood from the very first against the Vichy government headed by Philippe Pétain. The interwar decades had witnessed a narrowing of differences between the Catholic Church and the Republic. The Resistance experience crystallized Christian commitment to democratic principle, making possible at long last a wholehearted Catholic *ralliement*.

The two views, of course, are not altogether antithetical. The Catholic revival of the 1920s and 1930s was compatible with a variety of political choices, democratic and authoritarian, although on balance the scales tipped in favor of the latter. The catastrophes of the war years reweighted the options, this time to the advantage of the Christian Democrats. But whatever the ambivalences of Catholic culture and however such ambivalences got resolved, it should be remembered that Catholics were not just the objects of larger political forces. They in turn influenced events and policy, leaving an imprint not only on Vichy of course, but also on the political life of two Republics: the Third and, to a greater extent, the Fourth. Ghetto Catholicism accommodated itself to an ambient republican culture, but it gave as good as it got.

CIVIC MOBILIZATION

Catholic associational activism was not a creation of the interwar decades. The evangelization of the lower orders had been a preoccupation for many years, dating back to the foundation of the Association catholique de la jeunesse française (ACJF) in 1886. The organization, though, was paternalist in orientation, run by the well-bred with the object of bringing religion to the less fortunate. The experience of the war and its aftermath prompted a trio of new initiatives. The insurrectionary climate of 1918 and 1919 spurred Christian trade unionists, committed to a defense of working-class interests but not at the expense of religious principle or public order, to set up a national labor organization, the Confédération française

Catholics, the State, and the European Radical Right, 1919–1987, ed. R. J. Wolff and J. K. Hoensch (Boulder: University of Colorado Press, 1987), 67–91; and John Hellman, *Emmanuel Mounier and the New Catholic Left, 1930–1950* (Toronto: Toronto University Press, 1981). See also Hellman, *The Knight-Monks of Vichy France: Uriage, 1940–45* (Montreal: McGill–Queens University Press, 1993).

[5]Michel Winock, *"Esprit": Des intellectuels dans la cité (1930–1950)* (Paris: Seuil, 1996); and Bernard Comte, *Une Utopie combattante, L'Ecole des cadres d'Uriage 1940–1942* (Paris: Fayard, 1991).

des travailleurs chrétiens (1919). The next year saw the formation of Robert Garric's Equipes sociales. Garric, a war veteran, wanted to re-create in peacetime the social solidarity he had known at the front, and the Equipes, which brought together laborers and young Catholics in a spirit of common endeavor, were meant to achieve that end.[6] The kind of "go-to-the-masses" Catholicism that Garric preached, with its accent on youth and social exchange, was attractive to bright-eyed souls like writer, feminist, and political activist Simone de Beauvoir, who came from good families but hankered for something more than a conventional life. The Fédération nationale catholique des Scouts de France (SdeF), like the Equipes sociales, was founded in 1920, and it too devoted itself to the cultivation of team spirit, but with a more military and clerical twist. Throughout the interwar years, the post of chef Scout was occupied by a series of generals, and the movement took its spiritual inspiration from Paul Doncoeur and Marcel Forestier, both priests, the former a Jesuit, the latter a Dominican. Father Doncoeur presided over formation of scouting's elite wing, the Routiers, in the mid-1920s. Father Forestier was appointed the SdeF's chaplain general in 1936.[7]

Two circumstances—the first domestic in origin, the second foreign—helped to pick up the pace of Catholic activism. Catholic opinion had rallied to the Union sacrée and then to the Bloc national coalitions of the immediate postwar years. Such loyalty had yielded certain rewards. The separation of church and state was not imposed on the recovered provinces of Alsace-Lorraine. In 1920, on the occasion of Jeanne d'Arc's canonization, the Republic dispatched an official delegation to witness the ceremony. Dozens of deputies attended, but the standout was General Edouard de Castelnau in full-dress uniform, a war hero who not four years before had been passed over to succeed Joffre as commander in chief of western armies because he had been deemed too clerically minded. The warming of relations between the Catholic Church and the Republic culminated in the reestablishment of France's diplomatic ties to the Vatican in 1921.[8]

Then in 1924, all such progress threatened to come unstuck. Voters returned a leftist majority to office; the Cartel des Gauches promised a reversion to the secularizing ways of the pre–World War I era. Catholic opinion responded with a massive countermobilization that assumed organizational form as the Fédération nationale catholique (FNC) in 1924. General Castelnau took charge of the operation, assisted by Father Doncoeur and a cast of rabble-rousing public speakers, among them FNC vice president Philippe Henriot and that all-purpose champion

---

[6]Comte, *Utopie,* 33.

[7]Philippe Laneyrie, *Les Scouts de France: L'évolution du mouvement des origines aux années quatre-vingt* (Paris: Editions du Cerf, 1985).

[8]Harry W. Paul, *The Second Ralliement: The Rapprochement between Church and State in France in the Twentieth Century* (Washington DC: Catholic University of America Press, 1967).

of right-wing causes, Xavier Vallat. At its peak in the late twenties, the FNC boasted a membership approaching two million.[9]

An event of no less importance was the Vatican's resolution in 1926 to place the daily paper *Action française* under interdict. Pope Pius XI did not so much object to the monarchism of its editor, Charles Maurras, as to his emphasis on the primacy of the political; for what did a France wounded in spirit need?—not monarchist agitation but the healing power of Catholic action. The banning of the *Action française* signaled to Catholics that a nonpartisan, apostolic associationism was the direction in which to move, and their response was impressive and inventive: impressive in the sweep of new organizations formed, the Jeunesse ouvrière chrétienne (JOC) in 1927, the Jeunesse agricole chrétienne (JAC) in 1929, and the Jeunesse étudiante chrétienne (JEC) also in 1929; and inventive in the range of media employed: talk shows sponsored by the Fédération française de Radio-Famille, choral songfests sponsored by the JOC, and of course the abbé Courtois's illustrated youth magazine *Coeurs vaillants* which attracted a readership in the hundreds of thousands. Its secret? In 1930, the magazine began serialization of the adventures of Tintin: Boy Reporter, the invention of Belgian cartoonist Georges Remi (better known as Hergé).[10]

A new Catholic culture was in the making. It was sustained by an impressive associational scaffolding, and it spoke to the world in a variety of voices—journalistic, theological, literary, and artistic. For every audience, there was a review or newspaper. The stodgy stalwarts of the FNC could turn to *La France catholique* or *L'Echo de Paris,* but the young were just as well served: by *Coeurs vaillants,* by Garric and Father Forestier's *Revue des jeunes,* by a raft of scouting and Catholic action periodicals. For the high-minded, on the lookout for informed rumination or political commentary, the 1930s marked a kind of golden age with the founding of the Christian Democratic *L'aube* in 1932, Emmanuel Mounier's *Esprit* later that year, and in 1934, *Sept* (published under Dominican auspices).

Indeed, the decade was a golden age not just for the Catholic columnist, but for the independent Catholic theologian as well,[11] and here the names of Gabriel Marcel, Jacques Maritain, and Father Teilhard de Chardin come straightaway to mind. The first two were converts and the third an accomplished paleontologist who had a taste for cosmic meditation that did not always sit well with his church

[9]James McMillan, "Catholicism and Nationalism in France: The Case of the Fédération Nationale Catholique, 1924–1939," in *Catholicism in Britain and France since 1789,* ed. Frank Tallett and Nicholas Atkin (London: Hambledon Press, 1996), 151–63; and Aline Coutrot, "Les mouvements confessionnels et la société politique," in *Forces religieuses et attitudes politiques dans la France contemporaine,* ed. René Rémond (Paris: A. Colin, 1965), 135.

[10]Eugen Weber, *The Hollow Years, France in the 1930s* (New York: Norton, 1994), 187. See also Vincent Feroldi's *La Force des enfants, des Coeurs Vaillants à l'A.C.E.* (Paris: Editions ouvrières, 1987), ch. 5.

[11]Jacques Prévotat, "Théologiens laïcs des années trente," *Les Quatre Fleuves* 17 (1983): 49–69.

superiors. Much of Teilhard's work was not published in his lifetime, although it circulated among lay readers in manuscript form. These were men of profound Catholic faith who operated outside official church institutions, displaying a metaphysical élan that was bracing but also, from the hierarchy's point of view, at times troublesome.

Yet perhaps the most remarkable cultural development of the interwar years was the affirmation of a Roman Catholic presence in the arts, in literature above all; the work of Paul Claudel, François Mauriac, and Georges Bernanos is most notable. Bernanos, the youngest of the three, published *Journal d'un curé de campagne* in 1936, a haunting story of the spiritual wrestlings of a young, guileless country priest, which ends with the protagonist's death—one made holy by humility and a presumption of grace. The spirit could be transmuted not just into literature but also into music. The music might be popular as in the case of Tino Rossi's "Ave Maria" (1938), or modernist highbrow as in Arthur Honegger's score for *Jeanne d'Arc au bûcher* (1935), a dramatic oratorio created in collaboration with Claudel. Francis Poulenc, an old musical confederate of Honegger's, is best remembered as the composer of light, witty, and very French music, but after 1936 (a "hateful year" he is said to have called it), he turned to the writing of a series of choral works with powerful religious themes: *Litanies à la vierge noire* (1936), *Mass in G* (1937), and *Quatre motets pour un temps de pénitence* (1938/39).[12]

Even the domain of sacred art, weighed down by centuries of tradition, experienced a rejuvenation. After the Great War, the painters Maurice Denis and Georges Desvallières set up a workshop, the Ateliers d'art sacré, bringing to bear a palette of fresher, stronger colors on stained glass and ceramic work. The architect Auguste Perret set a new standard in church design, experimenting with reinforced concrete in the construction of Notre-Dame du Raincy (1922).[13] The devotees of *l'art sacré,* indeed, founded a magazine by that very name in 1935, underwritten by a mix of prominent lay and clerical personalities: Claudel, Denis, and the dramatist Jacques Copeau among the laymen; Fathers Doncoeur and Marie-Alain Couturier (a veteran of Denis's *Ateliers*) among the ecclesiastics.[14]

REFAIRE UNE CHRÉTIENTÉ

Father Doncoeur's phrase, "Refaire une chrétienté," sums up the renovative ambitions that inspired so many Catholic activists of the interwar decades. The new

[12]Benjamin Ivry, *Francis Poulenc* (London: Phaidon, 1996), 86, 90; and Frédéric Gugelot, *La Conversion des intellectuels au catholicisme en France (1885–1935)* (Paris: CNRS, 1998), 273–74.

[13]Gérard Cholvy and Yves-Marie Saint-Hilaire, *Histoire religieuse de la France contemporaine, 1880/1930* (Toulouse: Privat, 1986), 2:323–24.

[14]See "Comité de Rédaction," *Art sacré* 1 (July 1935). From 1937, Father Couturier coedited the periodical with R. P. Regamey.

Catholic culture did not reject out of hand the forms and means of communication modernity placed at its disposal. A readiness to engage with modernity, however, did not mean a capitulation to its ways. Catholics, however intent on self-transformation, still remained in critical opposition to the wider civic order, more intent on a reconquest of the public realm (*conquête* was in fact a favored term in the Catholic lexicon of the era) than on any form of power-sharing.[15]

Catholics did not doubt that the modern world had gone awry, attributing the initial false step to the Italian Renaissance. The Renaissance's paganism and aesthetic naturalism had alienated the flesh from the spirit, and the person from the community that nurtured him. The result was an atomistic pursuit of interest and pleasure that was at the source of all contemporary France's moral failings.[16] It was liberal individualism that lay behind what Mounier liked to call *le désordre établi* with its corrupt party politics and dubious parliamentary maneuverings.

What was needed was a new age of faith, and there were examples in the past to look to: golden age Spain and the French Middle Ages. Then, faith had burned with an unparalleled intensity. Saints and knights strode the earth, but they served in obedience to a wider purpose, to the human collectivity of which they were part, to the will of God whose instruments they were.

The heroes of these bygone ages had critical lessons to teach the modern-day believer, lessons of valor, risk, and adventure. The Catholic Scout movement was conceived as a twentieth-century reincarnation of "ce vieil idéal de la chevalerie chrétienne." Troops named themselves after champions of old, like the spotless Bayard, or the crusading Saint-Louis. Indeed, a crusading purity was taken to be the very essence of scouting. The English Scout pledged himself to cleanliness, but his SdeF counterpart went a step further, vowing to be "pure in body, thought, word, and deed." And the movement took as its emblem the *croix potencée* atop a shield. This had been Godefroy de Bouillon's blazon in crusading days, later taken up by the Knights of the Holy Sepulcher.[17] But the Scouts had no monopoly on such heraldic conceits. The members of JOC, called the Jocistes, had a coat of arms of their own, a young blade of wheat twined about a Maltese cross. This banner in

[15]Jacques Duquesne, *Les Catholiques français sous l'Occupation,* rev. ed. (Paris: Grasset, 1996), 72, 444.

[16]Jacques Maritain's *Humanisme intégral* (Paris: Aubier, 2000) opens with a critique of the anthropocentric humanism of the Renaissance. For a critique of Renaissance aesthetics, see Henri Charlier, "L'esprit sculptural," *Art sacré* 11 (1936). For a post–World War II variant, see Marie-Alain Couturier, *Sacred Art,* trans. Granger Ryan (Austin: University of Texas Press, 1989), 72, 102. The latter volume, edited by Dominique de Menil and Pie Duployé, republishes essays Couturier wrote for *Art sacré* in the late forties and early fifties. Menil had herself contributed to *Art sacré* before the war. She kept in contact with Couturier in subsequent years and is said to have purchased her first Cézanne on his advice in 1945. Such were the beginnings of the celebrated Menil collection, now housed in Houston, Texas.

[17]Laneyrie, *Scouts,* 94, 107, 109, 120. See also Pierre Assouline, *Hergé* (Paris: Plon, 1996), 68.

hand, they marched into spiritual battle, singing as they went the refrain of the "Chant de la JOC mondiale" (written 1927/28): "forts de nos droits, soyons vaillants/fiers, purs, joyeux et conquérants."[18]

Of course, the heroic ideal could lend itself to less combative treatment. Claudel's 1929 drama, the *Soulier de satin,* takes the story of Le Cid and resets it in late sixteenth-, early seventeenth-century Spain. There are infidels to fight and the hero must sacrifice love for duty, but Claudel's Rodrigue operates on a planetary scale: the scene shifts from Spain, to the New World, to North Africa. He is a visionary who imagines a globe made Christian, united in a higher love and submission to the divine scheme.

Saints too came in many shapes and sizes. Mounier thought of writing a thesis on the golden age Spanish mystic, Saint John of the Angels. Castilian Spain gripped the French imagination not just as a backdrop for noble deeds, but as the nourishing soil of a fierce faith, of an interior life that exalted.[19] For seekers of the interior life, though, what more compelling model was there than Saint Thérèse de Lisieux? Here was a modern-day French saint, a Carmelite nun canonized in 1925 not much more than a quarter century after her death. She may not have had the mystic's fire, but she had a simple candor and Christlike purity of heart. Edith Piaf was lifelong devotee of the saint's cult. Bernanos, who wanted no more than to remain true to the child he once had been, revered Saint Thérèse as the incarnation of *"l'esprit de l'enfance."*[20] To be sure, saints had other qualities to teach besides spiritual zeal or childlike humility. Take Saint Jeanne—the Scouts treated her as a martial figure on a par with the knights they so much admired. To Bernanos, she was France's last great soldier. Claudel on the other hand accented Jeanne's martyrdom, her agony at the stake as she gave up a life that had been consecrated to the unity of France.[21]

A crusading purity, spiritual simplicity and joy in God's love, and a devotion to France and the divine order of things were the qualities that the knights and saints of old exemplified. Yet it was not always necessary to look backward to find such paragons; there were contemporary counterparts: Maréchal Lyautey, for

---

[18]Roger Beaunez et al., *Jocistes dans la tourmente: Histoire des jocistes (JOC-JOCF) de la région parisienne 1937–1947* (Paris: Editions du "Témoignage chrétien," 1989), 207.

[19]Hellman, *Emmanuel Mounier,* 11, 27. The work of El Greco exercised a similar fascination and for much the same reason. It was Maurice Barrès who was responsible for rekindling public interest in the painter's work. Barrès had paid a visit to Toledo just before World War I. The sight of El Greco's *Burial of the Count of Orgaz* in the Church of Santo Tomé moved him to write of the painter's exaltation, his intensity, and his sense of the sublime; see *Greco ou le secret de Tolède* (1911; repr., Paris: Flammarion, 1988), 103, 104, 114. It is not without interest that the preface to this edition was authored by Jean-Marie Domenach.

[20]Georges Bernanos, *Les Grands Cimetières sous la lune* (1938; repr., Paris: Seuil, 1995), 227.

[21]Arthur Honegger, *Jeanne d'Arc du bûcher.* Lyrics by Paul Claudel (Paris: Editions Salabert, 1947).

example, the SdeF's *président d'honneur,* or Georges Guynemer, that latter-day
chevalier de l'air.[22] Hergé proposed the good Scout Tintin who picked his whole-
some way through a world abounding with secular villains: Bolsheviks, Chicago-
land gangsters, and a whole gallery of unscrupulous businessmen/criminals.[23]
Bernanos's country priest believed he had found a modern embodiment of Jeanne
d'Arc in the nephew of a neighbor, a motorcycle-driving soldier on leave from the
Foreign Legion.[24] As for saints, Bernanos populated his novels with them, hum-
ble country *curés* who in obscure villages lived out the most elemental and epic
spiritual confrontations.

Catholic activists looked to the past for models of good conduct, but this did
not mean there were no modern-day equivalents. And they approached collective
life in much the same spirit. The Middle Ages had known a sense of community,
long since corroded by a rampant individualism. In the interwar period, the shop
floor was rent by class struggle. Not so in the Middle Ages when the brotherhood
of labor had been sustained by guilds and corporate organization. Early twentieth-century theater audiences sat as isolated spectators, ranked by seat and box
number, separated from the stage by a proscenium arch. Not so in the Middle
Ages when the common folk had thronged to the cathedral steps to witness mystery plays or the reenactment of the Passion.[25] Modern women recited the rosary
during Mass and men just did not come. Then the liturgy had been vital, the Mass
a nourishment of faith, transforming the assembled into a true church, the mystical body of Christ.

Genuine spiritual community was all too rare a phenomenon in the modern
world, but Catholic activists did not despair, casting about for ways and occasions
that might lend themselves to a rekindled sense of mystical bonding. Such
impulses placed a special premium on the group experience: the *cercle d'études,* the
équipe sociale, the Scout troop. All such groups had a *chef* to be sure, but the true
leader did not just command but, by word and deed, helped to fuse the group into
a team. The sing-along was a means to that end: choral singing became a standard
feature at Jociste and Scout events, the overall effect often enhanced by an outdoor
setting in a sports stadium or forest clearing. The choral vogue even made its
impact felt in the fine arts over the course of the 1930s. Poulenc's *Mass in G* (1937)
was composed for a cappella choir, and the spoken chorus made a comeback in the

[22]Laneyrie, *Scouts,* 97, 120. See also Robert Wohl, "The Bards of Aviation: Flight and French Culture, 1909–1939," *Michigan Quarterly Review* 29 (1990): 303–27.

[23]See the plotlines of Hergé's first three Tintin serials: *Tintin au pays des Soviets* (1930), *Tintin au
Congo* (1931), and *Tintin en Amérique* (1932), published in Brussels in *Le petit vingtième,* both in separate issues and in album form.

[24]Bernanos, *Journal d'un curé de campagne* (1936; repr., Paris: Plon, 1974), 249–64.

[25]Jacques Copeau, "La représentation sacrée," *Art sacré* 18 (1937), 110–11.

theater as well, thanks in part to the promptings of Copeau who was inspired by ancient Greek examples.

Such hankerings for spiritual renewal were not without result. The Jocistes and Scouts contrived to stage mass events that left an enduring and transformative impression on participants. JOC officials mounted a three-day gala to commemorate the organization's tenth anniversary in 1937. An estimated eighty thousand turned out to take part in the event. The festivities on the second day were capped by a nighttime festival of labor, which featured a parade of metiers followed by a sudden blackout. A spotlight flashed, illuminating a forty-foot cross borne by a cohort of Jociste youth. A choir demanded, "But where then is the architect of *la Cité*?" to which the assembled crowd shouted in response "It is he."[26]

The Scouts had every bit as much flair for a public dramaturgy that mingled the sacred and the theatrical. One of Copeau's students, Léon Chancerel, assembled a theater company composed in the main of ex-Scouts, which took the name Comédiens-Routiers in 1931. The band offered up a mix of Molière and medieval mystery plays, and was remarkable on several counts: for its experimentation with acrobatics and masques, for its willingness to travel, and for the talent of its young troupers who included Hubert Gignoux, Jean-Pierre Grenier, and Olivier Hussenot, all of whom were destined to make a mark in French regional theater. Chancerel also had a hand in organizing amateur Scout theatricals. The performance put on by Scouts at Lourdes in 1938, a series of sketches written by Chancerel, was in many ways typical of such efforts. Its occasion was that year's national pilgrimage, and its subject was very much tailored to the event, for it dramatized the Virgin Mary's special relationship to France across the ages.[27] The Scouts were at it again in 1942, although this time it was not Chancerel's troupers at work but Doncoeur's Routiers. From across the land, elite units set out on pilgrimage to Le Puy to pay homage to the Virgin. There, ten thousand gathered under Doncoeur's watchful direction, reenacting the *chemin de Croix*, a dozen Scouts shouldering the cross followed by a host of their barefoot comrades.[28]

Indeed, collective celebration and pilgrimage, staged with attention to effects of music and theater, might help to reawaken a flagging sense of spiritual communion. But where such communion mattered most was in church itself. Various, albeit dispersed, experiments with the liturgy had been undertaken in the years

[26]*Jocistes dans la tourmente*, 35–36; and Pierre Pierrard, Michel Launay, and Rolande Trempé, *La J.O.C., Regards d'historiens* (Paris: Editions ouvrières, 1984), 75.

[27]Denis Gontard, *La Décentralisation théâtrale en France 1895–1952* (Paris: SEDES, 1973), 86; Daniel Lindenberg, "Révolution culturelle dans la révolution nationale: De Jacques Copeau à 'Jeune France': Une archéologie de la 'décentralisation' théâtrale," *Les Révoltes logiques* 12 (1980): 2–9; David Bradby, *Modern French Drama 1940–1990*, 2nd ed. (Cambridge: Cambridge University Press, 1991), 13; and Hubert Gignoux, "Théâtre Scout," *Art sacré* 35 (1938), 329.

[28]Cholvy and Saint-Hilaire, *Histoire religieuse*, 3:88.

preceding the war. The JOC from its earliest beginnings had engaged in choral
French-language singing at mass.[29] Father Doncoeur too had innovated, holding
Scout masses at historic sites or in woodland settings, using a tree stump or woven
branches for an altar. Theater had a part as well in the story. Copeau's strictures on
dramatic technique—his commitment to simplicity of set design, expressivity of
the body, and ensemble acting—had worked their way through the interwar theater world. When Jean-Louis Barrault staged Claudel's *Soulier de Satin* at the
Comédie française in 1943, it was a production very much in Copeau's spirit
(Copeau had in fact been the theater's director for a brief period in 1940/41).
Clergymen in the audience were bowled over by the poetry of the experience and
came away wondering how such effects might be applied to liturgical ends. It was
just such speculations that had inspired formation of the Centre de pastorale
liturgique the very same year. Father Doncoeur, it seems, was much taken with
the enterprise, seeing in it an instrument to realize a long-cherished project, the
fashioning of "a liturgy, simple, clear, *proche du peuple fidèle.*"[30]

As such cravings for liturgical reform indicate, it was not just the profane
world that stood in need of restoration, but the churches themselves. Critics
decried the tastelessness of church design and decoration, the fake Gothic and
bondieuserie saint-sulpicienne. What was needed was a new architecture simple in
its lines, a new ornamentation purified and sincere in its means of expression. That
is why Perret's pared down design for Notre-Dame du Raincy excited such enthusiasm among *art sacré* advocates. Yet, it was not just clean lines that they yearned for,
but also a sense of monumentality, of the whole. At the decorative arts exposition
of 1925, a half-dozen artists, among them Denis and Desvallières, collaborated in
the construction of a French village church, a religious *Gesamtkunstwerk* intended
to serve as both model and inspiration.[31] The innovators' agenda was clear. They
wanted to shake off the dead hand of the past in favor of *l'art vivant.* They wanted a
setting for prayer and contemplation that would be austere and direct, addressing
itself without sentimentality or excess of anecdote to the intuition of worshipers.
And they wanted structures that in their monumentality and rigor would express
the total life of the community.[32] It is not hard to affix a label to such a project, for

[29]Pierrard, Launay, and Trempé, *La J.O.C.,* 44–45.

[30]Bradby, *Modern French Drama,* 1–2, 23–28. See also Sabine de Lavergne, *Art sacré et modernité:
Les grandes années de la revue "l'Art sacré"* (Namur: Culture et vérité, 1992), 189–91.

[31]Cholvy and Saint-Hilaire, *Histoire religieuse,* 2:323–24; Emmanuel Bréon, "L'Art sacré s'expose,
1925–1931–1937," in *L'Art sacré au XXe siècle en France* (Boulogne-Billancourt: Centre cultural, 1993),
81–82.

[32]See Joseph Pichard, "Témoignage de notre temps, Promenades à travers les chantiers du Cardinal," *Art sacré* 14 (1936), 18; and Fr. M.-A. Couturier, "St.-Jacques de Montrouge," *Art sacré* 26 (1938),
34–35. For a later, comprehensive statement, see R. P. Regamey, *L'Art sacré, sa mystique et sa politique*
(Paris: Editions du Cerf, 1955).

it was a modern architecture to which they aspired. The adjective however was not to be bandied about lightly in a church that had locked horns with modernism in all its forms. Yet the periodical *Art sacré* did just that, publishing a call to artists to design "modern churches," a call issued by none other than Robert Mallet-Stevens, one of France's premier modern architects.[33]

A new church, it was hoped, would make for a new piety, no more the affected "rosewater" piety of old but a spirituality more vigorous, even more virile. There is no doubt that many Catholic activists worried about the feminization of the church.[34] Catholic action was in part about inducing men to take up a more central, active part in spiritual affairs. The patriarchal overtones of the era's Catholic activism are not hard to pick up. The first day of the Jocistes' tenth anniversary congress was given over to the theme of *le retour de la mère au foyer*. Catholics of all political persuasions advocated the cause of *allocations familiales*, state-paid allowances to families in which mothers did not work. Even Christian Democrats, the most "progressive" of the era's Catholic factions, came out for *le vote familial*, the apportionment of multiple votes to fathers of large families.[35]

No doubt Catholic activists wanted to shore up paternal authority, but the Christian family they dreamed of was not altogether traditionalist in cast. A father was meant to be *chef de famille*, but a *chef* in a family conceived of as a team, not as an inflexible hierarchy. Wives submitted, but it was a "submission of love which did not entail an abdication of personality."[36] The wife, moreover, was meant to be active outside the home, not on the job of course, but doing parish work or engaging in Catholic action. A pair of Catholic action groups was in fact set up for young marrieds, the Ligue ouvrière chrétienne (LOC) for husbands and the LOCF for wives, the two fusing in 1942 to form the Mouvement populaire des familles (MPF). There was concern too that female spirituality change with the times. Diocesan bulletins encouraged young women to practice retreat and embrace a Christocentric faith focused less on the baby Jesus than on the Savior's adult example. Was not a woman who made a Christian home, took part in civic action, and

[33]Robert Mallet-Stevens, "Pourquoi la France n'aurait-elle pas des Eglises Modernes?" *Art sacré* 10 (1936), 102.

[34]Gérard Cholvy, "Une image de la jeune fille entre les deux guerres: Les bulletins diocésains de la jeunesse catholique féminine," in *Education et images de la femme chrétienne en France au début du XXe siècle,* ed. Françoise Mayeur and Jacques Gadille (Lyon: Edition l'Hermès, 1980), 190; W. D. Halls, *Politics, Society and Christianity in Vichy France* (Oxford: Oxford University Press, 1995), 244; and Bréon, "La Peinture encadrée," in *L'Art sacré au XXe siècle,* 41.

[35]Henri Hatzfeld, *Du Paupérisme à la Sécurité sociale, essai sur les origines de la Sécurité sociale en France 1850–1940* (Paris: A. Colin, 1971), 172–84; Jean-Claude Delbreil, *Centrisme et démocratie chrétienne en France, le Parti démocrate populaire des origines au M.R.P., 1919–1944* (Paris: Publications de la Sorbonne, 1990), 134–35, 240–42, 249–50.

[36]Adrien Dansette, *Destin du catholicisme français, 1926–1956* (Paris: Flammarion, 1957), 425–26.

practiced her religion with a mature seriousness entitled to vote? Christian Democrats not only championed the *vote familial,* but also women's suffrage.[37]

France was rotten with individualism; the Catholic Church itself had grown
old, stodgy in its tastes and forms of piety. Catholic activists were determined to
cause a fresh wind to blow, an apostolic wind that would reenergize the faithful
and spur them to a conquest of the world. This was the Catholic answer to the
problems of the interwar decades, and believers did not hesitate to label it a superior form of humanism. Indeed, it is remarkable how often the words "humanism" and "human" crop up in the Catholic discourse of the period. Mounier
published an essay titled "Notre humanisme" in 1935. Maritain's magisterial
Humanisme intégral came out the next year. Teilhard de Chardin's *Le Phénomène
humain* was completed on the war's eve (although it did not appear in print until
the midfifties). And in late 1941, François Perroux and the Dominican Father
Louis Lebret organized a study group with the name Economie et humanisme.
Secular humanisms, whether liberal or Marxist, claimed to have a totalizing
vision of humankind's potential, but they were insensitive to the darker side of the
human nature and had no grasp at all of the transcendental ends of human existence. A Catholic humanism addressed all the concrete problems of the here-and-
now—problems of family and economy, of person and community—but it
remained ever cognizant of man's ultimate destiny outside himself in a loving
communion with a God of forgiveness.

CATHOLIC CULTURE AND THE CITY OF MAN
Whatever might be said about the Catholic mobilization of the interwar years, it
was neither modest in its ambitions nor backward in its means of action. But did it
have any impact on the wider national community? The answer, of course, is yes,
and that impact began to make itself felt already under the Third Republic. A confessional party, the PDP, had been founded by Catholics of Christian Democratic
persuasion in 1924. It was small, however, never mustering more than a score of
deputies in the chamber. Many in *bien-pensant* circles deemed it too "red." Yet,
whatever its occasional flirtations with the left, the PDP would not endorse socialist prime minister Léon Blum in 1936, finding more suitable ideological company
in the post–Popular Front Daladier administrations of 1938 through 1939. That a
center-right formation like the PDP was blackballed for its extremism is revelatory
of the state of Catholic opinion which found more congenial Colonel de La
Rocque's paramilitary Croix de Feu or other classic right parties like the Fédération républicaine. La Rocque, of course, styled the Croix de Feu a bulwark of

---

[37]Dansette, *Destin du catholicisme français,* 373–75. See also Cholvy's "Une image de la jeune
fille," 191–92, and Delbreil, *Centrisme,* 57.

Christian civilization, and the organization's militancy proved alluring to the likes of François Mitterrand (a "Catho-social" in the words of a friend) who was on the lookout for a formation that melded anticapitalism, anticommunism, and Christian action of a militant stripe.[38] As for the Fédération républicaine, it reaped substantial political dividends in the thirties from the declining fortunes of Castelnau's FNC, counting at least two FNC veterans, Henriot and Vallat, among its senior officers.

But it was not so much in the domain of party politics as in that of public policy that the new Catholic activism made a difference. The FNC's agitations in the twenties helped constrain the *cartel des gauches* to back down. Diplomatic relations with the Vatican were preserved, as was the church/state connection in Alsace-Lorraine. The secularizing swell that broke over France with the coming of the Third Republic had now crested.

At the time of the Spanish Civil War, France's Socialist government headed by Blum did not follow its initial impulse to lend military assistance to the Spanish loyalists, settling instead for a policy of collective noninterference. The reasons for the decision were manifold, but Blum was not insensitive to powerful currents in public opinion hostile to interventionism. One such current was Catholic. Castelnau hailed the conflict as a holy war. Franco was cast as a twentieth-century Le Cid and his soldiers as crusaders. True Spain, Mauriac announced, was the Spain of Saint Theresa of Avila and Saint John of the Cross, of Le Cid and El Greco.[39] There were to be sure Catholic voices who could not stomach the brutalities of the Francoist insurrection: the editorialists at *L'aube* and *Sept,* Bernanos, Mounier, and, in the long run, Mauriac too. But these were minority voices, and few among them went so far as to take the loyalists' part, refusing to choose sides in what was judged a fratricidal struggle.[40]

Blum was perhaps wary of Catholic opinion; the Daladier government that replaced Blum in 1938, however, was quite solicitous of Catholic support. In 1938, Daladier's administration enacted a series of laws and decrees on family policy that were extended and rationalized in the so-called Code de la famille of 1939. The Code was innovative on several counts, not least in its provision for a special allowance for unwaged mothers, the so-called *allocation pour la mère au foyer.* Republican legislators in the past had been more concerned about driving up birthrates than with favoring a particular family form, but no longer; the change may be

---

[38]Pierre Péan, *Une Jeunesse française, François Mitterrand 1934–1947* (Paris: Fayard, 1994), 33, 76.

[39]Cholvy and Saint-Hilaire, *Histoire religieuse,* 3:43–44; Mauriac, as cited in René Rémond, *Les Crises du catholicisme en France dans les années trente* (1979; repr., Paris: Editions Cana, 1996), 172.

[40]Hellman, *Emmanuel Mounier,* 118. See also Rémond, *Les Crises du catholicisme,* ch. 5; and Bernanos, *Les Grands Cimetières sous la lune.*

attributed to the growing clout of Catholic opinion in the councils of power.[41] And Daladier had more than one occasion to demonstrate a sensitivity to certain Catholic interests. Throughout the thirties, *Action française* had lobbied the Vatican to lift its ban, but Pius XI had demurred. His successor, Pius XII, was not so hesitant. Terms for lifting sanctions were worked out, and in July 1939 the Vatican removed *Action française,* repentant in certain respects but not in its Maurrasism, from the Index. Most remarkable of all, the Daladier government, which was consulted on the matter by the Holy See, saw fit to raise no objections.[42]

The new Catholic culture had become a force to contend with even before the war, tilting republican policy away from the militant secularism of old toward a family-minded conservatism. With the coming of Vichy, it became, not so much an influential contender, as a central player in the drama of public life. The major outlines of the story are well known.

There was much in Pétain's National Revolution to appeal to Catholics. Vichy promised to fortify the family and effect a rebirth of corporatism. It spoke the language of the Catholic revival, bandying about the terms "person" and "community" with all the authority of the initiated. The church's enemies were also the regime's: liberalism, parliamentarism, Freemasonry, "excessive" Jewish influence, and godless communism. Not least of all, Vichy proclaimed its determination to reeducate the nation's youth. This meant, in part, a repudiation of republican secularism in education, but more so, it meant a mobilization of the young in the nation's service, the training of new elites to spearhead the *redressement national* to come.

Vichy beckoned to Catholics, and few at the outset saw much reason not to respond. "Pétain, c'est la France, et la France aujourd'hui, c'est Pétain," intoned Cardinal Gerlier, archbishop of Lyon and a former ACJF president, in 1940. The rest of the church hierarchy did not much differ in its views. As for the activist laity, they were well represented in the senior ranks at Vichy. François Perroux counseled Pétain on constitutional affairs; Mounier's old philosophy professor at Grenoble, Jacques Chevalier, headed up the Ministry of Public Instruction. From 1941 through 1942, Vallat, late of the FNC, occupied the post of Commissioner-General for Jewish Affairs. And the FNC's star speaker Henriot ended up the voice of Radio Vichy and a minister of Information. He was gunned down by *résistants* in 1944; Cardinal Suhard, archbishop of Paris and a patron of the worker-priest movement, presided over the funeral services.

---

[41]Delbreil, *Centrisme,* 370; Susan Pedersen, *Family, Dependence, and the Origins of the Welfare State, Britain and France 1914–1945* (New York: Cambridge University Press, 1993), 386–91; and Jean-Jacques Dupeyroux, *Sécurité sociale* (Paris: Dalloz, 1965), 60.

[42]Cholvy and Saint-Hilaire, *Histoire religieuse,* 3:62–64. There was, however, one dissenting voice in the Daladier cabinet, that of the Christian Democrat Champetier de Ribes. See Paul, *Second Ralliement,* 174.

The Catholic cultural renaissance of the interwar years also supplied its fair share of recruits to the new order. Claudel penned an ode of praise to the Maréchal. In the summer of 1942, an exhibit was mounted in Paris to honor Hitler's favorite sculptor Arno Breker. The list of art world luminaries who agreed to serve on the French welcoming committee is striking: André Derain, Othon Friesz, Maurice de Vlaminck, formerly adherents of the avant-garde art movement known as the Fauves, for their preference for striking colors, and joining them, the architect of Notre-Dame du Raincy, Perret. In a less highbrow vein, Hergé, illustrator extraordinaire to Catholic youth, spent the war years turning out Tintin serials for the Brussels-based *Le Soir,* a collaborationist paper kept afloat by German funds.

Perhaps too much ought not to be made of such individual itineraries since numerous counterexamples can and will be cited. When the conduct of organizations is examined, the record looks every bit as ambiguous. Vichy solicited Catholic participation in setting up its so-called Corporation paysanne, and rural-based Catholic action groups, the JAC among them, proved willing to help out. The CFTC, on the other hand, rejected the regime's labor charter.[43] But it is in the domain of youth policy that the story gets most complicated.

At the Vichy youth administration, it was Catholics (and above all Catholic Scouts) who set the tone.[44] Pétain appointed a veteran of Garric's Equipes sociales, Georges Lamirand, to run the Secrétariat général de la jeunesse (SGJ), and Lamirand oversaw a host of institutional experiments. A youth labor service corps, the Chantiers de la jeunesse, was set up in 1940 under the leadership of an old Scout General de La Porte du Theil, seconded by Father Forestier in the post of head chaplain. The scouting influence was more indirect at the Ecole nationale des cadres, a 1940 creation invented by Major Pierre Dunoyer de Segonzac. Uriage, as the school came to be known after the château it made its home (which happened to be the family seat of the great Bayard), styled itself an elite institution, a training school for future *chefs.* Here, it was a Mounier-style personalism, rather than the scouting ethos, that enjoyed pride of place, although ex-Scouts, as well as graduates of the Equipes sociales, were numerous among the student population.

Two bodies, more autonomous in constitution although still dependent on SGJ subsidies, bear mentioning in the present context. The first, Henry Dhavernas's Compagnons de France, was a youth recreational and service organization. Dhavernas was himself a Scout official and brought a Scout's taste for group song to his work, forming a choral auxiliary, the Compagnons de la chanson.[45] The second, Jeune France, concentrated its efforts on cultural renovation. Founded by

---

[43]Duquesne, *Les Catholiques français,* ch. 9.
[44]Cholvy and Saint-Hilaire, *Histoire religieuse,* 3:85–86.
[45]Duquesne, *Les Catholiques français,* 217; and Halls, *Politics,* 296–97.

Pierre Schaeffer, a veteran Routier, it is best remembered for its work in radio and theater production. Schaeffer recruited ex-Comédiens-Routiers like Grenier and Hussenot, as well as a young newcomer named Jean Vilar, to serve in Jeune France's theater section. The organization extended its patronage to a variety of regional theater initiatives, among them Jean Dasté's *Les Quatre Saisons* (Dasté was Copeau's son-in-law) and André Clavé's *La Roulotte*.[46]

But what was ambiguous about all this? Few of the participants had much sympathy for liberalism or the defunct Republic, and they were willing enough to work under Vichy auspices. Yet they also had a taste for independence and a strong sense of patriotic mission. In the long run, these qualities led to clashes with Vichy authorities who were centralizing in outlook and craven in the face of the occupying power's ever more exigent demands. The Chantiers survived the life of the regime, but not Jeune France, Uriage, or the Compagnons, all of which were shut down between 1941 and 1944. Many of the survivors headed into the Resistance.

There is a salutary reminder here: however great the overlap between Vichy and prewar Catholic activism, the fit was never perfect. Indeed, there was a minority of Catholic *résistants* from the very beginning. The most significant group, the Témoignage chrétien, drew its cadres from PDP ranks, Christian Democrats who may have harbored reservations about the Third Republic but were serious in their commitment to democratic institutions. They were seconded by CFTC dissidents and by a band of hearty exiles: Maritain and Father Couturier in the United States, and Bernanos in Brazil (who proved himself yet once again a scourge of the *bien-pensants*). And the ranks of the Catholic Resistance swelled, as the Vichy government revealed its moral squalor. The Catholic Church and Scout hierarchies stuck by Pétain through good times and bad, but the bulk of the Catholic action apparatus, after an initial period of *Maréchalisme,* passed to the other side.

Catholic activists, as they broke out of the Vichy orbit, found themselves drawn into close proximity with competing, often alien currents—Communist, Gaullist, and Republican. For long-standing Christian Democrats, experience of a pluralist universe posed no special problem. But the Christian-Democratic Resistance recruited, not just from the ranks of the old PDP, but from Catholic Action as well, and for these young Catholics, joint effort with old antagonists proved an eye-opener. They emerged from the war, less fired by the rhetoric of *la conquête* and more willing to enter into a give-and-take exchange with *la cité*.[47]

[46]Bradby, *Modern French Drama*, 31. See also Véronique Chabrol, "L'ambition de 'Jeune France,'" in *La Vie culturelle sous Vichy*, ed. Jean-Pierre Rioux (Brussels: Complexe, 1990), 167; and Lindenberg, "Révolution culturelle dans la Révolution nationale," 8.

[47]Oscar L. Arnal, "Toward a Lay Apostolate of the Workers: Three Decades of Conflict for the French Jeunesse Ouvrière Chrétienne (1927–1956)," *Catholic Historical Review* 73 (1987): 214–15.

It is however possible to exaggerate how much the war experience reoriented the ghetto Catholicism of old. Not all Catholics were turned into good democratic pluralists at a stroke. Not Dunoyer de Segonzac, for example. He made his way to Algiers after breaking with Vichy, but found the atmosphere there distasteful, altogether too "Third Republic."[48] Nor did Bernanos ever ease up in his aversion to France's revolutionary past. Indeed, his last literary effort, the *Dialogues des Carmélites* (completed in 1949), tells the story of a convent of Carmelite nuns martyred at the hands of brutish Jacobins in 1794. Wartime experience cut deep inroads into Catholic culture's antipathy toward the republican tradition without wiping it away entirely. More to the point for the present discussion, certain underlying preoccupations remained the same. Catholics did not give up worrying about the fate of the family or confessional education in a secularizing world; they had no more liking than before for the cut-and-thrust of liberal capitalism; and in the cultural domain, they still spoke in a distinct idiom that placed a particular accent on the regional, the sacred, and the heroic.

In the war's aftermath, the Catholic laity stood poised to play an unprecedented part in reshaping public life; they seized on the opportunity, bringing to the task a set of concerns all their own, an agenda long in the making. At the Liberation, veterans of the Christian-Democratic Resistance constituted themselves into a confessional party, the Mouvement républicain populaire (MRP). Of the two hundred or so MRP officials elected in the various parliamentary votes of 1945/46, the vast majority had had prior experience in the PDP, the ACJF, or both.[49] The party, new as it was, exercised a decisive influence on postwar family and education policy that included the most generous family-allowance program to be found in Europe at the time; this was largely the work of MRP deputy turned minister of Health and Population, Robert Prigent. Prigent was an old Jociste who during the war had militated in the LOC-MPF before joining de Gaulle in North Africa. He was able to count on the assistance of a skilled subordinate and advisor, Alfred Sauvy, who is best remembered as the first director of the Institut national d'études démographiques, itself a postwar creation founded in 1945.[50] But perhaps the most striking of Catholic achievements in a France once more governed by republican institutions was the Barangé law of 1951. Named after its sponsor, MRP Deputy Charles Barangé, the law sanctioned public spending in support of

[48]Duquesne, *Les Catholiques français,* 225. He made the observation to de Gaulle, it seems, who responded with equanimity, "Que voulez-vous, la France est radicale-socialiste."

[49]Jean-Marie Mayeur, *Des Partis catholiques à la Démocratie chrétienne, XIXe–XXe siècles* (Paris: A. Colin, 1980), 167.

[50]Cholvy and Saint-Hilaire, *Histoire religieuse,* 3:131; Michel Chauvière, "Structure de sociabilité et travail de la socialité: Des associations familiales sous Vichy," in *Sociabilité, Pouvoirs et Société, Actes du Colloque de Rouen 24/26 novembre 1983* (Rouen: University of Rouen, 1987), 557–66; and Henry C. Galant, *Histoire politique de la Sécurité sociale française 1945–1952* (Paris: A. Colin, 1955), 65–69, 80–83.

private, confessional education, a symbolic break with the *foi laïque* of the old Third Republic.

In the domain of social relations, Catholic activists played a major role in the remodeling of agriculture. The JAC came into its own in the postwar decades. A *nouveau type de rural* emerged from its ranks, dynamic and confident. Young Catholic farmers plunged into agricultural organization, pushing the cooperative principle and by such efforts making a signal contribution to the modernization of the countryside, France's so-called silent revolution.[51] They plunged as well into agricultural syndicalism. Jacistes joined the nonconfessional Centre national des jeunes agriculteurs (CNJA) in sufficient number that they came to dominate its governing board. The CNJA in turn became one of the state's principal interlocutors in the formulation of agricultural policy. The arrangement may not have been just what corporate-minded intellectuals had dreamed of in the 1930s, but it was a form of corporatism nonetheless.

As for culture, the choral and theatrical experiments of the preceding years continued unabated. Claudel and Honegger's *Jeanne d'Arc au bûcher,* although composed in the thirties, did not make its debut in France until 1941 in a Jeune France presentation. The oratorio's greatest success, however, awaited the 1950 season. The Paris Opera mounted a full-stage production with Ingrid Bergman cast in the role of Joan, a stunning performance by all accounts that was followed by a world tour. Nor was it just Honegger's dissonant complexities that achieved world fame, but also (on a more popular note) the choirboy sounds of the Compagnons de la chanson. After the war, the Compagnons crossed paths with Piaf, performing a series of songs with her, among them the still memorable "Les trois cloches." The tune was a favorite at Jociste *veillées,* but in the United States too, for it was in the company of the Compagnons that Piaf made her American debut in 1947.[52]

In the world of the theater, Catholic-inspired critics like Copeau had long targeted the corrupt and superficial character of the Parisian boulevard stage. The postwar Republic proved itself responsive to such grievances. The Ministry of Fine Arts took up the cause of regional theater, extending its patronage to a network of state-subsidized *centres dramatiques* at Rennes, Saint-Etienne, etc. The Théâtre national populaire, directed from 1951 by Jean Vilar, was the capstone of this new theatrical edifice. No doubt many currents fed into these initiatives, but the Catholic influence was significant. So many of the new theater directors— Clavé at the Centre dramatique de l'Est, Gignoux at the Centre Dramatique de

---

[51] Yves-Marie Hilaire, "L'Association catholique de la jeunesse française: Les étapes d'une histoire (1886–1956)," *Revue du Nord* 66 (1984): 915.

[52] *Jocistes dans la tourmente,* 205; and Simone Berteaux, *Piaf: A Biography,* trans. June Guicharnaud (New York: Harper & Row, 1972), 257–68.

l'Ouest, Dasté at the Comédie de Saint-Etienne, even Vilar at the TNP[53]—had come out of the Catholic Scouts or Jeune France. They brought to their task a particular set of tastes, a taste for the French classics above all. More than half the dramas staged by the TNP in its first years were classics, and no production played to greater success than Corneille's *Le Cid* with Gérard Philipe in the title role. But these were classics made new again, reinterpreted by a generation of theater directors schooled in a Copeau-inflected aesthetic that eschewed effects in favor of austere staging and group acting.[54]

It was not just the profane arts that could be made new again, but the sacred as well. The war did not cause the aspiration toward a rejuvenation of Christian art to fade. In the early postwar years, plans were laid for construction of a Dominican chapel in the Provençal town of Vence. Father Couturier, having returned from the United States, assembled the design team: Perret for the architecture, and his friend Henri Matisse for the interior decoration. The Chapel of the Rosary, as it was called, was completed and consecrated in 1951. Matisse considered it his *chef d'oeuvre,* and well he might. He had worked in a variety of media, designing the stained glass, the wall ceramics, even the church vestments. Here was a decorative ensemble, an *espace religieux,* in Matisse's words, that combined light, simplicity of line, and a spare but telling application of pure color to create an overall effect of tranquil spirituality. Most remarkable of all was Matisse's representation of the Virgin and Child, the forms clarified to reveal an underlying geometry of ovals, circles, and curves. That old Communist Picasso was irritated with Matisse, whom he suspected of hypocrisy, for having taken on a religious assignment, but Matisse defended himself: "Yes, I do pray and you do too, you know it well."[55]

The sacred had a place in the postwar world, as did the heroic Christian ideal. Le Cid and Jeanne d'Arc were still figures to conjure with. Bernanos kept on adding to his portrait gallery of embattled curates and nuns. He died in 1949, but even then, the message of unflinching spiritual courage his heroes had to teach survived him and was indeed translated into a variety of new media—both by the filmmaker Robert Bresson who made a movie version of the *Journal d'un curé de campagne* in 1950, and by Poulenc who composed an opera based on the *Dialogues des Carmélites* that premiered at La Scala in 1957. As for the Scouts, the chivalric Routier gave way to a new model, the Raider Scout, a martial figure of an

---

[53]Although Vilar was at pains to distance himself from Copeau's religious agenda. See Emmanuelle Loyer, *Le Théâtre-Citoyen de Jean Vilar: Une utopie d'après-guerre* (Paris: Presses Universitaires de France, 1997), 156, 159.

[54]Bradby, *Modern French Drama,* 30–32, 88–93. See also Gontard, *Décentralisation.*

[55]Cited in Gilles Néret, *Henri Matisse* (Cologne: Taschen, 1996), 230. See also Couturier's diary entry of 17 July 1951, as quoted in Marcel Billot, ed., *La Chapelle de Vence, Journal d'une création* (Paris: Editions du Cerf, 1993), 401.

altogether modern sort who skied, knew judo, and sported a green commando beret.[56] Hergé's Tintin also got an update. After the war, Hergé began republication in album form of his old cartoons, purging them of certain dubious stereotypes. In a pair of midfifties serials, *Objectif lune* and *On a marché sur la lune,* Tintin as always comes across as the good Scout, but the good Scout now recast as earnest cold warrior. The setting is Eastern Europe; the goal, a landing on the moon; the enemy, an unnamed power whose agent Colonel Boris manages to suborn a decent but vulnerable rocket engineer recruited from America.

It makes sense to speak of a Catholic *ralliement* to republican principle in the twentieth century. The process, however, was at no time a smooth one. The first phase, begun in the 1890s, was interrupted by the Dreyfus affair. A second effort was mounted after the Great War, but Vichy brought it to an abrupt close. A third *ralliement* was attempted after World War II, and this time it proved a lasting success. The reasons why may well be debated. In part, it was because the war experience itself had burned out of ghetto Catholicism much of its authoritarian impulse. Activists were as never before prepared to come to terms with a pluralist and democratic regime. And on the secular side, much of the opposition to Catholic inclusion had been eroded. Had not Catholics proven themselves in the Resistance? It helped too that the Radical Party, once among the most die-hard of anticlerical forces, no longer counted for much on the postwar scene. Catholics poured into the breach and the onset of the Cold War strengthened their hand, making of them indispensable partners in any anticommunist coalition.

But the point is not just that once-marginalized Catholics now found a place for themselves in public life, but that in so doing, they made an original contribution to national policy and culture. A tight focus on the class struggle or the intellectual life of Saint-Germain-des-Prés might cause the curious onlooker to miss out on the phenomenon. Shift the gaze, however, to family or agricultural policy, to regional theater or children's literature, to the Vence of Matisse, the music of Poulenc, the heroes of Bernanos, and the picture looks altogether different. Such a claim may appear startling at first glance. From a late twentieth-century perspective, the French Catholic Church might well appear familiarly crisis-ridden: short of priests, anxious about shrinking congregations, and at loggerheads with an ambient "culture of death." But in the bracing post-Liberation years, it was other-

---

[56]For the rise and evolution of the Raider model, see Christian Guérin, *L'Utopie Scout de France, Histoire d'une identité collective, catholique et sociale 1920–1995* (Paris: Fayard, 1997), 311–39. Yet another utopia, after Uriage and the TNP.

wise. Then, a renaissance of faith had made of French Catholicism, in the words of one historian, "the most admired and redoubtable in Christendom."[57] How the French Catholic Church pitched from that moment of promise to the more troubled circumstances of the present time is an interesting story but not the business of the present essay. The argument made here is that Catholics for a multiplicity of reasons rallied to the Republic in the aftermath of World War II, and that the Republic in consequence took on a new and less secularist look. The Catholic reawakening, born of the interwar decades, changed the face of France, and indeed, as has been hinted, how France looked to the wider world.

[57]Etienne Fouilloux, *Les Chrétiens français entre crise et libération, 1937–1947* (Paris: Seuil, 1997), 257. The concluding chapters in this volume evoke to great effect the distinctive mix of effervescence and conservatism that characterized French Catholicism in the aftermath of the war.

The Right to Be Different

SOME QUESTIONS ABOUT THE "FRENCH EXCEPTION"

Carmen Bernand

THIS ESSAY AIMS TO EXPLORE the stakes and paradoxes of the "right to be different," as that right is claimed in France, both by the left wing (which, it should be noted, believes in a moderate form of multiculturalism that takes the republican French heritage into consideration), and by the right, which is at its most radical in the National Front. In concrete terms, what is meant by "cultural difference"? Is there a contradiction between that ideal and the French belief in the universal, which stems from the constitution of the First Republic? Indeed, it is through the individual that the French tradition gives rise to the universal; individual rights express mankind's transcendence, whereas collective rights are thought to obscure it. Following this reasoning, the Declaration of the Rights of Man would seem to run counter to the right to be different. Yet, at the twilight hour of republican evangelism, what power does such a position have? Under the pressure of diverse campaigns commemorating the "meeting of the two worlds" (the conquest of America), UNESCO, in 1992, declared the absolute importance of cultural factors. But what, for example, is to be said of the indigenous peoples integrated into France's overseas departments? How does one reconcile the claim for cultural specificity with the notion of universalism? In sum, what is to be done with the rights of man and with secularism in the context of religious and cultural pluralism?[1]

Moreover, can religious difference be separated from cultural difference? To do so is to suppose that the term "religion" possesses only an institutional sense, which removes it from other aspects of culture. Yet, religion is not merely identical with particular institutions, nor would the universality of the religious merge

---

This essay was translated from the French by Duane Rudolph.

[1]N. Rouland reviews these questions in "La tradition juridique française et la diversité culturelle," in *Droit et Société* 27 (Paris: Commission française pour l'UNESCO, 1994), 6 (also available at http://www.reds.msh-paris.fr/publications/revue/htlm/ds027/ds027-10.htm).

with the particularism of religious practices and doctrines.[2] French universalism condemns neither ways of life nor traditions nor behavior marked by belonging to a particular group. What French universalism rejects, however, is the spillage of such practices into the public sphere. Therefore, the true stake of such universalism is the dichotomy between the public and the private—the cleavage of individual behavior. In such a dichotomy is seen a radical distinction that characterizes modern societies, but above all French society.[3]

This essay will explore some themes related to religious differences from both an historical and an anthropological perspective by examining the cultural specificity of the French perception of difference. Such a particularity, which transcends religion, has nonetheless a religious dimension rooted in French history, a dimension that eventually contributed to the elaboration of the Declaration of the Rights of Man of 1789. The Declaration itself would serve as a model for international rights and would be echoed on 10 December 1948 in the Universal Declaration of Human Rights, which is the preamble to the Charter of the United Nations.[4] This essay will also examine the position of minorities in the constitution of national unity, and finally, the appearance of new modes of religious expression, which demands a new definition of what constitutes religion.

FRENCH UNIVERSALISM IN ITS HISTORICAL CONTEXT

In order to make a transition using the historical treatises on religious tolerance and the Edict of Nantes, it is useful to recall here, if only briefly, the appearance of a particular sensitivity regarding difference (cultural, social, physical, or religious) that is contemporary with the Declaration of the Rights of Man. Such sensitivity informed the remarkable movement that opposed the legitimacy of the authorities and questioned the political and religious basis of the social order. The movement wished to transcend the social positioning of individuals as members of various limited groups, that is, limited by social status, religion, ethnicity, or cultural background. The Enlightenment combined universalism and cosmopolitanism. What better illustration of this is there than the declarations of the philosopher Pierre Bayle, author of the famous *Historical and Critical Dictionary,* at the very beginning of the eighteenth century: "I am a citizen of the world. I am neither in the service of the Emperor, nor in the service of the King of France, but

---

[2]See Carmen Bernand and Serge Gruzinski, *De l'idolâtrie: Une archéologie des sciences religieuses* (Paris: Seuil, 1988).

[3]Mary Douglas, "The Cloud God and the Shadow Self," *Social Anthropology* 3 (June 1995): 83–94.

[4]Norbert Rouland, Stéphane Pierre-Caps, and Jean Poumarède, *Droit des minorités et des peuples autochtones* (Paris: Presses Universitaires de France, 1996), 198–200. The Charter of the United Nations—whose preamble is the Declaration—deals extensively with the rights of people to govern themselves, in the framework of the fight against colonialism.

in the service of truth."[5] It is therefore not surprising that the Enlightenment cast such an interested glance at social and cultural pluralism. Some examples, which are not exhaustive, taken from this new way of understanding difference, no longer seen in purely French terms, but in a more international context.

The collective notion of a "people" deserves some attention. The success of the term derives from its semantic ambiguity. At its most neutral, the notion means "all those living in a society, sharing a certain mixture of customs and inhabiting a defined territory." When positively overinvested, "people" refers to the nation, and more precisely, in the context of the Constituent Assembly, it means all those who are invested with rights and subject to the same laws. When negatively nuanced, "people" draws closer in meaning to the common people, though in this case it refers to the larger group. On the social level, the common people are seen as being in conflict with the ruling classes, and on the cultural level, they are in conflict with the elite. Therefore, should the representatives of the French people be understood as being part of the common people or of the nation more generally?

When "people" designates a collectivity of humans equal before the law, cultural and social differences lose their importance. An extreme example is that of Anacharsis Clootz, whose opinions isolated him during his speech at the Convention on 5 February 1793. Clootz declared that "the designations 'French' and 'universal' will become synonymous with greater reason than the names 'Christian' and 'Catholic,'" and he requested the suspension of the use of the name "French," "following the example of 'Burgundian' and 'Norman' for the sake of the designation 'human race.'"[6] However, from an anthropological perspective, the symbolic dimension of the "body of the nation" is in itself a cultural trait, and mention can only be made here of the parallelism between this idea and that of the "king's two bodies" in the Middle Ages, as analyzed by Ernst Kantorowicz.[7] To put it simply, the king was seen by medieval and early modern theorists of kingship as having a natural or mortal body, which was his own individual body, and a political and immortal body, which belonged to the nation. This dualistic notion of the king is transferred to the citizen in the post-Revolutionary period. Public adherence to the principles of the Republic guarantees the continuity of the state, now separated from both the Catholic Church and the king. In return, private expression of religious beliefs was tolerated, and religious pluralism even codified, in the forms of legal recognition of Jewish and Protestant religious practices, first under the

---

[5]Bayle, as quoted in J. P. Willaime, "Introduction," *Social Compass* 44 (1997): 197.

[6]Clootz, as quoted in Claude Nicolet, "Citoyenneté française et citoyenneté romaine: Essai de mise en perspective," in *Le modèle républicain,* ed. Serge Berstein and Odile Rudelle (Paris: Presses Universitaires de France, 1992), 29–30.

[7]Ernst H. Kantorowicz, *The King's Two Bodies: A Study in Medieval Political Theology* (Princeton, NJ: Princeton University Press, 1957).

Republic and later under Napoleon. This elaboration of what we might call "the citizen's two bodies" persists even today, although in modified form, as private religious practices remain free from constraints, but public religious expression is limited by law.

It is in the name of the group of citizens that religious minorities disappear as distinctive groups. The religious pluralism that resulted from the early phases of the Revolution underwent a short iconoclastic period, especially in 1793 and 1794, which affected the public manifestation of all religions, but principally of Catholicism. In the department of Hérault, for example, "no minister or preacher of any religion whatsoever may appear in public other than in civilian dress."[8] As for crucifixes, effigies, and other external shows of worship, they were destroyed in the entire department. Religious peace was imposed to put an end to resistance from the Vendée. Although the Catholic Church was subsequently able "to reenchant" the area through roadside crosses and statues of the Virgin Mary, such attempts were unable to thwart the iconoclasm (that is, the destruction of religious images) of the Third Republic. The Catholic Church was also unable to thwart the erection of monuments across France, after the Great War, for those who died for their country.

Concerning Islam, the revolutionary period retained as curious and as benevolent an attitude as that of the Enlightenment. The identity of men from lands under the Ottoman Empire is rarely described as "Muslim." In fact, before the beginning of the colonial adventure, the Ottoman Empire was cited as a model of tolerance to thwart its portrayal as evil by the Catholic priests. Protestants banished from France as a result of the Revocation of the Edict of Nantes obtained refuge in different European countries, as well as in the Maghreb and in Turkey. Liberal Catholics, hostile to partisans of the Counter-Reformation and destroyers of Jesuits, offered the most favorable images of Islam. As for the Deists, they condemned "all infamous superstition," that is, all dogma that augmented natural religion to the point of overburdening and obscuring it. The Deists considered Islam a natural religion. However, they blame the "three impostors," Moses, Jesus, and Mohammed, for the imposition of dogma.[9]

Religions were therefore judged by both Enlightenment and Revolutionary philosophers by the measure of liberty and human rights. They thus appeared to be all-encompassing and invasive systems—the most censured being Catholicism—that stifled the individual's freedom of thought. Today there is an echo of

[8]Minutes of the sessions of the Administrative Assembly of the Department of Hérault during the French Revolution (1790–1793), quoted in Gérard Cholvy, *La religion en France de la fin du XVIIIe à nos jours* (Paris: Hachette, 1991), 17.

[9]Jean-François Clément, "Les penseurs des Lumières face à l'Islam," *Social Compass* 44 (June 1997): 227–46.

the Enlightenment in the Catholic Church's criticism of sects that violate the rights of the individual. As the Catholic priest, Jacques Trouslard, specifies in a study by the Roger Ikor Center in 1995, "every belief is the prerogative of the individual's free choice and no one should be harassed for their religious convictions."[10] The cultural dimension of religions, the content of their representations, their enchantment of the world, their symbolic associations, however, were not taken into account by the movement of the Enlightenment that gave way to the Revolution.

In fact, Enlightenment philosophers saw cultural aspects of the Christian heritage as rustic backwardness. The Bretons—Catholic and hostile to the Republic—represented, more than any population group, this seemingly primitive pre-French culture. Through their Celtic origins, they were closest to the Gauls, and thus attracted a great amount of interest. They were consequently the object of study of a vast project organized in 1805 by the Celtic Academy. In the work of the Celtic Academy, the Breton religious past is reduced to tales and legends without religious significance. This secularization of past religious traditions is in keeping with post-Revolution republican ideals.

Apart from what is brought together under the rubric of archaeology, the Celtic Academy's study contains a list of regional practices. Though short-lived after the enforcement of the Civil Code, they are, for the most part, various forms of superstition. This study notes celebrations from this culture on the verge of extinction that are linked to both the agricultural and religious calendars and details all the ceremonies that lie outside "medical science" and "holy religion," both of which deal with man's misfortunes. The interest in these cultural characteristics derives from the assumption that they were in the process of disappearing. Before long, it was thought, standardization would replace local cultural idiosyncrasies. In this attitude is the same will to unify people that fueled the replacement of old measures—different from one province to the next—by a simple system with a universal basis: the metric system.[11] Monuments, whose place must be restored in "the general history of Gaul," are part of the sovereign people's heritage, not only as historical landmarks, but as a legacy to be passed on to subsequent generations. Though the opinion of the local inhabitants was solicited, when the study specified the importance of places of worship or even cited "miraculous"

---

[10]The Roger Ikor Center, *Les sectes: Etat d'urgence* (Paris: Albin Michel, 1995), 23–27. The Roger Ikor Center is also known as the Center for Documentation, Education, and Action Against Thought Control (the French term is *manipulations mentales*). The center has the support of the Ministry of Youth and Sports and the Ministry of Education.

[11]The Celtic Academy's questionnaires were reproduced in Arnold Van Gennep, *Manuel de Folklore français* (Paris: A. Picard, 1937), 3:12–18. Mona Ozouf commented on the scope of the study in "L'invention de l'ethnographie française: Le questionnaire de l'Académie celtique," *Annales ESC* 36 (March–April 1981): 210–30. See also Maurice Agulhon, *Histoire vagabonde* II (Paris: Gallimard, Bibliothèque des Histoires, 1988).

stones, it referred to the "people." In fact, the local population is consistently referred to by the term "people," meaning the "common people."

It is also in the revolutionary context, during the gestation period of universalism, that the Constituent Assembly began reforming the hospitals and assistance for the destitute. For example, La Rochefoucauld-Liancourt, the representative for Clermont in Beauvaisis, presented a report in 1791 on a bill regarding health and social services, and the eradication of begging. He recounted the causes of destitution and distinguished between the truly poor (the elderly, abandoned children, the disabled, and the unemployed) and the "falsely" poor. It was in humanity's name that the unsanitary conditions of the hospitals of Bicêtre and the Salepêtrière were denounced. It is clear from these reports that the committee saw certain basic rights—to health, food, dignity, and self-sufficiency—as inalienable for all people. We can see the germ of universalism in these reports.[12]

It was also in the name of humanity that scholars and explorers joined the Société des Amis de l'Homme in order to lay the foundation for an ethnography capable of enriching morality through the study of man in his primitive state in an extension of early modern theories of natural law, which already had posited certain human rights and privileges as universal to all mankind. Thus, the "Considerations of diverse methods to be followed in the observation of uncivilized peoples" that Joseph-Marie de Gérando addressed to the citizen Levaillant at the beginning of the nineteenth century fit within the framework of the universalist movement. The unknown islands of the Pacific were from then on "the cradle of mankind" and their peoples, hitherto despised "by our ignorant vanity," were "ancient and majestic monuments of the beginning of time."[13] They were thus considered to be the models of mankind untainted by cultural difference. This naive view of unfamiliar contours is now discredited, yet it informed the evolution of universalist ideas, based on the notion that fundamental similarities exist across cultures and among all mankind. This universalism in turn informed the debate surrounding human rights.

However, those of African descent in the Caribbean were often assimilated into French society.[14] It may be that their prior geographical and cultural displacement,

---

[12]For La Rochefoucauld-Liancourt's report, see Camille Bloch, *Procès verbaux et rapports du Comité de Mendicité de la Constituante, 1790–1791* (Paris: Imprimerie nationale, 1911), 777–82. The hospital conditions are denounced in the previous committee report; ibid., 758–77.

[13]Gérando's text can be found in Jean Copas and Jean Jamin, *Aux origines de l'anthropologie française: Les mémoires de la Société des Observateurs de l'Homme en l'an VIII* (Paris: Le Sycomore, 1978), 128–69. The society had a short life (1799–1805). It brought naturalists, historians, linguists, archaeologists, philosophers, and Hellenists together, but was divided by the proclamation of the Empire, when most of its members refused to rename the group "Société impériale des observateurs de l'homme."

[14]On the first abolition of slavery, see Lawrence C. Jennings, *French Anti-Slavery: The Movement for the Abolition of Slavery in France, 1802–1848* (Cambridge: Cambridge University Press, 2000). For

and their adaptation to new conditions of life demonstrated their capacity to assimilate into a new culture. During the eighteenth century, young slaves were sent to France for training as coopers, cooks, wigmakers, carpenters, and ironsmiths. They remained at port or in Paris for between one and three years. Their presence provoked rumors like that which circulated in the Caribbean in 1775 reporting an upcoming general emancipation. The rumors were spread from France's ports, such as Bordeaux, where many slaves lived. On the eve of the Revolution, many colonists were afraid of being overwhelmed by Afro-Caribbeans and free mulattos.

During the Revolution, the abolition of slavery was supposed to give way to a lack of differentiation between people who were both equal and alike since, theorists of race argued, belonging to a racial group was no longer a significant aspect of identity. Abbé Henri Grégoire, author of *The Essay on the Physical and Moral Regeneration of the Jews* (1788), was one of the founders of the Société des noirs. He obtained for free Afro-Caribbeans and mulattos the same legal and civil rights that were extended to whites. His concern was not protecting a specific culture from oblivion, but fighting against prejudice and discrimination. The colonists hanged the revolutionary cleric in effigy at Santo Domingo. Despite Grégoire's efforts, slavery was reinstated in 1802 and the concept of race continued to shape identity. A decree in 1805 proscribed mixed marriage and slavery was only abolished definitively in 1848. However, Abbé Grégoire continued to embody the universalist mind-set of the Enlightenment. Shortly before his death in 1826, he published the treatise, "On the Nobility of Skin, or On the Prejudice of Whites against the Color of Africans," a rich text praising interracial relations and expressing the author's admiration for the new republic of Haiti and faith in education's ability to destroy prejudice based on the idea of racial superiority.[15]

To recapitulate: the break with the ancien régime was based on the right to equality. The Revolutionary notion of equality broke groups into the individuals who composed them, and regrouped these individuals as citizens of the French nation. Freedom became the defining criterion of humanity. The French notion of freedom is anchored in its religious and cultural past, linked to monuments of that past and to a particular view of cultural difference. The free man's task is to bring the knowledge of freedom to those who lack it through teaching and work.

---

coverage of the antislavery movement during the Revolution, see Jean-Daniel Piquet, *L'Emancipation des Noirs dans la Révolution française (1789–1795)* (Paris: Karthala, 2002). On the problem of freed slaves and Afro-Caribbeans on the mainland, see Gabriel Debien, "Les affranchissements aix Antilles françaises aux XVIIe et XVIIIe siècles," *Annuario de Estudos Americanos* 24 (1967): 1177–1203; and Jean-Luc Bonniol, *La couleur comme maléfice: Une illustration créole de la généalogie des Blancs et des Noirs* (Paris: Albin Michel, 1992).

[15]Abbé Grégoire, *De la noblesse de la peau* (Grenoble: Editions Jerôme Millon, 1996), 82. The original edition was published in Paris by Baudouin Frères in 1826.

Therefore, the individuals freed from particular groups come together—or ideally should—in a common destiny based on the transmission of ideals and on collective action vis-à-vis supposed natural laws.

SECULARISM AND SACRED PRINCIPLES

The religious question intensified the Revolution. During the debates of 1789 and 1790, two ideological models were in opposition. The liberal model, expressed in the Declaration of the Rights of Man, depended on religious pluralism to promote a possible "expression of religious opinions" that would permit both the criticism of religion and the free choice of believers. The Jacobin model, embodied in the Civil Constitution of the Clergy, attempted to integrate Roman Catholicism—considered a public cultural service—into the new spatial and political organization of the constitution. The latter model dominated. The transfer of sovereignty to the nation marked the secularization of the political field. For the Protestants who had participated in the Estates General, the Constituent Assembly was to affirm their ability to work in all positions. Societal secularization was effected through institutions such as schools, health and welfare services, and the registry office.

This first step to secularization was essential, and Jean Baubérot is correct to affirm that from then on modern France's symbolic foundations fell outside religion, which maintained, however, right up to the Third Republic, a very strong hold on morality.[16] This is true from an institutional standpoint; however, it could be considered rather as a transfer of sacred references to the domain of the Republic. This is true because both the reference to humanity as the supreme principle and the spirit of the Declaration are tinged with religiosity—understood to mean the use of symbols having a sacred dimension, symbols that arouse powerful, lasting and profound impulses and tendencies.[17] Indeed, those symbols create the concepts governing the existence of men and societies. A representative for the Third Estate, a citizen Duquesnoy, declared, "It has been claimed that the Declaration aimed to substitute religious ideas...with moral ones that are either almost or completely unknown [to the people]." He added, "I would have liked the Declaration of Rights to have begun with a great and majestic religious concept that would be applicable to all religions, all opinions, all climates; that the sole idea of God's existence, for example, would have been the provenance of all moral truths and practices that would become a part of this declaration." For, as Duquesnoy continues,

[16]Jean Baubérot, "La laïcité française et ses mutations," *Social Compass* 45 (1998): 175–87. For a comprehensive history of secular schools and their roles in moral pedagogy, see also, Baubérot, *La morale laïque contre l'ordre moral* (Paris: Seuil, 1997).

[17]The definition of religiosity is taken from Clifford Geertz, "La religion comme système culturel," in *Essais d'anthropologie religieuse* (Paris: Gallimard, Essais, 1966), 19–66.

"The human being that has given his life to mankind has placed an invincible penchant in his heart, an irresistible societal need."[18]

Similarly, does the republican motto "Liberté, Egalité, Fraternité," readopted in 1848, not represent the supreme values of the nation? This triad of values derived from Masonic statements of their ideals.[19] Freemasonry cut across national and sectarian lines, as it was an international society and welcomed adherents of any religion. Its universalist principles had a profound effect on a number of French colonies, thereby extending the issues raised by secularism—eventually embraced by the Freemasons—and religious self-determination and practice to a wider Francophone world.[20] This meant that indigenous peoples and even slaves were demanding the same rights as French citizens, following the notion of universalism to its logical extreme and making human rights an international issue. This is a consequence of French republicanism that the Republic itself has yet to fully absorb. As the nineteenth century wore on, with republic following upon monarchy and empire following upon republic, Freemasons increasingly supported secular and republican principles, helping to forge the French Republic as it is now articulated: secular and, at least ideally, egalitarian. In the days after the institution of the Second Republic, a delegation from Masonic lodges, led by Father Bertrand, was received at the Hôtel de Ville by the members of the interim government. The delegation brought with it, in the name of all Masonic workshops, a declaration of its loyalty to republican principles.[21]

From the 1880s onward, the development of secular morals and the teaching of them in schools robbed the Catholic Church of its traditional role as the source of ethics and gave French secularism its unique qualities. In developing the modern French public school system ("secular, free, and obligatory"), Minister of Education Jules Ferry's great challenge was to construct neutral ethics concerning all religious transcendence.[22] This was possible because the subject of such ethical improvement was the sovereign people, the body of the nation, the supreme value, the collective ethos of France. The fact that it was spread through schools made

---

[18] Duquesnoy, quoted in Claude Langlois, "Religion, culte ou opinion religieuse: La politique des révolutionnaires," *Revue française de Sociologie* 30 (1989): 471–96.

[19] Margaret C. Jacob, *The Radical Enlightenment: Pantheists, Freemasons, and Republicans* (London: Allen and Unwin, 1981), 26.

[20] For example, see Caryn Cossé Ball, "French Freemasonry and the Republican Heritage," in *Revolution, Romanticism, and the Afro-Creole Protest Tradition in Louisiana, 1718–1868* (Baton Rouge: Louisiana State University Press, 1997), 145–86.

[21] Pierre Chevallier, *Histoire de la franc-maçonnerie française* (Paris: Fayard, 1974), 2:298–99. See also Philip Nord, "Freemasonry," in *The Republican Moment: Struggles for Democracy in Nineteenth Century France* (Cambridge: Harvard University Press, 1995), 15–30.

[22] Jean Baubérot, "L'Ecole publique et sa morale laïque," in *Histoire de la laïcité française* (Paris: Presses Universitaires de France, 2000), 48–63.

Portrait of Jules Ferry, from Jules Ferry, *Lettres, 1846–1893* (Paris: Calmann-Lévy, 1914). Reprinted with the kind permission of the Cornell University Library.

such secular ethics more pronounced in the mores and mentality of the French people than did the law of 1905 concerning the separation of church and state. Secular ethics contain diverse elements such as Christianity, Judaism, and philosophical anticlerical traditions, such as the works of Voltaire and their heritage. With the triumph of the Third Republic and the consolidation of the political system, the major symbolic text becomes the Declaration of the Rights of Man and of the Citizen of 1789. Therefore, secularism, firmly anchored in the universal principles of the declaration, represents both a rupture and the avoidance of the conflict that had pitted republican partisans and their detractors against each other.[23]

The sacred foundations of secularism were only to appear later (1946) in the constitution, which marked their decline. France stood out among all the countries of the European community by eliminating all religious instruction from its curriculum.[24] This French particularity has become more widespread, and today secularism has even affected Europe's churches, turning them into monuments of the historical past. Except for a few anticlerical milieus such as the Grand Orient de France and those associations close to it, society has subscribed to what Jean Baubérot has termed "the new secular pact,"[25] a general framework that regulates religious pluralism. In this movement of the "secularization of religion," the material vestiges of the Catholic Church today hold a position analogous to that held by Celtic monuments in the eyes of men at the beginning of the nineteenth century. Indeed, in order to fight against the deterioration of religious edifices, the Ministry of Culture and Communication published a report in 1987 entitled "Churches, Chapels and Temples in France: Belonging to All, Familiar, Yet Threatened," which shows the role of the idea of a "heritage," a universalist notion since it underlies the reference to the French people and, beyond that, to humanity.

Secular morals, however, became increasingly powerless to assert themselves. A great gulf grew between the generations in the transmission of republican values in the 1970s, probably as a result of the disenchantment that followed the political upheaval of May 1968, when students and workers rioted in the streets, demanding social reforms. This near revolt severely tested the efficacy and questioned the supposed egalitarianism of Republican institutions, revealing in particular the class distinctions that remained in French society. If the Catholic Church also suffered from this disrupted transmission, a new mysticism, impregnated with oriental traditions, emerged on the public scene and announced the beginning of a sectarian renewal. Religiosity was seen as a possible response to the inadequacies of republicanism and universalism (as an effacement of cultural and religious difference).

[23]Baubérot, "La laïcité française et ses mutations," 175–87.
[24]Langlois, "Religion, culte ou opinion religieuse," 471–96.
[25]Jean Baubérot, *Vers un nouveau pacte laïque* (Paris: Seuil, 1990).

After decades of secularism, confronted with complex questions such as cloning, artificial insemination, and the use of condoms in the fight against AIDS, state institutions turned to representatives of the main religious movements for advice. Today, civil religion has moved in the direction of ethics. What is more, the bicentennial celebrations of the French Revolution underscored the ethical heritage of the Declaration of the Rights of Man and of the Citizen. In the European Convention on Human Rights, democracy and human rights are presented as the very foundations of western societies.[26] But the role of religion relative to these ideals has yet to be adequately defined.

Once again, in the wake of the recent riots, as well as the debates over public display of religious symbols, such as the wearing of headscarves, the secular crisis raises the question of the dichotomy between the private and the public. The crisis corresponds, also, to a decline in the emotional and all-encompassing scope of the notion of the "French people." The "French people" seem to be defined more and more in contrast to immigrants, a phenomenon that signals a failure of French notions of universalism and assimilation, but that also signals a failure to see the French people as a group with its own particular and rich cultural heritage—like Bretons.

MINORITIES AND THE CASE OF INDIGENOUS PEOPLES

Perhaps because of this emphasis on secularism and universal ideals over cultural and religious pluralism, France has had some difficulty defining the place of ethnic groups, whether minorities or not. Passing from the Vichy period with its insistence on having one's roots in a territory to the detriment of republican egalitarianism, the French people have tended to emphasize the importance of natural communities such as the family and profession, and most importantly the peasantry. However, the increasing importance of folklore during this period was, to some extent, an antidote against what was seen as the decadent values of the citizenry. The virtuous lifestyle of the peasants—whether real or imagined—became a tool for national propaganda. Moreover, the emphasis on having one's roots in the country logically excluded foreigners and all those who did not possess land. Emblematic in this regard is the Statute for the Jews of 3 October 1940. Written in reaction to an influx of Jews from Germany and Eastern Europe, this law presented Judaism as a racial difference and Jews as not being of French nationality. Any individual with three Jewish grandparents or two Jewish grandparents and a Jewish spouse was considered, under this law, to be Jewish (the term was *de race juive*, "of Jewish race"). The state excluded Jews from public office and from careers in the

[26]Jean-Paul Willaime, "La Religion civile à la française et ses métamorphoses," *Social Compass* 40 (1993): 571–80.

press, radio, or theater. It also imposed quotas on the number of Jews allowed in other professions. Jews who performed military service, particularly in 1914–18, were allowed limited participation in public affairs. It should be noted that the term "race" in French is often used to designate nationality (the French "race"); at any rate, this state presented the Jews as not French. Their status was seen as a question of ancestry, rather than of religious practice.[27]

This emphasis on nationality has evolved somewhat into a less exclusionary model. But the emphasis on national unity over religious and cultural pluralism remains. The practice of religions as well as languages other than French is permitted in private, but not in the public domain. The negation of pluralism is to be found in article 2 of the Constitution: "France is an indivisible, secular, democratic, and social republic. It guarantees the equality of all its citizens before the law without distinction of race, origin, or religion. It respects all beliefs." This emphasis on unity and assimilation, echoing Revolutionary universalism, may explain France's continuing difficulties in dealing with immigrants and with indigenous peoples. As the first inhabitants of territories now occupied by France, indigenous peoples enjoy few privileges today and little compensation for the expropriation of their lands.[28]

From a juridical point of view, distinguishing between minorities and indigenous peoples is difficult. For example, Norbert Rouland states that "indigenous peoples are to be distinguished from minorities by virtue of their earlier historical presence established in relation to that of the dominant group." In the light of this definition, where are the Basques to be placed? Further, how much time is necessary for a people to warrant the designation "indigenous"? It seems that France can only tolerate minority discourse by weakening it, by depriving it of its collective dimension, and by reducing it to a simple matter of individual practice. This undermining of non-French cultural practices and beliefs is exacerbated by the unfavorable social and economic conditions imposed upon indigenous peoples. As with French anti-Semitism, in the case of indigenous peoples in French territories as well as that of immigrants in France, the insistence on assimilation into French culture is paradoxically accompanied by legal and social steps taken to isolate and marginalize these groups.

Despite its assimilatory discourse, during the colonial period, France put into place a system of judicial segregation. Until 1946, the French colonial empire consisted of two categories of inhabitants: national citizens, whose rights were fully

[27]André Kaspi, "Qu'est-ce qu'un Juif?" in *Les Juifs pendant l'Occupation* (Paris: Seuil, 1991), 54–67.
[28]Since 25 February 1982, Corsica has enjoyed a special status. The law of 13 May 1991 goes further than its predecessor by instituting a territorial collectivity of a unique kind, which brings Corsica closer to the status of an overseas territory (Territoire d'Outre-Mer or TOM). See Rouland, Pierre-Caps and Poumarède, *Droit des minorités et des peuples autochtones*, 314–16, 519–20.

protected by French law, and national subjects, who retained their private status of religious or customary origin, but were deprived of the greater part of their liberty and political rights. Quite simply put, cultural difference excluded colonized people from full status as French citizens. In fact, this rhetoric conceals the division between European and non-European French people. The plan was for the inhabitants of the Antilles, French Guyana, Reunion Island, the indigenous Jews of Algeria, who fell under the Crémieux Decree of 1870, the inhabitants of Tahiti (1880), and the nationals of the four Senegalese communes (1916), to become progressively assimilated as citizens.

In this context of colonialism, the right to be different adopts the concrete and judicial form of custom, that is, the cultural integration of traditional law effected by the colonizer and wielded also by the indigenous people. As long as custom remains moored in oral tradition, it can be negotiated. New stakes arise today, especially in New Caledonia, where attempts are being made to draft a customary code, which would amount to the creation of a differential law and to the consequent installation of juridical pluralism. This is done without recognizing that custom can turn against those who recast it in a colonial mold, as it takes into consideration collective traditional rights and consequently places emphasis on the ethnic group rather than on the individual.

In December 1992, the United Nations adopted the Declaration of the Rights of People Belonging to National or Ethnic Minorities. This raises the question of how French law should take cultural specificities into account. Under the French constitution, distinctions based on geographic origin (one of the demands of the inhabitants of the overseas territories) are unfounded.[29] In principle, therefore, indigenous people cannot exist in France, as there is only one French people. The case of Guyana's Amerindians illustrates well the conflict between French citizenship and being indigenous. Today, 320,000 Amerindians live in French Guyana. They are divided into several nations: the Galibi, the Palikur, the Arawak, the Wayana, the Wayapi, and the Emérillon. The First Republic made the Amerindians only temporary citizens, but biracial offspring of Indian and Afro-Caribbean unions were considered unworthy of such an honor. After more than two and a half centuries, the descendants of the Amerindians and Afro-Caribbeans who found refuge in Guyana—that is, the descendants of castaways—could have opted

[29]The outlying overseas territories consist of departments (DOM) and overseas territories (TOM). The DOMs are Guadeloupe, Martinique, French Guyana, and Reunion Island, which have been departments since 1946. Only the Amerindians of French Guyana are recognized as indigenous. The DOM are the oldest French colonies and are historically closely associated to the French nation. The TOMs are New Caledonia, Wallis and Futuna, and Polynesia. They are comprised of ethnically diverse populations of indigenous peoples with their own traditions and religions. Special territorial collectivities include Mayotte and Saint-Pierre-et-Miquelon. Mayotte was included in the Comoro Islands off Mozambique, once a TOM.

for French citizenship within the framework of the departmentalization of all the territories of French Guyana in 1967. Those who accepted this offer received subsidies such as family allowances and were included in the electoral process. Others, like the Wayana, refused citizenship. According to the criteria of the Institut National de Statistiques, they are "without nationality." Ironically, they live as French guests on their own land.

Due to their French citizenship, Amerindian citizens enjoy special status since they receive a family allowance and are registered on electoral lists. As indigenous people, however, they are tax-exempt and are also exempt from national service. This privilege is the cause of confrontation between the Amerindians and the Creoles, the mixed population in the majority, who demand in the name of equality that citizenship be applied to Amerindians both for their rights and for their duties. Converted to Christianity, but still practicing shamanism, Amerindians are now considered Europeanized.

The ethnologists Pierre and Françoise Grenand have reported various attitudes on the art of indigenous peoples to assimilation. Therefore, for the Galibi of the coast, French schools are supposed to educate their children in the same manner that whites and Creoles are educated so that they may eventually participate in the civil and administrative life of the island. For the Galibi, modern education and shamanism (reserved for the private sphere) would neither be in conflict nor would they be incompatible. Although they argue that the teaching of French should be done as a second language, Pierre and Françoise Grenand recognize that, in terms of employment prospects, French citizenship and acculturation present more of an asset than a liability.[30] Consequently, indigenous groups in this region are not clamoring for education in their native languages.

The most assimilated people of the Amerindians of French Guyana, the Galibi, founded the Association des Amérindiens de Guyane Française in 1970. Its leaders are young people who are acculturated as French, educated, and have converted to Christianity. In 1984, the president of the association, Felix Tiouka, spoke in defense of the Amerindians and brought up the concept of the "Amerindian people" (note the universalist collective noun). French citizenship, however, is not called into question, and participation in French political institutions flourishes. In 1989, after uphill political battles, the communities of Lower Mana obtained the right to establish communes. Inherent in this provision is an ambiguity as the term "commune" refers both to the Republic's abstract and rational division of the land, from which any regional, "provincial," or historical reference was banned, and also to the entire Amerindian ethnic group. Moreover, Amerindians are increasingly

---

[30]Pierre and Françoise Grenand, "Les Amérindiens de Guyane Française aujourd'hui: Eléments de compréhension," *Journal de la Société des Américanistes* 66 (1979): 361–82.

part of municipal councils. For the Amerindians, there is no contradiction between ethnicity and citizenship. However, with the advent of regionalization, the Creole community has extended its political ascendancy over French Guyana. The Creoles seem to be more adept at participation in republican institutions, perhaps because of their history of recourse to republican traditions in claiming their own rights,[31] perhaps because their republican ideals are not mitigated by affiliation with one particular ethnic or cultural identity. [32]

On the initiative of President Jacques Chirac, almost one hundred and fifty representatives of the Amerindian communities were welcomed inside the National Assembly, in Paris from 19 to 21 June 1996. The meeting was a well-thought-out political act by the government since the opening document insisted on the "strictly cultural nature" of the meeting. "Culture," in this sense, refers to a different way of life whose implicit support system is the ethnic group. The aim was to remind the Amerindians that they were a part of a France that was "one and indivisible." In the days following President Chirac's address, the Amerindians voiced their concerns about various instances of exclusion from the political process in their own region, for example, the absence of a representative from the Amerindian community on a pilot committee for the creation of a natural park in the south of French Guyana, a region whose population is mainly Indian.[33] France has neither fully assimilated these Amerindian populations as citizens, although on paper they have this status, nor has it accepted their cultural difference by granting them autonomy. As for the Jews before the Second World War and immigrants today, assimilation is both demanded of these groups and rendered impossible, as they are held at a distance from full access to the republican institutions (government, education) that would assure their equal rights as French citizens.

SECULARISM'S LAST STOP

In summer 1997, thousands of young people assembled in Paris to welcome the pope. Though played down by believers in a secular republic, the size of the gatherings indicated that secularism was threatened. The success of the papal visit was even more unforeseeable since it occurred dozens of years after the disillusioned report of the Catholic Church on the decline in religious practices. Bishops from northern France had depicted Catholicism as fragile in terms of congregation numbers and finances. As Monseigneur Michel Saudreau observed, believers

---

[31]See, for example, Bell, *Revolution, Romanticism, and the Afro-Creole Protest Tradition.*

[32]Pierre and Françoise Grenand, "Y a-t-il encore des sauvages en Amérique?" Chronique du Groupe d'Information sur les Amérindiens, *Journal de la Société des Américanistes* 78 (1992): 99–112.

[33]Jean-Claude Monod, Survival International–France, "Amérindiens à Paris: Les ambiguités d'une rencontre," *Journal de la Société des Américanistes* 82 (1996): 358–60.

were often considered "strange, bizarre people; eccentric." After the discussions, the bishops from northern France had taken it upon themselves to "begin the second evangelization of Europe at a new cost."[34]

From the standpoint of symbolic foundations such as "humanity," "sovereign people," and "freedom," secularism was equally threatened. It was threatened on the one hand by the Catholic Church's revival, which was visible both in the growth of standard pilgrimages to places such as Lourdes or Lisieux or to the Christian communities such as Tiazé.[35] On the other hand, secularism was also threatened by the growth of syncretic religious groups or groups developed on the margins of Christianity, often referred to in the French press under the umbrella term "cults" (*sectes*). It is difficult to establish a distinction between cults and religions. At any rate, the rise in adherence to a variety of religions signals a loss of faith in the secular republican project, which has not succeeded in including all French citizens—Catholic, Muslim, or of any faith. This failure is echoed by a failure to bring racial and ethnic differences into the universalist framework; clearly, ignoring or effacing these differences, or reducing them to individual cases of particularism, has not been effective.

Over the past few years, the theme of identity has been omnipresent in research in the social sciences. This interest correlates to a decline of confidence in the republican and secular project. Would it therefore be a postmodern phenomenon, as Mary Douglas suggests? For Douglas, identity in European countries is a personal and private matter and it refers to a unitary conception of the individual, whereas in many non-Western cultures, including African, many Amerindian, and a number of Asian cultures, the belief system states that a person can become an "alter-persona," and that the individual possesses one or many souls that can leave the body (see note 3). The notion of a shadow, of a double, is essential to many peoples of Western Africa and the Congo. Such systems of belief exemplify an articulation between the individual and the cosmos, that between the different parts of the body, the left and the right, the top and the bottom, there exists a code of correspondences. In many cases, identity seems to be a fixed idea in the framework of a group, be it "the ethnic group," or "the urban tribe." In many non-Western societies, the human being is considered to have a dual nature and to consist of a body and one or many souls. Corresponding to this representation of the individual is a

[34]Jean-Pierre Clerc, "Recevant les évêques du nord de la France, Jean Paul II met en garde contre 'la fausse mystique,'" *Le Monde*, 24 January 1987.

[35]For an excellent study on Lourdes, see Clara Gallini, *Il miracolo e la sua prova: Un etnologo a Lourdes* (Napoli: Ligouri Editore, 1998).

dual world: one is visible every day and the other is a phantasmic projection of the former. This notion of duality tends to disappear in developed countries, where it is replaced with the division between the "public" and "private." This division enables the secularization of Western societies by relegating religion to the domain of the private, thus separating it from the public domain.

This distinction between public and private does not seem functional however. Simply speaking, the private has been invaded by the public, and, inversely, what would have previously been considered a private matter—for example, the issue of the Islamic veil in France—has become a public matter. This duality gives way to a conception of the individual as being "combined," in what might seem to be a return to non-Western forms of spirituality and their formulations of individual identity. These formulations may offer a more productive model for integration of cultural difference into the framework of French republican secular universalism, a model of duality or pluralism that does not require effacement of one part of the individual's identity in favor of another. In this model, the designation of "French" would not preclude the expression of other forms of identity, religious or cultural.[36] Anthropologist Catherine Choron-Baix writes that the young Laotians who have come to France "create a dual opinion of the world for themselves, where religious sentiment is a private, very strongly affective and emotional sphere." "What we look for in the pagoda and in our rites," Laotians tell her, "is above all to recognize ourselves."[37] When a young girl states: "My mentality makes me French, my roots Tunisian," duality is expressed and it refers to a conception of the individual that is infinitely more complex than words could reveal.

Moreover, young French Muslims claim the right to live publicly as well as in Islam's collective manner, which is at the very basis of their culture. Indeed, Islam is not only a religion but also a community (*umma*) whose devotion to God is the basis of its believers' union with each other. The Koran is both a religious and juridical code that organizes the state and the ability of the people, their obligations and their successions, as well as the political structure of the community. These claims became apparent in France after the law of July 1946, a law dealing with "the settling process" of immigrants who remained in France, and advocating the reuniting of families.[38]

---

[36]Such a "combined" person appears in other contexts. For a discussion of this concept from the anthropological historical angle of the Americas, see Carmen Bernand and Serge Gruzinski, *Histoire du Nouveau Monde: Les métissages* (Paris: Fayard, 1993). See also, Leo Spitzer, *Lives in Between: Assimilation and Marginality in Austria, Brazil, West Africa 1780–1945* (Cambridge: Cambridge University Press, 1989).

[37]Catherine Choron-Baix, "Des forêts en banlieues: La transplantation du boudhisme Lao en France," *Archives des Sciences Sociales des Religions* 73 (1991): 29.

[38]Danielle Hervieu-Léger, "Les recompositions religieuses et les tendances actuelles de la sociologie des religions en France," *Social Compass* 45 (1998): 143–53.

Jean Baubérot has underscored the very strong tensions between the two poles that define secularism. He notes a freedom of conscience that regards atheists as being at the same level as believers, and a freedom of thought that is understood as a liberation from all overarching doctrines and from all particularities that would stop the individual from attaining the universal.[39] To the extent that this universalism, in the sense of a fundamental notion of human equality, guarantees basic human rights, it is still a necessary concept for the elaboration of a functional nation, whether France or any other country. To the extent that it requires the effacement of diverse cultural identities, at its limit it becomes self-destructive, a model that violates the very rights, in particular to freedom, that it is supposed to guarantee. A successful French nation, capable of juggling both the practice of social equality and the respect for religious and cultural diversity that this equality demands, will have to find the right equilibrium between liberty, equality, and fraternity, and not privilege the practice of one of these concepts over any of the others.[40]

[39]Baubérot, "La laïcité française et ses mutations," 182–86.
[40]Carmen Bernand, "La spiritualité de l'imperfection des alcooliques repentis: Etapes d'un voyage," *Communications* 62 (1996): 257–75.

Islam in a Secular Context
Catalyst of the "French Exception"

Jocelyne Césari

THE EMERGENCE OF ISLAM as a visible presence in French cities during the beginning of the 1980s was the source of several misinterpretations and misunderstandings, all of them prompted by the idea that Muslims were intensifying their religious practice or experiencing a return to religion. This increase of Islam's visibility in France was not, however, the sign of an appreciable increase in practice. Over the course of twenty years, Muslims have not become more observant or "more Muslim" but they have begun to practice Islam differently, reflecting not a change in their religious attitudes, but a change in attitude toward French society. First-generation immigrants, who once confined their observance to private spaces, now petition the authorities for more mosques.

Visibility concerns the viewer as much as the viewed: some behaviors are more visible than others, depending on the intensity of public interest in them. The more or less monolithic vision of Muslim populations that prevails in France is almost entirely due to France's troubled colonial past in North Africa, and Algeria in particular. Might it be possible, then, that the current discourse surrounding Islam in France reveals more about French preconceptions than about the reality of the Islamic religion? Indeed, French Islam's visibility is partly a result of France's own excessive attention to Muslims, particularly those of North African descent. Could it thus be the case that their presence exposes certain unresolved conflicts within France's collective memory of its own colonialism?

Whether or not this is the case, it is certain that the postcolonial situation of French Muslims helps to explain the various forms of Islamophobia that manifested themselves long before the term was applicable in other parts of Europe.[1]

[1]For further explication of this term, see Pnina Werbner, "Islamophobia, Incitement to Religious Hatred: Legislating for a New Fear?" *Anthropology Today* 21, no. 1 (2005): 5–9; Tariq Modood, "The Place of Muslims in British Secular Multiculturalism," in Nezar AlSayyad and Manuel Castells, eds., *Muslim Europe or Euro-Islam: Politics, Culture and Citizenship in the Age of Globalization* (Lanham:

Nonetheless, the postcolonial situation is inscribed within a metanarrative on Islam that ceaselessly plays out a confrontation between Islam and the West, and that exists throughout Europe.[2] Certain images and stereotypes—such as a Muslim propensity for violence or fanaticism, or Islam's incompatibility with modernity—none of them mutually exclusive, continue to influence the positions and political orientations taken in regard to "the second religion of France." These stereotypes encourage the public perception of an Islam that is constantly expanding and moreover manipulated by outside forces.

ISLAM IN FRANCE—VISIBLE BUT NOT A PRODUCT OF EXTERNAL INFLUENCE
Throughout the 1980s, the signs of Muslim practice that began to appear in urban spaces—*masjids, halal* butchers, headscarves worn in the public schools, Muslim plots in cemeteries—were all interpreted as symptoms of a "return to Islam." In reality, however, they demonstrated the changing attitudes of Muslims toward French society. For the most part, the advocates of a stronger Islamic presence in France, including members of the younger generation, have not become more devout, but rather have increasingly refused to limit the expression of their Muslim identity to the private sphere. The fact that what is a change of political *posture* has instead been interpreted as a "return to Islam" eloquently demonstrates the extent to which Islam carries a stigma in the French religious and cultural landscape. This mind-set may chiefly be attributed to the widespread reluctance to accept the fact that many North African immigrants have permanently settled in France.

Indeed, French hostility towards or stereotyping of Muslims can be understood through an analysis of the history of North African migration, both colonial and postcolonial. Due to certain historical particularities, North African migration, more than any other, was long considered to be temporary in nature. Both French and North African government officials shared this view. In addition, many of the migrants' own goals conformed to this expectation. The migrants saw their move as an opportunity to accumulate capital to reinvest in their country of origin. The failure of this project transformed their relationship to French society and led to a symbolic investment in Islam, which emerged as a kind of compensation for lost unity and the social consequences of being unable to return home. For young people born and educated in France, the public expression of Muslim identity may also be the result of a resistance to the values and norms of a society

---

Lexington Books, 2002), 113–30; Fred Halliday, "Islamophobia Reconsidered," *Ethnic and Racial Studies* 22 (Sept. 1999): 892–902; and Vincent Geisser, *La Nouvelle Islamophobie* (Paris: La Decouverte, 2003).

   [2]See Jocelyne Césari, *When Islam and Democracy Meet: Muslims in Europe and in the United States* (New York: Palgrave, 2004).

in which they feel that they are "illegitimate children." Nevertheless, in the past few years, identification with and involvement in Islam have been more than just a reaction to the postcolonial condition. The reclamation of Muslim identity is also a product of even more complex patterns of religious revivalism—patterns, for that matter, that also occur in religions besides Islam.

The emergence of a public Islam is often interpreted as the consequence of external influence, and thus as a potential source of political destabilization insofar as it coincides with the politicization of Islam around the Muslim world. In the 1980s and '90s, the politicization of Islam was concerned above all with the issue of Algeria. Islam's visibility in French society was thus conflated with the Algerian political situation. Today, in contrast, the increased visibility of Islam is associated with the spread of transnational *jihadi* groups such as Al Qaeda. This process creates a situation in which every form of religious practice is immediately suspect and open to charges of fundamentalism.

The tendency to interpret every visible manifestation of Muslim identity as an expression of fundamentalism is extremely widespread. Moreover, for outside French observers, the term "Islam" comes to designate a totalized ideal that prevents them from taking into account the individual liberties of each Muslim vis-à-vis revealed law. This perception of Islam has at least two consequences. First, it obfuscates the eminently modern relationship of young people to Islam. The vast majority of young Muslims who are born or educated in France think of Islam as a cultural and ethical point of reference, relatively detached from constraints of religious observance. They treat religion in a more or less secular fashion, assuming a believer/consumer role similar to that of young Catholics of the same age.[3] Second, this essentialist vision neglects the influence of cultural difference within the practice of Islam itself. There is a broad spectrum of ways of being Muslim, a result of the different cultural and historical contexts to which the Koranic message has been adapted. Thus the Islamic identity of North African Muslims may be very different from that of Muslims of Turkish, sub-Saharan African, or Asian descent. These differences are due not only to the great variety of cultural systems involved, but also to the public or political status of Islam in the countries of origin. This diversity partially explains the earlier difficulties in creating a federated Islamic authority in France. For a time (and occasionally still), religious leaders were more concerned with national or ethnic rivalries than with matters of religious interpretation. It is likely, however, that this situation will change with the advent of new religious elites born and educated in France. Nevertheless, these differences explain why topics such as socialization and Islamic education are such

[3]Jocelyne Césari, *Musulmans et Républicains: Les jeunes, l'islam et la France* (Brussels: Complexe, 1998).

highly charged issues in French discourse on Islam. What is at stake is precisely the creation of an institution that will assure the promotion of a properly *French* Islam. At the same time, the principal centers of propagation of Muslim *doxa* are in the Middle East, Asia, and North Africa. The challenge, therefore, is to understand what conditions French Islam requires before it can become autonomous and begin to find its own place as a minority religion—at the same time remaining part of the *'ummah* (the global community of believers).

There is, furthermore, the trap of superimposing facts of the international situation onto the French context—a trap that obliges Muslims to justify themselves endlessly in order to stem the downward spiral of suspicion. While it is true that some conservative transnational movements—such as the *Tabligh, Wahhabism,* or certain radical groups—attract a percentage of young French Muslims,[4] Muslim visibility in France is nevertheless not the effect of external manipulation. On the contrary, it is the definitive sign of Muslims' roots in French society. By considering all Muslim requests as merely the products of outside influence, French politicians and intellectuals fail to understand—or refuse to recognize—the crucial role that religion plays in the social integration of Muslims. The so-called exceptional nature of Islam is in fact a reflection of more general concerns about the status of religion in French public space, as well as of religion's ability to fill in gaps in the social and cultural domains.

ISLAM AND FRANCE—PROBLEMS REAL AND IMAGINED

The position of French government authorities toward Islam has evolved from one of indifference to one of strong concern. In 1976, the first laws governing the practice of Islam, initiated by Paul Dijoud, Secretary of State for Immigrant Workers, still took it for granted that all Muslims were migrant workers. Muslims were still perceived as outsiders in relation to French society, and legislation that concerned Muslim issues was ignored by most political leaders and attracted no controversy. The laws sanctioned the opening of Islamic chapels in workplaces, as well as the adjustment of work schedules for Muslim holidays. The additional plan to create Islam-themed radio and television programs—similar to the Jewish, Catholic, and Protestant programs that aired every Sunday—was not implemented until 1982.

At the beginning of the 1980s, however, the growing prominence of Islamic movements at the international level motivated a stronger political interest in Islam in France. Soon, the religious demands of French Muslims and the turmoil of the Islamic Revolution in Iran began to be connected in public discourse. Such an erroneous conflation of domestic and international issues continues to underlie

[4]See Césari, *When Islam and Democracy Meet.*

numerous stereotypes, commentaries, and analyses of Islam. In the 1980s, for example, requests for the building of mosques in factory areas and suburbs was not interpreted as the product of a social movement, but rather as the sign of external manipulation. It was at this point that the state began to take an interest in Islam—albeit one motivated exclusively by considerations of national security. At the time, government authorities considered the rector of the Mosque of Paris to be the representative of Muslim populations in general, and he was implicitly charged with protecting French Muslims from the spread of Islamic fundamentalism. His position in France was directly tied to the role played by Algeria in the contemporary Middle East crisis. In 1986, the Algerian government entered into negotiations with Iran for the liberation of French hostages in Lebanon. In a show of thanks, Minister of the Interior Charles Pasqua officially recognized the authority of the Algerian government over the Mosque of Paris in the following year.

In Search of a Representative Institution for French Islam
After 1988, the perception of Islam began to change yet again. In November 1989, Minister of the Interior and Secretary of State for Religious Affairs, Pierre Joxe, created a commission of six Muslim experts. In March 1990, this group was expanded under the name Conseil de réflexion sur l'Islam de France (CORIF). Its goal was to unify Muslim populations and to allow the government to interact with one well-informed interlocutor, rather than a multiplicity of sectarian or local representatives. To this end, Joxe only named the six original members after a series of consultations in France's large cities where Islamic organizations had taken root and in which religious leaders either had built or were planning to build mosques. The selection criteria for the first six experts were dictated by the wish to represent not only the different regions of France, but also the different national and ethnic currents of French Islam. The six chosen representatives then invited nine other organizational leaders to form CORIF.

In this way the French state, through the intervention of the minister of the interior, became an active participant in the organizing of French Islam. Several events contributed to the development of this initiative. First the Rushdie affair in Britain and then the 1989 controversy over the wearing of headscarves in French schools had made Islamic identification a political matter. In addition, the growing demand for places of worship in urban areas—an issue that mayors were neither capable of resolving nor legally entitled to decide upon—forced the state to take action in cases of discrimination or unequal treatment of Muslims.

But above all, the CORIF initiative responded to two objectives, albeit ones that were rarely articulated. First, the initiative was intended to disrupt the hegemony of the rector of the Mosque of Paris, by taking away his status as the sole officially recognized Muslim representative and neutralizing him within a larger group. Second, the government hoped that this group would be a first step towards a future representative council of Islam in France.

In appearing to be an attempt to put Islam under state supervision, the CORIF seemed to go against the spirit of the 1905 law of the separation of church and state. For this reason, the minister of the interior took pains at the time to make clear that he was "not Napoleon"[5] and that the government did not grant this committee any authority in terms of religious organization. Still, he justified the initiative by pointing out the unique situation of Islam in France: that the majority of Muslims in the country are French citizens, while almost all of the imams are foreign nationals. The government's project, then, represented an attempt to control religious expression by integrating all of the different currents and trends of Islam. Correspondingly, the choice of members for the expert committee revealed political more than religious criteria. Joxe argued that the members of this group were not representatives, but rather "prominent personalities."

With the change of legislative majority in March 1993, the CORIF was completely abandoned in favor of a strategy the government had already attempted once before: reliance on the Mosque of Paris. On 20 November 1993, Dalil Boubakeur, the rector of the mosque, initiated a Consultative Council of French Muslims, bringing together the most powerful figures of Islam in all France. Composed of twenty religious leaders, including the directors of organizations such as the Union des Organisations Islamiques de France (UOIF), Tabligh, and the National Council of French Muslims, its goal was to serve as a site of exchange and debate where members could discuss the status of Islam in France. This new group, supported by Charles Pasqua, hoped to create a statute governing the status of Islam. Quickly, however, the Mosque of Paris emerged as the main intermediary for this organization. Disagreements ensued between Dalil Boubakeur and the leaders of the UOIF, who challenged the rector's hegemony over Islam in France.

This controversy progressed in stages. In 1994, the Mosque of Paris was accorded complete control over the slaughtering of *halal* meat throughout the country. The next year, on 10 January 1995, Charles Pasqua officially recognized the Charter of the Muslim Religion. This document, ostensibly the product of a collective effort of the representative council, in fact represented only the stance of the Mosque of Paris.[6] This dominance of the Mosque of Paris serves to explain why the charter never became a key text in the organization of French Islam.

[5]Joxe was referring to the creation of representative Jewish institutions under the authoritarian patronage of Napoleon: Napoleon assembled the chief rabbis of the day in an attempt to give Judaism a status that would be in conformity with French law.

[6]In thirty-seven articles and five chapters, the charter asserted that Islam is not incompatible with Republican values and it propagated several minimal principles of organization, such as the neutrality of mosques and guidelines for the behavior of imams. The charter served no benefit other than as a symbolic act asserting that it is possible to be both a Muslim and a good French citizen. In no respect did it

If the Mosque of Paris could no longer be considered the primary agent of French Islam, however, the question of a suitable representative body remained unanswered. In October 1999, Jean-Pierre Chevènement reinitiated dialogue with Islamic leadership. These talks led to the signing of a document, on 28 January 2000, once again affirming the compatibility of Islam and the French Republic. The May 2002 presidential elections, marked by the victory of Jacques Chirac and the right-wing party, the UMP (between 23 April and 17 November 2002, known as the Union pour la majoritè présidentielle and after that as the Union pour un mouvement populaire) delayed the process yet again for several months. On 19 and 20 December 2002, however, the new minister of the interior, Nicolas Sarkozy, called together the main institutions of French Islam to create le Conseil Français du Culte Musulman (CFCM). This so-called historic agreement consisted in getting those Islamic associations involved in the previous delegation to give their assent to the document already approved by the minister of the interior and the three main Islamic organizations. This fact serves to explain why the board of directors of what was to become the French Council on Islam was not elected: the presidency went to Dalil Boubakeur; the two vice presidents were Fouad Alaoui, from the UOIF, and Mohmed Bechari, of the Fédération Nationale des Musulmans de France (FNMF).

In any event, the agreement confirmed the principle of vote by mosque for all future elections of the council, which have since included elections for its representative assembly, its administrative council, and its second board of directors (though some of the board remains to be appointed). On 6 and 13 April, 4,000 electors, representing more than 900 houses of worship, elected the CFCM's General Assembly, and 995 mosques chose 4,032 delegates to make up the regional electoral assembly. In the elections, the Mosque of Paris came out behind the FNMF, which has ties to Morocco, and the UOIF, which subscribes to the ideology of the Muslim Brothers. However, on 4 May 2003, the General Assembly of the CFCM confirmed the choice of the French government in reelecting Dalil Boubakeur as president of the new council. The 15 June 2003 elections for

---

aid the organization of Islam in France. The establishment of a federal body governing the different currents of Islam never took place. The charter recommended a national conference of imams responsible for coordinating all Muslim clerics in the country, while in each area a mufti would be named to oversee the imams of the region. The muftis of France were to constitute a *majlis,* or national council, composed of nine members. This group would oversee the activity of imams and issue fatwas. Throughout 1995, muftis assumed these functions in several regions of France. But the appointment of muftis did not succeed in federating Islam in France, since these officials were often considered regional representatives of the Mosque of Paris. In Marseille, the young and media-savvy Souheib Bencheikh arrived as mufti. The son of Cheikh Abbas, the former rector of the Mosque of Paris, Bencheikh advocated an Islam of openness and tolerance, and did not hesitate to call for a reform of Islam in order to adapt to life in France and in Europe.

regional council presidents confirmed the dominance of the UOIF, which, along with its allies, captured the presidency in eleven out of twenty-five regions, including the two most important: Île de France and Provence-Alpes-Côte d'Azur. This success demonstrates the lack of support and trust that the Mosque of Paris (seen as a puppet of the Algerian state) has among the Muslim population in France. The discrepancy between the results of the popular vote and the favorites of the French government led to the first crisis within the new council. The day after the elections, Boubakeur threatened to resign, only keeping his post due to pressure from the Ministry of the Interior.

The second serious crisis faced by the new council had to do with the head-scarf debate and the proposed ban on all visible signs of religion in the public schools. Upon the Stasi Commission's release of a study recommending the bill's approval, Boubakeur initially voiced CFCM's disagreement with this bill. However, after President Chirac's speech of 17 December 2003, supporting the Stasi Commission's position, Boubakeur changed his position and made an announcement asking Muslims to respect the law if it passed and urging them not to protest against it. Other members of the CFCM, on the other hand, such as Vice President Fouad Alaoui, expressed their disagreement with the proposed law (as representatives of the UOIF). These latter lent their support to the 17 January 2004 demonstration against the law, as to other forms of protest against the proposed law—which was indeed eventually adopted by Parlement on 15 March 2004.[7]

Since then, the council has only lost legitimacy. It was in this context that Fouad Alaoui, the secretary general of the UOIF, quit his post as vice president of the council in protest against the nomination of the head chaplain for prisons. Alaoui considered this nomination as undue interference in the council's affairs on the part of the French state. He returned to the council, and the 2005 elections emphasized continuity rather than change, so that the council remains stable.

FRENCH IMAMS—STATUS PENDING—THE CHALLENGE OF RELIGIOUS TRAINING
Whether they have involved a reliance on collectivities such as the CORIF or the current high council, or whether they have privileged one sole interlocutor such as the Mosque of Paris, these troubled negotiations between the French government and the Muslim community have been motivated by a single goal: to transform the Muslim population into an officially recognized minority religion. The situation is a historically anomalous one: for the first time, a large number of Muslims in France and throughout Europe are practicing their faith in a context

[7]The text of the Law on Secularity and Conspicuous Religious Behaviors and Symbols in Schools begins: "[C]omprising, in the application of the principle of secularism, the wearing, in public elementary, middle, and high schools, of symbols or clothing that display a religious affiliation." <http://www.legifrance.gouv.fr/WAspad/UnTexteDeJorf?numjo =MENX0400001L>.

of cultural and political pluralism. The question is therefore not one of conflict between the respective norms of Islam and the French Republic. Indeed, the majority of French Muslims accept the political norms of the secularized state, and even consider that the current situation provides an opportunity to observe their religion with more freedom than their country of origin would allow.[8]

The legal establishment of Islam as an official religion of France ought not to pose more difficulties than did the previous institutionalization of Judaism. Special dietary provisions, ritual slaughter, or chaplains in the military and prisons: all these form the basis of a voluminous body of law regulating the practice of Judaism in France. It would technically be easy to replicate the legal results of this first experience in the context of Islam. The obstacles to the organization of Islam in the Republican context are political rather than legal, the result of group and personal rivalries; neither do they have anything to do with the theological content of Islam, contrary to claims of critics who complacently evoke the lack of democratic principles in Islam.

In this respect, it is significant that CORIF never made efforts to provide a legislative basis for French Islam. Its primary work was directed toward setting a common date for the beginning of the fast of Ramadan: which did, however, allow the council to end the long-standing discord among religious authorities on this issue in 1991. The council also lobbied in favor of a 1991 circular issued by the Ministry of the Interior governing the creation of Muslim cemetery plots, which did not, however, radically differ from a 1975 circular on the same subject. The CFCM, for its part, has not proven itself to be any more productive.

The most delicate problem for the organization of French Islam is that of the status of imams, as well as imams' religious training. The title of imam does not reflect any official clerical responsibility in Islam, as do, for example, priests in the Catholic Church. The imam is simply the person who presents himself before the community to lead Friday prayer. However, although Sunni teaching considers each believer capable of discerning between good and evil and responsible for his/her acts before God, groups of specialists have held authority in interpreting the basic texts throughout Muslim history. These specialists of Islamic law (*ulema*), educated in the prestigious universities of Cairo and Tunis, do not hold the same sacramental functions as priests. Priests are ritually ordained by a hierarchically superior religious authority that assumes the role of intermediary between the believer and God. Imams do not serve as intermediaries in Islam. Still, they are recognized and respected figures of spiritual authority and play an important role

[8]Nevertheless, there are areas of conflict in regard to differences between Islamic civil law and the civil law of the secular state: specifically in laws relating to marriage, divorce, and child custody. Even in these cases, however, mechanisms for compromise are in place. See Césari, "Islam and Fundamental Rights in Europe." Report to the European Commission, DG Justice and Home Affairs, 2004.

in the French Muslim landscape. But since they are often of foreign nationality and have been educated abroad, they often encounter difficulties in attempting to meet the specific needs and expectations of French Muslims, particularly among the younger generations.

A more pressing concern, however, is that many imams have only a minimal education, yet are still expected to fulfill numerous roles. Imams must lead prayers, deliver the Friday sermon, visit families, oversee Koranic instruction, visit prisons and hospitals, and preside over funerals and weddings. It is impossible to know the exact number of imams in France today, but there are probably approximately as many imams as there are Muslim places of worship, which is estimated at between 1000 and 1500. For the most part, these imams have no official status and live off the contributions of their followers—if they are not subjected to the harassment of the administration upon renewing their visas. The condition of French Muslims is thus in the hands of religious leaders without significant education, without a regular salary, and without juridical recognition. In the midst of such disorder, French local and national authorities are understandably somewhat at a loss, and often do not know which imam they should be in dialogue with or direct their concerns to.

The first individuals to address the problem of training for imams were the directors of the UOIF, who, in 1991, opened a European Institute of Human Sciences at Château-Chinon, which included a training institute for imams and Islamic educators. With about 170 students (not all of them French nationals), the institute has however not yet proven capable of training the future religious personnel of France, particularly because French government officials hold it in some suspicion. Under the leadership of a French convert to Islam, Didier Ali-Bourg, the Centre d'Études et de Recherche sur l'Islam (CERSI) also opened in September 1993 in Paris, financed by contributions from the Gulf countries. It had almost 200 students, and had hoped to train organizational leaders and teachers, but its stated mission was never to train imams. After closing down its Paris location, it reopened in a new location in Seine-Saint-Denis. On 4 October 1993, Dalil Boubakeur inaugurated an Institute for the Training of Imams, which today claims fewer than twenty students. The reasons for this institute's failure are partly financial: since the French government cannot subsidize the costs of a religious institution and funding from the Algerian government has tapered off, it is difficult for the institute to provide a decent education for its students. In 2000, a third institute was founded under the supervision of the rector of the Great Mosque of Paris. [9]

---

[9]We should additionally mention two other training centers: l'Institut Français des Études et Sciences Islamiques (IFESI) in Boissy-Saint-Léger, and the Council of Imams in Mantes-la-Jolie.

It is also important to remember in this context that the principal centers of Islam where Muslim orthodoxy is now being developed are in the Middle East, Asia, and North Africa. It is unreasonable to imagine that European Islam can cut itself off totally from this external influence. The challenge, rather, is to know in which conditions French Islam will be able to attain autonomy and to construct a specific minority identity without cutting itself off from its roots. Henceforth the debate about Islam in France will be focused on the issue of imams, and whoever gains the upper hand over this elusive group of leaders will have obtained control over the religious direction of French Islam.

The professionalization of a competent corps of imams, recognized both in France and in the Muslim world, and capable of adapting to French cultural norms, is a more pressing issue now than ever, especially in the post–September 11 context. Today, leaders with the necessary qualifications are rare in France. Even though such leaders could have a positive influence on Islamic education, they are often treated as *persona non grata* by the French government. For example, Tariq Ramadan, grandson of Hassan El Banna (the founder of the Muslim Brothers), a Swiss citizen and professor of philosophy, enjoys great popularity among French youth, but was denied entry into France from November 1995 to May 1996. He has also been object of intense controversy in 2003, when he was suspected of holding anti-Semitic beliefs.[10] In general, it appears that the most competent religious authorities, as well as those whom young people most respect, are those who maintain their distance from institutional quarrels. This trend results in a growing gap between an "official" or "legal" Islam, endorsed by government leaders, and a "real" Islam, whose leaders are more in touch with ordinary Muslims' questions and aspirations.

The debate over the legal and social status of imams has intensified since September 11. Linked with the issue of terrorism in the public's mind, the religious conservatism of many imams is commonly seen as a sign of future political unrest. For example, the Algerian imam of Vénissieux, who had spoken out in favor of polygamy and the stoning of adulterous women, was deported from France on 21 April 2004 by the Ministry of the Interior. Despite a stay granted by the administrative court of Lyon, which questioned the grounds for this action, the imam's deportation was confirmed on 5 October 2004. In order to prevent such situations, a special ministerial committee was created in 2004 to present concrete solutions to the Home Ministry for the national training of imams. Educational programs in French culture for imams have also been created to aid in the fight against religious extremism. In this respect, a training program in

[10]See Césari, *When Islam and Democracy Meet*, 151–53.

French culture and civilization was planned to begin at the Sorbonne in the fall of 2005.[11] Similar programs have been instituted in Denmark and the Netherlands.

All these episodes in the relationship between Islam and the French government ultimately reveal a common motif. Whatever method the government chooses, it must find a way to integrate Islam into the framework of civil law while nonetheless carving out a separate contract for it. But the fact that many Muslims consider Islam to be a culture as well as a religion also raises the question of whether they will accept this separate contract, which can only ever be a partial fulfillment of their demands.

LAÏCITÉ IN QUESTION: BETWEEN LAW AND THE IMAGINARY
The appearance of headscarves in French schools shifted the public debate toward the most serious crisis of *laïcité* in French society since the initial separation of church and state. After 1989, one controversy followed upon another, giving way to conflict between high school students and school authorities. This conflict extended far beyond the schools, ultimately drawing in intellectuals, political figures, and religious authorities. Thus it must be asked: why does the issue of *laïcité* provoke such intense passions and fears?

The answer to this question lies in the striking divide between the dominant sociocultural vision of *laïcité* and its actual juridical content. In other words, the majority of French citizens perceive *laïcité* quite differently than the law in fact defines it. The real legal content of *laïcité* is twofold: first, it mandates the separation of government activities from any considerations of religion and thus the neutrality of public service; second, it guarantees freedom of religious expression to all religions.

Legally, the principle of *laïcité* regulates access to the public space, irrespective of religious affiliation, and prevents the state from interfering with this system. However, this is not society's expectation of the work that *laïcité* should do. The general public imagines *laïcité* to be a mechanism for the delegitimization of any public expression of religious adherence whatsoever, and of adherence to minority religions in particular. The repeated decisions of the Conseil d'État during the 1990s demonstrate this tension. On 2 November 1991, for example, the Conseil d'État was forced to overturn the decision of the administrative tribunal of Paris, which had upheld the College de Montfermeil's policy of excluding any student wearing a headscarf. The Conseil d'État justified this move by arguing that any absolute prohibition discriminating on the basis of a religious symbol was contrary to the principles of *laïcité*. A run of similar rulings followed, as the Conseil d'État reversed decisions of several administrative tribunals that had decided in

---

[11]"M. Boubakeur détaille la formation qui sera proposée aux Imams." *Le Monde*, 11 March 2005.

favor of schools, and against female students wearing headscarves. Two further examples of this trend are the ruling of 14 March 1994, which overturned the Court of Nantes's decision of 13 February 1992 in favor of a school that had expelled a headscarf-wearing student; and the ruling of 3 May 1994, which reversed a similar decision on the part of the Court of Orléans.

The 20 September 1994 circular of the minister of education, François Bayrou, stipulating that "the wearing of any ostentatious symbol of religious, political, or philosophical adherence is forbidden within the grounds of public schools," spawned yet more controversy due to its wording. What, in other words, is an "ostentatious symbol"? Isn't every symbol "ostentatious" by definition? Is it only the Islamic headscarf that is in question? Although these questions found no satisfactory answer, the legal debate over the headscarf escalated rapidly during the 1994–1995 school year. However, out of ninety-two administrative decisions upholding schools' policies of prohibiting the headscarf in this same academic year, more than half were eventually overturned.

Nevertheless, as a result of the continued controversy in the schools surrounding this issue—not to mention a new political climate in regard to the creation of a proper representative body for French Islam—the headscarf debate reached new levels of controversy in 2003 with the introduction of a bill to ban the "ostentatious" religious symbols in the public schools, which was eventually passed in March 2004. The Stasi Commission, a delegation of scholars and experts created in July 2003 on the initiative of the French presidency, came out in favor of the law. In a televised speech on 17 December 2003, President Chirac himself endorsed the commission's decision. Such a law seems to hope to bridge, by legislative means, the gap between public perception and the actual letter of the law. It presents an authoritarian conception of the law, which is henceforth charged with the protection of individual freedom—including the protection of individual freedom against the individual's will—and above all with imposing a definition of freedom of conscience based on an idealized and homogeneous vision of society. In other words: to be a modern citizen means to reject all public sign of religion. Thus the headscarf law seeks to "liberate" young Muslim women from the oppression of religious symbols.

How and why did the discrepancy arise between the legislative content of *laïcité* and society's perception of it? The origins of this snowballing misunderstanding lie in the painful history of *laïcité*'s beginnings. *Laïcité* is the product of a conflict between government power and church power, emerging from an inflammatory and reactive series of events. In France, early in the twentieth century, legislators' chief objective in engineering the separation of church and state was not the desire to regulate the domain of religion, but instead to sequester it from civil society, or even to repudiate it entirely. *Laïcité* thus emerged as much from a desire to "undo" the religious sphere as to negotiate its relation to public life. Further, it is important to remember that the key political figures of the Third Republic considered this principle to be the means by which they would cultivate a "new man": one committed to reason, science, and progress, in keeping with the prevailing intellectual context of positivism.

Positivism's influence on the architects of French secularism revealed to them, in effect, a new entity: the collective social being. In this way, they were able to establish the voluntary submission to the principles of positivist science and human progress as the basis of all democratic activity. They thus effected a complete epistemological about-face in French culture, the corollary of which was the rejection of all transcendental philosophies. This change implies even more than the principles of individual liberty, social equality, and religious neutrality; it also means the "will to place man as the source and the center of all necessity." In this manner, the history of the French Republic granted a radical character to the rejection of transcendent authority. French-style *laïcité* could never be what the first proponents of "liberty" had envisioned it to be: "an amicable separation of the spiritual and temporal spheres, the establishment of religious liberty."[12]

The founders of the French Republic drew from positivism a theoretical basis by which to legitimate their actions. This explains why the battle over *laïcité* has always been ideological as well as political. The corrupted understanding of *laïcité* as an explicit policy of anticlericalism, rather than one of state neutrality and religious tolerance, is a direct result of these beginnings. Because the original conception of *laïcité* implied "that we must assign to law only politico-social motivations and view religious belief as irrelevant to the achievement of the social goals of humanity,"[13] it provided fertile ground for an eventual battle between religious and antireligious forces.

The national school system, conceived as the state's primary vehicle by which to eliminate the influence of the Catholic Church on young people's spirits, bolstered this strict application of the separation of church and state. The schools were considered a means of combatting the outdated doctrine and message of the church.[14] The will to create a sense of national unity on a foundation of science and social morality was the chief motivation for the architects of *laïcité*.

---

[12]Claude Nicolet, *L'idée Républicaine en France* (Paris: Gallimard, 1982), 487.

[13]Nicolet, *L'idée Républicaine*, 488.

[14]This demonstrates a political application of the "society of three orders" articulated by Auguste Comte. Other Republicans, however, such as Jules Simon, argued for the necessity of absolute neutrality of the state in public school curricula. Simon contended that a temporal government should never serve as a spiritual guide or "director of conscience." See Pierre Chevallier, *La séparation de l'Eglise et l'Etat* (Paris: Fayard, 1981), 228. See also Jean Baubérot, *La Laïcité* (Paris: Presses Universitaires de France, 2000).

In order to create this sense of national unity, the Republic adopted as its main objective the elimination of all local ties, community allegiances, and forms of religious teaching, which, according to the positivist worldview, impeded the development of citizens who would make decisions solely on the basis of reason. This representation led to the limitation, to the greatest extent possible, of religion's access to the public sphere, even though the Law of 1905 recognized the right to collective expression of religious life. Thus, *laïcité* did not serve as a mechanism by which to regulate religion's access to the public sphere, but rather a way to eliminate its access almost entirely. In this context, the only legitimate setting for expressing religious adherence became either the home or the house of worship. This transformation of religion into a matter for the private sphere has two main consequences. First, religious groups are no longer allowed to initiate public service activities; and second, government-sponsored public services cannot be marked by any religious expression.

The newly private character of religion brings about a decline in its social legitimacy. As a result, the state, if it hopes to instill respect for freedom of thought and religion, no longer aims to help provide citizens with the "salvation goods." A rift thus grows between the practice of religion and its moral and social dimensions. Religion's lack of social legitimacy further means that religious groups cannot claim public funding, and that organizations sanctioned by the Law of 1905 must focus exclusively on the issue of religious practice.

Consequently, the current situation of French Muslims has raised the question of the legitimacy of the public funding of mosques and state aid for religious institutions (which Muslims have also asked for in certain cases). This unusual request on the part of French Muslims, which contradicts the principles of *laïcité*, is partially explained by the economic difficulties faced by many Muslim groups—difficulties created or at least exacerbated by a refusal to allow the intervention of foreign Muslim governments (or transnational religious groups) who would otherwise provide financial assistance. Since 11 September 2001, however, the issue of the funding of mosque-building projects has appeared less incongruous. A 2005 initiative on the part of the government, for example, created a foundation specifically for the financing of projects of mosque construction under the auspices of the CFCM.

QUESTIONING THE CIVIC ROLE OF THE PUBLIC SCHOOLS
At the time of the founding of the French Republic, the Republicans were not content simply to confine religion to the private sphere; they also hoped to found a countermorality that would owe nothing to the language of religion. Thus the law of 28 March 1882, in addition to establishing a system of compulsory, secular primary schools, also implemented a program of moral and civic instruction. The

secular morality taught in these schools was comprised of four basic tenets—
some of which would, however, prove difficult to accept today. They are:

- Universal morality is opposed to the particularity of religions.
- Science provides the foundation of morality.
- The structure of the *laïque* school system is inherently ethical, insofar as it encourages the intermingling of social groups and serves as a means of social promotion for the most deserving (through scholarships).
- The school is a breeding ground for civic spirit.

These dimensions of the *laïque* laws sketch the outlines of a "regenerating state"[15]—a state that, while not affiliated with religion, aimed to transform the individual and civil society through an ambitious politico-educational program. In this sense, it served as a counterchurch with monopolistic ambitions, with scientific knowledge providing its dogma. Such a vision is no longer feasible: its utopian conception of modernity is disintegrating, dramatically forcing us to examine the question of the foundations of the social bond. In an atomized society in which the ideas of accomplishment, achievement, and progress are challenged, what can serve as the basis for society's reflection on a shared future and a collective memory? The public schools can no longer provide a definitive, unambiguous answer to this question.

Indeed, a century after the law's passage, the landscape has changed considerably. The Catholic Church has finally accepted and adapted to the principle of *laïcité*. It has redoubled its educational aims and succeeded in compelling the state to recognize them through a powerful network of private foundations. Still, the terms of the relationship between church and state posited by the *laïque* revolution have not faced challenges in any fundamental way. Once restricted to the private sphere, religion has largely remained there. The space-time of social life is, to a great extent, disconnected from religious reference. The slow abandonment of religious practice throughout the twentieth century demonstrates how believers have adapted to this separation—which, although created in a setting of conflict, was nonetheless essentially consensual. Religious adherents less exotic than Muslims have fought against secularism in the past, particularly in the schools, which remain the most sensitive arena for issues of *laïcité*. Debate still rages over the introduction of courses on the science of religions and the history of religions into the school curricula; similarly, debate continues over the right to days off school to accommodate religious instruction; and controversy is currently brewing over the academic calendar, which observes Catholic holidays but does not give similar consideration to the holidays of minority religions. But these debates by and large

---

[15]Jean-Paul Willaime, "Le religieux dans l'espace public," *Projet* 225: 71–79.

resemble family discussions more than political conflicts. With the question of the headscarf, however, Islam, once perceived simply as the "religion of the Other," has come to the fore, calling the entire principle of *laïcité* into question.

The passionate nature of the reactions to such issues is chiefly due to many people's difficulty in accepting the fact that, henceforth, a significant number of French citizens are Muslims and want to identify themselves as such. French society is largely reluctant to accept this fact; as a result of France's violent colonial history, Islam often retains negative associations in the French collective imagination. Today, Islam also evokes unpleasant images in regard to the treatment of women. Women's status in Islam appears as the antithesis of the principle of nondiscrimination that theoretically governs relations between individuals in French society. This negative perception of Islam occasionally goes so far as to place the headscarf on a par with the swastika as a symbol of discrimination and hatred. Such views, however, only attest to a lack of understanding or even an intolerance of minority beliefs. In a controversial 1992 ruling, a member of the Conseil d'État wrote that the scarf expresses nothing in itself; it therefore cannot be equated with symbols such as the swastika, which are direct incitements to hate. The headscarf is only experienced as an assault on women's dignity within the reconstruction of everything one knows—or thinks one knows—about Islamic religion and society. But in fact, this interpretation of religious symbols without any consideration of those who actually wear it is in itself a violation of the principle of freedom of conscience.

In the end, the increased visibility of Islamic practice destabilizes the relationship between the public and private spheres by challenging the dominant conception of religion as solely a matter of private faith and practice. Many Islamic religious obligations concern the day-to-day life of individuals, from dietary regulations to the relations between men and women. The fact that Islam is not only a faith, but also a way of organizing everyday life—and that it is perceived as such by some of its followers—brings the question of the social dimension of religion back into the fore. Does religion not involve certain values that have an impact on public and social life? France's restrictive conception of freedom of conscience has no true equivalent among the other countries of Europe. Similar discriminatory practices against the headscarf, for example, can be found elsewhere in Europe, but, unlike in France, it is not supported by legislative measures. (Although in Germany, certain states—Baden-Württemburg in 2004 and later Berlin and Bavaria—did ban the wearing of the headscarf by public school teachers.)

Islam's entrance into the French religious landscape has destabilized a certain balance that has until now existed among the three main principles of *laïcité*: democratic unity, respect for religious pluralism, and freedom of conscience. From now on, however, the particular role of each of these principles will be the source of continued debate and controversy.

Bibliography

PRIMARY SOURCES

Actes du second concile national de France, tenu l'an 1801 de J[ésus] C[hrist] (an 9 de la République française) dans l'église métropolitaine de Paris. 3 vols. Paris: Imprimerie Chrétienne, 1801.

Actes et décrets du IIe Concile provincial d'Utrecht, tenu le 13 septembre M.DCCLXIII dans la chapelle de l'Eglise provinciale de Sainte Gertrude, à Utrecht. Utrecht: Au dépens de la compagnie, 1764.

Alembert, Jean Le Rond d'. *Sur la destruction des jésuites en France, par un auteur désintéressé.* N.p., 1765.

"Annales des Reverends Peres Capucins." Bibliothèque mazarine, ms. 2418.

Antraigues, Emmanuel-Louis-Henri, comte d'. *Dénonciation aux Français catholiques, des moyens employés par l'Assemblée nationale, pour détruire en France, la religion catholique.* London: Edward Pall-Mall, 1791.

Arbaleste, Charlotte d'. *Mémoires de Charlotte d'Arbaleste sur la vie de Duplessis-Mornay, son mari.* In Philippe Duplessis-Mornay, *Mémoires et correspondance.* Paris: Treuttel et Würtz, 1824.

Archives parlementaires de 1787 à 1860, première série (1787–1799). 94 vols. Edited by Marcel Reinhard and Marc Bouloiseau. Paris, 1867–1966.

Atti e decretti del concilio diocesano di Pistoia dell'anno 1786. Edited by Pietro Stella. 2 vols. Florence: Olschi, 1986.

Aubigné, Théodore Agrippa d'. *Oeuvres.* Edited by Henri Weber, Jacques Bailbé, and Marguerite Soulié. Paris: Gallimard, 1969.

———. *Histoire universelle.* Edited by André Thierry. 10 vols. Geneva: Droz, 1981–2000.

Babu, Jean. *Poésies de Jean Babu, curé de Soudan, sur les ruines des temples protestants de Champdeniers, d'Exoudun, de La Mothe-Sainte-Héraye (1663–1682).* Edited by Alfred Richard. Poitiers: P. Blanchier, 1896.

Barrès, Maurice. *Greco ou le secret de Tolède.* Paris: Flammarion, 1988.

Barruel, Abbé Augustin. *Question nationale sur l'autorité et sur les droits du peuple dans le gouvernement, par M l'abbé Barruel.* Paris: Crapart, 1791.

Beaunez, Roger, et al. *Jocistes dans la tourmente: Histoire des jocistes (JOC-JOCF) de la région parisienne 1937–1947.* Paris: Editions du "Témoignage Chrétien," 1989.

Bellegarde, Dupac de. *Histoire abrégée de l'église métropolitaine d'Utrecht, principalement depuis la révolution arrivée dans les 7 provinces unies des Pays-Bas, sous Philippe II, jusqu'à présent.* Utrecht: J. Schelling, 1784.

Benda, Julien. *La Jeunesse d'un clerc.* Paris: Gallimard, 1936.

Benoist, Elie. *Histoire de l'Édit de Nantes contenant les choses les plus remarquables qui se sont passées en France avant & après sa publication.…* 5 vols. Delft: A. Beman, 1693–94.

Bernanos, Georges. *Journal d'un curé de campagne*. Paris: Plon, 1974.

———. *Les Grands Cimetières sous la lune*. Paris: Seuil, 1995.

Bèze, Théodore de. *Histoire ecclesiastique des Eglises reformées au Royaume de France*. Anvers: Jean Remy, 1580.

Bonnaud, Jacques-Julien. *Découverte importante sur le vrai système de la Constitution du clergé, décrétée par l'Assemblée nationale*. Paris: n.d. This pamphlet has also been attributed to the abbé Barruel.

Bolgeni, Giovan Vincenzo. *Della carita o Amor di Dio Dissertazione*. Roma: Stampiera Salomini, 1788.

Chaupy, Bertrand Capmartin de. *Philosophie des lettres qui auroit pu tout sauver. Misosophie Votairienne qui n'a que tout perdre. Ouvrage inutile à la présente tenue des Etats, pour laquelle il avoit été entrepris, mais qui pourra servir à celle qui pourra lui succéder*. 2 vols. Paris: J. Beuchot, 1789–90.

Collection des pièces imprimées par ordre du Concile national de France. Paris: Imprimerie-Librairie Chrétienne, 1797.

Copeau, Jacques. "La représentation sacrée." *Art Sacré* 18 (1937).

Couturier, Fr. M.-A. "St.-Jacques de Montrouge." *Art Sacré* 26 (1938).

Couve, Benjamin. "L'Instruction Laïque." *Le Christianisme au XIXe siècle*, 5 January 1872.

Crespin, Jean. *Histoire des martyrs persecutez et mis à mort pour la verité de l'Evangile, depuis le temps des apostres jusques à présent (1619)*. Edited by Daniel Benoît and Matthieu Lelièvre. Toulouse: Société des livres religieux, 1889.

Decoppet, Auguste. *Nos libertés: Sermon… à l'occasion de la fondation de l'Association culturelle de l'Oratoire…* . Paris, 1906.

Dissertation sur le droit de convoquer les Etats-Generaux, tirée des capitulaires, des ordonnances, et les autres monumens de l'histoire de France. N.p., 1787.

Duchêne, Hervé, ed. *Notre Ecole Normale*. Paris: Les Belles lettres, 1994.

Dutoit, Marie. *Mme Edmond de Pressensé, sa vie d'après sa correspondance et son oeuvre*. Paris: Fischbacher, 1904.

Duvoisin, Jean-Baptiste. *La France chrétienne et vraiment libre*. N.p., 1789.

Edict et declaration du roy, sur la reduction de la ville de Paris soubs son obeyssance. Paris, 1594.

"Eloges historiques de tous les grands hommes et les illustres religieux Capucins de la Province de Paris,… 2e tome." BN, Ms. fr. 25046.

Filleau, Jean. *Décisions catholiques ou recueil general des arrests dans toutes les cours souveraines de France en éxécution, ou interpretation, des edits qui concernent l'exercice de la religion pretendue reformée…* . Poitiers: Veuve H. Braud, 1668.

Fontaine, Nicolas. *Mémoires pour servir à l'histoire de Port-Royal*. Utrecht: au dépens de la Compagnie, 1736.

Gignoux, Hubert. "Théâtre Scout." *Art Sacré* 35 (1938).

Grégoire, Henri. *Compte rendu par le citoyen Grégoire au concile national, des travaux des évêques réunis à Paris*. Paris: Imprimerie-Librairie Chrétienne, 1797.

———. *De la noblesse de la peau*. Grenoble: Editions Jerôme Millon, 1996.

———. *Mémoires de Grégoire, ancien évêque de Blois, député à l'Assemblée Constituante et à la Convention Nationale, Sénateur, membre de l'Institut, suivies de la Notice historique sur Grégoire d'Hippolyte Carnot*. Edited by Jean-Michel Leniaud. Paris: Editions de Santé, 1989.

————. *Réclamation des fidèles Catholiques de France au prochain concile national, en faveur de l'usage primitif de la langue vulgaire dans l'administration des sacrements et la célébration de l'office divine.* Paris: Brajeux, 1801.

————. *Traité de l'uniformité et de l'amélioration de la liturgie, présenté au concile national de 1801 par le citoyen Grégoire.* Paris: Imprimerie-Librairie, an X.

Hardy, Siméon-Prosper. "Mes loisirs, ou Journal d'événemens tels qu'ils parviennent à ma connoissance." 8 vols. BN, Nouv. Acq., Mss. Fr. 6687 (29–30 September 1789).

Inventaire des pièces d'archives françaises se rapportant à l'Abbaye de Port-Royal des Champs et son cercle et à la résistance contre la bulle Unigenitus et à l'appel, Ms 2767, Clément to Pierre-Jean Meindaerts, Archbishop of Utrecht, 13 September 1764. Het Utrechts Archief.

Jalabert, Philippe. *De la séparation des églises et de l'état au point de vue du Protestantisme français.* Dole, 1903.

Journal de François, bourgeois de Paris: 23 décembre 1588–30 avril 1589. Edited by Eugène Saulnier. Paris: E. Leroux, 1913.

La conférence entre un ministre d'état et un conseiller au parlement. N.p., n.d. In the Bibliothèque de Port-Royal (henceforth BPR), Collection Le Paige, Ms 915, no. 6.

Le Paige, Louis-Adrien. *Lettres adressées à mm. les commissaires nommés par le roi pour délibérer sur l'affaire présente du parlement au sujet du refus de sacrements, ou Lettres pacifiques au sujet des contestations présentes.* N.p., 1753.

————. *Lettres historiques sur les fonctions essentielles du parlement, sur le droit des pairs, et sur les loix fondamentaux du royaume.* 2 vols. Amsterdam, 1753–54.

L'Espine, Jean de. *Traicté de l'apostasie.* N.p., 1583.

L'Estoile, Pierre de. *Journal pour le règne de Henri IV.* 3 vols. Paris: Gallimard, 1948–1960.

————. *Mémoires-journaux: Journal de Henri IV, 1595–1607.* Paris: Librairie des Bibliophiles, 1879.

Le Témoignage: Journal de l'église de la Confession d'Augsbourg, 9 April 1870.

Lettre à M. xxx, chevalier de l'ordre de Malte, touchant en écrit "Sur la destruction des jésuites en France." France, 1765.

L'Hôspital, Michel de. *Discours pour la majorité de Charles IX.* Edited by Robert Descimon. Paris: Imprimerie nationale, 1993.

————. "Harangue prononcée à l'ouverture de la session des Etats généraux à Orléans le 13 décembre 1560" ("Discours d'Orléans"). In *Discours pour la majorité de Charles IX.* Edited by Robert Descimon. Paris: Imprimerie nationale, 1993.

Maultrot, Gabriel-Nicolas. *Les droits de la puissance temporelle, défendue contre la seconde partie des Actes de l'Assemblée du clergé de 1765 concernant la religion.* Amsterdam, 1777.

————. *Origines et justes bornes de la puissance temporelle suivant les livres saints et la tradition sainte.* 3 vols. Paris: Le Clère, 1789.

"Memoire pour les temples de Niort et de Cherveux," AN TT 260 (10), 1198–99.

"Memoire pour monseigneur le chancelier touchant les exercises de fief en Poictou" (1681), AN TT 262.

Mey, Abbé Claude, Gabriel-Nicolas Maultrot, et al. *Maximes du droit public François.* 2 vols. Amsterdam: Marc-Michel Rey, 1775.

————. *Apologie de tous les jugemens rendus par les tribunaux séculiers en France contre le schisme.* 2 vols. France, 1752.

Migault, Jean. *Les dragonnades en Poitou et Saintonge: Le journal de Jean Migault.* Le Poiré sur Vie: Imprimerie graphique de l'ouest, 1988.

"Niort, au sujet de la demolition du temple, 1684," AN TT 260 (10), 1204–5.

Nouvelles ecclésiastiques, ou Mémoires pour servir à l'histoire de la constitution Unigenitus. Utrecht, 1728–1803, 19 March 1760.

Pascal, Blaise. *Provinciales,* published as pamphlets in 1656–57. Published in English as *The mystery of Jesuitism: Discovered in certain letters written upon occasion of the present differences at Sorbonne between the Jansenists and the Molinists: Displaying the pernicious maximes of the late Casuists: With additionals.* 3rd ed. London: Printed for Richard Royston..., 1679.

"Pièces concernant les contestations relatives à la démolition de temple dudit lieu (Cherveux)" and Proces-verbal de Messieurs de Basville et de Jaucourt touchant la proximité du temple de Cherveux a l'eglise parroisialle, 17 juillet et 3 aoust 1689," AN TT 240 (24), 1339–46, 1356–78.

Pressensé, Edmond de. *Une église séparée de l'état: Notice historique sur l'église Taitbout à Paris, et discourse pronouncés a l'occasion du cinquantenaire de sa chapelle le 6 mai 1890.* Paris, 1890.

Pressensé, Mme. Suchard de. *L'Oeuvre de Mme. de Pressensé.* Paris: Fischbacher, 1903.

Procès apostolique de la bienheureuse soeur Marie de l'Incarnation. Archives du Carmel de Pontoise.

"Proces-verbal de la descente faitte par...Basville...au bourg de Cherveux, 20 avril 1684," AN TT 260 (10), 1196–97.

"Proces-verbal de M. de Basville et de M. de Jaucourt touchant la proximité du temple de Niort 17 juillet 1683," AN TT 260 (10).

Quick, John. *Synodicon in Gallia Reformata, or, the Acts, Decisions, Decrees and Canons of those Famous National Councils of the Reformed Churches in France.* London, 1692.

Quinet, Edgar. *La révolution.* Alençon: Belin, 1987.

———. *Le christianisme et la Révolution française.* Paris: Fayard, 1984.

Rabelais, François. *Gargantua.* Paris: Gallimard, 1955.

Recherches historiques et dogmatiques, de ce que a interessé la doctrine chrétienne depuis le Concile de Trente, BPR, RV 108=38 (8292), no. 23.

"Recueil des délibérations du Concile national du clergé de France en 1797," BN, Nouv. Acq., Mss Fr. 2779, sessions on 14 August and 7 September, fols. 8–12, 34–35.

Reinach, Salomon. *Bibliographie de Salomon Reinach.* Paris: Les Belles lettres, 1936.

———. *Cultes, mythes et religions.* 5 vols. Paris: E. Leroux, 1905–23.

———. *Cultes, mythes, et religions.* Edited by Hervé Duchêne. Paris: R. Laffont, 1996.

———. *Le mirage oriental.* Paris: G. Masson, 1893.

———. *L'Origine des Aryens: Histoire d'une controverse.* Paris: E. Leroux, 1892.

———. *Orpheus: Histoire générale des religions.* Paris: Picard, 1909.

Renan, Ernest. *Oeuvres complètes.* Edited by Henriette Psichari. 10 vols. Paris: Calmann-Lévy, 1947–61.

Réveillaud, Eugène. "L'Agonie du budget des cultes." *Le Signal,* 1 December 1883.

———. "Une grande question toujours en suspens." *Le Signal,* 10 April 1886.

"Requeste et pieces pour le sindic du clergé de Poitiers," AN TT 262.

Robert, Charles. *De l'Instruction obligatoire.* Paris: Hachette, 1871.

Seyssel, Claude de. *La Monarchie de France et deux autres fragments politiques.* Edited by Jacques Pujol. Paris: Librairie d'Argences, 1961.

"Sommaire des raisons que ceux qui font profession de la religion refformée ont de se plaindre de l'arrest du seiziesme septembre 1634 donné par nos seigneurs de parlement tenants les grands jours en la ville de Poictiers." Archives Départmentales de Vienne C 49.

Stegmann, André, ed. *Edits des guerres de Religion…* . Paris: J. Vrin, 1979.

Stella, Pietro, ed. *Atti e decreti del concilio diocesano di Pistoia dell'anno 1786,* reprinted from the Bracali edition. 2 vols. Florence: Olschki, 1986.

Tamburini, Pietro. *Lettere teologico-politiche sulla presente situazione delle cose ecclesiastiche.* 2 vols. Pavia: Stampiera di Baldassara Comini, 1794.

Thou, Jacques-Auguste de. *Histoire universelle…* . The Hague: Henri Scheurleer, 1740.

Tremblay, Augustin-Charles-Jean Clément du. *Journal de correspondances et voyages d'Italie et d'Espagne pour la paix de l'église en 1758, 1768 et 1769 par M. Clément, alors trésorier de l'église d'Auxerre, et depuis évêque de Versailles.* 3 vols. Paris: Longuet, 1802.

Trial, Louis. *La séparation des églises et de l'état.* Paris, 1905.

Vinet, Alexandre, et al. *Alexandre Vinet d'après sa correspondance inedite avec Henri Lutteroth.* Paris: Fischbacher, 1891.

Vinet, Alexandre. *Essai sur la conscience et sur liberté religieuse.* Paris and Geneva: Henry Servier, 1829.

———. *La Liberté des cultes.* 2nd ed. Paris: Chez les éditeurs, 1852.

———. *Lettres d'Alexandre Vinet et de quelques-uns de ses correspondants.* Lausanne: Bridel, 1882.

———. *Liberté religieuse et questions ecclésiastiques.* Paris: Chez les éditeurs, 1854.

———. *Mémoire en faveur de la liberté des cultes.* Paris: Servier, 1826.

SECONDARY SOURCES

Ackerman, Robert. *The Myth and Ritual School: J. G. Frazer and the Cambridge Ritualists.* New York: Garland, 1991.

Alfaric, Prosper. *Jean Macé, fondateur de la Ligue française de l'enseignement.* Paris: Ligue française de l'enseignement, 1955.

Allier, Raoul. *La cabale des dévots.* Paris: A. Colin, 1902.

———. *Le Bilan de la séparation pour les églises protestantes.* Paris, n.d.

Almog, Shmuel. *Antisemitism through the Ages.* Oxford: Pergamon Press, 1998.

Amphoux, Henri. *Michel de L'Hôspital et la liberté de conscience au XVIe siècle.* Paris: Librairie Fischbacher, 1900.

Appolis, Emile. *Le "tiers parti" catholique au dix-huitième siècle.* Paris: Picard, 1960.

Aquarone, Alberto. "Giansenismo italiano e rivoluzione francese prima del Triennio giacobino." *Rassegna storica del Risorgimento: Organo della Società nazionale per la storia del Risorgimento italiano* 39 (1962): 559–624.

Arnal, Oscar L. "Toward a Lay Apostolate of the Workers: Three Decades of Conflict for the French Jeunesse Ouvrière Chrétienne (1927–1956)." *Catholic Historical Review* 73 (1987): 221–27.

Assouline, Pierre. *Hergé.* Paris: Plon, 1996.

Auspitz, Katherine. *The Radical Bourgeoisie. The Ligue de l'enseignement and the Origins of the Third Republic, 1866–1885.* Cambridge: Cambridge University Press, 1982.

Babelon, Jean-Pierre. *Henri IV.* Paris: Fayard, 1982.

Bannon, Patrick, ed. *Les sectes en France: Rapport parlementaire. Preface by Alain Gest.* Paris: Opinion Publiques, 1995.

Barnes, Andrew E. "*Ces Sortes de Pénitence Imaginaires:* The Counter Reformation Assault on *Communitas.*" In *Social History and Issues in Human Consciousness: Some Interdisciplinary Connections.* Edited by Andrew Barnes and Peter Stearns, 67–84. New York: New York University Press, 1989.

———. "From Ritual to Meditative Piety: Devotional Change in French Penitential Confraternities from the 16th to the 18th Centuries." *Journal of Ritual Studies* 1 (1987): 1–26.

———. *The Social Dimension of Piety: Associative Life and Devotional Change in the Penitent Confraternities of Marseilles (1499–1792).* New York: Paulist Press, 1994.

Basch, Françoise. *Victor Basch ou la passion de la justice: De l'affaire Dreyfus au crime de la milice.* Paris: Plon, 1994.

Baubérot, Jean. "La laïcité française et ses mutations." *Social Compass* 45 (1998): 175–87.

———. *La Laïcité.* Paris: Presses Universitaires de France, 2000.

———. *La morale laïque contre l'ordre moral.* Paris: Seuil, 1997.

———. "Problèmes du Protestantisme français face à la séparation des églises et de l'état." *Etudes théologiques et religieuses* 47 (1972): 271–312.

———. *Le Retour des Huguenots: La Vitalité protestante, XIXe–XXe siècle.* Paris: Cerf, 1985.

———. "La tolérance dans la France actuelle." In *Tolérance et intolérance de l'édit de Nantes à nos jours.* Edited by Guy Saupin. Rennes: Presses Universitaires de Rennes, 1998.

———. *Vers un nouveau pacte laïque.* Paris: Seuil, 1990.

Baumgartner, Frederic J. *Radical Reactionaries: The Political Thought of the French Catholic League.* Geneva: Droz, 1976.

Becker, Annette. *La Guerre et la foi, de la mort à la mémoire 1914–1930.* Paris: A. Colin, 1994.

Becker, Jean-Jacques, ed. *Les Juifs de France: De la Révolution française à nos jours.* Paris: Liana Levi, 1998.

Benbassa, Esther. *Une diaspora sépharade en transition: Istanbul, XIXe–XXe siècle.* Paris: Cerf, 1993.

Benedict, Philip. *Rouen during the Wars of Religion.* Cambridge: Cambridge University Press, 1981.

———. "*Un roi, une loi, deux fois:* Parameters for the History of Catholic-Reformed Coexistence in France, 1555–1685." In *Tolerance and Intolerance in the European Reformation.* Edited by Ole Peter Grell and Bob Scribner, 65–93. New York: Cambridge University Press, 1996.

Bergin, Joseph. *Pouvoir et fortune de Richelieu.* Paris: R. Laffont, 1987.

Berkovitz, Jay. "Jewish Scholarship and Identity in Nineteenth Century France." *Modern Judaism* 18 (1998): 1–33.

Bernand, Carmen, and Serge Gruzinski. *De l'idolâtrie: Une archéologie des sciences religieuses.* Paris: Seuil, 1988.

———. *Histoire du Nouveau Monde: Les métissages.* Paris: Fayard, 1993.

Berstein, Serge, and Odile Ruddelle, eds. *Le modèle républicain.* Paris: Presses Universitaires de France, 1992.

Berteaux, Simone. *Piaf: A Biography.* Translated by June Guicharnaud. New York: Harper & Row, 1972.

Billot, Marcel, ed. *La Chapelle de Vence, Journal d'une création.* Paris: Editions du Cerf, 1993.

Birnbaum, Pierre. "La citoyenneté en péril: Les juifs entre intégration et résistance." *La France de l'affaire Dreyfus.* Edited by Pierre Birnbaum, 526–27. Paris: Gallimard, 1994.

———. *The Jews of the Republic: A Political History of State Jews in France from Gambetta to Vichy*. Stanford: Stanford University Press, 1996.

———. "Les Juifs et l'Affaire." In *Les Juifs de France: De la Révolution française à nos jours*. Edited by Jean-Jacques Becker and Annette Wieviorka, 75–101. Paris: Liana Levi, 1998).

Blanning, Timothy C. W. *Reform and Revolution in Mainz, 1743–1803*. Cambridge: Cambridge University Press, 1974.

Bloch, Camille. *Procès verbaux et rapports du Comité de Mendicité de la Constituante. 1790–1791*. Paris, 1991.

Boegner, Marc. *Un demi-siècle de séparation des églises et de l'état: Essai de bilan*. Paris: Firmin-Didot, 1955.

Bonniol, Jean-Luc. *La couleur comme maléfice: Une illustration créole de la généalogie des Blancs et des Noirs*. Paris: Albin Michel, 1992.

Boucher, Jacqueline. *Société et mentalités autour de Henri III*. Lille: Presses de l'Université de Lille, 1981.

Boyer, Alain. *L'Islam en France*. Paris: Presses Universitaires de France, 1998.

Bradby, David. *Modern French Drama 1940–1990*. 2nd ed. Cambridge: Cambridge University Press, 1991.

Bradley, James E., and Dale K. Van Kley, eds. *Religion and Politics in Enlightenment Europe*. Notre Dame, IN: University of Notre Dame Press, 2001.

Bréon, Emmanuel. *L'Art sacré au XXe siècle*. Boulogne-Billancourt: Centre culturel, 1993.

Bridel, Philippe. *Alexandre Vinet: Sa personne et ses idées*. Paris: La Cause, 1912.

Broersma, J. *Antonius de Haen, 1704–1776: Leven en werk*. Assen: Vrije Universiteit van Amsterdam, 1963.

Buisson, Ferdinand, ed. *Nouveau dictionnaire de pédagogie et d'instruction publique*. Paris: Hachette, 1911.

Burke, Edmund. *Reflections on the Revolution in France*. Indianapolis: Bobbs-Merrill, 1955.

Burke, Peter. "History as Social Memory." In *Memory: History, Culture and the Mind*. Edited by Thomas Butler, 97–112. Oxford: Oxford University Press, 1989.

Bury, J. P. T. *Gambetta and the National Defense*. London: Longman, 1936.

———. *Gambetta's Final Years: "The Era of Difficulties," 1877–1882*. London: Longman, 1982.

Calais, Henri de. *Histoire de la vie, de la mort et des miracles du R. P. Honoré Bochart de Champigny, Capuchin*. Paris: Veuve Poussielgue-Rusard, 1864.

Cameron, Keith, ed. *From Valois to Bourbon: Dynasty, State, and Society in Early Modern France*. Exeter: University of Exeter Press, 1989.

Carroll, James. *Constantine's Sword: The Church and the Jews*. New York: Houghton Mifflin, 2001.

Certeau, Michel de. *La fable mystique XVIe–XVIIe siècle*. Paris: Gallimard, 1982.

———. "Politique et mystique. René d'Argenson (1596–1651)." *Revue d'ascétique et mystique* 39 (1963): 45–82.

———. "The Formality of Practices. From Religious Systems to the Ethics of the Enlightenment (the Seventeenth and Eighteenth Centuries)." In *The Writing of History*. Translated by Tom Conley, 147–205. New York: Columbia University Press, 1988.

Césari, Jocelyne. "Islam and Fundamental Rights in Europe." Report to the European Commission, Director General of Justice and Home Affairs, 2004.

————. *Musulmans et Republicains: Les jeunes, l'islam et la France*. Brussels: Complexe, 1998.

————. *When Islam and Democracy Meet: Muslims in Europe and in the United States*. New York: Palgrave, 2004.

Chadwick, Owen. *The Popes and the European Revolution*. Oxford: Clarendon Press, 1981.

Charuty, Giordana. "L'invention rituelle du catholicisme pentecôtiste français et italien." *Social Compass* 24 (1987): 437–63.

Châtellier, Louis. *L'Europe des dévots*. Paris: Editions de la Maison des sciences de l'homme, 1987.

Chauvière, Michel. "Structure de sociabilité et travail de la socialité: Des associations familiales sous Vichy." In *Sociabilité, Pouvoirs et Société, Actes du Colloque de Rouen 24/26 novembre 1983*, 557–66. Rouen: University of Rouen, 1987.

Chédozeau, Bernard. "Les traductions de la Bible, le jansénisme, et la Révolution." In "Jansénisme et Révolution." Edited by Catherine Maire. Special issue, *Chroniques de Port-Royal* 39 (1990): 219–39.

Chevallier, Pierre. *La séparation de l'église et de l'école: Jules Ferry et Léon XIII*. Paris: Fayard, 1981.

Cholvy, Gérard. *La religion en France de la fin du XVIIIe à nos jours*. Paris: Hachette, 1991.

Cholvy, Gérard, and Yves-Marie Saint-Hilaire. *Histoire religieuse de la France contemporaine, 1880/1930*. Toulouse: Privat, 1986.

Chomarat, Jacques. *Grammaire et rhétorique chez Erasme*. Paris: Belles lettres, 1981.

Choron-Baix, Catherine. "Des forêts en banlieues: La transplantation du boudhisme Lao en France." *Archives des Sciences Sociales des Religions* 73 (1991): 29.

Christin, Olivier. "Sortir des guerres de Religion: L'autonomisation de la raison politique au milieu du XVIe siècle." *Actes de la Recherche en Sciences Sociales: Histoire de l'Etat* (March 1997): 24–38.

Church, William. "The Decline of French Jurists as Political Theorists," *French Historical Studies* 5 (1967): 1–40.

————. *Richelieu and Reason of State*. Princeton: Princeton University Press, 1972.

Cochrane, Eric. *Florence in the Forgotten Centuries, 1527–1800: A History of Florence and the Florentines in the Age of the Grand Dukes*. Chicago: University of Chicago Press, 1973.

Compayre, Gabriel. *Jean Macé et l'instruction obligatoire*. Paris: Delaplane, n.d.

Comte, Bernard. *Une Utopie combattante, L'Ecole des cadres d'Uriage 1940–1942*. Paris: Fayard, 1991.

Conway, Martin. *Catholic Politics in Europe, 1918–1945*. London: Routledge, 1997.

Copas, Jean, and Jean Jamin. *Aux origines de l'anthropologie française: Les mémoires de la Société des Observateurs de l'Homme en l'an VIII*. Paris: Le Sycomore, 1978.

Cordey, Henri. *Edmond de Pressensé et son temps*. Lausanne, 1916.

Cottret, Bernard. *1598, L'Édit de Nantes: Pour en finir avec les guerres de religion*. Paris: Le Grand livre du mois, 1997.

Cottret, Monique. *Jansénisme et lumières: Pour un autre dix-huitième siècle*. Paris: Albin Michel, 1998.

————. *La Bastille à prendre: Histoire et mythe de la forteresse royale*. Paris: Presses Universitaires de France, 1986.

Coutrot, Aline. "Les mouvements confessionnels et la société politique." In *Forces religieuses et attitudes politiques dans la France contemporaine*. Edited by René Rémond, 123–52. Paris: A. Colin, 1965.

Couturier, Marie-Alain. *Sacred Art*. Translated by Granger Ryan. Austin: University of Texas Press, 1989.

Couturier, Marie-Alain, Pierre Jivonne, and Pie-Raymond Régamey. *L'Art sacré, sa mystique et sa politique*. Paris: Editions du Cerf, 1955.

Crouzet, Denis. *La Sagesse et le malheur: Michel de L'Hospital chancelier de France*. Seyssel: Champ Vallon, 1998.

———. *Les Guerriers de Dieu: La violence au temps des troubles de religion*. Seyssel: Champ Vallon, 1990.

Dammig, Enrico. *Il movimento giansenista a Roma nella seconda metà del secolo XVIII*. Vatican City: Bibliotteca Apostolica, 1945.

Dansette, Adrien. *Destin du catholicisme français, 1926–1956*. Paris: Flammarion, 1957.

Dartigue, Henry, ed. *Annuaire protestant: Année 1937*. Paris: Fischbacher, 1937.

Davis, Natalie Zemon. *Society and Culture in Early Modern France*. Stanford: Stanford University Press, 1975.

Dean, Rodney J. *L'église constitutionnelle, Napoléon et le Concordat de 1801*. Paris: R. J. Dean, 2004.

Debien, Gabriel. "Les affranchissements aux Antilles françaises aux XVIIe et XVIIIe siècles." *Annuario de Estudios Americanos* 24 (1967): 1177–1203.

Delbreil, Jean-Claude. *Centrisme et démocratie chrétienne en France, le Parti démocrate populaire des origines au M.R.P., 1919–1944*. Paris: Publications de la Sorbonne, 1990.

Desan, Suzanne. *Reclaiming the Sacred: Lay Religion and Popular Politics in Revolutionary France*. Ithaca: Cornell University Press, 1990.

Descimon, Robert. *Qui étaient les Seize? Mythes et réalités de la Ligue parisienne (1585–1594)*. Paris: Klincksieck, 1983.

Descimon, Robert, and Christian Jouhaud. *La France du premier XVII siècle*. Paris: Belin, 1996.

Dessoye, Arthur. *Jean Macé et la fondation de la ligue de l'enseignement*. Paris: Marpon et Flammarion, 1883.

Deyon, Solange. *Du loyalisme au refus: Les protestants français et leur député-général entre la Fronde et la Révocation*. Villeneuve-d'Ascq: Université de Lille, 1976.

Dez, Pierre. *Histoire des protestants et des églises réformées du Poitou*. La Rochelle: Imprimerie de l'Ouest, 1936.

Diefendorf, Barbara. "An Age of Gold: Parisian Women, the Holy League, and the Roots of Catholic Renewal." In *Changing Identities in Early Modern France*. Edited by Michael Wolf, 169–90. Durham: Duke University Press, 1997.

———. *Beneath the Cross: Catholics and Huguenots in Sixteenth-Century Paris*. New York: Oxford University Press, 1991.

———. "Reconciliation and Remembering: A *Devôt* Writes the History of the Holy League." In "Clémence, oubliance et pardon en Europe, 1520–1620." Special issue, *Cahiers d'histoire* 16 (1996): 69–79.

———. "The Huguenot Psalter and the Faith of French Protestants." In *Culture and Identity in Early Modern Europe (1500–1800): Essays in Honor of Natalie Zemon Davis*. Edited by Barbara Diefendorf and Carla Hesse, 41–64. Ann Arbor: University of Michigan Press, 1993.

Dompnier, Bernard. "La logique d'une destruction: L'église catholique, la royauté et les temples protestants (1680–1685)." In *Révolution française et "vandalisme révolutionnaire": Actes du colloque international de Clermont-Ferrand, 15–17 décembre*

1998. Edited by Simone Bernard-Griffiths, Marie-Claude Chemin, and Jean Ehrard, 343–51. Paris: Universitas, 1992

———. *Le venin de l'hérésie: Image du protestantisme et combat catholique au XVIIe siècle.* Paris: Le Centurion, 1985.

Douglas, Mary. "The Cloud God and the Shadow Self." *Social Anthropology* 3 (June 1995): 83–94.

Dubief, Henri. "Réflexions sur quelques aspects du premier réveil et sur le milieu où il se forma." *Bulletin de la Société du protestantisme français* 114 (1968): 373–402.

Dulong, Claude. *La Fortune de Mazarin.* Paris: Perrin, 1990.

Dumont, Paul. "Le français d'abord." In *Salonique 1850–1918, la ville des juifs et le réveil des Balkans.* Edited by Gilles Veinstein, 208–25. Paris: Autrement, 1993.

Dupeyroux, Jean-Jacques. *Sécurité sociale.* Paris: Dalloz, 1965.

Dupront, Alphonse. *Du Sacré: Croisades et pèlerinages: Images et langages.* Paris: Gallimard, 1990.

Duquesne, Jacques. *Les Catholiques français sous l'Occupation.* Paris: Grasset, 1996.

Efron, John. *Defenders of the Race: Jewish Doctors and Race Science in Fin-de-Siècle Europe.* New Haven, CT: Yale University Press, 1994.

Encrevé, André, ed. *Les Protestants.* Vol. 5 of *Dictionnaire du monde religieux dans la France contemporaine.* Edited by Jean-Marie Mayeur and Yves-Marie Hilaire. Paris: Beauchesne, 1993.

Encrevé, André. *Les Protestants en France de 1800 à nos jours: Histoire d'une réintégration.* Paris: Stock, 1985.

Fantappiè, Carlo. *Riforme ecclesiastiche e resistenze sociali.* Bologna: Mulino, 1986.

Feitlowitz, Marguerite. *A Lexicon of Terror: Argentina and the Legacies of Torture.* New York: Oxford University Press, 1998.

Feroldi, Vincent. *La Force des enfants, des Coeurs Vaillants à l'A.C.E.* Paris: Editions ouvrières, 1987.

Fierro,Alfred, André Palluel-Guillard, and Jean Tulard, eds. *Histoire et dictionnaire du consulat et de l'empire.* Paris: Laffont, 1995.

Fouilloux, Etienne. *Les Chrétiens français entre crise et libération, 1937–1947.* Paris: Seuil, 1997.

Fuhrmann, Paul T. *Extraordinary Christianity: The Life and Thought of Alexander Vinet.* Philadelphia: Westminster, 1964.

Galant, Henry C. *Histoire politique de la Sécurité sociale française 1945–1952.* Paris: A. Colin, 1955.

Gallini, Clara. *Il miracolo e la sua prova: Un etnologo a Lourdes.* Napoli: Ligouri Editore, 1998.

Garrisson, Francis. *Essai sur les commissions d'application de l'Édit de Nantes, première partie: Règne de Henri IV.* Montpellier: P. Déhan, 1964.

Garrisson, Janine. *L'Édit de Nantes et sa révocation: Histoire d'une intolérance.* Paris: Seuil, 1985.

Gazier, Augustin. *Etudes sur l'histoire religieuse de la Révolution française, d'après des documents originaux et inédits.* Paris: Armand Colin, 1887.

———. *Histoire générale du mouvement janséniste depuis ses origines jusqu'à nos jours.* 2 vols. Paris: Honoré Champion, 1924.

Geertz, Clifford. *Essais d'anthropologie religieuse.* Paris: Gallimard, Essais, 1966.

Geisser,Vincent. *La Nouvelle Islamophobie.* Paris: La Découverte, 2003.

Gennep, Arnold Van. *Manuel de Folklore français*. Paris: A. Picard, 1937.

Giuntella, Vittorio E. *Le dolci catene, testi della contro-rivoluzione cattolica in Italia*. Rome: Istituto per la Storia del Risorgimento Italiano, 1988.

Goldstein, Jan, and John W. Boyer, eds. *Nineteenth-Century Europe: Liberalism and Its Critics*. Chicago: University of Chicago Press, 1988.

Gontard, Denis. *La Décentralisation théâtrale en France 1895–1952*. Paris: SEDES, 1973.

Graetz, Michael. *The Jews in Nineteenth-Century France: From the French Revolution to the Alliance Israélite Universelle*. Translated by Jane Marie Todd. Stanford: Stanford University Press, 1996.

Grenand, Pierre, and Françoise Grenand. "Les Amérindiens de Guyane Française aujourd'hui: Eléments de compréhension." *Journal de la Société des Américanistes* 66 (1979): 361–82.

———. "Y a-t-il encore des sauvages en Amérique?" In "Chronique du Groupe d'Information sur les Amérindiens." Special issue, *Journal de la Société des Américanistes* 78 (1992): 99–112.

Guérin, Christian. *L'utopie Scout de France: Histoire d'une identité collective, catholique et sociale 1920–1995*. Paris: Fayard, 1997.

Gugelot, Frédéric. *La Conversion des intellectuels au catholicisme en France (1885–1935)*. Paris: CNRS, 1998.

Halbwachs, Maurice. *Les cadres sociaux de la mémoire*. Paris: Mouton, 1975.

Halliday, Fred. "Islamophobia Reconsidered." *Ethnic and Racial Studies* 22, no. 5 (Sept. 1999): 892–902.

Halls, Wilfred Douglas. *Politics, Society and Christianity in Vichy France*. Oxford: Oxford University Press, 1995.

Hanlon, Gregory. *Confession and Community in Seventeenth-Century France: Catholic and Protestant Coexistence in Aquitaine*. Philadelphia: University of Pennsylvania Press, 1993.

Harding, Robert R. "The Mobilization of Confraternities against the Reformation in France." *Sixteenth Century Journal* 11 (1980): 92–98.

Hart, Mitchell. "Racial Science, Social Science, and the Politics of Jewish Assimilation." *Isis* 90 (1999): 268–97.

Hatzfeld, Henri. *Du Paupérisme à la Sécurité sociale, essai sur les origines de la Sécurité sociale en France 1850–1940*. Paris: A. Colin, 1971.

Hause, Steven C. "A Pastoral Family in French Politics: Edmond, Elise, and Francis de Pressensé." *Proceedings of the Western Society for French History* 18 (1990): 383–91.

Hayat, Pierre, ed. *Ferdinand Buisson: Education et république*. Paris: Kime, 2003.

Hayden, J. Michael. *France and the Estates General of 1614*. Cambridge: Cambridge University Press, 1974.

Hellman, John. *Emmanuel Mounier and the New Catholic Left 1930–1950*. Toronto: Toronto University Press, 1981.

———. *The Knight-Monks of Vichy France: Uriage, 1940–45*. Montreal: McGill–Queens University Press, 1993.

Hermon-Belot, Rita. *L'abbé Grégoire: La politique et la vérité*. Paris: Seuil, 2000.

Hervieu-Léger, Danielle. "Les recompositions religieuses et les tendances actuelles de la sociologie des religions en France." *Social Compass* 45 (1998): 143–53.

Holt, Mack P. *The French Wars of Religion, 1562–1629*. Cambridge: Cambridge University Press, 1995.

Hunt, Lynn, David Lansky, and Paul Hanson. "The Failure of the Liberal Republic in France, 1795–1799: The Road to Brumaire." *Journal of Modern History* 51 (December 1979): 734–59.

Imbert, Hugues. *Histoire de Thouars*. Niort: Clouzot, 1871.

Ivry, Benjamin. *Francis Poulenc*. London: Phaidon, 1996.

Jean-François Clément, "Les penseurs des Lumières face à l'Islam," *Social Compass* 44 (1997): 227–46.

Jolly, Jean, ed. *Dictionnaire des parlementaires français… 1889–1940*. Paris: Presses Universitaires de France, 1960.

Jouhaud, Christian. "Imprimer l'événement: La Rochelle à Paris." In *Les Usages de l'Imprimé (XVe–XIXe siècles)*. Edited by Roger Chartier, 381–438. Paris: Fayard, 1987.

———. *La Main de Richelieu ou le pouvoir cardinal*. Paris: Gallimard, 1991.

———. "La tactique du lierre: Sur 'L'Etat au miroir de la raison d'Etat' de Marcel Gauchet." *Miroirs de la raison d'Etat, Cahiers du Centre de Recherches Historiques* 20 (April 1998): 39–47.

Joutard, Philippe, Jacques Poujol, and Patrick Cabanel. *Cévennes terre de refuge, 1940–1944*. Montpellier: Les Presses du Languedoc, 1994.

Joutard, Philippe. "The Museum of the Desert, the Protestant Minority." In *Realms of Memory: Rethinking the French Past*. Vol. 1, *Conflicts and Divisions*. Edited by Pierre Nora. English edition edited with a foreword by Lawrence D. Kritzman. Translated by Arthur Goldhammer, 354–55. New York: Columbia University Press, 1996.

Julia, Dominique, "L'affaiblissement de l'Église gallicane." In *Histoire de la France religieuse*. Edited by Le Goff and Rémond, 3:35–36.

Kaiser, Wolfgang. *Marseille au temps des troubles, 1559–1596: Morphologie sociale et luttes de factions*. Translated by Florence Chaix. Paris: Editions de l'Ecole des hautes études en sciences sociales, 1992.

Koehler, Ellen A. "Religious Liberty and *Civisme moral*: Alexandre Vinet, French Protestantism, and the Shaping of Civic Culture in 19th Century France." PhD diss., University of California–Davis, 2002.

Krumenacker, Yves. *Les protestants du Poitou au XVIIIe siècle (1681–1789)*. Paris: H. Champion, 1998.

Kuntz, H. "La Séparation des églises et de l'état et la proposition de Francis de Pressensé." *Revue chrétienne* 3 (1903): 450–73.

L'Archiviste, *Drumont et Dreyfus: Etudes sur la "Libre Parole" de 1894 à 1895*. Paris: V.-L. Stock, 1898.

La Trémoïlle, Louis, duc de. *Les La Trémoïlles pendant cinq siècles*. 5 vols. Nantes: E. Grimaud, 1895.

La Viguerie, Jean de. *Christianisme et révolution: Cinq leçons d'histoire de la Révolution française*. Paris: Nel, 1986.

Labriolle, Charles de. "Le concile d'Embrun de 1727, révélateur de la société du 18e siècle." *Bulletin de la Société d'études des Hautes Alpes* (1966): 143–56.

Labrousse, Elisabeth. *"Une foi, une loi, un roi?" Essai sur la révocation de l'Édit de Nantes*. Geneva: Labor et Fides, 1985.

———, ed. *Avertissement aux protestans [sic] des provinces (1684)*. Paris: Presses Universitaires de France, 1986.

Lacouture, Joseph. *La politique religieuse de la Révolution*. Paris: Picard, 1940.

Laneyrie, Philippe. *Les Scouts de France: L'évolution du mouvement des origines aux années quatre-vingt.* Paris: Editions du Cerf, 1985.

Langlois, Claude. "La rupture entre l'Eglise catholique et la Révolution." In *The Transformation of Political Culture, 1789–1848.* Edited by François Furet and Mona Ozouf, 375–90. Vol. 3 of *The French Revolution and the Creation of Modern Political Culture.* Oxford: Pergamon Press, 1989.

———. "Religion, culte ou opinion religieuse: La politique des révolutionnaires." *Revue française de Sociologie* 30 (1989): 471–96.

Latreille, André. *L'église catholique et la Révolution française.* 2 vols. Paris: Hachette, 1946–50.

Laurent, Marcel. "Jean Soanen, évêque de Senez devant le 'Concile' d'Embrun (1727)." *Revue d'Auvergne* 82 (1968): 94–112.

Lavergne, Sabine de. *Art sacré et modernité: Les grandes années de la revue "l'Art sacré."* Namur: Culture et vérité, 1992.

Le Goff, Jacques, and René Rémond, ed. *Histoire de la France religieuse.* Paris: Seuil, 1988–91.

Leclercq, Dom Henri. *L'église constitutionnelle, juillet 1790–avril 1791.* Paris: Letouzey et Ané, 1934.

Lelièvre, Claude, and Christian Nique, eds. *Bâtisseurs d'école: Histoire biographique de l'enseignement en France.* Paris: Nathan, 1994.

Lièvre, Auguste-François. *Histoire des protestants et des églises réformées du Poitou.* 3 vols. Poitiers: Grassart, J. Cherbuliez, 1856.

Ligou, Daniel. "Un vandalisme oublié: La destruction des temples réformés par l'autorité royale au XVIIe siècle." In *Révolution française et "vandalisme révolutionnaire": Actes du colloque international de Clermont-Ferrand, 15–17 décembre 1998.* Edited by Simone Bernard-Griffiths, Marie-Claude Chemin, and Jean Ehrard, 333–41. Paris: Universitas, 1992.

Lindenberg, Daniel. "Révolution culturelle dans la révolution nationale. De Jacques Copeau à 'Jeune France': Une archéologie de la 'décentralisation' théâtrale." *Les Révoltes logiques* 12 (1980): 2–9.

Lods, Armand. "Situation financière des églises protestantes pendant l'exercice 1911." *La Revue de droit* 29 (1912): 193–98.

———. *Traité de l'administration des cultes protestantes.* Paris: Grasset, 1896.

———, ed. *La Législation des cultes protestantes, 1787–1887.* Paris: Grassart, 1887.

Loyer, Emmanuelle. *Le Théâtre-Citoyen de Jean Vilar, Une utopie d'après-guerre.* Paris: Presses Universitaires de France, 1997.

Luria, Keith. "Rituals of Conversion: Catholics and Protestants in Seventeenth-Century Poitou," In *Culture and Identity in Early Modern Europe.* Edited by Barbara Diefendorf and Carla Hesse, 65–82.

———. *Sacred Boundaries: Religious Coexistence and Conflict in Early-Modern France.* Washington DC: Catholic University of America Press, 2005.

———. "Separated by Death? Burials, Cemeteries, Confessional Boundaries in Seventeenth-Century France." *French Historical Studies* 24, no. 2 (Spring 2001): 185–222.

Maguire, Robert J., and France Beck. "Un document inédit de l'affaire Dreyfus." *Les Cahiers Naturalistes* (1993): 326–34.

Maire, Catherine. *De la cause de Dieu à la cause de la nation: Le jansénisme au XVIIIe siècle.* Paris: Gallimard, 1998.

Maistre, Joseph de. *De l'église gallicane dans son rapport avec le souverain pontif.* Lyon: J.-B. Pélagaud, 1862.

Mallet-Stevens, Robert. "Pourquoi la France n'aurait-elle pas des églises modernes?" *Art Sacré* 10 (1936).

Manceron, Claude, ed. *La Révolution française: Dictionnaire biographique.* Paris: Renaudot, 1989.

Margolf, Diane. "Adjudicating Memory: Law and Religious Difference in Early Seventeenth-Century France." *Sixteenth Century Journal* 27 (1996): 399–418.

Marion, Marcel. *Dictionnaire des institutions de la France aux XVIIe et XVIIIe siècles.* New York: B. Franklin, 1968.

Maritain, Jacques. *Humanisme intégral.* Paris: Aubier, 2000.

Marrus, Michael. *The Politics of Assimilation: A Study of the French Jewish Community at the Time of the Dreyfus Affair.* Oxford: Oxford University Press, 1971.

Martimort, Aimé-Georges. *Le gallicanisme de Bossuet.* Paris: Editions du Cerf, 1953.

Martin, Victor. *Le gallicanisme et la réforme catholique: Essai historique sur l'introduction en France des décrets du concile de Trente (1563–1615).* Paris: Picard, 1929.

Maury, Léon. *Le Réveil religieux dans l'église réformée à Genève et en France, 1810–1850.* Paris, 1892.

Mayeur, Françoise, and Jacques Gadille, eds. *Education et images de la femme chrétienne en France au début du XXe siècle.* Lyon: Edition l'Hermès, 1980.

Mayeur, Jean-Marie. *Des Partis catholiques à la Démocratie chrétienne, XIXe–XXe siècles.* Paris: A. Colin, 1980.

McMahon, Darrin. "Enemies of the Enlightenment: Anti-*Philosophes* and the Birth of the French Far Right, 1778–1830." PhD diss., Yale University, 1997.

McManners, John. *Church and State in France, 1870–1914.* New York: Harper, 1972.

———. *The French Revolution and the Church.* New York: Harper & Row, 1969.

McMillan, James F. "Catholicism and Nationalism in France: The Case of the Fédération Nationale Catholique, 1924–1939." In *Catholicism in Britain and France since 1789.* Edited by Frank Tallett and Nicholas Atkin, 151–63. London: Hambledon Press, 1996.

Merrick, Jeffrey. *The Desacralization of the French Monarchy in the Eighteenth Century.* Baton Rouge: University of Louisiana Press, 1990.

Michel, Marie-José. "Clergé et pastorale janséniste à Paris, 1669–1730." *Revue de l'histoire moderne et contemporaine* 27 (April–June 1979): 177–97.

Miller, Samuel J. *Portugal and Rome, c. 1748–1830: An Aspect of the Catholic Enlightenment.* Rome: Università Gregoriana, 1978.

Modood, Tariq. "The Place of Muslims in British Secular Multiculturalism." In *Muslim Europe or Euro-Islam: Politics, Culture and Citizenship in the Age of Globalization.* Edited by Nezar AlSayyad and Manuel Castells, 113–30. Lanham, MD: Lexington Books, 2002.

Monod, Gustave. *La Famille Monod: Portraits et souvenirs.* Paris, 1890.

Monod, Henri. *La Famille Monod.* Lyon, 1909.

Monod, Jean-Claude. "Amérindiens à Paris: Les ambiguités d'une rencontre." *Journal de la Société des Américanistes* 82 (1996): 358–60.

Mousnier, Roland Mousnier. *The Assassination of Henri IV: The Tyrannicide Problem and the Consolidation of the French Absolute Monarchy in the Early 17th Century.* Translated by Joan Spencer. New York: Scribner, 1973.

Muratori, Lodovico Antonio. *Della regolata divozione de' Christiani, trattato di Lamindo Pritanio* [pseudo.]. Trent: Monauni, 1766.

Negroni, Barbara de. *Intolérances: Catholiques et Protestants en France, 1560–1787*. Paris: Hachette, 1996.

Néret, Gilles. *Henri Matisse*. Cologne: Taschen, 1996.

Nicolet, C. *L'idée républicaine en France*. Paris: Gallimard, 1982.

Nielsen, Donald A. *Three Faces of God: Society, Religion, and the Category of Totality in the Philosophy of Emile Durkheim*. Albany: State University of New York Press, 1999.

Nord, Philip. *The Republican Moment: Struggles for Democracy in Nineteenth-Century France*. Cambridge: Harvard University Press, 1995.

O'Brien, Charles. "Jansénisme et tolérance civile à la veille de la Révolution." In "Jansénisme et Révolution." Edited by Catherine Maire. Special issue, *Chroniques de Port-Royal* 39 (1990): 131–45.

Olender, Maurice. *Les langues du paradis: Aryens et sémites, un couple providentiel*. Paris: Seuil, 1989.

Osen, James L. *Prophet and Peacemaker: The Life of Adolphe Monod*. Lanham, MD: University Press of America, 1984.

Ozouf, Mona. "L'invention de l'ethnographie française: Le questionnaire de l'Académie celtique." *Annales ESC* 36 (March–April 1981): 210–30.

Pacteau, Severine de Luze. "L'église réformée de Bordeaux et la séparation des églises et de l'état." *Annales du midi: Anthologie du centenaire* 2 (1989): 755–71.

Parker, David. "Sovereignty, Absolutism, and the Function of the Law in Seventeenth-Century France." *Past and Present* 122 (1989): 36–74.

Paul, Harry W. *The Second Ralliement: The Rapprochement between Church and State in France in the Twentieth Century*. Washington DC: Catholic University of America Press, 1967.

Paxton, Robert O. "France: The Church, the Republic, and the Fascist Temptation, 1922–1945." In *Catholics, the State, and the European Radical Right, 1919–1987*. Edited by Richard Wolff and Jorg Hoensch, 67–91. Boulder: University of Colorado Press, 1987.

Péan, Pierre. *Une Jeunesse française, François Mitterrand 1934–1947*. Paris: Fayard, 1994.

Pecquet, Marguerite. "La Compagnie des Pénitents Blancs de Toulouse." *Annales du Midi* 84 (1972): 213–24.

———. "Des Compagnies de Pénitents à la Compagnie du Saint-Sacrement." *XVIIe siècle* 69 (1965): 6–13.

Pedersen, Susan. *Family, Dependence, and the Origins of the Welfare State, Britain and France 1914–1945*. New York: Cambridge University Press, 1993.

Pessin, Alain. *Le mythe du peuple et la société française du XIXe siècle*. Paris: Presses Universitaires de France, 1992.

Phillips, Henry. *Churches and Culture in Seventeenth-Century France*. Cambridge: Cambridge University Press, 1997.

Pichard, Joseph. "Témoignage de notre temps: Promenades à travers les chantiers du Cardinal." *Art Sacré* 14 (1936).

Pickering, W. S. F. *Durkheim's Sociology of Religion: Themes and Theories*. London: Routledge & Kegan Paul, 1984.

Pierrard, Pierre, et al. *La J.O.C., Regards d'historiens*. Paris: Editions ouvrières, 1984.

Pignatelli, Giuseppe. *Aspetti della propaganda cattolica a Roma da Pio VI a Leone XII*. Rome: Istituto per la Storia del Risorgimento Italiano, 1974.

Plongeron, Bernard. *L'abbé Grégoire ou L'arche de la fraternité, 1750–1831.* Paris: Letouzey et Ané, 1989.

———. "Recherches sur l'Aufkläring catholique en Europe occidental, 1770–1830." *Revue d'histoire moderne et contemporaine* 16 (1969): 555–605.

———. *Théologie et politique au siècle des lumières, 1770–1820.* Geneva: Droz, 1973.

Poliakov, Léon. *The Aryan Myth: A History of Racist and Nationalist Ideas in Europe.* London: Basic Books, 1974.

Polman, Pontien. *Katholieke Nederland in de Achttiende Eeuw.* 3 vols. Hilversum: Paul Brand, 1968.

Préclin, Edmond. *Les jansénistes et la Constitution civile du clergé: Le développement du richérisme, sa propagation dans le bas clergé.* Paris: Librairie universitaire J. Gamber, 1929.

Prévotat, Jacques. "Théologiens laïcs des années trente." *Les Quatre Fleuves* 17 (1983): 49–69.

Rabut, Elisabeth. *Le roi, l'église et le temple: L'exécution de l'Édit de Nantes en Dauphiné.* Grenoble: La Pensée sauvage, 1987.

Rambert, Eugène. *Alexandre Vinet: Histoire de sa vie et de ses ouvrages.* 5th ed. Lausanne: Payot, 1930.

Raphaël, Freddy. "Les juifs de l'Ancien Régime." In *Histoire de la France religieuse.* Edited by Le Goff and Rémond, 62–71.

Rémond, René. *Les Crises du catholicisme en France dans les années trente.* Paris: Editions Cana, 1996.

Reymond, Bernard. *A la redécouverte d'Alexandre Vinet.* Lausanne: L'Age d'homme, 1990.

Richard, Gaston. *La Vie et l'oeuvre de Raoul Allier.* Paris: Berger-Levrault, 1948.

Richet, Denis. *De la Réforme à la Révolution: Études sur la France moderne.* Paris: Aubier, 1991.

Rioux, Jean-Pierre, ed. *La Vie culturelle sous Vichy.* Brussels: Complexe, 1990.

Robert, Daniel. *Les Eglises Réformées en France, 1800–1830.* Paris: Presses Universitaires de France, 1961.

Roberts, John Morris. "The French Origins of the 'Right.'" *Transactions from the Royal Historical Society* 23 (1973): 27–53.

Roberts, Penny. "The Most Crucial Battle of the Wars of Religion? The Conflict over Sites for Reformed Worship in Sixteenth-Century France." *Archiv für Reformationsgeschichte* 89 (1998): 247–67.

Rodrigue, Aron. *French Jews, Turkish Jews: The Alliance Israélite Universelle and the Politics of Jewish Schooling in Turkey, 1860–1925.* Bloomington: University of Indiana Press, 1990.

———. *Images of Sephardi and Eastern Jewries in Transition, 1860–1939: The Teachers of the Alliance Israélite Universelle.* Seattle: University of Washington Press, 1993.

———. "Léon Halévy and Modern French Jewish Historiography." *Jewish History and Jewish Memory: Essays in Honor of Yosef Hayim Yerushalmi.* Edited by Elisheva Carlebach, John Efron, and David Myers, 413–27. Hanover, NH: University Press of New England, 1998.

———. "Les enfants de Crémieux: Devenir de l'Alliance Israélite Universelle." *Les Cahiers du Judaïsme* 1 (1998): 94–100.

———. "Rearticulations of French Jewish Identities after the Dreyfus Affair." *Jewish Social Studies: History, Culture, Society,* n.s. 2, no. 3 (1996): 1–24.

Roger Ikor Center. *Les Sectes: Etat d'urgence.* Paris: Albin Michel, 1995.

Rogier, Louis J. *Terugbliken Uitzicht: Verspreide Opstellen van L. J. Rogier.* Hilversum: Paul Bland, 1964.

Rosa, Mario. *Riformatori e ribelli nel '700 religioso italiano.* Bari: Dedalo, 1969.

Rouland, Nobert, Stéphane Pierré-Caps, and Jacques Poumarède. *Droit des minorités et des peuples autochtones.* Paris: Presses Universitaires de France, 1996.

Rürup, Reinhard, and Thomas Nipperdey. "Antisemitismus: Entstehung, Funktion und Geschichte eines Begriffs." In *Emanzipation und Antisemitismus: Studien zur "Judenfrage" der bürgerlichen Gesellschaft.* Edited by Reinhard Rürup, 95–144. Göttingen: Vandenhoeck & Ruprecht, 1975.

Said, Edward. *Orientalism.* New York: Vintage, 1978.

Salvatorelli, Luigi. *Il pensiero politico italiano dal 1700 al 1870.* N.p.: Giulio Einaudi, 1949.

Saupin, Guy, ed. *Tolérance et intolérance de l'édit de Nantes à nos jours.* Rennes: Presses Universitaires de Rennes, 1998.

Saupin, Guy, Rémy Fabre, and Marcel Launay, eds. *La tolérance: Colloque international de Nantes (mai 1998).* Rennes: Presses Universitaires de Rennes, 1999.

Scherer, Edmond. *Alexandre Vinet: Notice sur sa vie et ses écrits.* Paris: Ducloux, 1853.

Schneider, Robert. "Mortification on Parade: Penitential Processions in Sixteenth- and Seventeenth-Century France." *Renaissance and Reformation,* n.s. 10 (1986): 123–46.

———. *Public Life in Toulouse, 1463–1789: From Municipal Republic to Cosmopolitan City.* Ithaca: Cornell University Press, 1989.

Sciout, Ludovic. *Histoire de la Constitution civile du clergé et de la persécution révolutionnaire (1790–1801).* 4 vols. Paris, 1872–81.

Sedgwick, Alexander. *The Travails of Conscience: The Arnauld Family and the Ancien Régime.* Cambridge: Harvard University Press, 1998.

Simon-Nahum, Perrine. *La cité investie: La "science du judaïsme" français et la République.* Paris: Editions du Cerf, 1991.

Sluhovsky, Moshe. *Patroness of Paris: Rituals of Devotion in Early Modern France.* Leiden: Brill, 1998.

Spicer, Andrew. "'Qui est de Dieu oit la parole de Dieu': The Huguenots and Their Temples." In *Society and Culture in the Huguenot World, 1559–1685.* Edited by Raymond A. Mentzer and Andrew Spicer, 175–92. Cambridge: Cambridge University Press, 2002.

Spiertz, Mathieu Gerardus. *Eglise catholique des Provinces-Unies et la Saint-Siège pendant la deuxième moitié du XVIIe siècle.* Louvain: Publications Universitaires de Louvain, 1975.

Spitzer, Leo. *Lives in Between: Assimilation and Marginality in Austria, Brazil, West Africa 1780–1945.* Cambridge: Cambridge University Press, 1989.

Stella, Pietro. "L'oscurimento della verità nella chiesa dal sinodo di Pistoia alla bolla 'Auctorem fidei' (1786–1794)." *Salesianum rivista trimestrale di cultura ecclesiastica* 43 (1981): 731–56.

Strenski, Ivan. *Durkheim and the Jews of France.* Chicago: University of Chicago Press, 1997.

Sutherland, Nicola M. *The Huguenot Struggle for Recognition.* New Haven: Yale University Press, 1980.

Tackett, Timothy. *Religion, Revolution, and Regional Culture in Eighteenth-Century France: The Ecclesiastical Oath of 1791.* Princeton: Princeton University Press, 1986.

Tallon, Alain. *La Compagnie du Saint-Sacrament (1629–1667)*. Paris: Cerf, 1990.

Taveneaux, René. "Les anciens constitutionnels et l'église d'Utrecht: À propos de quelques inédits d'Henri Grégoire et de Joseph Monin." In *Jansénisme et réforme catholique*, 177–93. Nancy: Presses Universitaires de Nancy, 1993.

Todorov, Tzevan. *On Human Diversity: Nationalism, Racism and Exoticism in French Thought*. Cambridge: Harvard University Press, 1993.

Traver, Emilien. *Histoire de Melle*. Melle, 1938. Reprint, Marseille: Lafitte, 1980.

Turchetti, Mario. "'Concorde ou tolérance?' de 1562 à 1598." *Revue historique* 274 (1985): 341–55.

Van Kleef, Bastien Abraham. "Das Utrechter Provinzialkonzil vom Jahre 1763." In "Die Zeit vor dem Konzil." Special issue, *Internationale kirchliche Zeitschrift* 49 (1959): 197–228.

———. *Geschiedenis van de Oud-Katholieke Kerk van Nederland*. 2nd ed. Assen: Gorkum, 1953.

Van Kley, Dale K. "Church, State, and the Ideological Origins of the French Revolution." *Journal of Modern History* 51 (Dec. 1979): 629–66.

———. *The Damiens Affair and the Unraveling of the Old Regime, 1757–1770*. Princeton: Princeton University Press, 1984.

———. "The Debate over the Gallican Clergy on the Eve of the French Revolution: A Supplementary Introduction to Section III of the Pre-Revolutionary Debate." In *The Pre-Revolutionary Debate*. Edited by Jeremy Popkin and Dale K. Van Kley. Section 5 of *The French Revolution Research Collection*. Edited by Colin Lucas. Oxford: Pergamon Press, 1989.

———. "The Estates General as Ecumenical Council: The Constitutionalism of Corporate Consensus and the Parlement's Ruling of September 25, 1788." *Journal of Modern History* 61 (March 1989): 1–52.

———. *The Jansenists and the Expulsion of the Jesuits from France, 1757–65*. New Haven: Yale University Press, 1975.

———. *The Religions Origins of the French Revolution: From Calvin to the Civil Constitution, 1560–1791*. New Haven: Yale University Press, 1996.

Van Lessel, Peter J. "Il Paesi Bassi e il sinodo di Pistoia." In *Il sinodo di Pistoia del 1786: Atti del Convegno per il secondo centenario Pistoia-Prato, 25–27 settembre 1986*. Edited by Claudio Lamioni, 401–9. Rome: Herder, 1991.

Vaussard, Maurice. *Jansénisme et gallicanisme aux origines religieuses du Risorgimento*. Paris: Letouzey et Ané, 1959.

———. *L'epistolario di G. M. Pujati col canonico Clément di 7 di ottobre 1776–19 di dicembre 1786*. Venice: Fondazione Giorgio Cini, 1964.

Viénot, John. *Histoire de la réforme française de l'Édit de Nantes à sa révocation*. Paris: Fischbacher, 1926.

Vovelle, Michel. *La Révolution contre l'église: De la raison à l'Etre suprême*. Paris: Editions complexes, 1988.

———. "La politique" In *Histoire de la France religeuse*. Edited by Le Goff and Rémond, 73–108.

Wanegffelen, Thierry. *L'Edit de Nantes: Une Histoire européenne de la Tolérance du XVIe au XXe siècle*. Paris: Livre de poche, 1998.

Weber, Eugen. *The Hollow Years, France in the 1930s*. New York: Norton, 1994.

———. *My France: Politics, Culture, Myth.* Cambridge: Belknap Press of Harvard University Press, 1991.

Weiss, Nathanaël, Charles Read, and Henri Bordier. "Poursuites et condemnations à Paris pour hérésie de 1564 à 1572, d'après les registres d'écrou de la Conciergerie du Palais." *Bulletin de la Société de l'histoire du protestantisme français* 50 (1901): 640.

Wemyss, Alice. *Histoire du Réveil, 1790–1849.* Paris: Les Bergers et Les Mages, 1977.

Werbner, Pnina. "Islamophobia, Incitement to Religious Hatred: Legislating for a New Fear?" *Anthropology Today* 21, no. 1 (2005): 5–9.

Wieviorka, Annette. "Les années noires." In *Histoire de la France religieuse.* Edited by Le Goff and Rémond, 197–247.

Willaime, Jean-Paul. "La Religion civile à la française et ses métamorphoses." *Social Compass* 40 (1993): 571–80.

———. "Le religieux dans l'espace public." *Projet* 225: 71–79.

———. "Religious and Secular France between Northern and Southern Europe." *Social Compass* 45 (1998): 155–74.

Winock, Michel. *"Esprit": Des intellectuels dans la cité (1930–1950).* 1975. Reprint, Paris: Seuil, 1996.

Wohl, Robert. "The Bards of Aviation: Flight and French Culture, 1909–1939." *Michigan Quarterly Review* 29 (1990): 303–27.

Wolfe, Michael. "Amnesty and *Oubliance* at the End of the French Wars of Religion." In "Clémence, oubliance et pardon en Europe, 1520–1620." Special issue, *Cahiers d'histoire* 16 (1996): 184.

Yvert, Benoît, ed. *Dictionnaire des ministres de 1789 à 1989.* Paris: Perrin, 1990.

Index

absolutism, 77, 80–84, 100–109, 125–40
Acarie, Barbe, Marie de l'Incarnation, 43–44, 48, 84
Action français, 182, 192
agriculture, 196
Alaoui, Fouad, 227, 228
d'Alembert, Jean Le Rond, *Encyclopédie,* 103–4
Alexander VII, 101
Ali-Bourg, Didier, 230
Alliance Israélite Universelle, 161, 162, 176, 177
Allier, Raoul, 158–59
America, 111
Amerindians, 215–16
amnesty, 24, 45–46
Anne of Austria, 65
anthropology, 161, 171–73, 203–4
anti-Semitism
    and assimilation, xxiii–xxix
    Comité de Défense contre l'Antisémitisme, 167
    and new nationalism, 166–67, 175–77
    Statute for the Jews (1940), 212
Appolis, Emile, 115
d'Arbaleste, Charlotte, 34
archaeology, 165–66
Archetto, 113
architecture, 188–89
d'Argenson, comte , and Compagnie du Saint-Sacrement, 88–89
Arnauld family, 86
    Antoine, 87; *la fréquente communion,* 96
    Mother Angélique, 85
arts *(l'arte sacré),* 183, 193, 196–97
Aryans, 170–71
asceticism, 44
Assembly of Notables, 13
Association catholique de la jeunesse française (ACJF), 180–83, 192
Association des Amérindiens de Guyane Française, 215
Astorri, Girolamo, 121, 122
d'Aubigné, Théodore-Agrippa, *Les Tragiques,* xviii, 35, 37
Augustinians/Augustinianism
    and Catholic Enlightenment, 114–15
    Jansenist view of, 95–96, 98, 110

    as neo-Gallicans, 115
    propaganda of, 113
    theological works of, 116

Barangé, Charles, 195
Barrault, Jean-Louis, 188
Baubérot, Jean, xv, 208, 211, 219
Bayle, Pierre, 202
Bayrou, François, 233
Beauvoir, Simone de, 181
Bechari, Mohmed, 227
"Belleville Manifesto," 152
Benedict, Philip, 38
Benedict XIV (pope), 115
Bernanos, Georges, 185, 186
    Dialogues des Carmélites, 195
    Journal d'un curé de campagne, 183
Berruyer, Isaac, 98, 103
Bérulle, Pierre de, 94
Bèze, Théodore de, 34
Bible
    adherence to, under January Edict, 8
    vernacular translation of, 102–3, 115
    1 Corinthians, 14
    Psalms, 13, 34
Blum, Léon, 190, 191
Boissy d'Anglas, François, 158
Bonaparte, Napoleon, 143
Boubakeur, Dalil, 226–28, 230
Bresson, Robert, 197
Bretons, 205
Buisson, Ferdinand, 153, 159
Burke, Peter, 32, 32n

Calvinists. *See* Protestants/Huguenots; Reformed Church
Camus, Armand-Gaston, 124
Capuchins, 42
    expulsion from Rheims, 47
    nuns, 44
    at siege of La Rochelle, 76
Carmelite nuns, 44, 45
Carvalho e Melho, Sebastian, 110
Castelnau, Edouard de, 181, 191
Catherine de Médicis, 1, 22
    on freedom to preach, 5
Catholic Church
    Augustinianism of, 95–96, 98

Contributors

CARMEN BERNAND is professor of anthropology at the University of Paris, X, a member of the Institut de France, and author of many articles and books on South America and religious questions in the context of anthropology, including *De l'Idolâtrie: Une archéologie des sciences religieuses* (with Serge Gruzinski); *Les Incas, peuple du soleil; Histoire du Nouveau Monde* (with Serge Gruzinski); *Pindilig: Un village des Andes équatoriennes; La Solitude des Renaissants: Malheur et sorcellerie dans les Andes;* and *Buenos Aires, 1880–1936.*

JOCELYNE CÉSARI is a research associate in the Center for Middle Eastern Studies at Harvard University, where she has served as a chair of the seminar "Islam in the West" and where she is now coordinator of the Provost Interfaculty Program on Islam in the West. She has published thirteen books and more than fifth articles in European and American journals. Her most recent book, *European Muslims and the Secular State,* was published in 2005. She has published multiple articles in European and American books and journals. Césari received her PhD in political science from the University of Aix-en-Provence in France and has served as a senior research fellow and associate professor at the French National Center for Scientific Research at the Sorbonne, Paris, since fall 1992. She has received grants to write the reports "Islam and Fundamental Rights" and "The Religious Consequences of September 11, 2001, on Muslims in Europe" for the European Commission.

DENIS CROUZET is professor of history at the University of Paris, IV, the Sorbonne. He has authored numerous books, including *Les Guerriers de Dieu: La violence au temps des troubles de religion; La Nuit de la Saint-Barthélemy: Un rêve perdu de la Renaissance; La Genèse de la Réforme française: 1520–1560; La Sagesse et le malheur: Michel de l'Hôspital, Chancelier de France; Jean Calvin: Vies parallèles; Charles de Bourbon, Connétable de Bourbon;* and *Le Haut Coeur de Catherine de Médicis.* He is the author of hundreds of articles, particularly on the Wars of Religion in France.

BARBARA DIEFENDORF is professor of history at Boston University, and is the author of three books on early modern France, *Paris City Councillors in the Sixteenth Century: The Politics of Patrimony; Beneath the Cross: Catholics and*

Huguenots in Sixteenth-Century Paris; and *From Penitence to Charity: Pious Women and the Catholic Reformation in Paris.* She is coeditor of *Culture and Identity in Early Modern Europe, 1500–1800: Essays in Honor of Natalie Zemon Davis* and has authored a number of journal articles and book chapters on the social, political, and cultural history of early modern Europe.

STEVEN C. HAUSE is professor of history, senior scholar in the humanities, and codirector of European studies at Washington University in St. Louis. He is the author and coauthor of three previous books on the history of the women's rights movement in modern France, which have won four research prizes: *Women's Suffrage and Social Politics in the French Third Republic* (with Anne R. Kenney); *Hubertine Auclert, the French Suffragette;* and *Feminisms of the Belle Epoque* (with Jennifer Waelti-Walters). He is coauthor with William Maltby of a series of books on the history of western civilization, the latest being *Essentials of Western Civilization: A History of European Society.* His essays on various aspects of modern European history have appeared in numerous journals, including *American Historical Review* and *French Historical Studies.*

CHRISTIAN JOUHAUD is director of studies at the Ecole des Hautes Etudes des Sciences Sociales, as well as director of research at the Centre National de la Recherche Scientifique. He has authored a number of books, including *Mazarinades: La Fronde des mots; La Main de Richelieu ou le pouvoir cardinal; La France du premier XVIIe siècle* (with Robert Descimon); and *Les Pouvoirs de la littérature: Histoire d'un paradoxe.* He is editor and coeditor of a number of volumes on seventeenth-century history and also author of more than a hundred articles on early modern history and culture. He is currently preparing two book-length studies: one on the "journée des dupes" (November 1630) and one on the French seventeenth century as a preconstructed object.

KATHLEEN LONG is professor of French at Cornell University and author of articles and books on Renaissance literature and culture, including *Another Reality: Poetry and the Imagination in the Works of Ovid, Petrarch, and Ronsard; High Anxiety: Masculinity in Crisis in Early Modern France* (edited volume); and *Hermaphrodites in Renaissance Europe* (forthcoming). She is currently preparing a book-length study of literary representations of religious violence.

KEITH LURIA is professor of history at North Carolina State University. He is the author of *Sacred Boundaries: Religious Coexistence and Conflict in Early Modern France* and *Territories of Grace: Cultural Change in the Seventeenth-Century Diocese of Grenoble,* as well as of numerous articles on religion in seventeenth-century France.

PHILIP NORD is professor of history at Princeton University. He has authored three books: *The Politics of Resentment: Shopkeeper Protest in Nineteenth-Century Paris*; *The Republican Moment: Struggles for Democracy in Nineteenth-Century France*; and *Impressionists and Politics: Art and Democracy in the Nineteenth Century*, as well as numerous articles on modern European history. He is currently at work on a new project titled *The Modern French State: Institutional and Cultural Reform, 1930–1950*.

ARON RODRIGUE is the Eva Chernov Lokey Professor in Jewish Studies at Stanford University. He has published numerous articles and books on a wide range of Jewish history, including *Jews and Muslims: Images of Sephardi and Eastern Jewries in Modern Times*; *French Jews, Turkish Jews: The Alliance Israélite Universelle and the Politics of Jewish Schooling in Turkey, 1860–1925*; *Ottoman and Turkish Jewry: Community and Leadership* (edited volume); *Images of Sephardi and Eastern Jewries in Transition: The Teachers of the Alliance Israélite Universelle, 1860–1939*; *A Sephardi Life in Southeastern Europe: The Autobiography and Journal of Gabriel Arié, 1863–1939* (with Esther Benbassa); and *Sephardi Jewry: A History of the Judeo-Spanish Community, 14th–20th Centuries* (with Esther Benbassa).

DUANE RUDOLPH, who translated Denis Crouzet's, Christian Jouhaud's, and Carmen Bernand's essays, is an assistant professor at the University of Hawai'i. He is currently revising a book-length study on Renaissance dystopias.

DALE K. VAN KLEY is professor of history at the Ohio State University. He is the author or editor of many articles and books, including *The Jansenists and the Expulsion of the Jesuits from France, 1757–1765*; *The Damiens Affair and the Unraveling of the Ancien Régime, 1750–1770*; *The French Idea of Freedom: The Old Regime and the Declaration of Rights of 1789*; *The Religious Origins of the French Revolution: From Calvin to the Civil Constitution, 1560–1791*; and *Religion and Politics in Enlightenment Europe* (coedited with James E. Bradley).